THE FATHERS
OF THE CHURCH

A NEW TRANSLATION

VOLUME 103

THE FATHERS OF THE CHURCH

A NEW TRANSLATION

EDITORIAL BOARD

Thomas P. Halton
The Catholic University of America
Editorial Director

Elizabeth Clark
Duke University

Joseph T. Lienhard
Fordham University

Frank A. C. Mantello
The Catholic University of America

Kathleen McVey
Princeton Theological Seminary

Robert D. Sider
Dickinson College

Michael Slusser
Duquesne University

Cynthia White
The University of Arizona

Robin Darling Young
The Catholic University of America

David J. McGonagle
Director
The Catholic University of America Press

FORMER EDITORIAL DIRECTORS

Ludwig Schopp, Roy J. Deferrari, Bernard M. Peebles,
Hermigild Dressler, O.F.M.

Cornelia Horn, Joel Kalvesmaki
Staff Editors

ORIGEN
COMMENTARY ON THE EPISTLE TO THE ROMANS BOOKS 1–5

Translated by
THOMAS P. SCHECK

THE CATHOLIC UNIVERSITY OF AMERICA PRESS
Washington, D.C.

Copyright © 2001
THE CATHOLIC UNIVERSITY OF AMERICA PRESS
All rights reserved
Printed in the United States of America

The paper used in this publication meets the minimum requirements of the American National Standards for Information Science—Permanence of Paper for Printed Library Materials, ANSI Z39.48—1984.

LIBRARY OF CONGRESS CATALOGING-IN-PUBLICATION DATA
Origen.
   [Commentary on the Epistle to the Romans. Book 1–5. English]
   Commentary on the Epistle to the Romans. Books 1–5 / Origen ; translated by Thomas P. Scheck.
      p. cm. — (The fathers of the church ; v. 103)
   Translated from Rufinus' Latin translation of the original Greek.
   Includes bibliographical references (p.   ) and indexes.
   ISBN 0-8132-0103-9 (alk. paper)
   ISBN 978-0-8132-1736-9 (pbk.)
   1. Bible. N.T. Romans—Commentaries—Early works to 1800.
   I. Scheck, Thomas P., 1964– II. Title. III. Series.
BR60.F3 O675
[BS2665]
270 s—dc21
[227/.10

2001028018

CONTENTS

Abbreviations	vii
Select Bibliography	ix
Introduction	1

COMMENTARY ON THE EPISTLE TO THE ROMANS

Preface of Rufinus	51
Preface of Origen	53
Book 1	60
Book 2	102
Book 3	178
Book 4	237
Book 5	303

INDICES

General Index	381
Index of Holy Scripture	394
Index of Origen's Works	407

ABBREVIATIONS

General

ACW   Ancient Christian Writers. New York: Newman Press, 1946– .
AGLB   *Vetus Latina: Die Reste der altlateinischen Bibel. Aus der Geschichte der Lateinischen Bibel.* Freiburg: Herder, 1957.
ANF   Ante Nicene Fathers. 1890. Reprint, Grand Rapids, Mich.: Erdmanns, 1994.
BAGD   *A Greek-English Lexicon of the New Testament and Other Early Christian Literature.* 5th ed. Chicago: University of Chicago Press, 1979.
CCL   Corpus Christianorum, Series Latina. Turnhout: Brepols, 1954– .
ChH   *Church History.* Chicago: American Society of Church History, 1932– .
CWE   Collected Works of Erasmus. Toronto: University of Toronto Press, 1974– .
DCB   *A Dictionary of Christian Biography.* Ed. W. Smith and H. Wace. London: J. Murray, 1887.
FC   Fontes Christiani. Freiburg: Heider, 1991– .
FOTC   The Fathers of the Church. Washington, D.C.: The Catholic University of America Press, 1947– .
GCS   Die griechischen christlichen Schriftsteller der ersten drei Jahrhunderte. Leipzig: J. C. Hinrichs, 1897–1949. Berlin: Akademie-Verlag, 1953– .
JThS   *Journal of Theological Studies.* London, 1899– .
LCC   The Library of Christian Classics. Philadelphia: Westminster Press, 1953–66.
LCL   Loeb Classical Library. Cambridge, Mass.: Harvard University Press. London: W. Heinemann, 1899– .
L&S   *A Latin Dictionary.* Ed. C. T. Lewis and C. Short. 1879. Reprint, Oxford: Oxford University Press, 1975.
LXX   Septuagint.
MT   Masoretic Text.
NPNF   A Select Library of Nicene and Post-Nicene Fathers of the

	Christian Church. 1890. Reprint, Grand Rapids, Mich.: Erdmanns, 1994.
NRSV	Bible: New Revised Standard Version.
PG	Patrologiae Cursus Completus: Series Graeca. Ed. J.-P. Migne. Paris, 1857–66.
PL	Patrologiae Cursus Completus: Series Latina. Ed. J.-P. Migne. Paris, 1878–90.
SP	*Studia Patristica.*
SPCK	Society for Promoting Christian Knowledge.
TDNT	*Theological Dictionary of the New Testament.* Ed G. Kittel. Grand Rapids, Mich.: Eerdmans, 1964–76.
TS	*Theological Studies.* Baltimore, 1940– .
TU	Texte und Untersuchungen zur Geschichte der altchristlicher Literatur. Leipzig: J. C. Hinrichs, 1882–1949; Berlin: Akademie-Verlag, 1953– .
VC	*Vigiliae Christianae.* Amsterdam: North-Holland Pub. Co., 1947– .
Vulg.	Latin Vulgate.
ZThK	*Zeitschrift für Theologie und Kirche.* Tübingen, 1891– .

Works of Origen

Comm in Cant	*Commentary on Song of Songs*
Comm in Jn	*Commentary on John*
Comm in Ps	*Books on the Psalms*
Orat	*De Oratione* = *Treatise on Prayer*

Aside from those noted above, abbreviations of patristic texts follow G. W. H. Lampe, ed. *A Patristic Greek Lexicon.* Oxford: Oxford University Press, 1961.

SELECT BIBLIOGRAPHY

Texts and Translations

Balthasar, H. Urs von, ed. *Origen: Spirit and Fire. A Thematic Anthology of His Writings.* Trans. Robert J. Daly. Washington, D.C.: The Catholic University of America Press, 1984; reprint 2001.
Bray, G., trans. and ed. *Ancient Christian Commentary on Scripture. New Testament VI: Romans.* Downers Grove, Ill.: Intervarsity, 1998.
Origen. *Philocalia.* Trans. G. Lewis. Edinburgh: T & T Clark, 1911.
Origene. *Commento alla Lettera ai Romani.* Trans. F. Coccini. 2 vols. Casale Monferrato, 1985–86.
Origenes. *Commentarii in epistulam ad Romanos/Römerbriefkommentar.* Ed. and trans. Theresia Heither. 5 vols. FC 2 (1–5). Freiburg im Breisgau: Herder, 1990–96.
———. *Der Römerbriefkommentar des Origenes: Kritische Ausgabe der Übersetzung Rufins. Buch 1–3.* Ed. C. P. Hammond Bammel. AGLB 16. Freiburg im Breisgau: Herder, 1990.
———. *Der Römerbriefkommentar des Origenes: Kritische Ausgabe der Übersetzung Rufins. Buch 4–6.* Ed. C. P. Hammond Bammel. Zum Druck vorbereitet und gesetzt von H. J. Frede und H. Stanjek. AGLB 33. Freiburg im Breisgau: Herder, 1997.
———. *Der Römerbriefkommentar des Origenes: Kritische Ausgabe der Übersetzung Rufins. Buch 7–10.* Ed. C. P. Hammond Bammel. Aus dem Nachlaß herausgegeben von H. J. Frede and H. Stanjek. AGLB 34. Freiburg im Breisgau: Herder, 1998.
Ramsbotham, A. "Documents: The Commentary of Origen on the Epistle to the Romans." *JThS* 13 (1912): 209–24, 357–68; *JThS* 14 (1913): 10–22.
Robinson, J. A., ed. *The Philocalia.* Cambridge: Cambridge University Press, 1893.
Scherer, J., ed. *Le Commentaire d'Origène sur Rom. III.5–V.7, d'après les extraits du Papyrus n 88748 du Musée du Caire et les fragments de la Philocalie et du Vaticanus graecus 762. Essai de reconstitution du texte et de la pensée des tomes V et VI du 'Commentaire sur l'Épître aux Romains.'* Bibliothèque d'Étude 27. Cairo: Institut français d'Archéologie orientale, 1957.
Tollinton, R. B., trans. *Selections from the Commentaries and Homilies of Origen.* London: SPCK, 1929.

Secondary Sources

Bammel, C. P. "Adam in Origen." In *The Making of Orthodoxy: Essays in Honour of Henry Chadwick*, ed. R. Williams, 62–93. Cambridge: Cambridge University Press, 1989.
———. "Augustine, Origen and the Exegesis of St. Paul." *Augustinianum* 32 (1992): 341–68.
———. Review of *Translatio Religionis: Die Paulusdeutung des Origenes*, by Theresia Heither. *JThS*, n.s., 44 (1993): 348–52.
———. "Justification by Faith in Augustine and Origen." *Journal of Ecclesiastical History* 47 (1996): 223–35.
Bardenhewer, O. *Geschichte der altkirchlichen Literatur*. 5 vols. Freiburg im Breisgau: Herder, 1913–32.
Bigg, C. *The Christian Platonists of Alexandria*. 1886. Reprint, New York: AMS Press, 1970.
Boyd, W. J. P. "Origen on Pharaoh's Hardened Heart: A Study of Justification and Election in St. Paul and Origen." *SP* VII, Part I. Ed. F. L. Cross. TU 92 (1966): pp. 434–42.
Chadwick, H. "Origen, Celsus, and the Stoa." *JThS* 48 (1947): 34–49.
———. "Rufinus and the Tura Papyrus of Origen's Commentary on Romans." *JThS*, n.s., 10 (1959): 10–42.
Cranfield, C. E. B. *A Critical and Exegetical Commentary on the Epistle to the Romans*. 2 vols. Edinburgh: T. & T. Clark, 1975, 1985.
Crouzel, H. *Origen: The Life and Thought of the First Great Theologian*. Trans. A. S. Worrall. San Francisco: Harper and Row, 1989.
Daniélou, Jean. *Origen*. Trans. W. Mitchell. London and New York: Sheed and Ward, 1955.
Fairweather, W. *Origen and Greek Patristic Theology*. Edinburgh: T. & T. Clark, 1901.
Florovsky, G., "Origen, Eusebius, and the Iconoclastic Controversy." *ChH* 19 (1950): 77–96.
Fremantle, W. F. "Hieronymus." *DCB* 3:29–50.
———. "Rufinus." *DCB* 4:555–61.
Gorday, P. *Principles of Patristic Exegesis: Romans 9–11 in Origen, John Chrysostom, and Augustine*. Studies in the Bible and Early Christianity, vol. 4. New York: The Edwin Mellen Press, 1983.
Hammond, C. P. "The Last Ten Years of Rufinus' Life and the Date of His Move South from Aquileia." *JThS*, n.s., 28 (1977): 372–429.
———. "Notes on the Manuscripts and Editions of Origen's Commentary on the Epistle to the Romans in the Latin Translation of Rufinus." *JThS*, n.s., 16 (1965): 338–57.
Hammond Bammel, C. P. "Philocalia IX, Jerome, Epistle 121, and Origen's Exposition of Romans VII." *JThS*, n.s., 32 (1981): 50–81.
———. *Origeniana et Rufiniana*. *AGLB* 29. Freiburg im Breisgau: Herder, 1996.

———. *Der Römerbrieftext des Rufin und seine Origenes-Übersetzung. AGLB* 10. Freiburg im Breisgau: Herder, 1985.
Hanson, R. P. C. *Allegory and Event.* Richmond, Va.: John Knox Press, 1959.
———. *Origen's Doctrine of Tradition.* London: SPCK, 1954.
Harnack, A. von. *Geschichte der altchristlichen Literatur bis Eusebius.* 2 vols. Leipzig: J. C. Hinrichs, 1958.
———. *Der kirchengeschichtliche Ertrag der exegetischen Arbeiten des Origenes.* TU 42. Leipzig: J. C. Hinrichs, 1919.
Heither, T. *Translatio Religionis: Die Paulusdeutung des Origenes in seinem Kommentar zum Römerbrief.* Bonner Beiträge zur Kirchengeschichte, vol. 16. Cologne: Böhlau, 1990.
Hildebrand, Stephen M. "The Letter Kills but the Spirit Gives Life: Romans 7 in the Early Works of Augustine and in Rufinus's Translation of Origen's Commentary." *Augustinian Studies* 31:1 (2000): 19–39.
Kannengiesser, C., and W. L. Peterson, eds. *Origen of Alexandria: His World and His Legacy.* Notre Dame: University of Notre Dame Press, 1988.
Kelly, J. N. D. *Early Christian Creeds.* 3d edition. New York: David McKay Company Inc., 1972.
———. *Early Christian Doctrines.* Revised edition. New York: Harper & Row, 1978.
Koch, H. *Pronoia und Paideusis: Studien über Origenes und sein Verhältnis zum Platonismus.* Berlin: Walter de Gruyter & Co., 1932.
Lampe, G. W. H. *The Seal of the Spirit.* London: Longmans, Green and Co., 1951.
Lange, N. R. M. de. *Origen and the Jews.* Cambridge: Cambridge University Press, 1976.
Lieske, P. A. *Die Theologie der Logos-mystik bei Origenes.* Münster in Westfalen: Aschendorff, 1938.
Lubac, H. de. *Medieval Exegesis.* Volume 1: *The Four Senses of Scripture.* Trans. M. Sebanc. Grand Rapids, Mich.: Eerdmans, 1998.
Melanchthon, P. *Selected Writings.* Trans. C. L. Hill. Minneapolis: Augsburg, 1962.
Metzger, B. M. *A Textual Commentary on the Greek New Testament.* 1971. Corrected edition, Stuttgart: United Bible Societies, 1975.
Molland, E. *The Conception of the Gospel in the Alexandrian Theology.* Oslo: I kommisjon hos J. Dybwad, 1938.
Murphy, F. X. *Rufinus of Aquileia (345–411): His Life and Works.* Washington, D.C.: The Catholic University of America Press, 1945.
Neuschäfer, B. *Origenes als Philologe.* 2 vols. Basel: Friedrich Reinhardt Verlag, 1987.
Norris, F. W. "Universal Salvation in Origen and Maximus." In *Universalism and the Doctrine of Hell: Papers presented at the Fourth Edinburgh*

Conference in Christian Dogmatics, ed. N. M. de S. Cameron, pp. 35–72. Grand Rapids, Mich.: Baker, 1991.

Quasten, J. *Patrology*. 4 vols. Utrecht-Antwerp: Spectrum, 1975.

Roukema, R. *The Diversity of Laws in Origen's Commentary on Romans*. Amsterdam: Free University Press, 1988.

———. "Jews and Gentiles in Origen's Commentary on Romans III 19–22." *Origeniana Quarta, Die Referate des 4. Internationalen Origeneskongresses* (Innsbruck, 2–6 September 1985), ed. Lothar Lies (Innsbruck: Tyrolia 1987), pp. 21–25.

Sanday, W., and A. C. Headlam. *A Critical and Exegetical Commentary on the Epistle to the Romans*. International Critical Commentary. New York: Charles Scribner's Sons, 1903.

Schelkle, K. H. "Kirche und Synagoge in der frühen Auslegung des Römerbriefs." *Theologische Quartalschrift* 134 (1954): 290–318.

———. *Paulus, Lehrer der Väter: Die altkirchliche Auslegung von Römer 1–11*. Düsseldorf: Patmos, 1956.

———. "Staat und Kirche in der patristischen Auslegung von Rm 13:1–7." *Zeitschrift für die neutestamentliche Wissenschaft und die Kunde des Urchristentums* 44 (1952–53): 223–36.

Schlarb, R. *Wir Sind mit Christus Begraben: Die Auslegung von Römer 6,1–11 im Frühchristentum bis Origenes*. Tübingen: J. C. B. Mohr (Paul Siebeck), 1990.

Smith, A. J. "The Commentary of Pelagius on 'Romans' Compared with that of Rufinus." *JThS* 20 (1919): 127–77.

Souter, A. *The Earliest Latin Commentaries on the Epistles of St. Paul*. Oxford: Oxford University Press, 1927.

Teichtweier, G. *Die Sündenlehre des Origenes*. Studien zur Geschichte der katholischen Moraltheologie, vol. 7. Regensburg: Verlag Friedrich Pustet, 1958.

Turner, C. H. "Greek Patristic Commentaries on the Pauline Letters." In *Dictionary of the Bible*, ed. J. Hastings, 484–531. New York: Charles Scribner's Sons, 1909.

Verfaillie, C. *La doctrine de la justification dans Origène d'après son commentaire de l'Épître aux Romains*. Thèse de la Faculté de théologie catholique de l'Université de Strasbourg. Strasbourg, 1926.

Vogt, H. J. *Das Kirchenverständnis des Origenes*. Bonner Beiträge zur Kirchengeschichte, vol. 4. Cologne: Böhlau Verlag, 1974.

Völker, W. *Das Vollkommenheitsideal des Origenes*. Tübingen: J. C. B. Mohr, 1931.

———. "Paulus bei Origenes." *Theologische Studien und Kritiken: eine Zeitschrift für das gesamte Gebiet der Theologie* 102 (1930): 258–79.

Wagner, M. M. *Rufinus the Translator: A Study of his Theory and his Practice as Illustrated in his Version of the Apologetica of St. Gregory Nazianzen*. Washington, D.C.: Catholic University Press, 1945.

Westcott, B. F. "Origenes." *DCB* 4:96–142.

Wiles, M. F. *The Divine Apostle: The Interpretation of St. Paul's Epistles in the Early Church.* London: Cambridge University Press, 1967.
Williams, N. P. *The Ideas of the Fall and of Original Sin.* London: Longmans, Green and Co., 1927.
Windisch, H. *Taufe und Sünde im ältesten Christentum bis auf Origenes.* Tübingen: J. C. B. Mohr, 1908.

INTRODUCTION

INTRODUCTION

Background of Origen's *Commentary on the Epistle to the Romans*

1. Text, Acknowledgments & Dedication

The history of detailed exegesis on Paul's Letter to the Romans begins with the *Commentary on the Epistle to the Romans* by Origen of Alexandria, written around 246 and presented here for the first time in English translation. The work is Origen's only biblical commentary to survive in a coherent form from beginning to end, though it has been reduced to half its original length in Rufinus of Aquileia's abbreviated Latin translation (only fragments of the Greek archetype have survived). Thus it presents an exceptional opportunity to observe Origen's exegetical method at work in interpreting a single self-contained book of the Bible.

The uniqueness of Origen's *Commentary* has been noted by scholars who have studied it in detail. One leading patristic scholar describes it as a "magnificent creation, full of accurate linguistic observations, concordance-like compilations of references, acute theological exegesis, and Spirit-filled interpretation."[1] It has also won the sincere, though condescending, admiration of specialists on Romans: "The reader is astonished not only at the command of Scripture but at the range and subtlety of thought which it displays. The questions raised are often remarkably modern."[2]

As the oldest surviving commentary on Romans, written by

---

1. K. H. Schelkle, *Paulus, Lehrer der Väter: Die altkirchliche Auslegung von Römer 1–11* (Düsseldorf: Patmos, 1956), p. 413.

2. W. Sanday and A. C. Headlam, *A Critical and Exegetical Commentary on the Epistle to the Romans*, International Critical Commentary (New York: Charles Scribner's Sons, 1903), p. xcix.

the most important Christian theologian between St. Paul and St. Augustine, it is a work of considerable importance. From the standpoint of the history of NT interpretation, Origen's work "stands out in splendid isolation at the fountain-head of the tradition of Greek exegesis."[3] For it precedes the next surviving Greek commentary on Romans, namely the exegetical homilies of John Chrysostom (345?–407), by 150 years. In its Latin translation, Origen's *Commentary* exerted a significant influence on subsequent Christian thought.

My translation is based on the critical edition of the *Commentary* which has been published in three volumes by the late Caroline P. Hammond Bammel.[4] To facilitate cross-referencing, the Migne column numbers appear in square brackets. Also, the reader should note that I have used the Migne chapter enumeration (which differs at times from the Hammond Bammel edition) and have numbered the sub-paragraphs. I would like to acknowledge my debt to the editor of the critical edition. The foremost authority on Origen's *Commentary on the Epistle to the Romans*, the history of its manuscript tradition, and its reception, Hammond Bammel died suddenly, before she could fulfill her promise to present the English-speaking world with her own translation.[5] The giant fell while clearing the field of stumps and boulders, so that a dwarf could walk freely and without hindrance over those smooth places.

I am also indebted to Theresia Heither whose German translation, explanatory footnotes, and introductions have proven to be a tremendous source of helpful information.[6] Without the herculean labors of Heither as a translator and especially of

---

3. M. F. Wiles, *The Divine Apostle: The Interpretation of St. Paul's Epistles in the Early Church* (London: Cambridge University Press, 1967), p. 6.

4. Origenes, *Der Römerbriefkommentar des Origenes: Kritische Ausgabe der Übersetzung Rufins*, Ed. C. P. Hammond Bammel. 3 vols. (Freiburg im Breisgau: Herder, 1990–98). The last two volumes were issued posthumously. Hammond Bammel lived to complete the textual apparatus for Books 1–5 in their entirety. Her works appear under three different authorial designations: C. P. Hammond, C. P. Bammel, and C. P. Hammond Bammel.

5. Hammond Bammel in Origenes, *Römerbriefkommentar*, 1:5 n. 2.

6. Origenes, *Commentarii in epistulam ad Romanos/Römerbriefkommentar*, ed. and trans. Theresia Heither, 5 vols., FC 2 (1–5) (Freiburg im Breisgau: Herder, 1990–96).

Hammond Bammel as a critical editor, I would have been lost, "overwhelmed as much by the greatness of his thoughts as by the immensity of the waves."[7]

I am grateful to several other scholars who offered me their assistance. D. A. Carson encouraged the whole project and gave helpful criticisms at every stage of writing. Joseph Lienhard and the late Dr. John C. Olin offered valuable criticisms of the Introduction. Ronald E. Heine and Thomas Halton made many suggestions that greatly improved many passages. The librarian LaDonna Schluterbusch tracked down needed works through Interlibrary Loan. Finally, I am most grateful to Joel Kalvesmaki, Staff Editor of The Fathers of the Church, for his excellent skills in Latin and English. There is hardly a page in the work that has not benefited from his scrutiny. The translation is dedicated to my wife Susan and to our four small sons, Peter (6), Luke (5), Mark (2), and John (1 month).

2. Origen's Life[8]

Origen of Alexandria (185–254) was born to Christian parents in Alexandria, Egypt, the eldest of seven children. His father Leonides was put to death in 202 in a persecution instigated by the Roman Emperor Septimius Severus (193–211).[9] Eusebius records that when Origen learned that his father had been imprisoned, his whole being was inflamed with the desire for martyrdom, but his mother thwarted his purpose by hiding his clothes from him, thus forcing him to remain at home. Prevented from joining his father, he sent him a letter in prison, exhorting him not to waver in his allegiance to Christ for the sake of his family; in other words, he must not commit apostasy in order to be released. Eusebius was in possession of this and many other letters of Origen that have subsequently perished.

7. Preface of Rufinus (2).
8. The best source for the life of Origen is Eusebius of Caesarea (260–339), *Ecclesiastical History*, bk. 6.
9. The Edict is documented in secular sources where it is shown to have been directed primarily against proselytism: "He [Severus] forbade men from converting to Judaism under heavy penalties. He passed the same legislation with respect to the Christians." *Severus* 17.1 in *Historia Augusta*.

After the execution of Leonides, the family's property was confiscated. The eighteen-year-old Origen thus took over responsibility for the family, now without means, and began his activity as a teacher of catechesis and literature, evidently an occupation his father held prior to his martyrdom.[10] Eusebius asserts that Origen had studied under Clement of Alexandria (150?–220?), and it is beyond all doubt that Origen had read his books and "absorbed his point of view."[11] In Alexandria Origen instructed educated Christians as well as members of heretical sects. With the latter he refused to pray, according to Eusebius. Origen's hostile stance toward heretics is a defining feature of his personality and life work. He wrote as a churchman and "never aimed at anything but defending the faith against heretics."[12]

Eusebius records that the young Origen castrated himself as a means of guarding his chastity since many of his pupils were female.[13] One scholar has wryly remarked that this incident is "the only thing the general public usually knows about Origen."[14] Some modern researchers have exhibited skepticism about this episode, suspecting that Eusebius may have uncritically recorded a slanderous rumor circulating about Origen.[15] That the tradition about Origen's castration is preserved by Eusebius of Caesarea, who was an ardent admirer of Origen and knew men who had known Origen, is strong evidence in favor of its historicity.

The edict of Severus forbade conversions, i.e., the baptism of pagans, but those such as Origen who were already Christians were normally not affected, provided they did not openly defy

---

10. Jerome, *On Illustrious Men* 54 (= FOTC 100:77–81).

11. Chadwick in Origen, *Contra Celsum*, (Cambridge: Cambridge University Press, 1953), p. ix. In the *Commentary* there are numerous allusions to Clement's writings.

12. J. Daniélou, *Origen*, trans. W. Mitchell (London and New York: Sheed and Ward, 1955), p. 8.

13. Eusebius, *Ecclesiastical History* 6.8.1–2.

14. Crouzel, *Origen: The Life and Thought of the First Great Theologian*, trans. A. S. Worrall (San Francisco: Harper and Row, 1989), p. 9 n. 32.

15. Cf. H. Chadwick, *The Early Church*, The Pelican History of the Church 1 (Harmondsworth: Penguin Books, 1971), p. 109.

the authorities.[16] Origen was not intimidated. His life and doctrine were responsible for "myriads" of conversions, and at least six of his converts/pupils were killed in this persecution. Origen placed himself in great danger by visiting them in prison and accompanying them to the execution site. His own house was watched and he was forced to go underground with frequent changes of residence.

It is known that Origen made a visit to the ancient and famous Church of Rome and that he heard St. Hippolytus preach a sermon there.[17] Around 215 he journeyed to Arabia. Upon his return a war had broken out in Alexandria. Caracalla had been the butt of jibes from the student population, which greeted him as "Geticus," a pun on the triumphal title of honor, "Gothicus," i.e., "victor over the Goths," because he had assassinated his brother Geta.[18] Enraged, Caracalla sacked the city, closed the schools, and exiled the faculty. According to Eusebius this was the occasion of Origen's first departure from Alexandria to Caesarea, about the year 216.[19] There may be a cryptic allusion to this incident in the *Commentary*.[20]

From about 230 he stayed at Caesarea in Palestine, though he continued to travel a fair amount. Under the persecution of Decius, the first truly universal persecution of Christians, Origen was imprisoned. Eusebius had access to authentic letters of Origen in which he recounted the severe tortures inflicted upon him in prison. Origen was released and died shortly afterwards in 254 at the age of 69 or 70. His body was laid to rest in Tyre and his tomb was still being reverently shown at the end of the thirteenth century.

For a more detailed summary of Origen's life and writings, see Quasten, *Patrology*, 2:37–101.

---

16. Cf. C. Bigg, *The Christian Platonists of Alexandria* (1886; reprint, New York, AMS Press, 1970), p. 117 (page citations are to the reprint edition); H. M. D. Parker, *A History of the Roman World from A.D. 138 to 337*, revised with additional notes by B. H. Warmington (London: Methuen & Co., 1958), p. 137.

17. Eusebius, *Ecclesiastical History* 6.14.10–11; Daniélou, *Origen*, p. 20.

18. Cf. *Geta* 6.6 in *Historia Augusta*.

19. Eusebius, *Ecclesiastical History* 6.19.15–19. In this summary I have relied on Crouzel, *Origen*, pp. 14–15.

20. Preface of Origen (9).

3. Origen's Errors and Condemnation

Some of Origen's views were later condemned as heretical by the Church. Even during his lifetime Origen had been charged of heresy.[21] Pope Anastasius I, bishop of Rome (399–401), issued a letter to John, bishop of Jerusalem, approving of the condemnation passed by a synod of anti-Origenist bishops in Egypt of his writings. The pope virtually anathematized Rufinus (Origen's translator) and claimed that Origen's object was to disintegrate the Christian faith. Amazingly, the pope admitted not only that he had never read Origen's writings, but that he had never heard of the man he was condemning. Ecclesio-political machinations were obviously at work here, rather than definite knowledge of Origen's views. The pope had come under the influence of Jerome and Marcella (one of Jerome's anti-Origenist friends) and was seeking to satisfy their wishes. Marcella's motivation is called into question in that she had supplied the Roman bishop with an edition of Rufinus's translation of Origen's *De Principiis* that contained forgeries.[22] Such realities would seem to mitigate the authority of Anastasius's condemnation of Origen.

A century and a half later in 543, the Emperor Justinian (527–65) issued an edict denouncing Origen by name. A list of his doctrines was formally condemned at the Fifth Ecumenical Council in 553. According to Crouzel, this Council had virtually no authority as regards Origen, since it was really aimed at the Origenists of the day, who had turned Origen's speculations into dogmas.[23] Nevertheless, Origen's name was listed among the heretics, and several points in Origen's theology were rejected by Church authority. Among the condemned doctrines were his Christological subordinationism; his eschatological speculation, which included the conjecture that all rational beings including Satan and the demons may eventually be restored to grace;[24] the doctrine of pre-existence of souls; his

---

21. Cf. *Princ* 1.6.1; *Hom in Lk* 25.
22. Rufinus complains of this in his *Apology against Jerome* 1:19 = NPNF2, 3:444.
23. Crouzel, *Origen*, p. xii.
24. This doctrine was called, by its Greek name, the *apocatastasis*; cf. Acts 3.21.

theory about previous worlds and future world cycles; his speculation that the final state of salvation may be disembodied; and his purgatorial understanding of hell. I refer the reader to the works of Daniélou and Crouzel for detailed discussion of these matters.

4. Origen's Influence

In spite of posthumous anathematizations against him, his condemnation never really "took." In both the East and the West Origen had many admirers, including Gregory Thaumaturgus, Pamphilus the Martyr, Eusebius of Caesarea, Athanasius, Didymus the Blind, Ambrose, the early Jerome, Rufinus, Basil the Great, Gregory Nazianzus, Gregory of Nyssa, John Chrysostom, Evagrius Ponticus, and John Cassian. His admirers did not deny his errors, but viewed them as those of a pioneer, not a heretic. Origen's defenders noticed that he had spoken tentatively and never with the intention to violate the Church's rule of faith. In most cases his erroneous opinions were simply questions brought forward for the sake of discussion, not dogmatic assertions, and usually with the intention of refuting Gnostic heresies, leading him somewhat unwittingly to advocate extreme or unconsidered views. Origen's supporters also pointed out that certain disputed teachings in Origen, such as the doctrine of the pre-existence of the soul, were still being debated in the Church as late as the fifth century. Consequently, they said, it would be unfair to condemn Origen on this point, since the Church itself had not yet settled that matter in his lifetime.

Many were attracted to Origen because of his universally acknowledged holiness and his unparalleled zeal in studying Scripture. Origen's writings reveal a man whose heart was aflame with a consuming love for Jesus Christ and for his Church. One senses not only penetrating biblical insight but a sincerity and modesty that is rare among learned men. His life was godly, and he had endured prison and torture for the sake of Christ. "Though he does not bear the conventional title of Saint, no saintlier man is to be found in the long line of ancient

8   INTRODUCTION

Fathers of the Church."[25] One of Origen's modern translators has fittingly summarized his life in these words:

He was humble and free from envy, caring neither for power nor wealth. He bore unmerited suffering, from friends and foes alike, without complaint. His life, from beginning to end, was hard and strenuous. His courage never failed, and he died in reality a martyr's death. He loved truth with a sincerity and devotion rarely equaled, and never excelled.[26]

5. Occasion and Date of Origen's Commentary

Although it is not mentioned in Eusebius's *Ecclesiastical History*, Origen's *Commentary* is one of his last and most mature works.[27] He wrote it during his Caesarean period, around the year 246.[28] The mention of Gothicus[29] would be decisive in determining the *terminus a quo* for the *Commentary*, if it could be proven to be a reference to the emperor Gordian III (238–44), the first to bear this title (unofficially) after his victory over the Goths in 242. *Victor Gothorum* was inscribed on his tomb.[30] Unfortunately, Rufinus tells us that he has appended the discussion in which Gothicus is mentioned from a source outside the *Commentary*.[31] Moreover, it is also possible that Origen merely intends this to be a facetious reference to Caracalla (211–17).

---

25. F. J. A. Hort, *Six Lectures on the Ante-Nicene Fathers* (1895; reprint, New York: Books for the Libraries Press, 1972), p. 126.
26. Butterworth in Origen, *On First Principles*, p. v.
27. H. Urs von Balthasar, ed. *Origen: Spirit and Fire. A Thematic Anthology of His Writings*, trans. Robert J. Daly (1984; reprint, Washington, D.C.: The Catholic University of America Press, 2001), p. 197 n. 1.
28. Heither in Origenes, *Commentarii*, 1:11, dates it at 243–44; A. von Harnack, *Geschichte der altchristlichen Literatur bis Eusebius*, 2 vols. (Leipzig: J. C. Hinrichs, 1958), vol. 2, part 2:41, puts it at 244. Cf. Chadwick in Origen, *Contra Celsum*, p. xiv n. 2, "The [Romans] commentary is often dated exactly in 246, but the evidence is quite insufficient."
29. Preface of Origen (9).
30. Cf. *Gordiani Tres* 34.3 in *Historia Augusta*. The Goths had invaded the Danubian frontiers in 238. Claudius II (268–70) was the first Roman emperor who officially assumed the triumphal title "Gothicus," or, more precisely, on whom the title was bestowed by the Senate. Cf. H. Wolfram, *History of the Goths*, trans. Thomas J. Dunlap (Berkeley: University of California Press, 1979), p. 55.
31. Preface of Origen (11).

INTRODUCTION   9

In that case it would not tell us anything about the date of writing. Origen himself refers to the *Commentary* in his last works, *Commentary on Matthew* 17.32 and *Against Celsus* 5.47 and 8.65, thus establishing a *terminus ad quem* (248) for the work.

The timing of the appearance of Origen's *Commentary* (ca. 246) is interesting. Rome, the capital city of the Roman Empire, celebrated her millennium on April 21, 248.[32] This was the outstanding event of the reign of Philip I (244–49), who may have been the first Christian emperor.[33] The millennium was magnificently commemorated with the traditional pagan religious ceremonies and extravagant games in the Circus Maximus.[34] Some scholars have identified this event with the occasion of Origen's apologetic work *Against Celsus*, dated at 247–48. Origen regarded Paul as the most important apostle, a man who wrote Romans at the peak of his spiritual maturity.[35] Origen sensed that anti-Christian sentiment was on the rise in the mid-240s and that a persecution was imminent. He predicted that the secure existence of Christians would soon come to an end, "when those who attack Christianity in every possible way regard the multitude of believers as responsible for the rebellion which is so strong at this moment, thinking that it is because they are not being persecuted by the governors as they used to be."[36] Chadwick suggests that this feeling came about in connection with the renewal of pagan pride resulting from Rome's millennial celebrations.[37] Perhaps the *Commentary* was written in anticipation of Rome's approaching 1000-year Jubilee, as an enthusiastic outcropping of Christian pride over the inspired document addressed to the church in the Eternal City.

---

32. Parker, *A History of the Roman World from A.D. 138 to 337*, p. 153.
33. Cf. Crouzel, *Origen*, p. 3f.
34. M. Grant, *The Roman Emperors. A Biographical Guide to the Rulers of Imperial Rome, 31 BC–AD 476* (New York: Charles Scribner's Sons, 1985), p. 153.
35. He calls Paul the *Apostolorum maximus* in *Hom in Nm* 3.3. Cf. Preface of Origen (3–7).
36. *Cels* 3.15, trans. Chadwick.
37. Chadwick in Origen, *Contra Celsum*, p. xv.

6. Life and Work of Rufinus of Aquileia

Because Origen's *Commentary* has survived (except for short Greek fragments) in the Latin translation of Rufinus, it is fitting to introduce Origen's translator as well. Together with St. Jerome, Tyrannius Rufinus of Aquileia (345–411) made the writings of Origen available to the Latin West. Rufinus, like Origen, was never canonized, and a shadow was cast over him in subsequent centuries owing to the malicious and unjust attacks on his character and orthodoxy by St. Jerome. Yet Rufinus is one of the noblest and most productive figures of Christian antiquity. He dedicated the latter part of his life to the unselfish task of translating the works of Greek theologians into Latin. "Through his labors . . . a considerable part of the works of the great Alexandrian have floated down across the ocean of the Dark Ages, and, while lost in their native Greek, have in their Latin garb come to enrich the later civilization of the West."[38] As a translator Rufinus became one of the most important educators of the Latin Middle Ages, although to the present day his significance has scarcely been appreciated or fully measured. "More than any other figure in the fields of hermeneutics, exegesis, and spirituality, he would be the grand master."[39]

Rufinus was born into a Christian family in Concordia, not far from Aquileia. Athanasius (296–373) had popularized monasticism in the West and spent a year in Aquileia around the year of Rufinus's birth. By 370 there was an ascetic community in Aquileia and Rufinus joined it upon his return from Rome, where he had studied. He became a monk and was baptized in Aquileia around 370. In 372 or 373 he went to Egypt, a Greek-speaking part of the Empire, where he met Didymus the Blind, who introduced him to Origen's works.[40] Following Athanasius's death in 373 there was an outbreak of persecution

---

38. Fremantle, "Prolegomena on the Life and Works of Rufinus," NPNF2, 3:405.

39. H. de Lubac, *Medieval Exegesis*, vol. 1: *The Four Senses of Scripture*, trans. M. Sebanc (Grand Rapids, Mich.: Eerdmans, 1998), p. 159.

40. See Rufinus's brief biography of this saintly man in his *Ecclesiastical History* 11.7.

INTRODUCTION   11

by the Arians against orthodox Christians in Egypt. Rufinus himself was thrown into prison and afterwards he and many other confessors were banished from Egypt by their Arian persecutors.[41]

After his sojourn in Egypt, Rufinus moved to Palestine with a wealthy patroness and sister in Christ, Melania. Together they established on the Mount of Olives a monastic foundation devoted to ascetic practices, to scholarly pursuits such as the copying of manuscripts of Christian and pagan classics, to teaching, and to showing hospitality to visitors of the Holy Land. Palladius relates, "They passed their life, offending none, and helping almost the whole world."[42] It was during this period of eighteen to twenty years that Rufinus was ordained by John, bishop of Jerusalem. The last years of Rufinus's life, during which he carried out his great Latin translations, were spent in Aquileia, Rome, and Sicily, where he died.

In the heat of the Origenist controversy, St. Jerome vilified Rufinus, St. Ambrose, and St. John Chrysostom, attempting to blacken the reputation of all three men for subsequent generations. Only in the case of Rufinus has the cloud of suspicion lingered till the present day.[43] The more objective ancient Christian historians held a different assessment. Palladius described Rufinus as a man of noble birth and manners, very strong in following out his own independent resolutions. "No one of the male sex was ever gentler, and he had the strength and the calmness of one who seems to know everything."[44] In the late fifth century Gennadius saw clearly that Jerome had unjustly attacked Rufinus. He describes Rufinus as a brilliant and gifted teacher of the Church who gave to the Latins a very large part of the library of the Greek writers. "He also replied in two volumes to him who decried his works [St.

41. Cf. Rufinus, *Apology to Anastasius* 2 = NPNF2, 3:430.
42. *Lausiac History* 46, trans. Fremantle in citation, NPNF2, 3:406.
43. For detailed coverage of Rufinus's life and involvement in the Origenist controversy, see F. X. Murphy, *Rufinus of Aquileia (345–411): His Life and Works* (Washington, D.C.: Catholic University of America Press, 1945), and J. N. D. Kelly, *Jerome: His Life, Writings, and Controversies* (New York: Harper & Row, 1975).
44. Palladius, *Lausiac History*, NPNF2, 3:410.

Jerome], showing convincingly that he [Rufinus] had exercised his powers through the insight given him by God and for the good of the Church, and that it was through a spirit of rivalry that his adversary had employed his pen in defaming him."[45] John Cassian considered Rufinus "a man of Christian philosophy, a portion of the learned body of the Church scarcely to be contemned."[46] And Cassiodorus regarded him as a most eloquent translator, who translated Origen's *Commentary* even more eloquently.[47]

7. *Rufinus's Translation of Origen's* Commentary

Rufinus translated Origen's *Commentary* in 406/7. The question of provenance is disputed. The translation was carried out either in Aquileia or in southern Italy. Earlier scholarship favored Aquileia as the place of writing and dated Rufinus's move south into Italy in 407/8.[48] Recently, however, C. P. Hammond has argued that Rufinus's complaints in the Epilogue reflect disputes going on in Rome at the time.[49] It is certain that Rufinus had already completed the translation of Origen's *De Principiis* and the homilies on *Psalms, Genesis, Exodus, Leviticus, Joshua,* and *Judges.*[50] He announces that his next project, which can be dated to 407, will be the translation of *Clement's Recognitions.*[51]

Rufinus tells us in the Preface that a certain Heraclius has asked him to translate Origen's *Commentary*. For this otherwise unknown monk he also translated Origen's homilies on *Genesis, Exodus,* and *Leviticus.*[52] Judging from the length of these works,

---

45. Gennadius, *List of Ecclesiastical Writers* 17 = NPNF2, 3:389.

46. Murphy, *Rufinus of Aquileia*, p. 222.

47. M. M. Wagner, *Rufinus the Translator: A Study of his Theory and his Practice as illustrated in his Version of the Apologetica of St. Gregory Nazianzen* (Washington, D.C.: Catholic University of America Press, 1945), p. 2.

48. E.g., Fremantle, Westcott, Murphy, Kelly.

49. Hammond, C. P., "The Last Ten Years of Rufinus' Life and the Date of His Move South from Aquileia," *JThS*, n.s., 28 (1977): pp. 401ff.

50. As he states in the Epilogue (1–2).

51. Epilogue (5).

52. Epilogue (1).

INTRODUCTION   13

Heraclius must have been in frequent contact with Rufinus over a long period of time.⁵³ He requested that Rufinus abridge the work to half the space, since the original Greek text, which comprised fifteen books, exceeded forty thousand lines. A Latin book corresponds to more than two Greek books, which explains how Rufinus's abbreviated version of fifteen Greek volumes could comprise ten Latin books.⁵⁴ C. H. Turner has calculated that 40,000 Greek lines, at a rate of sixteen syllables per verse occupies 25,000 half-lines (there being two columns to a page) when translated into Latin. This is twice the length of Rufinus's Latin translation.⁵⁵ Thus Rufinus kept his word to Heraclius: He compressed the Greek work to precisely half the space.

Rufinus's open admission of having substantially abbreviated the work is of importance in assessing his reliability as its translator.⁵⁶ For this possibly explains why the surviving Greek fragments of the *Commentary* only rarely show word-for-word correspondence with Rufinus's Latin translation: He has omitted half of the original. The lack of congruence between any given Greek fragment and Rufinus's Latin version may not necessarily impugn Rufinus's reliability as a translator, since the fragment might have been not translated by Rufinus.

In the Preface Rufinus complains that his translation task was made difficult because Origen's text had been "interpolated." The question arises: Is he repeating the complaint he made in the preface to *De Principiis*, that heretics have falsified Origen's writings with their own interpolations? Or does he mean that volumes are missing from the booksellers' copies of Origen's massive work?

Scholars are divided on Rufinus's explanation.⁵⁷ Rufinus

53. Cf. Hammond, "Last Ten Years," p. 403.
54. C. P. Hammond Bammel, *Der Römerbrieftext des Rufin und seine Origenes-Übersetzung, AGLB* 10 (Freiburg im Breisgau: Herder, 1985), p. 173.
55. C. H. Turner, "Greek Patristic Commentaries on the Pauline Letters," in *Dictionary of the Bible*, ed. J. Hastings (New York: Charles Scribner's Sons, 1909), p. 491.
56. For a detailed analysis of Rufinus's general translation procedure and reliability, see Ronald Heine's Introduction in Origen, *Homilies on Genesis and Exodus*, FOTC 71:27–39.
57. Preface (2).

seems to be complaining of books missing from the original work rather than intentional falsifications of the existing text. According to this view, the sense of *interpolare* would be "to interrupt," "to break the continuity" (by subtraction).[58] This would mean that Rufinus had to supply the material missing from his copy of the *Commentary* from Origen's other exegetical works, wherever relevant discussions could be found. And yet he speaks of volumes missing from the libraries of nearly *(fere)* everyone. Does this mean he had access to libraries that contained the entire work? It does seem that "interpolations" in the strict sense cannot be entirely excluded from Rufinus's intention in this passage, since he has complained of this on other occasions. Moreover, this meaning of *interpolare* agrees with its only other use in the *Commentary* in 10.43, where it is applied to Marcion's critical endeavors.

8. The Lemmata & Biblical Citations

B. F. Westcott was the first to observe that Rufinus used an Old Latin[59] version for the lemmata[60] of the *Commentary*. Rufinus did not make a new translation of the lemmata in Origen's Greek version of Romans.[61] Hammond Bammel suggests that the reason he did this was that the lemmata in Origen's Greek *Commentary* were abbreviated.[62] Even if they were fully present in the original, however, it is not certain that Rufinus would have translated these cue headings *de novo*. Beyond doubt he saved himself considerable labor by simply supplying

---

58. H. Chadwick, "Rufinus and the Tura Papyrus of Origen's *Commentary on Romans*," *JThS*, n.s., 10 (1959): pp. 38–41.

59. The Old Latin version refers to ancient (2d–3d century) translations of the Bible in use prior to Jerome's more famous edition, the Latin Vulgate. One of its unique features was that its OT was a translation of the LXX (i.e., the Alexandrian Greek translation of the Hebrew OT), not of the Hebrew. Its NT translation was based upon a "Western" text type. In contrast, Jerome's Latin version was a new translation of the Hebrew.

60. The lemmata are the cue phrases or head words which contain the text of Romans to be explained in each section of the *Commentary*. They are given in italics in this translation.

61. B. F. Westcott, "Origenes," *DCB* 4:116.

62. Hammond Bammel, *Römerbrieftext*, p. 57.

an existing Latin translation for the lemmata and other scriptural citations, rather than creating a new one. The Old Latin wording would have been familiar to his readers. Especially for the OT quotations, this version was well-suited to his purpose, since it was a translation of the LXX, the Bible Origen used. Though Rufinus used an existing Old Latin text for the cue headings, for the body of the *Commentary* he simply translated the Greek text of Origen's *Commentary*. This has resulted in disagreements between the wording of the lemmata and Origen's discussion, which was based on the Greek text of Romans. At times Rufinus failed to adjust Origen's explanation to the wording of the Old Latin lemmata and vice versa.[63] Rufinus's method resembles that of a modern translator of patristic literature who uses an existing English translation for the biblical citations without always checking the citations against the original. Such a procedure may create textual difficulties for readers of the original, but it saves much work for the translator. The point is particularly important from the perspective of NT textual criticism: "Unless Origen's Greek reading is expressly noted, the reading given must be regarded as a Latin reading and not as Greek."[64]

If Rufinus produced his translation in Aquileia, his text of Romans may have been a Latin version current in the Aquileian church.[65] Hammond Bammel theorizes a Roman provenance for Rufinus's translation and she suggests that it might have been a Roman version.[66]

---

63. One can listen to Rufinus comparing and correcting the Old Latin to the Greek text in 1.5.1; 2.6.5; 2.13.25; 2.14.18; 3.1.6; 3.1.12; 3.2.4; 3.6.5; 3.8.12; 4.1.20; 4.2.11; 5.1.37; 5.8.3; 5.10.17; 6.7.17; 6.8.11; 6.12.3; 7.4.7; 7.4.14; 9.1.9; 9.1.14; 9.2.2; 9.2.10; 9.2.11; 9.3.2; 9.10.1; 9.11.1; 9.12.1; 9.42.3; 10.2.2; 10.11.3; 10.12.2; 10.15.3; 10.19.1. For a detailed discussion of these readings, see Hammond Bammel, *Römerbrieftext*, pp. 212–30. They concern the following verses: Rom 1.4; 2.8; 3.4; 3.5; 3.16; 3.19; 3.25; 5.14; 6.11; 7.6; 7.13; 8.3; 8.22; 12.2; 12.3; 12.6; 12.11; 12.13; 15.16; 15.17; 15.30; 16.5; 16.25–27.

64. Westcott, "Origenes," p. 116.

65. So Kelly in Rufinus, *A Commentary on the Apostles' Creed*, ACW 20 (London: Newman Press, 1955), p. 20.

66. Hammond, "Last Ten Years," p. 421 n. 2.

9. The Augustinian/Pelagian Background to Rufinus's Translation

There is a relationship between Rufinus's translation and the beginnings of the Pelagian controversy. Hammond Bammel conjectures that Pelagius and Rufinus knew each other and were on amicable terms while the latter was completing his translation. "Rather than defending Rufinus against the charge that he was associated with the genesis of Pelagianism, we should be ready to acknowledge the stimulation of his influence in person as well as through his translations on the creative thought of his generation."[67] Texts from Origen's *Commentary* played a critical role in the Pelagian controversy. Indeed, Pelagius himself was one of the first and most enthusiastic pillagers of Rufinus's translation.[68] Rufinus's translation was also used by St. Augustine.[69]

Bammel argues that Rufinus was inspired to translate this particular work of Origen as a reaction to Augustine's harsh views, in which the human race was conceived as a mass of perdition. Rufinus wanted to make Origen's sharply contrasting exegesis of Romans available to the Latin West to offset Augustine's interpretations.[70] Both sides of the Pelagian controversy cited passages from it to support their interpretation of the disputed themes: divine grace and human responsibility, free will, the relationship between predestination and foreknowledge, the possibility of sinlessness, the propagation of Adam's sin. Since the Pelagian and anti-Pelagian camps had not yet become entrenched, Rufinus could translate Origen without inhibitions.

There seems to be a near-consensus among modern scholars that the general point of view of Origen's *Commentary* cannot

---

67. Hammond, "Last Ten Years," p. 427.
68. Cf. T. Bohlin, *Die Theologie des Pelagius und ihre Genesis* (Uppsala: Almqvist & Wiksells, 1957), p. 103, "It appears to us that Pelagius found rich and central material for his doctrine of grace nowhere so much as in Origen's *Commentary on Romans.*"
69. C. P. Bammel, "Augustine, Origen and the Exegesis of St. Paul," *Augustinianum* 32 (1992): pp. 341–68; C. P. Bammel, "Justification in Augustine and Origen," *JEH* 47 (1996): p. 231.
70. Bammel, "Augustine, Origen and the Exegesis of St. Paul," p. 358.

fairly be designated as Pelagian. Hammond Bammel cites two reasons for this.

First of all, a chief component of Pelagianism is the denial of Origen's well-known opinion that every human being already at birth is found in a fallen condition. Secondly, the statements of the commentary are so diverse that one could prove both Pelagian and typically Augustinian views through quotations from Rufinus's translation.[71]

I shall return to this question below.[72]

10. The Greek Fragments of Origen's Original Commentary

The Greek fragments of Origen's *Commentary* are very short. The longest contains less than a complete chapter of the *Commentary*. They are found in the following: 1) Basil's *De Spiritu Sancto* 29.73; 2) Socrates' *Ecclesiastical History* 7.32.17;[73] 3) the "chain of extracts" or *Catena*;[74] 4) the *Philocalia;* 5) and the *Tura Papyrus*, discovered in 1941.[75] This last source preserves the longest continuous text of the *Commentary*, passages concerning Romans 3.5–5.5. Here it is possible to test the reliability of Rufinus's work, at least in some cases.

In an appendix to his magisterial study of the patristic interpretation of Romans, K. H. Schelkle makes a detailed comparison of the Greek fragments with Rufinus's Latin translation.[76] He calls into question the traditional suspicion of Rufinus's reliability and the preference for the Greek fragments, concluding

71. Hammond Bammel, *Römerbrieftext*, p. 47 n. 14.
72. See Introduction (12).
73. The quotation is from Book 1 of the *Commentary* but does not correspond to Rufinus's translation. Socrates is discussing the Nestorian controversy and claims that Origen had used the title *theotokos*, "mother of God" with reference to Mary in his *Commentary*. To Socrates this was proof of two things: The tradition supported the controversial title for Mary and Nestorius was not very well read in ecclesiastical literature.
74. These are collections of excerpts from miscellaneous Greek patristic commentaries. The Origen-fragments have been critically edited by A. Ramsbotham, "Documents: The Commentary of Origen on the Epistle to the Romans," *JThS* 13 (1912): pp. 209–24, 357–68; *JThS* 14 (1913): pp. 10–22.
75. J. Scherer, éd., *Le Commentaire d'Origène sur Rom. III.5–V.7*, Bibliothèque d'Étude, vol. 27 (Cairo: Institut français d'Archéologie orientale, 1957).
76. Schelkle, *Paulus, Lehrer*, pp. 443–48.

that the reliability of the fragments must be contested. Schelkle denies that they can even be regarded as genuine pieces of Origen's original *Commentary*. They are instead excerpts from the *Commentary*, i.e., summaries of longer passages, and they have been shaped into a unique form by the excerptor.[77] The excerpts create their own wording according to the key-words and thoughts of Origen's interpretation.[78]

Schelkle offers reasons why Rufinus may have abbreviated the material found in certain fragments: some for dogmatic reasons, some to avoid unnecessary repetition. But according to Schelkle, the most decisive point in favor of the reliability of Rufinus's Latin translation is its breadth and detail. The *Catenae* do not cite biblical passages word-for-word and tend to cite a single passage of the Bible in support of an idea, whereas Rufinus quotes word-for-word, interprets the passage, and furnishes additional quotations. The *Catena* string together thoughts in a sentence according to some key word, whereas Rufinus has worked these thoughts out in detail. And it is not possible to explain this relationship by saying that Rufinus expanded the original text which is authentically represented by the *Catena*, and that he filled it in out of his own head. For the content of the exegesis is too meaningful to be regarded as Rufinus's padding. Moreover, such a theory would make it impossible to explain why Rufinus needed to reduce the extent of Origen's interpretation, as he himself says in his Preface, if the *Catena* represented the original text of Origen. Instead, it is evident that Rufinus has preserved the original text in its larger context, whereas the scholiast greatly abbreviated the original text.[79]

If Schelkle's investigation is correct, it seems that Rufinus's Latin translation has been vindicated, at least in large part. It offers us the best source and most reliable witness for Origen's thoughts, though Rufinus has expressed these thoughts in his own words. Even Scherer, who thinks that Rufinus has substituted his own exegesis at several points, admits, "The translation is often accurate, exact, and in large measure faithful."[80]

77. Ibid., p. 444.   78. Ibid., p. 448.
79. Ibid., p. 444.
80. Scherer, *Commentaire d'Origène*, p. 88.

It is certain that Rufinus has left out large blocks of text. It is very likely that he has reformulated (or updated) heterodox-sounding passages, particularly those pertaining to the Trinity, since his translations assume that heretics had falsified some passages in Origen's works.[81] We are moreover well advised to keep in mind Hammond Bammel's cautions to the effect that in his translations of Origen, Rufinus has spoken with his own voice to the readers of his time. He has reflected upon the thoughts of Origen and expressed them in his own words for his readers. We are listening to a Latin speaker, schooled in rhetoric, of the time around 400; no longer do we hear a Greek, educated in philosophy, of the first half of the third century. Rufinus's language was less polished and less technical than Origen's.

> His readers were at a lower intellectual level than Origen. The difficult concepts had to be explained and simplified for them. . . . Rufinus's aim was to edify his readers, not to show off his erudition; thus he often simplifies problems or covers over difficulties. Inevitably his standpoint was different from that of Origen.[82]

These *caveats* notwithstanding, it is to Origen's interpretations we are listening in the *Commentary*, not to Rufinus's. A sure method of confirming this is to compare the exegesis found here with that of Origen's other writings. To facilitate this task I have incorporated in the footnotes most of the references to parallel passages in Origen's other writings found in Heither's and Hammond Bammel's editions. I have tried to supplement these with references found in secondary works and with those discovered in the course of my own study of Origen's writings.

11. How Well Did Origen Understand Paul?

Because Origen supplies an abundance of material in his *Commentary* and often leaves to the reader the decision to pick

---

81. He justifies this (dubious) suspicion in his *Apology against Jerome* and in his *Book on the Adulteration of Origen's Writings*.
82. Hammond Bammel, *Römerbrieftext*, pp. 44f.

the best interpretation of the several he has offered,[83] the question of determining how well Origen understood Pauline theology is complicated by Origen's humility as an exegete. His *Commentary* is more of a humble investigation with the reader than a forceful imposition of a pattern on Paul's thought.[84] Therefore, speaking generally, the work "is better suited for illustrating the range of Origen's ideas than for answering questions about what his view was on particular disputed topics."[85]

Yet there is a more serious difficulty in formulating the problem this way. The question presumes to know Paul's thought, then asks whether Origen subscribed to this understanding. This procedure is methodologically false. We also need to remember that neither Origen nor any other Church Father occupied themselves with the question about Paul's specific contribution to Christian theology.[86] The Fathers did not distinguish "Pauline theology" from others, e.g., Petrine, Matthean, or Johannine. Since Origen placed weight on the divine, not the human, author of Scripture, only "biblical" theology mattered to him. To the Fathers, any attempt to isolate Paul's theology would have been reminiscent of the program Marcion had outlined.

Marcion is one of Origen's most important opponents in the *Commentary*. The heretic from Pontus preferred Paul's writings to the rest of the NT, but he interpreted them as being contrary to the other books of Scripture. In striking ways Marcion anticipated the modern school of NT interpretation. According to Marcion, the Jesus depicted in the four Gospels as the fulfiller of the OT prophecies had been a creation of the early Church and a corruption of the primitive tradition. In order to recover the "historical Jesus," the unique views of Paul and Luke had to

---

83. Cf., e.g., 1.4.1; 1.4.4; 2.7.9; 4.1.7; 4.2.9; 5.8.9; 5.9.11; 6.12.11; 7.5.6; 7.5.7; 7.12.7; 8.10.3; 10.42.1.

84. In this connection Bammel notes a stark contrast to Augustine's exegesis of Paul. See Bammel, "Augustine, Origen and the Exegesis of Paul," p. 351.

85. C. P. Hammond Bammel, "Philocalia IX, Jerome, Epistle 121, and Origen's Exposition of Romans VII," *JThS*, n.s., 32 (1981): p. 77.

86. Cf. T. Heither, *Translatio Religionis: Die Paulusdeutung des Origenes in seinem Kommentar zum Römerbrief*, Bonner Beiträge zur Kirchengeschichte, vol. 16 (Cologne: Böhlau, 1990), pp. 1–4; E. Dassmann, *Der Stachel im Fleisch: Paulus in der frühchristlichen Literatur bis Irenäus* (Münster: Aschendorff, 1979), p. 20.

be isolated and a new canon had to be defined. Consequently, Marcion rejected the OT in its entirety. He discarded all the books of the NT in their received form. He saved for his new church only mutilated portions of Luke's Gospel and Paul's letters. Yet he did not hesitate to cut away entire books from the received Pauline canon such as 1 Timothy, 2 Timothy, Titus, and Hebrews. Marcion then arbitrarily erased scores of theologically offensive passages in the "authentic" letters of Paul and Luke's Gospel. In 10.43 Origen reports that Marcion had entirely deleted the doxology of Rom 16 and had cut to pieces chapters 15 and 16 from his edition of Romans.

For Marcion, as for Luther, the Bible contained a "canon within a canon." It centered around his arbitrary interpretation of Paul's writings and his "revised" edition of Luke. In spite of the many attempts in the modern period to rehabilitate Marcion, his critical endeavors "embody *a priori* theological judgments not founded on any historical, linguistic, or textual criteria we would recognize as valid."[87] It hardly needs to be said that Origen rejected such a procedure. Origen viewed the witness of the biblical writings as a theological unity, since God was the ultimate author of these documents. To Origen the whole Bible had been verbally inspired by the Holy Spirit and was therefore exempt from error and contained nothing that was superfluous.[88]

Thematic Essay on Origen's *Commentary on the Epistle to the Romans*

12. Introduction

Up to now Origen's longest and most detailed exercise in biblical exegesis has been undeservedly neglected.[89] Even in the abbreviated form preserved in Rufinus's translation, Ori-

87. J. Trigg, *Origen: The Bible and Philosophy in the Third-Century Church* (Atlanta: John Knox Press, 1983), p. 48.
88. Cf., e.g., 1.5.2; 1.8; 1.9.3; 2.6.1; 4.11.2; 5.3.5; 5.8.8; 5.10.18; 6.5.6; 7.7.4f.; 9.41.8; 10.25.
89. H. Crouzel calls it the *parent pauvre*, "the poor relation," of Origen's great works, i.e., one that is regarded as holding a subordinate or inferior position. H. Crouzel, "Literature on Origen 1970–1988," *JThS* 49 (1988): p. 506.

gen's *Commentary* is more than one-third longer than *De Principiis*.[90] The reason for the neglect seems to be threefold. First, there has been uncertainty about the reliability of Rufinus's translation. This has caused some scholars to distrust it and others to excuse themselves from studying it. Second, until 1998 no complete critical edition existed. In the nineteenth century Migne reproduced without change the edition of Dom Delarue.[91] This situation has now been corrected by the late C. P. Hammond Bammel. Third, no modern language translations existed until 1985. The Italian scholar F. Cocchini was the first to translate the work into a modern language.[92] She was followed by T. Heither, who produced a German translation. Both were based on the Migne text. To my knowledge there is not yet a French translation.

Disregard for what is undoubtedly Origen's greatest exegetical achievement has resulted in imbalanced and misleading depictions of his thought. Entire monographs on Origen have been written with virtually no engagement with his *Commentary*. Yet the *Commentary* is one of Origen's longest and most mature works. It is the only commentary of Origen that we possess in a coherent form from beginning to end.[93] His work is characterized by its opposition to Gnostic, i.e., predestinarian, interpretations of Paul. Above all Origen defends Paul against the "doctrine of natures," i.e., the belief that all human beings are born with unalterable natures, either good or evil, and thus bound for either salvation or damnation, and that no conduct of theirs during this life can alter their destiny.[94] Origen successfully re-

90. Hammond, "Last Ten Years," pp. 428–29 provides a table showing the number of columns in Migne occupied by Rufinus's translations of Origen's works: *Hom in Jgs*, 40; *Hom in Pss*, 90; *Hom in Ex*, 100; *Hom in Gn*, 117; *Hom in Jos*, 123; *Com in Cant*, 136; *Hom in Lv*, 169; *Hom in Nm*, 220; *Princ* I–IV, 296; *Com in Rom*, 455.

91. C. P. Hammond Bammel, *Römerbrieftext*, pp. 133f.

92. Origene, *Commento alla Lettera ai Romani*, 2 vols., trans. F. Coccini (Casale Monferrato, 1985–1986).

93. C. P. Hammond Bammel, "Die Fehlenden Bande des Römerbriefkommentars des Origenes," in *Origeniana Quarta, Die Referate des 4. Internationalen Origeneskongresses* (Innsbruck, 2–6 September 1985), ed. Lothar Lies (Innsbruck: Tyrolia 1987), p. 16.

94. This definition was given by R. P. C. Hanson, *Allegory and Event* (Richmond, Va.: John Knox Press, 1959), p. 142.

futes this teaching, claiming that a genuine freedom of will always abides in rational beings.

Provoked in part by Marcion's repudiation of the OT and desecration of the New, Origen emphasizes the unity and integrity of the whole Christian canon.[95] He also stresses the harmony between Law and Gospel. The contrast between Origen's interpretive categories and those of modern, chiefly Protestant, interpreters is obvious. This may be in part due to Origen's failure to apprehend correctly some aspects of Paul's thought. What is undeniable is that there are real and apparent similarities between certain Protestant theological formulae, especially those of Calvinism and Lutheranism, and the assertions of Gnostic and Marcionite exegesis. E. Molland has observed:

> In all the works of Origen there is hardly a passage where he conceives of the relation of the Law and Gospel in the Pauline terms of νόμος [law] and χάρις [grace], the role of the Law being to convince mankind of sin and bring all men under the judgement of God, whereas redemption comes by Grace through the Gospel. Of this idea, which is so central in theological thinkers like Marcion and Luther and has determined their whole conception of the Gospel, there are but very faint traces in Origen. . . . Origen thus conceives of the difference and contradiction of the Law and the Gospel in quite other terms than those of judgement and grace, viz., in the terms of imperfect and perfect religion.[96]

This passage illustrates the chasm standing between Origen's teaching and Protestant theology, especially the Lutheran antithesis between Grace and Law. Another point of divergence is Origen's repudiation of the natural predestinarian doctrine of his Gnostic opponents, a doctrine which seems to resemble that of the double-predestinarianism of Calvinism. Whether this implies head-to-head opposition between Origen and Augustine is difficult to say. It is at least clear that Rufinus perceived tension between Origen's interpretation of Romans and Au-

---

95. Not only had Marcion "thrown away" the OT, in 10.43.2 Origen reports that he had completely deleted *(penitus abstulit)* the doxology (Rom 16.24–25) and cut to pieces *(desecuit)* the last two chapters of Romans, from Rom 14.23 until the end, in his version of the NT. Cf. Bammel 10.43.7–11 = PG 14:1290.

96. E. Molland, *The Conception of the Gospel in the Alexandrian Theology* (Oslo: I kommisjon hos J. Dybwad, 1938), p. 121.

gustine's, so much so that his translation was intended to provide a foil for the African Church father's views.

Modern scholars have reached different verdicts on the question of whether Origen really understood the historical context in which Romans was written. P. Gorday thinks that Origen did not show any sign of an historical perspective on the life of the primitive Church. "Specifically this means that in his exegesis of Paul he did not try to set the Apostle within a context of debate, particularly of inter-churchly debate, arising from the problems of the apostolic age."[97] Gorday exemplifies "inter-churchly debate" by claiming that the epistle of James was probably written as a criticism of the letter to the Romans.[98] Such a dismissive assessment of Origen goes further in revealing the Marcionite sympathies of some modern interpreters than it does in impugning Origen's interpretation of Paul. It is of course true that Origen failed to understand the "inter-churchly debate" of the first century, according to the principles and insights of the Tübingen school of NT interpretation. Origen read James and Paul as complementary rather than contradictory to one another, since they were both apostles. Whether this implies that his exegesis of Romans is therefore insensitive to first century historical realities is another question. That Origen's *Commentary* shows awareness that Paul was writing a real letter to real addressees has been calmly defended by the editor of the critical edition.[99]

13. Principal Theme

Origen highlights as one of Paul's main themes in Romans the transfer of religion from Judaism to Christianity, from the letter to the spirit, in terms both of salvation history and of the

---

97. P. Gorday, *Principles of Patristic Exegesis: Romans 9–11 in Origen, John Chrysostom, and Augustine*, Studies in the Bible and Early Christianity, vol. 4 (New York: The Edwin Mellen Press, 1983), p. 48.

98. Gorday, *Principles of Patristic Exegesis*, p. 43.

99. Cf. C. P. Bammel's criticism in her review of T. Heither's monograph *Translatio Religionis* in *JThS*, n.s., 44 (1993): pp. 348–52, "Heither ignores the fact that Origen was aware that Paul was writing a real letter to real addressees, and therefore characterizes the literary form of Romans as a drama."

INTRODUCTION   25

transformation of the individual.[100] Origen claims that the key to unlocking Romans is understanding Paul's use of homonyms, i.e., expressions such as "law," "Jew," "circumcision," "death," etc., used repeatedly, but with divergent meanings.[101] Origen summarizes the content of Romans at the beginning of his explanation of chapter 12, where he says that the essence of religion has been transferred from the Jews to the Gentiles, from the letter to the Spirit, from shadow to truth.[102]

Origen understands that Paul's aim in Romans is to show how salvation came first to those who lived according to the law before the coming of Christ and then how, on the basis of Israel's unbelief, salvation would be bestowed upon the Gentiles through the coming of the Savior. Further, Paul wants to show that not entirely all Gentiles come to salvation but only those who have believed; nor is the entire nation of Israel rejected but a remnant of believers are being saved.[103]

14. Justification, the Doctrine of Natures, Freedom, and Merit

Origen understands justification as the reception of the righteousness of God, which he identifies with Jesus Christ (cf. 1 Cor 1.30). This righteousness makes human beings just, beings in whom the justice of God dwells.[104] With this in mind he cites 1 Cor 1.30 ("God has made Christ our justice") more than thirty times in the *Commentary*. Christ is the righteousness through which all become righteous.[105] Origen argues that to attain salvation the Jews need to realize that Jesus Christ is the key to the meaning of the Scriptures and, through this realiza-

---

100. T. Heither identifies this theme as central to Origen's *Commentary* in *Translatio Religionis*, pp. 57ff., as do P. Gorday, *Principles of Patristic Exegesis*, p. 284, and Molland, *Conception of the Gospel*, p. 121.
101. Cf. R. Roukema, *The Diversity of Laws in Origen's Commentary on Romans* (Amsterdam: Free University Press, 1988), p. 9. Origen "made homonymity the key of his interpretation of this epistle."
102. 9.1.1: Bammel 9.1.1–5 = PG 14:1202.
103. Cf. 3.1.3: Bammel 3.1.25–28 = PG 14:923.
104. Cf. 3.1.9; 3.7.10: Bammel 3.1.87ff. = PG 14:924; 3.4.118–29 = PG 14:944. Cf. T. Heither, *Römerbriefkommentar* 2:16.
105. 3.6.5: Bammel 3.3.79 = PG 14:939.

tion, receive him as their righteousness. The Gentiles need to accept the whole body of Scripture which they had not known before and thereby be justified, i.e., made just through the indwelling Christ, who is justice. For both groups, faith means moving from their previous status into new ground and, in the process, adopting a new shape for their religious lives. Origen understands genuine faith necessarily to involve adhesion to revealed truths. For he considers the faith of the heretics to be a would-be faith.[106] Yet faith is not a mere sentiment, but a moral life, since without its practical fruits it cannot justify. To be sure faith involves trust in Christ's saving power, but it must necessarily become effective in good works.[107]

Origen's discussions of justification are usually embedded in polemic against false interpretations of Paul's teaching. A brief survey of the anti-Gnostic thrust of the *Commentary* will give us insight into Origen's exegetical principles, especially his stress on the unity of the Bible's message. Also it will remind us of a central theme in Origen's theology: the necessity of human cooperation in salvation, a cooperation that extends to all that pertains to salvation: election, interior transformation, and perseverance.[108]

Origen declares in the Preface the two chief reasons why Paul's Letter to the Romans is more difficult to understand than his other letters: first, because Paul makes use of unclear and confused expressions in this letter; second, because in Romans Paul stirs up many questions of the kind which the heretics like to "prop themselves up with," as they claim that the cause of a person's actions is not his own purpose and free will but the possession of different kinds of natures.[109] Supported by a few words from Paul's letter, Origen asserts, the heretics

---

106. 10.5.5: Bammel 10.5.38–39 = PG 14:1256.
107. Cf. 8.1.3: Bammel 8.1.52–60 = PG 14:1159.
108. Cf. C. Verfaillie, *La doctrine de la justification dans Origène d'après son commentaire de l'Épître aux Romains*, Thèse de la Faculté de théologie catholique de l'Université de Strasbourg (Strasbourg, 1926), pp. 63–67.
109. Origen also wrote his treatise *On Prayer* in defiance of heretics who "propped themselves up" on Rom 8.29–30 to teach unconditional predestination, the impossibility of falling from one's election, and the needlessness and vanity of prayer; cf. *Orat* 5.5. See also *Princ* 3.1.7ff.

attempt to subvert the meaning of Scripture in its entirety, which teaches that God has given man freedom of choice.[110] Defending the Christian religion against the heretical doctrine of natures preoccupies Origen throughout the *Commentary*. To his mind this is a fatal doctrine which plunges all of religion and morality into ruin.

Shortly into the treatise Origen confronts a heretical interpretation of Rom 1.1c, where Paul describes himself as "set apart for the gospel of God."[111] Origen reports that the heretics invoke this text calumniously when they say that Paul was set apart because goodness was inherent in his nature.[112] On the contrary Origen affirms that Paul was set apart based upon God's foreknowledge of his future merits. It was neither by chance nor by reason of his possession of a special nature, but justly and deservedly that Paul was set apart. The causes within himself and the merits for the sake of which he was entitled to this were known to God, who knows and foreknows all things. For God had foreseen Paul's apostolic labors, sufferings, and merits, mentioned in such texts as 1 Cor 15.10 and 2 Cor 11.26–27. In advance God knew of Paul's fear of his own damnation should he cease to preach the gospel or fail to restrain his own body (cf.1 Cor 9.16; 1 Cor 9.27). On the basis of this foreknowledge, God chose him.

According to Origen, individuals (including the Apostle Paul himself) are capable of falling out of the state of grace, and God's enemies can become his friends if they are reconciled. He confronts the heretical understanding of Rom 5.10–11 (Marcion and Valentinus are named) and says that no substance is constitutionally hostile to God. If it were, reconciliation would be impossible.[113] The static doctrine of natures fails to reckon with the possibility of conversion, i.e., movement toward or away from salvation. In 2.10 Origen again engages the proponents of the doctrine of natures while commenting on Rom 2.15–16. He says that this Pauline text reveals that each

---

110. Preface of Origen (1): Bammel 1.1(Praefatio).7–9 = PG 14:833.
111. 1.3.1: Bammel 1.5(3).1–4 = PG 14:843–44.
112. 1.3.1: Bammel 1.5(3).7–8 = PG 14:844.
113. 4.12.1: Bammel 4.12.5–11 = PG 14:1002.

person is going to be judged, not by the privilege of possessing a special nature, but by one's own thoughts, as one accused or excused by the testimony of one's own conscience.[114] Later, Origen refers again to those who come from the school of Valentinus and Basilides, who think that there is one nature of souls that must always be saved and cannot perish, and another nature that must always perish and can never be saved. But Paul plainly states that the branches of the good olive tree were broken off deservedly, on account of their unbelief, for they were in need of the vengeance of the divine severity. Paul also says that the branches of the wild olive tree, which the heretics assert are of a ruined nature, were grafted into the root of the olive tree's fertility.[115] This contradicts the Gnostic teaching. A little earlier in 8.7, Origen names the trio Marcion, Basilides, and Valentinus as originators of these depraved doctrines.[116] In contrast to these schools, the orthodox teach that all rational creatures possess one kind of nature, which is equally suited for salvation and damnation.[117] Paul's two-tree analogy, Origen affirms, should be interpreted by Mt 12.33, "Make a tree good and its fruit will be good."[118] This text shows that it is the freedom of will, not natural constitution, that determines the nature of the tree. For Jesus wanted to show that good or evil trees are made, not born.[119]

According to Origen the heretics "prop up" their doctrine of good and evil natures with Rom 9.20–23.[120] But they fail to let that text be informed by 2 Tim 2.20–21, where Paul says that vessels prepare themselves for honorable or dishonorable use

---

114. 2.10.2: Bammel 2.7(9–10).89–95 = PG 14:894
115. 8.11.2: Bammel 8.10.15–23 = PG 14:1191.
116. 8.8.7: Bammel 8.7.85–89 = PG 14:1181. He seems to have associated all three with the doctrine of natures. H. Crouzel, *Origen*, pp. 153f., observes that the objections Origen makes to the trio Basilides-Valentinus-Marcion are somewhat stereotyped and do not reflect a very deep first-hand knowledge of these teachers.
117. 8.11.3: Bammel 8.10.22–26 = PG 14:1191.
118. 8.11.4: Bammel 8.10.40–42 = PG 14:1192.
119. 8.11.4, 5, 7: Bammel 8.10.42–43 = PG 14:1192; cf. also Bammel 8.10.46–47 = PG 14:1192; Bammel 8.10.82–89 = PG 14:1193.
120. 7.17.6; 9.2.16: Bammel 7.15.56–61 = PG 14:1148–49; Bammel 9.2.154–63 = PG 14:1212.

INTRODUCTION 29

by their own free will, namely by cleansing themselves from the defilements of sin. Origen's exegetical method often is to explain difficult and obscure texts of Scripture by clearer ones elsewhere in Paul's writings, in the Gospels, or in the OT. As a churchman his intention is to stress the unity and integrity of the entire Christian canon. For him this includes both the Bible of Israel and the new Christian writings, taken as a single narrative with a single message.

Origen says that nonsense is made of the heretical doctrine of natures by Paul's issuing of commands to believers, which implies that the matter lies within our own power.[121] Paul's order, "Do not let sin reign in your mortal body" (Rom 6.12), assumes the existence of free will and of our ability to avoid sin.[122] Obedience rests with us;[123] we present ourselves freely, with no one forcing us; therefore we must cease blaming the devil, our enslaved natures, or the course of the stars for our sins.[124] All of Paul's commands presume that everyone is capable of paying out to righteousness and sanctification the service he was previously paying out to the devil, once one's purpose has been converted to better things. This could not be done at all, Origen asserts, if, "as some think," one's nature were fighting against this, or if the course of the stars were resisting.[125]

15. Analysis

Schelkle has noted that Hermas (*Similitudes* 8.6.1ff.) was the first to explain predestination on the basis of God's foreknowledge, and that Pelagius followed Origen in seeing "calling" based upon *praevisa merita*, foreseen merits.[126] It is possible to reproach Origen for his theory of election, made defective by his ostensible acceptance of antecedent human merit, and many have done so, especially those who read him through the

---

121. 6.1.4: Bammel 6.1.28–31 = PG 14:1056.
122. 6.1.4: Bammel 6.1.31–33 = PG 14:1056.
123. 6.3.3: Bammel 6.3.17–18 = PG 14:1060.
124. 6.3.5: Bammel 6.3.39–44 = PG 14:1060.
125. 6.4.2: Bammel 6.4.36–42 = PG 14:1063–64.
126. Schelke, *Paulus, Lehrer*, p. 18 n. 2

spectacles of the Pelagian crisis. Indeed, he was accused of being a forerunner to Pelagius in subsequent centuries by hyper-Augustinian theologians.[127] Origen does, at times, seem to speak of faith and conversion as a merit which deserves to be counted for righteousness.[128] While it is not my intention to defend Origen's unconsidered and unclear views, when we study the totality of Origen's thought and pay close attention to the context of his polemic, we notice that he was engaged in different problems than those of Augustine and Pelagius.

Origen's affirmation of free will and an election based upon antecedent human merit was grounded in his biblically-inspired opposition to Gnostic thought, in which salvation or damnation was attributed to unalterable natures, either good or evil. Origen's aim was to demonstrate the necessity of human cooperation and human activity in the process of salvation, not to deny that the grace of God is the ultimate source of those merits and of that activity. Interpreters should be hesitant to characterize as a coarse and slavish works-oriented program the pre-Augustinian theological explanations of predestination as the result of foreknowledge. For when reading individual Fathers it is always important to consider both the context of their polemic and their entire doctrine of grace and freedom.[129] Consider the words of H. J. McSorley:

When the (pre-Augustinian) Fathers argued that free will was necessary for merit or demerit, they were not seeking to extol the power of man to merit his salvation. They were simply taking seriously the scriptural teaching that God judges all men according to their works, and from this theological standpoint—from the revealed truth of the coming judgment of God—they insisted against their pagan contemporaries, Marcion above all, that the God who judges is the good God and that man had to have free will if a judgment of God is to be at all meaningful and just. One misunderstands the patristic teaching on free will, then, if one interprets it as mere moralism or as an assertion of autonomous humanism. It was much more an assertion of the jus-

---

127. By, e.g., Luther, Melanchthon, Calvin, Beza, and Jansen.
128. 4.1.12; 4.3.2, 3: Bammel 4.1.151–52 = PG 14:963
129. Both Schelkle, *Paulus, Lehrer*, p. 19 n. 1, and Hammond Bammel, *Römerbrieftext*, p. 47 n. 14, have issued this caution.

tice and the holiness of the one God, the recognition of the original goodness of his creation and a confession of the biblical faith in the coming judgment of our works by God.[130]

Parallel to his stress on the necessity of cooperation and antecedent merit is Origen's insistence on the fallen condition of human beings and on the necessity of grace for salvation. He claims that in their fullness, justice or righteousness belongs to God alone. Human beings, in whom is unrighteousness, come to participate in God's justice by accepting the revelation that changes them from their fallen state and reunites them to God in the union of love.[131] Origen insists that the grace of faith is absolutely indispensable to justification. Not even one who has kept the law of nature perfectly and who has no consciousness of sin whatsoever can be justified unless he or she possesses the grace of faith. For faith is reckoned as righteousness.[132] Since Origen presupposes that faith itself is a gift of God, given by grace through the Holy Spirit, he deems the grace of God absolutely necessary for salvation.[133] Such texts led Verfaillie to conclude, "It would certainly be an extreme injustice to classify among the precursors of Pelagianism a writer who, by insisting so forcefully on the necessity of grace, has refuted in advance the principal error of that system."[134]

Furthermore, Origen's *Commentary* contains striking statements in which he seems to repudiate merit altogether. Von Balthasar described Origen's comments on Rom 4.1–8 as a "strongly Augustinian passage," in which "the apologetics of freedom against a naturalistic Gnosticism recedes into the background and gives way to a genuinely Pauline theology of faith."[135] Verfaillie has perceptively noted that this passage implicitly contains a definition of merit as such, that which would

---

130. H. J. McSorley, *Luther: Right or Wrong? An Ecumenical-Theological Study of Luther's Major Work, The Bondage of the Will* (New York: Newman Press; Minneapolis: Augsburg Publishing House, 1969), p. 61.
131. Cf. 3.1.7; 9.6.3: Bammel 3.1.87ff. = PG 14:924.
132. 4.5.7: Bammel 4.5.108–12 = PG 14:977.
133. 4.5.3: Bammel 4.5.21–25 = PG 14:974–75.
134. Verfaillie, *Doctrine de la justification dans Origène*, pp. 66f.
135. 4.1.14: Bammel 4.1.157–63 = PG 14:963–64. Von Balthasar, *Origen: Spirit and Fire*, p. 197 n. 1.

demand from God repayment as something due *(quod ex debito remunerationem Dei deposcat)*, and that Origen is strongly inclined not to admit merit in this sense.[136]

Origen says that because all have come under sin it is certain that they are likewise estranged from the glory of God, "because they were able neither to receive it in any respect whatsoever nor to merit it."[137] He goes on to say that the righteousness of God reaches to all who believe, whether Jew or Greek, and justifies those who have been cleansed from their past crimes and makes them capable of receiving the glory of God. "And it supplies this glory not for the sake of their merits nor for the sake of works, but freely to those who believe."[138] Clearly merit means to Origen something less than justice in the strict sense, as if one were speaking of two equal and independent parties. For in these passages he denies that justification is given for the sake of merit. His intention in affirming merit (in other passages) does not entail the exact equivalence of desert and reward.[139]

Another passage in the *Commentary* supports the above interpretation. Origen comments on Rom 6.23, "The wages of sin is death," and calls attention to the fact that Paul did not go on to say in similar fashion: But the wages of righteousness is eternal life. Instead he says, "'But the gift of God is eternal life,' in order [not only] to teach that the wages, which are assuredly comparable with a debt and a reward, are a repayment of punishment and death, but to establish eternal life in grace alone."[140] In formulating this contrast between gift and wage, grace and debt, Origen is implying that the initiative in bestowing salvation ultimately rests with God alone, whose capital precedes our efforts. Thus his earlier insistence on the necessity of human merit must presuppose the more fundamental necessity of divine grace. Verfaillie may be right to find in Origen's words here an anticipation of Augustine's dictum: *Eorum coronando*

---

136. Verfaillie, *Doctrine de la justification dans Origène*, p. 116.
137. 3.7.13: Bammel 3.4.149–51 = PG 14:945.
138. 3.7.13: Bammel 3.4.157–58= PG 14:945.
139. Wiles, *Divine Apostle*, pp. 118–19.
140. 4.1.15: Bammel 4.1.177–82 = PG 14:964.

merita coronas dona tua, "By crowning their merits, you crown your own gifts."[141]

16. Origen's Use of the Expression "Justification by Faith Alone"

In the *Commentary* Origen uses the expression, or an approximation of the expression, "justification by faith alone," on numerous occasions, both approvingly and disapprovingly. These passages were hotly disputed during the age of the Reformation. The Magisterial Protestants (Luther, Melanchthon, Calvin, Beza) cited the texts in which Origen repudiated the "formula" of "justification by faith alone" to show that Origen was no true Christian but a Pelagian or even a pagan. Catholic polemicists (Eck, Cochleus, Pyghius), on the other hand, pillaged the same texts to show that Luther, Melanchthon, and Calvin were theological innovators, since the ancient Church, as represented by Origen, repudiated the chief article of the Protestants. Subsequent to these initial controversies, in the late sixteenth and early seventeenth centuries the disciples of the Magisterial Protestant Reformers (e.g., Cranmer, Bullinger, Chemnitz, and the anti-Calvinist Anglican theologian Richard Montague) fastened on passages in Origen where he used the formulation "justification by faith alone" approvingly. Their aim was to prove to Catholic theologians that the Protestant doctrine of justification by faith alone was not an innovation but was rooted in the ancient tradition. What few theologians of this period saw clearly was that Origen was engaged in a set of problems wholly different from the intra-Christian, intra-ecclesial discussions of "faith and works" that dominated the debates of the Scholastic and Reformation periods. Consequently, few recognized that it was naïve to expect Origen to fit neatly into the categories of subsequent periods.

17. Origenes Contra "Iustificatio Sola Fide"

While explaining Rom 2.6, Origen polemicizes against the Gnostic doctrine of natures. He says that Paul's words about the

---

141. Verfaillie, *Doctrine de la justification dans Origène,* p. 117.

righteous judgment of God in the first place refute the heretics who claim that the natures of human souls are either good or evil. They need to realize that God pays back to each one not on account of his nature but on account of his works. "In the second place let believers be edified so as to not entertain the thought that, because they believe this alone can suffice for them. On the contrary, they should know that God's righteous judgment will pay back to each one according to his own works."[142]

In this passage Origen addresses two groups: the heretics and Christian believers. He repudiates the heretical doctrine of salvation by natures and says that it is overthrown by Paul's appeal to a final decisive judgment based upon works. With believers in mind he rejects the view that justification is by faith alone, apparently because certain Christians were denying a future judgment based upon works. By speaking with approval of a just retribution that applies both to recompense and to punishment, Origen seems to presuppose that the works of the justified Christian have a value and that they secure eternal life for him.[143]

Heither fails to comment on this passage either in her German translation or in her monograph, *Translatio Religionis*. Evidently out of ecumenical concerns, she endeavors to interpret Paul and Origen as advocates of the doctrine of justification by faith alone. She chooses to focus her study on those passages in which Origen defends this formulation and she summarizes Origen's thought, "Solely through faith alone is there access into the grace of God, which gives man reconciliation and justification. Works grow out of faith, as branches and fruits from the root."[144] While there is support for this view in Origen's *Commentary*,[145] the failure to address passages like that of 2.4, in which Origen plainly denies that faith alone suffices for justification, results in a somewhat reductive depiction of Origen's complete thought. For when Origen later speaks of justification by faith "alone," it is clear that he has added a

---

142. 2.4.7: Bammel 2.4.140–43 = PG 14:878.
143. Cf. Verfaillie, *Doctrine de la justification dans Origène*, p. 115.
144. Heither, *Römerbriefkommentar* 2:21.
145. 4.1.18: Bammel 4.1.216–24 = PG 14:965, which I shall discuss below.

qualification to the Pauline text which should be interpreted in light of his previous affirmation that justification is by both faith and works.

In several passages Origen insists that faith and works are linked inextricably. "For one without the other is condemned, seeing that faith without works is called 'dead' (Jas 2.17, 26); and that no one is justified before God by works without faith." He cites Mt 7.24 and Lk 6.46 as evidence that "everywhere faith is joined with works and works are united with faith."[146] Faith is the beginning of justification, but it needs to be perfected through good works. Both elements are rooted in each other and need to be brought to perfection.[147]

In 8.2 Origen again shows awareness of persons who do not seem to be heretics, but who do not understand the inextricable link between faith and good works. He refers to them as he expounds Rom 10.9, where it is evident that Origen rejects their theology, insisting that belief in Christ's resurrection and public confession of his lordship profits one nothing if his resurrection is not realized in the life of the believer. In fact for us Christ is still in the tomb and no reconciliation with God has taken place if we have not subjected ourselves to his lordship by embracing the virtues.[148] This passage does not support Heither's assertion that for Origen reconciliation with God is effected by faith alone.[149] After all, Origen plainly says that faith can be present but, without the advantages of good works, effectual reconciliation with God does not take place.

Related to this is Origen's statement that it is impossible for one who is justified to have indwelling unrighteousness. For the proof of true faith is that sin is not being committed, and where sin is being committed, there you have proof of unbelief.[150] In 4.7 he says that it is impossible for righteousness to be reckoned to one who has any unrighteousness dwelling in him, even if one believes in him who raised the Lord Jesus from the

---

146. 2.13.23; 2.12.4: Bammel 2.9(12–13).403–8 = PG 14:908; cf. Bammel 2.9(12– 13).62– 63 = PG 14:900.
147. Cf. 3.10.5: Bammel 3.8(11).81–82 = PG 14:957.
148. 8.2.8: Bammel 8.2.131–34 = PG 14:1164.
149. Heither, *Translatio Religionis*, p. 235.
150. 4.1.6: Bammel 4.1.70–72 = PG 14:961.

dead. If we do not lay aside the old man with his unrighteous deeds, faith cannot be reckoned as righteousness.[151] When this renewal occurs, faith is deservedly reckoned as righteousness to those who believe.[152] For it is only to the deserving, i.e., those in whom sin is dead and the virtues are operational, that the verdict of "no condemnation" (Rom 8.1) will be reckoned, granted that the effective attainment of the virtues is a gradual process.[153] For if, Origen says, after receiving forgiveness of past sins, we again transgress and do not wash these sins away with tears of repentance, Christ's advocacy will do us no good, since Jesus "cannot call darkness light and what is bitter sweet."[154] He is both advocate and judge.[155] Origen says in 5.10 that to be alive to God in Christ Jesus (Rom 6.11) means to be alive to God in all the virtues: wisdom, peace, righteousness, and sanctification, all of which are identified with Christ (cf. 1 Cor 1.30; Eph 2.14).[156] Essentially Origen understands the infusion of righteousness into the believer as the presence of Christ himself, who is identical with all the virtues.

There are clear parallels between Origen's identification of the indwelling Christ with the virtues, especially righteousness *(dikaiosune)*, and his discussion of the attributes *(epinoiai)* of the Son in his *Commentary on John*.[157] For Origen it seems that Christ did not merely possess the various virtues accidentally or contingently, but he is identical with them. Wiles has rightly perceived that this important conception of Origen may point to his most fundamental resolution of the problem of faith and works in his *Commentary*. He summarizes Origen's thought as follows:

Our relationship to Christ is automatically our relationship to wisdom, righteousness, truth and all the other virtues. To be 'in Christ' is to be 'in' all the virtues; to have Christ in us is to have them in us. To be 'in Christ' is the same as to serve him, and to be his servant is to be the ser-

---

151. 4.7.6: Bammel 4.7.75–83 = PG 14:986.
152. 4.7.5, 7: Bammel 4.7.93–99 = PG 14:986.
153. 6.11.2: Bammel 6.11.29–33 = PG 14:1092.
154. 7.10.3: Bammel 7.8.32–33 = PG 14:1130.
155. 7.10.3: Bammel 7.8.41–42 = PG 14:1131.
156. 5.10.18: Bammel 5.10.264–66 = PG 14:1055.
157. This is discussed in chapter 10 of Marguerite Harl, *Origène et la fonction révélatrice du Verbe incarné* (Paris 1958).

vant of all the virtues. To put on Christ is to put on all the virtues, and conversely to put on the armor of God is to put on Christ. Clearly therefore according to this analysis there can be for Origen no faith without works. Faith in Christ does not need to be supplemented by the virtuous life; it *is* [emphasis Wiles's] the adoption of the virtues. Thus the connection between faith and works is a logically necessary one.[158]

In my view Wiles has identified the epicenter of Origen's solution to the problem of faith and works. For a justified Christian to continue in sin and lack inherent justice and good works is not so much a regrettable alternative as a logical impossibility.[159]

Thus, because Origen conceives justification to be an effective sanctification in which sin is expelled and grace is established in the believer's soul, it cannot be attributed to faith alone. For such a justification brings the Christian's renewal, leading to his inherent righteousness. Origen views justification as the translation of the believer's soul from the state of sin to the state of righteousness. It begins with the remission of sins but embraces the sanctification of the soul. These two aspects are inseparable. Verfaillie accurately observes that although Origen does not pose the question of knowing if justice is imputed or inherent, one can see that the spiritual realism of his psychology favors the latter conception.[160]

This perception is relevant to the Catholic-Protestant debate over the nature of justification and the question of which side is really supported by Origen. Verfaillie does not seem to be in error when he says that nothing could be further from Origen's thought than the Protestant doctrine which admits no other condition for justification but faith alone. "Not only does he affirm with the Church the equal necessity of faith and works; but to this elementary catholic teaching his theological analyses already carry a felicitous precision."[161] In addition to the affirmation of the equal necessity of faith and works, Origen also teaches that one can never have certitude of the state of grace.

158. Wiles, *Divine Apostle*, p. 114.
159. On the other hand, Origen makes it clear that he rejects the claims of rigorists who deny that believers will ever sin and say that if one sins, it is proven that one does not believe. Cf. 2.7.8: Bammel 2.8.345–50 = PG 14:889.
160. Verfaillie, *Doctrine de la justification dans Origène*, p. 110.
161. Verfaillie, *Doctrine de la justification dans Origène*, p. 68.

Therefore he regards it premature to affirm here that someone is definitely justified.[162] It is no wonder that the first Protestants were repulsed by Origen and utterly repudiated him as an interpreter of Paul.

A second motif in Origen's polemic against the expression "justification by faith alone" is found in 3.7. While explaining Rom 3.21 he calls attention to the fact that Paul does "not put down to faith alone the single cause of the disclosure of the righteousness of God, but he associates with it both the law and the prophets. The reason for this is that faith alone, apart from the law and the prophets, does not disclose the righteousness of God nor, on the other hand, do the law and the prophets disclose it apart from faith. Thus the one is rooted in the other so that perfection comes from both."[163] This passage is clearly directed against Marcion's school, which, by the words "justification by faith alone," evidently was advocating a Christianity that rejected the law and the prophets. This sect seems to have promoted the view that its adherents were saved by the NT faith, i.e., religion,[164] alone and not by the Old Covenant religion.

In summary, Origen seems to oppose the formulation "justification by faith alone" for two principal reasons. First, it fails to describe justification as a total renewal of the inner man, resulting in the believer's deserved commendation as inherently just. It thus dissolves the unity of faith and works and severs Christ from his virtues or attributes. But Scripture makes clear that Christ is identical with his *epinoiai* and that justification depends on both faith and good works. Gnostic and even some Christian exegetes used the "faith alone" formulation to deny the doctrine of a future judgment according to works, but Origen repudiates this tactic. Second, Marcion's exegesis had apparently used the same expression to repudiate the faith and religion of the Old Covenant. Origen is to have nothing to do with such a dissolution of scriptural unity.

---

162. 3.2.13: Bammel 3.2.185–89 = PG 14:932–33. Cf. Verfaillie, *Doctrine de la justification dans Origène*, p. 114.
163. 3.7.12: Bammel 3.4(7).140–44 = PG 14:945.
164. *Fides* and *religio* are closely related terms in Origen's *Commentary*. Cf. 1.9.4: Bammel 1.11.27 = PG 14:855.

18. Origenes Pro "Iustificatio Sola Fide"

On the other hand, there are striking statements in Origen's *Commentary* where Origen insists that justification is by faith alone. In 3.9 Origen paraphrases Paul in Rom 3.28, "He is saying that the justification of faith alone suffices, so that the one who only believes is justified, even if he has not accomplished a single work."[165] This nearly seems to be a formal contradiction to his words in 2.4, "Let believers . . . not entertain the thought that, because they believe this alone can suffice for them."[166] What is all the more interesting is that, in keeping with his usual pattern, Origen seeks to establish the harmoniousness of Paul's words with the rest of Scripture. Where else in the Bible, Origen asks, do we find someone who has been justified by faith alone without works of the law?[167] The thief on the cross comes to his mind. He called out, "Lord Jesus, remember me when you come into your kingdom!" (Lk 23.42). Origen notes that in the Gospels nothing else is recorded about his good works, but for the sake of this faith alone Jesus said to him, "Truly I say to you: Today you will be with me in paradise" (Lk 23.43). Origen then applies the words of Paul to the case of this thief and tells the Jews that their boasting is excluded through the law of faith. For through faith this thief was justified without works of the law since the Lord did not require in addition to this that he should first accomplish works, nor did he wait for him to perform some works when he had believed. By his confession alone Jesus, who was about to begin his journey to paradise, received the thief as a justified traveling companion.[168]

---

165. 3.9.2: Bammel 3.6(9).22–24 = PG 14:952.
166. 2.4.7: Bammel 2.4.141–42 = PG 14:878.
167. Heither, *Römerbriefkommentar*, 2:132 n. 72, claims that the two examples Origen invokes of persons justified by faith alone, namely that of the thief and of the sinful woman, are given as *Extremfälle*, "exceptional cases," which are intended to support the radical statement of Paul. Likewise Verfaillie, *Doctrine de la justification dans Origène*, p. 88, also speaks of the case of the thief as being *exceptionnel*.
168. 3.9.3: Bammel 3.6(9).30–39 = PG 14:953. The *sola fide* is also attested in the original Greek; cf. Scherer, *Commentaire*, p. 91:164.4–9. Scherer criticizes

To defend this teaching Origen then cites a second scriptural example, namely, the story of the sinful woman who anointed Jesus' feet (Lk 7.37–39). He insists that it was on the basis of no work of the law but for the sake of faith alone that Jesus said to her, "Your sins are forgiven you." Origen notes that there are many passages in the Gospels in which we read that the Savior used this phrase and said that the faith of the believer was the cause of salvation.[169]

These texts seem to suggest that Origen can accept and even defend the expression "justification by faith alone" if by this one means that the initial gift of forgiveness of sins is received by faith alone and not on account of works of the law. When the sinner's first remission of sins is in view and its relation to works of the law, Origen seems to concede that faith alone is the cause of justification. But the complexity and range of Origen's views will become clearer as we look at other passages.

The "faith alone" formulation is again used by Origen in 3.10, in which he names heretics. He is explaining Rom 3.29–30 and claims that the Apostle's words are an inextricable knot for the heretics, but are easily explainable for churchmen.[170] The circumcision refers to Jewish believers, and the uncircumcision refers to those who have been called to faith from the Gentiles. "For the very same God justifies members of both peoples who believe . . . not upon the privilege of circumcision or uncircumcision, but in consideration of faith alone."[171] This passage shows again that Origen can apparently support the formulation "justification by faith alone" even in a context in which the dangerous doctrine of natures is also in sight. Yet clearly the works he intends to exclude by the adjective "alone" are ceremonial works such as circumcision. But lest this understanding of justification be misinterpreted as a ticket to licentiousness, Origen immediately raises the question: If justifica-

---

Rufinus's translation here of being exceptionally clumsy, feeble, and listless, in comparison with the sharply articulated force of Origen's Greek.

169. 3.9.4: Bammel 3.6(9).48–52 = PG 14:953.

170. A comparison with *Cels* 5.61 shows that the unnamed heretics discussed here are probably the followers of Valentinus.

171. 3.10.1: Bammel 3.7(10).19–21 = PG 14:955.

tion is by faith alone, and works of the law contribute nothing to justification, what happens if someone who hears this should become lax and negligent in doing good, if indeed faith alone suffices for him to be justified? Origen answers that such a person has rejected the grace of justification. For the gift of forgiveness is not a license to sin, since forgiveness applies to past sins, not future ones.[172]

We can sketch Origen's view of justification in the following terms. The initial justification or remission is by faith alone and not by works of the law. It grants complete forgiveness of all past sins, but not future. But justification can be forfeited through laziness and negligence. To put it another way and in Origen's own words, the baptismal circumcision of the believer will be reckoned as the uncircumcision of unbelief if a Christian afterwards becomes a transgressor of Christ's law, since faith without works is dead (Jas 2.26) and the lot of the evil steward is with the unbelievers (Lk 12.46).[173] Yet the qualifying epithet "alone" may be added to Paul's teaching on justification by faith, provided that works of the law and works anterior to initial justification are envisioned as being excluded by the word "alone" and provided that this is not misconstrued as though Paul were granting baptized believers a licence to sin in the future.

19. Works of the Law

Origen's conception of "works of the law" needs to be elucidated, since a more precise definition of this expression will help clarify Origen's intention in excluding "works" from justification. On several occasions Origen emphasizes that the works which Paul says contribute nothing to justification are primarily ceremonial works. In 8.6 while explaining Rom 11.6 he says that "the works which Paul repudiates and frequently criticizes are not the works of righteousness which are commanded in the law, but those in which they boast, who keep the law according to the flesh; that is to say, the circumcision of the

---

172. 3.9.4: Bammel 3.6(9).56–60 = PG 14:953.
173. 2.12.4: Bammel 2.9(12–13).59–63 = PG 14:900.

flesh, the sacrificial rituals, and the observance of Sabbaths and new moon festivals (cf. Col 2.18). These and works of a similar nature are the works by which he says no one can be saved."[174] Similarly, in 3.9 Origen cites the parable of the tax collector (Lk 18.1off.) as evidence that boasting that arises from works of the law avails nothing, "because it does not embrace the humility of the cross of Christ."[175] Thus to Origen the added adjective "alone" seems to be intended primarily to exclude the Jewish works of the law. It does not have in view the virtues of the indwelling Christ or the works of righteousness that result in a believer becoming inherently just in the inner man and deservedly justified in the final judgment. This passage also confirms that moral works are deemed by Origen as absolutely necessary for salvation.[176]

And yet, significantly, in both of the above passages (8.6 and 3.9) Origen immediately extends this repudiation of boasting beyond mere Jewish boasting over works of the law to entirely all religious boasting. Inspired by Gal 6.14, he insists that not only is all Judaic boasting in works of the law excluded, so is the Christian's boasting over his own virtues. In light of texts like Mt 5.28, Prv 20.9, 1 Cor 1.21, and Is 64.6, Origen concludes that the Christian's virtues of chastity, wisdom, and righteousness cannot provide him valid grounds for boasting, since the only legitimate boasting is based upon faith in the cross of Christ, which excludes all boasting that derives from the works of the law.[177] Schelkle was impressed by how strictly Origen interpreted Paul's repudiation of all boasting done by Jews or Christians. He noted that subsequent Fathers did not adopt Origen's total repudiation of religious boasting.[178]

---

174. 8.7.6: Bammel 8.6.111–18 = PG 14:1178.
175. 3.9.6: Bammel 3.6(9).79–81 = PG 14:954.
176. Cf. Verfaillie, *Doctrine de la justification dans Origène*, p. 82, "Works are so necessary in his eyes that he limits the *sine operibus* [without works] of Saint Paul to the ritual law. This implicitly safeguards moral works."
177. 3.9.7: Bammel 3.6(9).81–101 = PG 14:954.
178. Schelke, "Kirche und Synagoga in der frühen Auslegung des Römerbriefs," *Theologische Quartalschrift*, 134 (1954): p. 311.

20. Perfect and Imperfect Faith, Comparative Justification

The complexity and range of Origen's views can be further demonstrated by other passages in which he speaks of faith and justification. In 4.1 Origen states that there are differing degrees of faith within people, both in quantity and quality. When Abraham's faith was credited to him for righteousness, this was the culmination of many antecedent episodes in his life in which he had demonstrated faith. When his faith is reckoned to him as righteousness, his faith is being declared perfect.[179] For sometimes faith is in part, sometimes it is perfect. Nor is faith, in Origen's view, the only virtue that can be reckoned as righteousness. So can wisdom, gentleness, humility, love, piety, mercy, etc.[180] In listing faith as simply one of the virtues that justify, Origen's thought was still inspired by biblical texts. For example, Ps 106.31 says that Phineas's zeal was credited as righteousness.

Origen also observes that faith is not invariably reckoned as righteousness in every believer. For example, of the Israelites it says, "They believed in God and in his servant Moses" (Ex 14.31), but nowhere does it say that this faith was reckoned as righteousness, as was said about Abraham.[181] To Origen this shows that they did not possess the perfection of faith, collected together from many parts into one whole, which deserved to be reckoned as righteousness, as in Abraham's case. Faith can only be reckoned as righteousness in one who believes completely and perfectly.[182]

While explaining Rom 3.9ff. Origen asks whether Paul's words, "There is no one righteous," are not contrary to the other texts of Scripture which testify to many righteous persons. Origen cites Ezek 16.51–52 to show the solution to this problem, namely, that justification is comparative in nature. For that text says Sodom has been justified in comparison with Jerusalem.[183] Because Jerusalem had been committing so many

---

179. 4.1.10: Bammel 4.1.121–24 = PG 14:962–63.
180. 4.1.12; 4.6.5: Bammel 4.1.141–45 = PG 14:963; Bammel 4.6.166–67 = PG 14:983–84.
181. 4.1.12: Bammel 4.1.145–52 = PG 14:963.
182. 4.1.16: Bammel 4.1.192–93 = PG 14:964.
183. 3.2.10: Bammel 3.2(2–5).142–50 = PG 14:931–32.

wicked deeds, in comparison with her crimes even Sodom has been justified. Similarly, when the psalm and Paul say, "No one living will be justified in your sight," this is not to be taken in an absolute sense but a comparative one. In comparison with God, no one will be justified except Christ alone. But in comparison with other men, one may be justified. He then goes on to state his apprehension that in comparison with some church members, various pagans might be deemed just.[184]

The pagan's lack of faith excludes him from justification in the sense of receiving the remission of his past sins through faith and baptism, since he has neither of these.[185] But he can still be justified in the sense of being inherently just, and he will be recompensed for his justice. Origen is far from saying that all the deeds of unbelievers are sins. He admits that their good works have value and will receive reward, though eternal life is reserved for believers.[186]

Origen supplies two lucid illustrations by which he dramatizes his conception of the human being's justification before God, in the first of which he uses the "faith alone" formulation, but this time with emphasis on the unity between faith and works.

[T]he Apostle fittingly says that only on the basis that he believes in him who justifies the ungodly, righteousness would be reckoned to a man, even if he has not yet produced works of righteousness. For faith which believes in the one who justifies is the beginning of being justified by God. And this faith, when it has been justified, is firmly embedded in the soil of the soul like a root that has received rain so that when it begins to be cultivated by God's law, branches arise from it which bring forth the fruit of works. The root of righteousness, therefore, does not grow out of the works, but rather the fruit of works grows out of the root of righteousness, that root, of course, of righteousness which God also credits even apart from works.[187]

184. 3.2.12: Bammel 3.2(2–5).173–82 = PG 14:932.
185. 2.7.6–7: Bammel 2.5.299–311 = PG 14:888.
186. Bammel, "Justification in Augustine and Origen," p. 228, says, "He [sc. Origen] agrees that works cannot give justification without faith, although in general he takes a more favorable view than Augustine does of the prospects of Gentiles who obey natural law." Cf. Verfaillie, *Doctrine de la justification dans Origène*, p. 39.
187. 4.1.18: Bammel 4.1.216–24 = PG 14:965.

INTRODUCTION   45

K. Schelkle calls Origen's exposition here "very clear—and catholic."[188] Heither fastened on this passage in her depiction of Origen as a defender of Paul's "radical" doctrine of justification by faith alone. She claims that Origen "solves" the problem of faith and works in this passage. "Faith obtains the righteousness out of which works emerge; and this relationship is not reversible. Only upon the way of faith does man obtain forgiveness of sins, reconciliation with God."[189] This seems to be an accurate summary of Origen's meaning in this passage. But the danger in proposing, by one single passage in his writings, that Origen "solves" the problem of faith and works is that it tends to simplify Origen's thought by failing to take other passages into consideration. It seems to me that Origen has already made clear in other texts that good works can effect reconciliation with God and that not all faith is capable of doing so. The most we can say from the current passage is that it confirms that Origen has in view works antecedent to faith when he says that faith alone justifies.

Origen returns to the pericope about the thief on the cross, but this time to emphasize once again the unity of faith and works of righteousness in justification. Origen says that this thief had fulfilled Rom 6.5–6, in that he had been planted together in the likeness of Christ's death and of his resurrection.[190] Origen had earlier used the thief on the cross as an example of one justified by faith alone without works. This passage makes clear that even in the case of the thief, both his faith and his works contributed to his justification. Initially he was justified by faith alone in the sense that Jesus freely forgave him his past crimes and demanded no antecedent works before this first justification. But his faith immediately became effective in the just works of publicly confessing the lordship of Christ and rebuking the other thief who was blaspheming. In the end this robber deserved to be justified. By God's wonder-

188. *Sehr klar—und katholisch.* Schelke, *Paulus, Lehrer,* p. 128. He goes on to note, however, that immediately after Origen, an un-Pauline theology of "faith as a work" arose in Chrysostom and Ambrosiaster.
189. Heither, *Translatio Religionis,* p. 235; cf. Hammond Bammel in Origenes, *Römerbriefkommentar,* 2:132 n. 72.
190. 5.9.3, 7: Bammel 5.9.27–30, 83–90 = PG 14:1043, 1045.

ful gift of life to him he was made just and worthy of paradise through his active adhesion to the living Christ.

Significantly, Heither does not discuss this passage in *Translatio Religionis* or refer to it anywhere in the notes of her translation. The reason for this may be that it does not fit neatly into her construction of Origen as an advocate of the "radical" Pauline doctrine of justification by faith alone. She seems very concerned to make Origen relevant to modern dialogue on justification between Catholic and Protestant interpreters of the NT. The danger with this approach is that it can tend to impoverish or simplify Origen's thought by excluding from consideration important passages such as this one. In my view Verfaillie has a better grasp of Origen's overall thought. He seems to take more seriously Origen's emphasis on the necessity of human cooperation, the possibility of genuine merit, and the role of good works in uniting the soul with God. He summarizes Origen's theology of works as follows.

> This meritorious character of our acts has its source in the grace of justification and completes the conception of it. Liberated from the death of sin, the Christian soul is united to Christ who gives it a new life and through this new life he gives the means of bearing fruit pleasing to God.[191]

This liberation by divine grace was even experienced by the thief on the cross, who was made worthy of Paradise through his fruitful union with Christ.

21. Conclusion

In the 16th century the Lutheran theologian Phillip Melanchthon summarized Origen's understanding of justification in the *Commentary* by saying that Origen "seems to be proposing justification by faith as synecdoche: We are justified by faith, that is, by a perfect faith embracing all the virtues. We are justified by mercy, i.e., a perfect mercy embracing all the other virtues."[192] This seems to be fair and accurate. But in my

---

191. Verfaillie, *Doctrine de la justification dans Origène*, p. 117.
192. P. Melanchthon, *The Church and the Authority of the Word* (1539), in *Selected Writings*, trans. C. L. Hill (Minneapolis: Augsburg, 1962), p. 150.

INTRODUCTION   47

view Melanchthon was wrong when he associated Origen's position with that of Pelagius: "But this is no different from saying that men possess the remission of their sins for the sake of their works and their own virtues and are just."[193] In Lutheran theology any affirmation of free will, the saving necessity of merit, virtue, cooperation, or good works was dismissed as Pelagian. Any denial that faith alone sufficed for justification, no matter what historical context provoked that denial, was registered as paganism.

Bammel has pointed out that the difficulty involved here has an Augustinian source. In connection with the texts from Origen's *Commentary* in which he notices that not all faith can justify and that faith is one of many necessary virtues, she says:

> Much of this must have seemed to Augustine to distract from the main point of Paul's words. For Augustine justification by faith applies to the transition made from law to grace or from the letter to the spirit at the point of conversion or baptism, when the believer with no antecedent merits is received and justified by God's mercy. To suggest that one needs a number of acts of faith or that one can count faith as one among other virtues does not fit with this picture.[194]

This does not necessarily mean that Augustine's categories are decisive for Christian theology or that Protestantism was fair in its caricature of Origen as a Pelagian. Perhaps Origen has identified a complexity in Paul and in the Bible that escaped Augustine's notice.[195]

Origen's understanding of justification as something capable of being increased, decreased, or lost altogether appears to foreshadow the definitions put forward at the Council of Trent. Verfaillie noted that Origen in his *Commentary* anticipated the

---

193. Ibid.
194. C. P. Bammel, "Justification in Augustine and Origen," p. 231.
195. Cf. C. P. Bammel, "Augustine, Origen and the Exegesis of St. Paul," p. 352: "There are two possible reactions to the contrast between Augustine and Origen. One is to conclude that Augustine has understood the central point of Paul's theology, whereas Origen has not. The other is to regard Augustine as having imposed his own theological preconceptions onto Paul without regard for the complexity of Paul's thought or the historical context in which he was writing. If I say a little in support of the second viewpoint this is not to deny that there is a certain validity in the first."

following principal affirmations of the Council of Trent's decree on justification: an original fall but not a total corruption of humanity, the necessity and efficacy of the redemptive work, its application through the indivisible cooperation of God and man, the effective sanctification of the soul through grace, and the meritorious value of its actions in view of glory. "Such are the doctrines opposed by the Church to the Reformed. Yet they are all already found clearly in the writings of Origen."[196] The intense hostility of Luther, Melanchthon, Calvin, and Beza to Origen's theology confirms that the Magisterial Protestants themselves recognized that an unbridgeable chasm existed between themselves and him.

To Origen justification is more than a remission and more than a renewal. It is the reception of Christ himself, our justice (1 Cor 1.30) who makes us just. It begins with a bestowal of forgiveness of past sins that takes place at the moment of faith and baptism. But it is identical with the process of sanctification so that it can increase, decrease, or be repudiated through negligence.[197] With reference to the initial remission, he allows the qualification of the epithet "alone" to the formulation "justification by faith," provided that one understands principally that Jewish works of the law are being excluded by the qualifying word "alone." He grants additionally and significantly that all religious boasting, both Jewish and Christian, is excluded through the cross of Christ and will not avail in the final judgment. But with regard to final justification, he conceives it to be conditional upon the renewal of the inner man, i.e., upon the believer's meritorious performance of works of righteousness through divine grace, a contingency which implies that justification is not by faith alone. Origen is saved from moralism, legalism, and Pelagianism by his "overriding doctrine of divine Grace."[198]

---

196. Verfaillie, *Doctrine de la justification dans Origène*, p. 119.

197. 9.3.4: Bammel 9.3.46–59 = PG 14:1214.

198. B. Drewery, *Origen and the Doctrine of Grace* (London: The Epworth Press, 1960), pp. 163f.

COMMENTARY ON THE EPISTLE TO THE ROMANS
BOOKS 1–5

PREFACE OF RUFINUS

ALTHOUGH I WANTED to touch along the coastline of a tranquil shore in my small boat and draw out tiny fish from the pools of the Greeks, you compel me, brother Heraclius,[1] to unfurl the sails for the high seas and, once I had set aside the task I had to translate the homilies[2] Adamantius[3] wrote in his old age, you persuade us to set forth in our language his fifteen books in which he discussed Paul's Letter to the Romans.

(2) In these books, as he pursues the Apostle's thought, he is taken out into such a deep sea that anyone who follows him out there encounters enormous fear lest he be overwhelmed as much by the greatness of his thoughts as by the immensity of the waves.[4] Moreover you do not consider the fact that my breath is too weak to fill up such a magnificent trumpet of eloquence. The greatest difficulty of all, however, was that the books themselves have been tampered with.[5] For some of the volumes of the work are missing from the libraries of nearly everyone—indeed, I am unsure how this came about. To fill in these things and restore complete continuity to the Latin work does not come from my natural talent but, just as you who demand these things believe, probably by God's favor. And yet,

---

1. See Introduction (7).
2. Cf. Epilogue of Rufinus (6).
3. Origen is often referred to as Adamantius, "Man of Steel" or "Man of Adamant"; cf. Eusebius, *Ecclesiastical History* 6.14.10 and Jerome, *Ep* 43. Eusebius says that he was known by this name even during his lifetime and that the epithet denoted the firmness with which Origen stood like a rock against heretics. Jerome thought it signified Origen's unwearied industry in producing innumerable books.
4. Cf. *Hom in Gn* 9.1.
5. *Interpolati sunt ipsi libri.* See Introduction (7). The only other appearance of *interpolare* in the *Commentary* occurs in 10.43.2, where it is used to describe Marcion's work of tampering with the Scriptures.

lest I be spared any labors, you add that I am supposed to abridge this entire fifteen-volume work, a Greek text which has reached the length of some forty thousand lines or more, and, if possible, compress it to half the space.[6]

(3) These instructions were hard enough, as if imposed by a man who seems unwilling to appreciate the work load involved. Nevertheless I shall set out in the hope that by your prayers the things which seem to me to be humanly impossible might become possible as God assists me. But now, with your permission, let us listen to Origen himself, as he composes the Preface of the work at hand. [M833]

6. See Introduction (7).

PREFACE [OF ORIGEN]

T SEEMS TO ME that there are two reasons why the letter that was written to the Romans is considered to be harder to understand than the Apostle Paul's other letters. First, because he makes use of expressions which sometimes are confused and insufficiently explicit.[1] Second, because he stirs up very many questions in the letter and the heretics, especially propping themselves up on these, are accustomed to add that the cause of each person's actions is not to be attributed to one's own purpose but to different kinds of natures.[2] And, from a handful of words from this letter they attempt to subvert the meaning of the whole of Scripture, which teaches that God has given man freedom of will.[3]

(2) Therefore, first praying to God, "who teaches man knowledge"[4] and "who gives the word of wisdom through the Spirit"[5] and who "enlightens every man coming into this world,"[6] that he might deem to make us worthy "to understand parables and obscure words and the sayings and riddles of the wise,"[7] only then shall we touch the Introduction of the *Commentary on Paul's Letter to the Romans*.

(3) I want to say by way of a preface what is usually observed by the diligent, that the Apostle seems to have been more perfect in this letter than in the others.[8] To be sure when he was

---

1. Cf. 1.9.6; 1.13.1–2; 6.3.2.
2. Cf. 1.3.1; *Princ* 3.1.7ff. See Introduction (14).
3. *Arbitrii libertatem.* "Free will" is the traditional rendering of *liberum arbitrium* (lit. "free choice") and will be used in this translation. According to Bigg, *Christian Platonists,* p. 79, the term "free will" was coined by Tertullian in *On the Soul* 21. Origen was this doctrine's greatest ancient defender against gnostic determinism. Cf. 1.3.1–4; 2.4.7; 2.10.2; *Hom in Ezek* 1.3.
4. Ps 94.10.
5. 1 Cor 12.8.
6. Jn 1.9.
7. Prv 1.6.
8. Cf. 10.14.3.

writing First Corinthians he was someone in great progress, yet he declares something about himself which sounds like a man who is wavering when he says, "but I punish my body and reduce it to slavery, so that after proclaiming to others I myself should not be rejected."[9] Moreover, when writing to the Philippians he reveals that thus far there was less perfection in himself than that which he subsequently attained when he claims to be conformed to the death of Christ "if somehow" he might attain "the resurrection from the dead."[10] For he would not have said "if somehow" if the matter appeared to him at the time to be of undoubted certainty. But also, in what follows in the same epistle he reveals the same thing when he says, "Not that I have already attained this or have already become perfect, but I press on to take hold of that in which I am held by Christ. Brothers, I do not yet consider that I have taken hold of it."[11] But if anyone thinks this has been said out of humility, let him see in what follows what great things he relates in regard to his own progress when he says, "but this one thing I do: forgetting what lies behind and straining forward to what lies ahead of me, with [M834] purpose I pursue the prize of the upward call of God in Christ Jesus";[12] and after this he says, "Let those of us then who are perfect be of this mind."[13] By these words he reveals that there is a twofold perfection: one which consists in the satisfying of the virtues,[14] according to which he says that he is not perfect; the other is when someone advances so far that he is not able to fall away or to look backwards,[15] according to

9. 1 Cor 9.27.
10. Cf. Phil 3.10–11.
11. Phil 3.12–13.
12. Phil 3.13–14.
13. Phil 3.15.

14. Heither, *Translatio Religionis*, p. 31, notes that Origen's conception of "virtue" does not correspond to Stoic and Aristotelian views which were incorporated into Scholasticism. Instead Origen understands virtues to be the expressions of the living Christ dwelling within man.

15. Cf. 5.10.15; 6.5.6; 10.10.3 Wiles, *Divine Apostle*, pp. 20–21, perceptively observes with regard to Origen's allowance for spiritual development in Paul's letters, "[M]ore often Origen speaks in simple and unqualified terms of Paul's perfection, and it is worthy of note that he can base this belief on words from the very same chapter of 1 Corinthians as that which he also used to illustrate the lowest stage of Paul's spiritual progress. The idea of gradual spiritual development is never really integrated into the main body of his thought about Paul's person."

which he was saying, "Let those of us then who are perfect be of this mind."[16]

(4) How then will it be demonstrated that he wrote Second Corinthians as an even more perfect man than he was when writing First Corinthians? Without doubt this is shown by what is related in this letter when he says, "We suffer affliction, but are not crushed; we are perplexed, but not driven to despair; we suffer persecution, but are not forsaken; we are struck down, but not destroyed, always carrying around the death of Jesus in our body, so that the life of Jesus Christ may also be made visible in our body."[17] In him who was always carrying around the death of Jesus in his own body, certainly never did the flesh lust against the spirit,[18] but rather the flesh had been subjected to him since it had been put to death in the likeness of Christ's death.[19]

(5) Now if anyone should say to us that these observations do not seem true because there was not much time between the first letter and the second, it is possible to know this very plainly from the fact that in the first letter Paul compelled the man who had been defiled with the atrocious crime of incest to be ejected and handed over to Satan for the destruction of the flesh in order that the spirit might be saved.[20] Yet now in the second letter Paul calls this man back and associates him with the members of the church.[21] Surely he would not have done this unless, with the passing of time, he had clearly observed worthy fruit of repentance[22] in the man and the flesh had already suffered the destruction which the Apostle had ordered, namely, mortification to sin and the vices so that he was at last alive to God.[23] Therefore since there would have been enough time for the incestuous sinner to receive the salvation of his spirit through the praiseworthy destruction of the flesh,[24] how is it possible to deny that the Apostle was pursuing perfection at a much swifter pace?

16. Phil 3.15.
17. 2 Cor 4.8–10.
18. Cf. Gal 5.17.
19. Cf. Rom 6.5.
20. Cf. 1 Cor 5.5.
21. Cf. 2 Cor 2.8.
22. Cf. Lk 3.8.
23. Cf. Rom 6.11.
24. Cf. 1 Cor 5.5.

(6) But that would have been his progress in the Corinthian letters; yet we may gather how much more lofty and eminent he is when writing to the Romans from the passages of this letter in which he says, "Who will separate us from the love of Christ? Will affliction, [M835] or distress, or persecution, or famine, or nakedness, or peril, or sword? As it is written, 'For your sake we are exposed to death all day long; we are accounted as sheep for the slaughter.' But in all these things we overcome because of him who loved us. For I am convinced that neither death, nor life, nor angels, nor rulers, nor authorities, nor things present, nor things to come, nor powers, nor height, nor depth, nor any other creature, will be able to separate us from the love of God which is in Christ Jesus our Lord. I am speaking the truth in Christ, I am not lying, my conscience bears witness to me in the Holy Spirit."[25] Will it appear that he has said, "I punish my body and reduce it to slavery, so that after proclaiming to others I myself should not be rejected,"[26] with the same loftiness of mind with which he says here, "for in all these things we overcome,"[27] and, "I am convinced that neither death, nor life, nor angels, nor rulers," and the other things he has described, "will be able to separate us from the love of God"?[28]

(7) So then, having formulated these things to the best of our ability concerning his now more perfect understanding in this letter, we shall now make the by-no-means absurd suggestion that he is evidently writing this letter from Corinth. Although there are a great number of other indications, still it is more clear by what he says, "I commend to you your sister Phoebe, a servant of the church at Cenchreae."[29] Cenchreae is the name of a place near Corinth, in fact the port of Corinth itself. Therefore it seems that the letter was written from Corinth, both from that and from this, where he says, "Gaius, my host, greets you."[30] Paul mentions this Gaius when he writes to the Corinthians stating, "I thank God that I baptized none of you

---

25. Rom 8.35–9.1.   26. 1 Cor 9.27.
27. Rom 8.37.
28. Rom 8.38–39. Cf. 7.12.12 and 10.14.3.
29. Rom 16.1. This phrase is rendered differently in the lemma to Rom 16.1. See 10.17.1.
30. Rom 16.23.

except Crispus and Gaius."[31] A similar indication is also given from this when he says, "Erastus the treasurer of the city greets you."[32] Paul spoke of this Erastus when writing his second letter to Timothy, "Erastus remained in Corinth."[33] From all these things, the most certain indications seem to be gathered that Romans was written from Corinth.

(8) This letter yields no small difficulties in interpretation because many things are woven into this epistle concerning the law of Moses, about the calling of the Gentiles, about Israel according to the flesh and about Israel which is not according to the flesh, about the circumcision of the flesh and of the heart, about the spiritual law and the law of the letter, about the law of the flesh and the law of the members, about the law of the mind and the law [M836] of sin, about the inner and the outer man. It is enough to have mentioned these individual themes since in these it seems the contents of the letter are contained. But now let us hasten to his explanations as far as the Lord considers us worthy to disclose the way to us.[34]

(9) The first question which seems to rise for us concerns the name of Paul himself: Why is he who was called Saul in the Acts of the Apostles[35] now called Paul? In the Holy Scriptures we find that names were changed in some of the men and women of antiquity so that Abram was re-named Abraham, Sarai was renamed Sarah, and Jacob, Israel.[36] In the Gospels too, Simon was renamed Peter, and the sons of Zebedee were named the Sons of Thunder.[37] We read that this was done at God's command. However, nowhere do we find anything like this in the case of Paul. Because of this, some people think that the Apostle may have assumed this name for himself on behalf of the consul Paul whom, in Cyprus, he had subjugated to faith in Christ.[38] Just as rulers were accustomed to be named for the peoples whom they had conquered, for instance those called

---

31. 1 Cor 1.14.
32. Rom 16.23.
33. 2 Tm 4.20.
34. In the original *Commentary*, Origen's Preface evidently ended here. Rufinus has supplied the next three paragraphs from another work of Origen (now lost), as he himself tells us below (11).
35. Cf. Acts 7.58; 9.1.
36. Cf. Gn 17.5; 17.15; 35.10.
37. Cf. Mk 3.16–17.
38. Cf. Acts 13.6–12.

Parthicus[39] were named after the Parthians and those called Gothicus[40] were named after the Goths, in a similar way the Apostle would have been named Paul once Paul had been subjugated. Not even we think that this explanation is to be discarded entirely.

(10) However because no such custom is detected in the Holy Scriptures, let us rather seek a solution in those things which are our patterns. In the Scriptures, then, we find some people who use two names and others who use even three names. For example, Solomon himself is called Jedediah,[41] Zedekiah is called Jehoiachin,[42] Uzziah is called Azariah[43] and you shall find many others as well in the books of Kingdoms and Judges who are called by two names. Nor do the Gospels reject this practice. For even Matthew reports this about himself, "As Jesus was passing by, he found a certain man by the name of Matthew sitting at the tax booth."[44] Luke, however, says of the same person that when Jesus was passing by "he saw a certain tax collector by the name of Levi and said to him, 'Follow me'."[45] Moreover, in the list of the apostles, after many other names, Matthew himself says, "Matthew the tax collector, and James [the son] of Alphaeus, and Lebbaeus,[46] and Simon the Cananaean."[47] Yet Mark reports it this way, "Matthew the tax collector, and Thomas, and James [the son] of Alphaeus, and Thaddeus."[48] This same man whom Matthew has called Lebbaeus, Mark recorded as [M837] Thaddeus. But Luke records it this way, "Matthew, Thomas, James, and Judas, [son] of James."[49] Consequently the very same fellow whom Matthew called Lebbaeus and Mark called Thaddeus, Luke writes as Ju-

---

39. According to *Historia Augusta*, this cognomen was assumed by Marcus Aurelius (s.v. 9.2); Lucius Verus (s.v. 7.2); Severus (s.v. 16.2, 6); Caracalla (s.v. 6.5; 10.6; *Geta* 6.6); Severus Alexander (s.v. 56.9); and after Origen's lifetime by Aurelian (s.v. 30.5) and Probus (s.v. 11.9).

40. See Introduction (5). 41. Cf. 2 Sm 12.25.
42. Cf. 2 Kgs 25.7, 27. 43. Cf. 2 Kgs 15.1–7, 32–34.
44. Mt 9.9. 45. Lk 5.27.

46. Modern editions of the Bible read "Thaddeus." "Lebbaeus" is testified in some Greek manuscripts. Cf. Metzger, *A Textual Commentary on the Greek New Testament*, corrected ed. (Stuttgart: United Bible Societies, 1975), p. 26.

47. Mt 10.3–4. 48. Mk 3.18.
49. Lk 6.15–16.

das, [son] of James. Now it is certain that the evangelists have not erred in the names of the apostles, but because it was customary for the Hebrews to use two or three names, each author employed different designations for one and the same person. According to this custom, therefore, it appears to us that Paul also used two names and while he was ministering to his own people he was called Saul because it seemed more colloquial to his native country, but he was called Paul when [M838] composing laws and precepts for the Greeks and Gentiles. For the Scripture that says, "Saul, who was also called Paul,"[50] shows very plainly that he is not being designated Paul there for the first time, but rather this had been an old designation.[51]

(11) These things, although not included by the author of the work, we have set down in the Preface (which I think not inappropriate) because the beginning of the discourse seemed to demand it. Now let us follow the rest of the body of the commentary, abridging it[52] as well as we can.[53]

50. Acts 13.9.
51. Origen gives a different explanation of Paul's double name in *Orat* 24.2, where he associates Paul's name change with qualitative changes that occurred within Paul's soul.
52. Cf. Preface of Rufinus (2).
53. This paragraph stems from Rufinus. He appears to have inserted the discussion about the origin of Paul's name from another passage in Origen's writings (now lost). Cf. Hammond Bammel, *Römerbrieftext*, p. 189.

BOOK ONE

PAUL, A SLAVE OF JESUS CHRIST.[1] We have already spoken about Paul. Now let us try to find out why he is called a slave here, seeing that elsewhere he writes, "For you did not receive a spirit of slavery to fall back again into fear, but the Spirit of adoption, by whom we cry, 'Abba! Father!'"[2] And again, "Because you are sons, God has sent the Spirit of his own Son into our hearts, crying, 'Abba! Father!' So you are no longer a slave but a son."[3] Why, therefore, does he declare himself to be a slave to people to whom he has previously said, "You are no longer a slave but a son"? We shall not be in error if we consider it to be an expression of that humility which the Lord taught when he said, "Learn from me, for I am meek and humble in heart."[4] Nor is the truth of Paul's freedom violated by this. For he himself says, "For though I am free from all, I have made myself a slave to all."[5] He serves Christ, then, not in a spirit of slavery but in the Spirit of adoption because being a slave of Christ is more distinguished than any freedom. Or it may be that he utters these words as an imitator of him who had said, "Behold I am among you not as one reclining at the table but as one who serves";[6] and of him who "emptied himself, taking the form of a slave."[7] Just as he himself becomes one under the law for those who are under the law, and for those who are without the law he himself even becomes one without the law,[8] so also, if he becomes a slave for the sake of those who are still slaves and who have not yet been led through the Spirit of adoption to the freedom of sons, it will not seem contradictory.

1. Rom 1.1.
2. Rom 8.15.
3. Gal 4.6–7.
4. Mt 11.29.
5. 1 Cor 9.19.
6. Lk 22.27.
7. Phil 2.7.
8. Cf. 1 Cor 9.20–21.

(2) We can add the following to these things: When this same Apostle writes to the Corinthians and gives instructions about marriage and chastity, he inserts some things concerning freedom and slavery, as if on external authority, saying, "Were you a slave when called? Do not be concerned. Even if you can gain your freedom, make use of it instead. For whoever was called in the Lord as a slave is the Lord's freedman; likewise, whoever was free when called is a slave of Christ. You were bought with a price; do not become slaves of men."[9] To at least some people these words appear to have been introduced illogically. For why is [M839] mention made of slavery and freedom in the midst of instructions about marriage and chastity? But we understand Paul's thought in this way: He is calling a man a slave who has been bound to the matrimonial state because "the wife does not have authority over her own body, but her husband does; and the husband does not have authority over his own body, but his wife does."[10] This is why he says of them in another passage, "the brother or sister is not subjected to servitude in such cases";[11] obviously because in other cases he would understand them to be subjected to servitude. Therefore a person who comes to Christ while married is called a slave, to whom he says, "Were you a slave when called? Do not let it be of consequence to you. Even if you can gain your freedom, make use of it instead."[12] The reason he says this is because among married persons the freedom of continence of one partner can endanger the chastity of the other. For they are not obligated except by mutual consent for a time in order to be free for prayer. Then they ought to return again to the same lest Satan tempt them owing to their lack of self control.[13] Therefore he who has been called a slave on account of the marriage bond is the Lord's freedman. A freedman is neither entirely free nor is he entirely a slave. Consequently, he who is a slave owing to marriage, if he becomes free respecting the rest of the virtues, if he takes hold of the freedom of faith, patience, mercy, and

9. 1 Cor 7.21–23.
10. 1 Cor 7.4.
11. 1 Cor 7.15.
12. 1 Cor 7.21.
13. Cf. 1 Cor 7.5.

righteousness, he is called the Lord's freedman, inasmuch as he is free for the sake of the virtues of his mind, and he is a slave for the sake of marital obligation. He is indeed free who comes to Christ without a wife through the purity of continence, however he is made a slave of Christ when he serves the virtues completely.

(3) Paul, then, if certain traditions are true, was called while in possession of a wife, concerning whom he speaks when writing to the Philippians, "I ask you also, my loyal mate, help these women."[14] Since he had become free by mutual consent with her,[15] he calls himself a slave of Christ. But if, as others think, he had no wife, nonetheless he who was free when he was called is yet a slave of Christ. In fact what does it mean to be a slave of Christ? It means that one is a slave of the Word of God, of wisdom, righteousness, truth, and of absolutely all the virtues which are identical with Christ himself.[16]

(4) But if it seems fitting, let us add this: Just as knowledge and prophecy and other gifts of the Holy Spirit[17] which are now being given to the saints are given "in a mirror" and "in a riddle,"[18] so also the freedom which is now offered to the saints is not yet full freedom but "as in [M840] a mirror and in a riddle,"[19] and for this reason saints call themselves slaves in comparison with that freedom which shall be granted "face to face."[20] For who is there placed in the flesh who is able to attain such complete freedom that he no longer serves the flesh in any respect whatsoever? In the same way it is not possible for someone who has been placed in a body to possess the adoption of sons completely.[21] If only one could at least attain in this mortal life to this, that whoever completely becomes a slave of Christ would serve neither flesh, nor blood, nor vainglory, nor greed, nor wrath, nor envy, but Christ alone, that is to say, all

---

14. Phil 4.3. Cf. Clement, *Stromateis* 3.6.53.1–2; Eusebius, *Ecclesiastical History* 3.30.1. Origen suggests in 4.6.7 that Paul may have been married.
15. Cf. 1 Cor 7.5.
16. Cf. 1 Cor 1.30; Jn 14.6. See also 2.5.6; 3.7.14.
17. 1 Cor 12.8–10; 13.8–12.   18. Cf. 1 Cor 13.12.
19. 1 Cor 13.12.   20. Cf. 1 Cor 13.12.
21. Cf. 7.2; 7.3.2ff.; 7.5.9.

the virtues simultaneously. These are the things concerning that which is written, "Paul, a slave of Jesus Christ."

2. *Called to be an apostle.*[22] The word "called" can be viewed as a general term because it applies to all who believe in Christ. However each person individually is called either an apostle, prophet, teacher, a man free from a wife, or a slave to the marriage bond,[23] according to what God foresees and chooses. And for the sake of the diversity of grace, that which has been written, "Many are called but few are chosen,"[24] is fulfilled. Nevertheless one should recognize that it is possible for someone to be a called apostle or a called prophet or a called teacher and, should he neglect the grace of his calling, to fall away from it. This is precisely what happened in the case of Judas, who had been called to be an apostle but, by neglecting the grace of his calling, changed from being an apostle to a traitor.[25] He was indeed called to be an apostle but he was not chosen to be an apostle. Moreover the prophet who is reported in the Third Book of Kingdoms to have prophesied about Jeroboam was called to be a prophet. But whether he was also chosen you yourself must ascertain since, although forbidden to eat bread in Israel, he ate and was subsequently killed by a lion.[26] There are also many called to be teachers in all of God's churches and called to be ministers, but I do not know who among them are chosen teachers and chosen ministers. In this way as well there are, in my opinion, certain people who are indeed called to suffer for Christ and yet they are not chosen. That is to say, they are called to be martyrs but are not chosen to be martyrs, since there are those who do not hold out to the end in the endurance of confession after the struggles of tortures and prisons. And there is also the virgin who is called but is not chosen a virgin, [M841] namely the one who will not be holy in body and spirit.[27] There is also the shepherd who is called but is not chosen a shepherd, who indeed presides over the flock, enjoys

22. Rom 1.1.
23. Cf. 1 Cor 12.28; Eph 4.11; 1 Cor 7.27.
24. Mt 22.14.
25. Cf. Lk 6.16.
26. Cf. 1 Kgs 13.9, 19, 24.
27. Cf. 1 Cor 7.34.

its milk, and is covered with its wool, but he does not search for the weak and bind up the lame and employ the strong with labor.[28] In the same way there is someone called to be abstinent but [M842] is not chosen to be abstinent, certainly anyone who fasts in a sullen manner, distorting his countenance in order to please men.[29] You will, in like manner, find many persons at each level of the spiritual gifts who are called, but few who are chosen.[30]

3. *Set apart for the gospel of God.*[31] In Paul's case [M843] not only is a general calling to apostleship described[32] but also a choosing according to the foreknowledge of God,[33] which followed immediately, through which he is said to be set apart for the gospel of God. In this manner he says elsewhere about himself, "But when God, who set me apart from my mother's womb, was pleased to reveal his Son in me."[34] The heretics,[35] however, invoke this text for the purpose of calumny, saying that Paul was set apart from [M844] his mother's womb because goodness was inherent in his nature; just as, in contrast, it says in the Psalms of those who are evil in nature, "For they have been set apart as sinners from the womb."[36]

(2) But we maintain that Paul was not chosen due to chance or a special nature, but rather he himself gave the reasons for his own election as found in himself and in the One who "knows all things before they take place."[37] Nor are the sinners who are set apart from the womb set apart by an unjust judgment. [M845] After all, look at the immediate context and see what the divine text says concerning them. For it is written, "They have been set apart as sinners from the womb; they have gone astray from their birth, they have spoken lies."[38] If we understand in what sense sinners have gone astray from their mothers' wombs and have spoken lies, we shall equally un-

---

28. Cf. Ezek 34.3–4; Zec 11:16; and below, 2.8.4.
29. Cf. Mt 6.16.
30. Cf. Mt 22.14.
31. Rom 1.1.
32. Cf. 1.2.
33. 1 Pt 1.2.
34. Gal 1.15–16. Cf. *Orat* 5.4; 6.3, 5.
35. Cf. Preface of Origen (1).
36. Ps 58.3.
37. Dn 13.42 LXX.
38. Ps 58.3.

derstand at once that they are set apart from the womb deservedly.

(3) It says then that Paul was set apart for the gospel and set apart from his own mother's womb. The reasons for this and the merits which entitled him to be set apart for this purpose were seen by the One from whom man's mind does not escape.[39] For God foresaw that Paul was going to labor harder than all the others in the gospel;[40] that, despite hunger and thirst, cold and nakedness, dangers from thieves, dangers from rivers, dangers at sea, he was going to preach the gospel of Christ,[41] knowing that it would have been woe to him if he did not preach the gospel;[42] and that he was going to punish his body and reduce it to slavery, so that, after proclaiming to others, he himself should not be rejected.[43] Therefore, seeing in advance these things and many other similar things in him, God set Paul apart for the gospel from his mother's womb on account of these matters. For if, as [M846] the heretics think, he had been chosen either by uncertain fate or by the privilege of possessing a superior nature, surely he would never have expressed the fear that, if he were not to hold the restraints on his own body, it could potentially come to pass that he would be rejected[44] or that woe would be his if he were to cease from proclaiming the gospel.[45]

(4) After all, later in the letter he himself explains this more fully when he says, "For those whom he foreknew he also predestined to be conformed to the image of his Son."[46] Plainly showing that those whom God foreknew would become the kind to conform themselves to Christ by their sufferings, he even predestined them to be conformed and similar to his image and glory. Therefore there precedes a foreknowledge of them, through which is known what effort and virtue they will

---

39. Cf. 1 Kgs 8.39; 1 Chr 28.9.
40. Cf. 1 Cor 15.10.
41. Cf. 2 Cor 11.26–27.
42. Cf. 1 Cor 9.16.
43. 1 Cor 9.27.
44. Cf. 1 Cor 9.27.
45. 1 Cor 9.16. Schelkle, *Paulus, Lehrer,* p. 18 n. 2, notes that Hermas (*Similitudes* 8.6.1ff.) was the first to explain predestination on the basis of God's foreknowledge. Pelagius followed Origen in seeing "calling" based upon *praevisa merita* "foreseen merits."
46. Rom 8.29.

possess in themselves, and thus predestination follows, yet foreknowledge should not be considered the cause of predestination. For while men requite merit to each individual based upon past accomplishments, for God this is determined from future ones; and a person is very impious not to concede to God that what we see in the past he can see in the future.[47]

(5) "Set apart," he says, "for the gospel of God." Other passages of Scripture speak of the gospel of Christ, [M847] as the evangelist Mark writes, "The beginning of the gospel of Jesus Christ, as it is written in Isaiah the prophet."[48] In truth since Christ is the Word, and "in the beginning he was with God, and the Word was God,"[49] then the gospel of God and the gospel of Christ signify one and the same thing.[50] For the Lord himself says "I and the Father are one."[51] And again he says to the Father, "All which is mine is yours, and what is yours is mine; and I have received glory in them."[52] Accordingly the gospel of the Father is the gospel of the Son. Yet Paul also says, "my gospel which I proclaim among the Gentiles."[53] He says this perhaps as a coheir of Christ[54] and just as if a coheir in the gospel. For elsewhere he says additionally that the gospel belongs to many persons. For example to the Galatians [Corinthians][55] he writes, "But even if our gospel is veiled."[56] "Our" means everyone who are coheirs of Christ. And indeed, in accordance with the fact that he himself is its proclaimer, Paul rightly calls it his own gospel.[57]

4. *Which he had promised beforehand through his prophets in the Holy Scriptures.*[58] Whether this ought to be interpreted simply as referring to the gospel promised by God in the prophetic Scrip-

---

47. Cf. 7.8.6.
48. Mk 1.1–2.
49. Cf. Jn 1.1.
50. Cf. 6.13.3.
51. Jn 10.30.
52. Jn 17.10.
53. Gal 2.2; cf. Rom 2.16; 16.25; 2 Tm 2.8.
54. Cf. Rom 8.17.
55. Origen has made a mistake here by citing from memory, unless the mistake belongs to Rufinus. The passage is from 2 Corinthians. For other mistaken citations, see 1.5.5; 5.3.8; 9.2.6; 9.23.2; 10.14.5.
56. 2 Cor 4.3.
57. Cf. 2.10.1.
58. Rom 1.2.

tures, or to the distinction of another gospel which John calls in the Apocalypse "eternal,"[59] which is to be revealed at that time when the shadow passes away and the truth comes and when death shall be swallowed up[60] and eternity restored, I leave for you the reader to consider.[61] Those eternal years spoken of by the prophet evidently correspond with this eternal gospel: "I kept in mind the eternal years."[62] With the eternal gospel can also be associated the book of life, in which the names of the saints are said to be written down,[63] as can those books which, in Daniel, were opened when the court was seated,[64] or those in Ezekiel the prophet which are said to be inscribed on the inside and outside,[65] and all the things that are recounted as having been written not with ink but with the Spirit of the living God.[66]

(2) Although it may be risky to commit this discussion to paper, nevertheless the sayings and riddles of the wise[67] ought not to be leisurely passed over but should be contemplated as in a mirror[68] with the subtle acuteness of the entire mind, to the extent the matter allows this.

(3) He who was the Word who became flesh[69] [M848] appeared to those who were in flesh, as the Apostle says, "For he was revealed in flesh, was justified in the spirit, and appeared to angels."[70] That which appeared to angels did not appear to them apart from the gospel; nor to us men, to whom it says he was sent to preach the good news to the poor, to release the captives in remission, and to proclaim the accepted year of the Lord.[71] Well then, if, when he appeared to us men, he did not appear apart from the gospel, it seems consistent to declare that he did not appear to the angelic order apart from the

---

59. Cf. Rv 14.6.
60. Cf. 1 Cor 15.54.
61. Cf. *Comm in Jn* 1.7; *Princ* 3.6.8; 4.3.13; Jerome, *Ep* 124.2.
62. Ps 77.5. Cf. 5.1.41; *Comm in Cant* 3; *Comm in Mt* 15.31.
63. Cf. Phil 4.3; Rv 3.5; 17.8; 21.27. See also *Comm in Jn* 5.7; *Hom in Lk* 11.
64. Cf. Dn 7.10. See 9.41.3 below and *Hom in Gn* 13.4; *Hom in Ezek* 2.3; *Comm in Mt* 14.9.
65. Cf. Ezek 2.10.
66. Cf. 2 Cor 3.3.
67. Cf. Prv 1.6.
68. Cf. 1 Cor 13.12.
69. Cf. Jn 1.14.
70. 1 Tm 3.16.
71. Cf. Is 61.1–2; Lk 4.18.

gospel, possibly the one called by John the "eternal gospel,"[72] as we have taught above.[73]

(4) Now whether we should also assume that such a thing was accomplished by him among the other heavenly orders of beings, that he appeared to each of them in their own form and announced peace, since he indeed made peace through the blood of his cross not only with things on earth but also with the heavenly beings,[74] this too is a question you yourself must investigate.[75]

(5) "Which he promised through his prophets in the Holy Scriptures." One should understand the things predicted about Christ through the prophets as things which have been predicted about the gospel as well, even though the evangelist Mark appears to make a distinction between Christ and the gospel when he says, "He who has left father and mother," etc., "for my sake or for the sake of the gospel."[76] But even if one demands promises strictly of the gospel you will find them abundantly in the prophets. For example, "The Lord shall give the word with much power to those who preach the gospel";[77] and, "How beautiful are the feet of those who proclaim the gospel tidings."[78] Also regarding this is, "Their sound went forth in all the earth and their words unto the end of the world";[79] and, "His word runs swiftly."[80] There is also a promise of the gospel in Jeremiah, "Behold I am sending many shepherds[81] and many hunters, and they shall catch them upon every mountain and upon every hill."[82] This is what Paul is now speaking of when he says that God "promised [it] through his prophets in the Holy Scriptures."

72. Rv 14.6.   73. Cf. 1.4.1.
74. Cf. Eph 2.17; Col 1.20. See also 5.7.6; *Hom in Lv* 1.3; Jerome, *Ep* 124.12.
75. For other passages where the reader is directly addressed like this, see 1.4.1; 2.7.9; 4.1.7; 4.2.9; 5.8.9; 5.9.11; 7.5.6; 7.5.7; 7.12.7; 8.10.3; 10.42.1.
76. Mk 10.29.   77. Ps 68:11.
78. Is 52.7; Rom 10.15.   79. Ps 19.4.
80. Ps 147.15.
81. The original text speaks of fishers, not shepherds, which is how Origen cites it elsewhere. Cf. *Hom in Jer* 16.1; *Comm in Cant* 3. Heither in Origenes, *Commentarii*, 1:94 n. 23, suggests that perhaps Rufinus was using a text which had replaced *piscatores* with *pastores*.
82. Jer 16.16.

5. *Concerning his Son.*[83] He who was a son according to the flesh came indeed from the seed of David. Undoubtedly, he became that which previously was not, according to the flesh. According to the Spirit, however, he existed first, and there was never a time when he was not.[84] It should be noted that [M849] he did not say, "who has been predestined Son of God in power according to the Spirit of holiness," but, "who has been destined the Son of God."[85] Let no one think that we are scrutinizing the words used here more carefully than the matter allows. For even though it is customary to find "predestined" in the Latin copies,[86] the correct translation here is "destined" and not "predestined." For only a person who is in existence can be destined; but to be predestined applies to someone who is not yet in existence, such as those, concerning whom the Apostle says, "Those whom he foreknew these he also predestined."[87] Accordingly those who do not yet exist can be foreknown and predestined, but he who is and who always is, is not predestined but destined.[88] We should mention this on account of those who utter blasphemies against the only begotten Son of God and, ignorant of the distinction between "destined" and "predestined," they imagine that he ought to be counted among those who were predestined to exist when they previously did not exist. But he was never predestined to be the Son, but he always was, just as also the Father. So then, he who always is, is destined, as we have said, not predestined. But one

---

83. Rom 1.3.
84. This formulation also occurs in *Fr in Heb* 1.8 (= von Balthasar, *Origen: Spirit and Fire,* p. 77). The Greek formula is attributed to Origen by Pamphilus, *Apology* 1.3. Arius, whose teaching was condemned by the Council of Nicaea, 325, became infamous for his slogan, ἦν ποτε ὅτε οὐκ ἦν, "There was a time when he was not," referring to the time before the Son was created. Origen's expression clearly anticipates the Nicene and Athanasian definitions. Cf. Bigg, *Christian Platonists,* p. 167, "There is no shadow of a doubt that for Origen the Son is co-eternal and co-equal with the Father." Cf. 10.8.5; *Princ* 1.1.2; 1.2.9; 4.4.1.
85. Rom 1.4.
86. The discussion of Latin witnesses in the *Commentary* comes from Rufinus.
87. Rom 8.29.
88. Cf. 3.8.9. Schelkle, *Paulus, Lehrer,* p. 22, notes that Greek biblical philology carefully distinguished ὁρισθέντος, "destined," from προορισθέντος, "predestined." Cf. Eusebius, *Contra Marcellum* 1.2.

who is predestined did not yet exist at the time he was predestined, but he began at some point in time.[89] The Apostle is therefore making a critical distinction when he refers to him as "made of the seed of David according to the flesh," but calls him destined "the Son of God in power according to the Spirit of holiness."

(2) Furthermore when he said "Son of God" he did not add the words, "in power," superfluously,[90] by this indicating that he is the Son substantially according to the Spirit of holiness. For Christ is called "the power of God and the wisdom of God,"[91] which is also named "the breath of the power of God, and the purest emanation of the glory of the Almighty" and "the splendor of eternal light and the image of God's goodness."[92] Now the next question is: If that which is born from David's seed is according to the flesh, but that which is destined in power, according to the Spirit of holiness, is the Son of God and substantially God, how ought we to understand the soul of Jesus, which is by no means named with the flesh and [M850] the Spirit of holiness, or even with the substance of the divine power? Elsewhere the Savior himself says of his soul, "My soul is grieved unto the point of death,"[93] and, "now is my soul troubled."[94] This is the soul he lays down of his own accord;[95] and yes, in fact it even descended to the underworld, concerning which it is also said, "You will not abandon my soul in the underworld."[96] For it is beyond any doubt that this soul was not generated from the seed of David. For it says that what was made from the seed of David is according to the flesh.

(3) Since therefore the soul is evidently included neither in

---

89. Erasmus's clarification of this passage (CWE 56:11) is most helpful: "Origen seems to have thought that 'predestine' has a double aspect of futurity and 'destine' merely a single. For if I 'destine' a bride for a son of mine already born, the person for whom I destine belongs to the present time, what I am destining belongs to the future. But if I resolve to dedicate to the study of theology the son who will be born first, then both the person and the thing belong to future time; and Origen would have the world 'predestine' refer to cases of the latter type."

90. Cf. 1.8; 1.9.3.
91. 1 Cor 1.24.
92. Wis 7.25–26.
93. Mt 26.38.
94. Jn 12.27.
95. Cf. Jn 10.17–18.
96. Ps 16.10; Acts 2.27.

that which is according to the flesh nor in that which is destined to be the Son of God in power according to the Spirit of holiness, it is my belief that the Apostle is using his customary habit in this passage,[97] knowing that the soul is always midway between the spirit and the flesh and that it joins itself either to the flesh, thus becoming one with the flesh, or it associates itself with the spirit and becomes one with the spirit.[98] Consequently if it is joined with the flesh men become fleshly; but if it unites with the spirit they become spiritual. And for that reason he does not explicitly designate the soul but only the flesh and the spirit. For he knows that the soul inevitably attaches itself to one of these two aspects, as in those to whom he writes, "But you are not in the flesh but in the spirit,"[99] and, "Whoever unites himself with a prostitute is one body,"[100] here calling "prostitute" the flesh or body. "But whoever unites himself with the Lord is one Spirit."[101] So then Paul, now aware that the soul of Jesus, united with the Lord and attaching to him, was one Spirit of holiness with him, thus does not designate it explicitly lest he should break apart the unity of Jesus.[102] For "what God has joined together let man not separate."[103] He is in truth called the "Spirit of holiness" according to the fact that he makes holiness available to all, just as it is written elsewhere about him, "who has become wisdom for us from God, and righteousness and holiness and redemption."[104]

(4) Still, some people[105] attack us by raising the most aggravating questions. For example: How can Christ be descended from the seed of David when it is an established fact that he was not born of Joseph, in whom Joseph's lineage as a descendant of David [M851] is adduced?[106] Although it is vexing to respond to these people in the manner of a treatise, the following

---

97. Cf. 1.10.2; 1.18.5.
98. Cf. *Princ* 2.8.4.
99. Rom 8.9.
100. 1 Cor 6.16.
101. 1 Cor 6.17.
102. Cf. 1 Jn 4.3. The same textual reading is attested in Irenaeus, *Against Heresies* 3.16.8. See also *Princ* 2.6.3.
103. Mt 19.6.
104. 1 Cor 1.30.
105. The Ebionites are probably intended here. Cf. Heither in Origenes, *Commentarii*, 1:100 n. 28.
106. Cf. Mt 1.6–16; Lk 3.23–31.

shall nevertheless be answered from our side: "Before Mary, who was betrothed, and Joseph came together, she was found to be with child from the Holy Spirit."[107] Now according to the law she was united to her own fellow tribe member and kinsman.[108] And although it was told to her by the angel, "For behold Elizabeth your kinswoman shall herself give birth to a son in her old age";[109] yet Elizabeth is said to be descended from the daughters of Aaron,[110] nevertheless it will be affirmed on our side that the term "kinsman" may be appropriately and interchangeably applied not only to fellow tribe-members but also to everyone who are of the race of Israel. In this way the Apostle himself speaks likewise of all Israelites, "who are my kinsmen according to the flesh."[111] These types of responses and others similar to them may be given. To what extent they may actually be effective against the assertions of those who press us concerning the testimonies from the Scriptures, the reader shall have to test.

(5) All the same, in our view these matters should instead be understood by using the spiritual or allegorical method of interpretation. According to this method there is no problem in Joseph being called the father of Christ even though he is not at all his actual father.[112] For it is also recorded by Matthew in the genealogy that Jehoshaphat begat Joram, and Joram begat Uzziah.[113] Yet in the fourth book of Kingdoms it is written that Joram begat Ahaziah, and Ahaziah begat Joash, and Joash begat Amaziah. Amaziah in fact begat Azariah, who is sometimes called Uzziah, and Azariah begat Jotham.[114] Hence Uzziah, who is also called Azariah, is said to be a son of Amaziah in the third[115] book of Kingdoms,[116] and yet in Matthew's account he

---

107. Mt 1.18.
108. Cf. Nm 36.8–9. For the tradition that Mary too was of Davidic descent, cf. Ignatius of Antioch, *Ephesians* 18.2; Justin, *Dialogue with Trypho* 43, 45, 100, 120; Tertullian, *Against Marcion* 4.1; *Against the Jews* 9; Eusebius, *Ecclesiastical History* 1.7.17.
109. Lk 1.36. 110. Cf. Lk 1.5.
111. Rom 9.3.
112. Cf. Lk 2.33, 48; Jn 1.45; 6.42. See also *Hom in Lk* 17.1; *Hom in Lv* 12.4.
113. Mt 1.8.
114. Cf. 2 Kgs 8.25; 11.2; 14.1; 15.1, 7, 32, 34; 1 Chr 3.11–12. See above Preface of Origen (10).
115. Migne, "fourth." 116. 2 Kgs 15.1.

is recorded as a son of Joram.[117] Three generations in between have been skipped. The explanation of this matter is certainly not established by the historical but by the spiritual understanding. It is not the time for us to deal with these matters in passing. Instead they will be investigated in their proper place.[118] It suffices us for the moment to respond to those who oppose us that, just as Jesus is said to be a son of Joseph, from whom he was not generated, and Uzziah is said to be generated from Joram, from whom he was not generated, so also is it possible to understand that Christ was of David's seed according to the flesh. We would say that whatever defense and proof they produce in the case of Joram and Joseph should be accepted as well in the case of David.

6. *From the resurrection from the dead, Jesus Christ our Lord.*[119] For the person who reads the following Scripture, "It was fitting that he, through whom and in whom all things exist, in bringing many sons to glory, should make the author of their salvation perfect through sufferings,"[120] it is not difficult to perceive how he who is said to have been made from David's seed according to the flesh is, from the resurrection from the dead, [M852] the Son of God.[121] The resurrection is indeed the end of Christ's sufferings, and because after the resurrection "he dies not again and death will no longer have dominion over him";[122] and it also says, "even though we knew Christ according to the flesh, now we know him no longer in that way";[123] therefore everything that is in Christ is now the Son of God.[124]

(2) But how this relates to him who has been destined the Son of God in power is something that constrains our comprehension; unless it be that because of the inseparable unity of

---

117. Mt 1.8.
118. An interpretation of the genealogy in Origen's *Comm in Mt* is not preserved. See, however, *Hom in Lk* 28.
119. Rom 1.4. 120. Heb 2.10.
121. Rom 1.3–4. 122. Rom 6.9.
123. 2 Cor 5.16.
124. Apparently he means that after the resurrection Christ, in all his aspects, i.e., body/flesh, soul, spirit, may now be designated the Son of God or Logos. Cf. *Cels* 2.9; 3.41.

the Word and flesh, everything that is of the flesh is attributed to the Word also, since also the things which belong to the Word are foretold in the flesh. For we often find the designations "Jesus" and "Christ" and "Lord" referred to both natures. For example, "Our one Lord Jesus Christ through whom are all things";[125] and again, "For if they would have known they would never have crucified the Lord of majesty."[126]

(3) Christ is called the first or "firstborn from the dead."[127] We need to investigate whether he alone is the firstborn or first from the dead and has no other sharers with him in this status of firstness. The Apostle says about this, "For he raised us up with Christ and, at the same time, made us sit with him in the heavenly places."[128] It may be the case that those who are said to be raised up with Christ and seated with him in heavenly places are the firstborn or first from the dead, like those individuals who are said to have been raised with him when "the tombs were opened and the bodies of many saints appeared and entered into the holy city."[129] Possibly the Apostle is speaking about such persons when he calls that city "the church of the firstborn ones"[130] which, he mentions, is written in heaven.[131]

7. *Through whom we have received grace and apostleship to bring about the obedience of faith among all the Gentiles for the sake of his name.*[132] He claims to have received grace and apostleship through Christ inasmuch as he is mediator of God and men.[133] "Grace and apostleship." "Grace" must refer to the endurance of labors, "apostleship" to the authority of proclamation. Even Christ himself is called an apostle,[134] i.e., one who has been

---

125. 1 Cor 8.6.
126. 1 Cor 2.8. Here we see an early example of the doctrine of the *communicatio idiomatum*, "the sharing of the attributes," which became important in later theology. Because Christ is a unified person, divine and human, the attributes of the divine nature may be attributed to the human nature and vice versa. Cf. *Princ* 2.6.3.
127. Col 1.18; Rv 1.5.   128. Eph 2.6.
129. Cf. Mt 27.52–53. See below, 5.1.37; 5.10.3.
130. Heb 12.23.   131. Cf. 8.5.2.
132. Rom 1.5.   133. Cf. 1 Tm 2.5.
134. Cf. Heb 3.1.

sent[135] from the Father, since he himself claims to have been sent to preach good news to the poor.[136] Everything which is his, therefore, he gives to his disciples as well. It is said that grace has been poured out on his lips.[137] [M853] He also gives grace to his own apostles with which they may say as they labor, "I have labored harder than all of them; but not I but the grace of God with me."[138] And because it has been said about him, "Therefore since we have a high priest and apostle of our confession, Christ,"[139] he gives to his disciples the dignity of apostleship in order that they also might become apostles of God. For the Gentiles who were "foreigners to the covenant of God and the way of life of Israel"[140] were not able to believe the gospel except through the grace which had been given to the apostles. It is said that through this grace, as the apostles preach, men obey through faith, and the sound of Christ's name arising out of their grace is recounted as having gone forth unto all the earth[141] so that it has even reached those who are in Rome. The Apostle says to them, "among whom you also have been called of Jesus Christ."[142] Paul is said to be called an apostle;[143] the Romans are indeed called, but not as apostles, but called to be saints in the obedience of faith.[144] We have already spoken above about the variety of the callings.[145]

8. *To all God's beloved in Rome: Grace to you and peace from God our Father and the Lord Jesus Christ.*[146] In my opinion, this blessing of peace and grace which the Apostle Paul bestows on God's beloved to whom he is writing is nothing less than the blessing given by Noah to Shem and Japheth[147] which has been fulfilled through the Spirit in those who have been blessed.[148] Likewise

---

135. The word ἀπόστολος, "apostle," is derived from ἀποστέλλω, "I send." Cf. *Comm in Jn* 20.19; 32.17.
136. Cf. Lk 4.18.
137. Cf. Ps 45.2.
138. 1 Cor 15.10.
139. Cf. Heb 3.1; 4.14.
140. Cf. Eph 2.12.
141. Rom 10.18; Ps 19.4.
142. Rom 1.6.
143. Rom 1.1.
144. Rom 1.7; 1.5.
145. Cf. 1.2.
146. Rom 1.7. The words "called saints" are missing from the lemma of this section, but Origen mentions them at the end of 1.7.1.
147. Cf. Gn 9.26–27.
148. Cf. 10.7.3; *Hom in Lv* 16.1.

it is also the blessing in which Abraham was blessed by Melchizedek[149] and Jacob by his father Isaac[150] and the twelve patriarchs by their father Israel;[151] or the blessing of Moses with which he blessed the twelve tribes of Israel.[152] Therefore I regard the blessing with which the Apostle blessed the churches of Christ not inferior to any of these other blessings. For he himself says concerning himself, "I think that I too have the Spirit of God."[153] Consequently the Apostle is writing in the Spirit and he blesses in the Spirit. It is through that Spirit, then, that those who are blessed by the Apostle shall obtain blessings, provided that those upon whom his blessing comes are found worthy. Otherwise what is written shall come to pass, "If a son of peace is there, your peace will come on him; but if not, your peace will return to you."[154] What is written about peace applies also to grace since he joins grace and peace together. Nevertheless one should recognize that the Apostle does not observe this custom when he writes to all the churches. To be sure he writes in a similar way to [M854] the Corinthians in the first and second letter, and to the Galatians and to the Ephesians and to the Philippians.[155] To the Colossians, however, he says, "Grace be with you and peace from God our Father,"[156] and he does not add, "and from our Lord Jesus Christ." First Thessalonians has the following, "Grace be with you and peace,"[157] and nothing more. But in the second letter, "Grace be with you and peace from God the Father and the Lord Jesus Christ."[158] In First and Second Timothy he writes, "Grace, mercy, and peace from God the Father and Christ Jesus our Lord";[159] yet to Titus he says, "Grace and peace from God the Father and Christ Jesus our Savior."[160] And even though observations of this sort may appear too inquisitive, nevertheless he who believes there is nothing superfluous in the Holy Scriptures shall not regard these differences and variations as matters of insignificance.

---

149. Cf. Gn 14.18–20.
150. Cf. Gn 27.28–29.
151. Cf. Gn 49.1–28.
152. Cf. Dt 33.
153. 1 Cor 7.40.
154. Lk 10.6.
155. Cf. 1 Cor 1.3; 2 Cor 1.2; Gal 1.3; Eph 1.2; Phil 1.2.
156. Col 1.2.
157. 1 Thes 1.1.
158. 2 Thes 1.2.
159. 1 Tm 1.2; 2 Tm 1.2.
160. Ti 1.4.

9. *First, I thank my God through Jesus Christ for all of you, because your faith is proclaimed in the whole world.*[161] When writing to certain people the Apostle says he gives thanks for all of them, as he does now in writing to the Romans. However when he writes to others he indeed gives thanks but does not add the words, "for all." You shall discover if you look carefully that when he says he gives thanks "for all" he does not amplify on particular faults or serious charges of disgraceful conduct among them; but when he singles out certain people or makes an accusation he does not add to the thanksgiving that he gives thanks "for all." This is the case in the letters to the Corinthians and to the Colossians.[162] Indeed in Galatians he does not write a thanksgiving at all because he is amazed at them that they are "so quickly turning away from him who called them unto another gospel."[163]

(2) Thus his first expression in this letter starts with a word of thanksgiving. Now to give thanks to God is to offer a sacrifice of praise; and for that reason he adds, "through Jesus Christ," as through a great high priest.[164] For whoever wants to offer a sacrifice to God should know that he must offer it through the hands of a high priest.[165]

(3) Nor should the words "my God" be taken as superfluous. For this expression cannot be anyone's except these saints of whom God is called, just as the God of Abraham or Isaac or Jacob.[166] The man whose belly is his god[167] or for whom greed is god or the one for whom worldly glory and the ostentation of the world or the power of perishable things is god cannot say that God is his own.[168] For whatever each person [M855] worships above all else is his god.

(4) But let us see what it is for which the Apostle gives thanks to his God. He says, "because your faith is proclaimed in the whole world." If we interpret the words "in the whole world" in a simple sense it would seem to denote that in many places of the world, that is, of this earth, the faith and religion of those

---

161. Rom 1.8.
162. 1 Cor 1.4; Col 1.3.
163. Gal 1.6.
164. Cf. Heb 3.1.
165. Cf. Heb 8.3. See also *Hom in Nm* 11.9; *Cels* 7.46; *Orat* 10.2.
166. Cf. Ex 3.6.
167. Cf. Phil 3.19.
168. Cf. *Hom in Jer* 5.2; 7.3; *Hom in Jgs* 2.3.

who are in Rome is being proclaimed.[169] But if, as in not a few other passages, the world denoted here is the one which consists of heaven and earth and everything in them, then it is possible to understand that the powers, of whom it is said, "they have joy over one sinner who repents,"[170] are rejoicing far more over the conversion and faith of the Romans, when the angels who ascend and descend on the Son of Man announce it to them.[171] For they too are amazed at the conversion of the nations and that the sound of the apostles of Christ Jesus has gone forth into the whole earth.[172] After all, they even rejoice as they behold the struggles of the saints in this world, as the Apostle says, "For we have become a spectacle to the world, both to angels and to men."[173]

(5) Yet it is also possible to understand this verse in the following way: That faith which the Romans possess is the very same and no different than that which is being proclaimed and believed in the whole world and which also will be preached not only on earth but also in heaven. For Jesus has made peace through his own blood not only with the things on earth but also with the things in heaven.[174] And at the name of Jesus not only do earthly beings bow the knee but also heavenly beings and those which live in the underworld.[175] This is what it means when it says that their faith is being proclaimed in the whole world. Through this faith the entire world is being subjected to God.[176]

(6) We take note, of course, that to the word "first" he does not relate anything like, "and in the second place."[177] However we said in the Preface[178] that Paul's style of speaking is incomplete. Possibly, however, it may be completed when he says later, "Now, I want you to know, brothers."[179]

10. *For God, whom I serve in my spirit in the gospel of his Son, is my witness.*[180] God is a witness for his saints since they also are

169. Cf. 3.6.6.
170. Cf. Lk 15.10.
171. Cf. Jn 1.51.
172. Cf. Rom 10.18; Ps 19.4.
173. 1 Cor 4.9. Cf. 4.1.4; *Mart* 18.
174. Cf. Col 1.20; 2 Pet 1.1.
175. Cf. Phil 2.10.
176. Cf. Rom 3.19.
177. Cf. 4.9.1; 4.12.5.
178. Cf. Preface of Origen (1).
179. Rom 1.13.
180. Rom 1.9.

BOOK 1, CHAPTER 10

witnesses of God according to what he says through the prophet, "You shall be my witnesses and I am a witness, says the Lord."[181] Moreover the Savior says to the disciples, "You will be my witnesses in Jerusalem, and Samaria, and to all the ends of the earth,"[182] according to which it is written, "Everyone who confesses me, I also will confess him before my Father."[183]

(2) Let us now see why it is that he says, "whom I serve in my spirit." To serve in the spirit seems to me to be similar to, yes and even something more than, to worship in the spirit.[184] As [M856] the Lord himself said to the Samaritan, "Woman, the hour will come, and is now here, when the true worshipers will worship the Father in spirit and truth."[185] But Paul not only worships in the spirit, but he also serves in the spirit. For who can worship without affection? But to serve pertains to one who is constrained by affection. Accordingly the Apostle serves God not in the body or in the soul but in his best part, in the spirit. For when he writes to the Thessalonians he makes known that these three aspects are in man when he says, "May your whole body, soul, and spirit be preserved on the day of our Lord Jesus Christ."[186] And Daniel says, "Praise the Lord you spirits and souls of the righteous."[187] In accordance with this the Apostle everywhere prefers the spirit and repudiates the flesh or that which belongs to the flesh. After all, he himself praises the spirit of the law but spurns the letter as if flesh when he says, "The letter kills but the spirit gives life."[188] But also when he says, "For where the law was weak through the flesh, God sending his own Son in the likeness of sinful flesh,"[189] doubtless he is calling the "flesh of the law" the "letter of the law." For through the letter the law is weak so that it may not be fulfilled.[190] For who could fulfill what is written about the Sabbath, "You shall not move from your place on the Sabbath"?[191] For how was it possible for

---

181. Is 43.12 LXX.
182. Acts 1.8.
183. Mt 10.32.
184. Cf. Jn 4.23.
185. Jn 4.23.
186. 1 Thes 5.23. Cf. 1.5.3; *Princ* 4.2.4;
187. Dn 3:86 LXX.
188. 2 Cor 3.6.
189. Rom 8.3.
190. Cf. 2.9.1; 6.12.2.
191. Cf. Ex 16.29. In *Princ* 4.3.2 Origen gives a Jewish explanation of this passage from Exodus; noted by N. R. M. de Lange, *Origen and the Jews* (Cambridge: Cambridge University Press, 1976), p. 40.

someone, deep down inside, not to move from his place? Or what about the laws concerning leprous diseases that break out on thread or on a wall or on a hide or the thousands of other laws?[192] It is on account of these laws that the law is weak according to the letter, that is, according to the flesh. For that reason, the Apostle says, "For the law is spiritual."[193] Consequently he who understands that the law is spiritual serves God in the spirit. Whence also he says to others, "For if you live according to the flesh, you will die," that is to say, according to the letter which kills; "but if by the Spirit you put to death the deeds of the flesh, you will live."[194]

(3) It must now of course be asked whether we are also to believe that the fathers of old, the patriarchs and prophets, since they likewise attained perfection, served God in the spirit.[195] Since also "Abraham longed to see the day" of Christ; "and he saw it and was glad."[196] And Moses and Elijah appeared in glory, speaking with Jesus on the mountain.[197] In this the law and the prophets are shown to harmonize with the Gospels and to shine forth with the same glory when viewed and interpreted spiritually.[198]

11. *How without ceasing I make mention of you always in my prayers, asking that by God's will I may somehow at last at some time have a successful journey [M857] in coming to you.*[199] When Paul says that he prays without ceasing for those to whom he is writing, being mindful of his own command, he fulfills in deed what he has commanded in word.[200] He says that he prays that by God's will he may somehow at some time at last have a successful journey and may come to the Romans. One should keep in

---

192. Cf. Lv 13.48ff.; 14.37ff. See also *Hom in Gn* 2.6.
193. Rom 7.14.   194. Rom 8.13.
195. Cf. 6.7.7.   196. Cf. Jn 8.56.
197. Cf. Mt 17.3; Lk 9.30–31. See also 2.5.4; *Comm in Mt* 12.38; *Hom in Lv* 6.2.
198. Cf. Heither in Origenes, *Commentarii*, 1:119 n. 42, "Thus the question posed above which had been formally left unanswered is decided in the affirmative: The Fathers also served God in the spirit, for the law and the prophets are spiritual at their core."
199. Rom 1.9–10.   200. Cf. 1 Thes 5.17.

mind that when the Apostle of God sets out on a holy work, i.e., the work of the gospel, he waits until, by means of prayers, he procures not only a successful journey for himself but also a success that comes about by the will of God. How much more, then, this should be the case with us, who do not possess such a great task or confidence of merit. When we are disposed to undertake something we must request from God success for the journey.

(2) I think, however, that the Apostle wanted this to be understood, that the success of a journey is not always accomplished by the will of God. After all, even Balaam had a successful journey while going to Balak to curse the people of Israel,[201] but this success was not by the divine will.[202] Moreover many people experience successful outcomes in secular affairs and rejoice in their successes, but such success is not by the will of God except when there is need of our journey, as the Apostle specifies here.

12. He says, *For I am longing to see you so that I may impart to you some spiritual gift to strengthen you, that is, that we may be mutually encouraged by each other's faith, both yours and mine.*[203] First of all, we must learn that to long to see Christian brothers is an apostolic work, but for no other reason except that we might confer to them some spiritual gift if we are able and, if we are not able, that we might receive one from them. For apart from this reason the longing to go around to the brothers is not commendable. When he says, "so that I may impart to you some spiritual gift," he is evidently making known that there are gifts which are not spiritual.[204] Certainly the gift of faith is spiritual, and the gift of wisdom and knowledge and likewise virginity. But when he speaks of marriage and virginity he says, "But each has his own gift from God, one having one kind and another a different kind."[205] Thus he indeed calls marriage a gift, since as it is written, "A wife is prepared for the husband by the Lord,"[206]

---

201. Cf. Nm 22.7ff.   202. Cf. 9.1.14; *Hom in Nm* 13.8.
203. Rom 1.11–12.
204. Cf. Sir 20.10. See also *Comm in Mt* 14.16.
205. 1 Cor 7.7.   206. Prv 19.14.

but this gift is not spiritual. Many other things as well can be called gifts of God such as wealth, bodily strength, outward beauty, and earthly kingdoms. For these too are granted by God, as even Daniel says, "For he sets up kings and deposes them,"[207] but these gifts are not spiritual. Blessed are those, therefore, to whom the Apostle wants to impart a spiritual gift for the strengthening of faith so that they might no longer be infants [M858] nor borne along by every wind of teaching.[208] When this is accomplished by Paul, he himself receives encouragement seeing his own work strong and stable, and they who become sharers in the apostolic grace[209] are also encouraged.

13. *I want you to know, brothers, that I have often intended to come to you but thus far have been prevented, in order that I may have some fruit even among you as also among the other nations, the Greeks and barbarians, the wise and foolish, I am a debtor; thus for my part I am eager to proclaim the gospel to you also who are in Rome.*[210] There is a hyperbaton[211] in this passage and it is a rhetorical ellipsis. We can render the hyperbaton as follows: "I want you to know, brothers, that I have often intended to come to you in order that I may have some fruit both among you as also among the other nations, the Greeks and barbarians, the wise and foolish, but thus far I have been prevented." But the rhetorical ellipsis may be completed in the following way: In the place where he says, "also among the other nations, the Greeks and barbarians, the wise and foolish," it appears that the words "to whom" are missing. What follows should read this way, "to whom I am a debtor." The logical order might be, "Just as I have fruit among the other nations, the Greeks and barbarians, the wise and foolish, to whom I am a debtor, thus for my part I am eager to proclaim the gospel to you also who are in Rome; for I have never

---

207. Dn 2.21.   208. Cf. Eph 4.14.
209. *Gratia,* which means both "grace" and "gift."
210. Rom 1.13–15.
211. A transliterated term stemming from Greek rhetoric (cf. Quintilian, *Training of an Orator* 8.6.62–7; 9.3.91). It refers to a transposition of words from their natural order, or a confusion in the order of the words. See B. Neuschäfer, *Origenes als Philologe,* 2 vols. (Basel: Friedrich Reinhardt Verlag, 1987), pp. 230–32.

BOOK 1, CHAPTER 13 83

been ashamed to preach the gospel among any nation because the power of God is in it for salvation to all who believe, first for the Jew and then for the Greek."[212] For in the gospel the righteousness of God is revealed which had been concealed previously, being hidden in the law. But it is revealed to those who go from the faith of the old covenant to the new faith of the gospel; just as it was predicted in the prophet: The "righteous," even if he is still under the law, by believing in God and in his servant Moses,[213] "lives out of faith."[214] And when he comes to the gospel from the faith of the law he is led to faith in Christ and thus advances from faith to faith.[215]

(2) These things should be said as far as pertains to the logical coherence of the words of the Apostle. But now, let us investigate what contributes to understanding. He shows his love for the Romans when he says, "For I have often intended to come to you." If we think that what he adds, "but thus far I have been prevented," means that he has been prevented by God, it is shown through this as well that it matters to God where each of the apostles ought to go or not to go, and that by a kind of superintendence he allows the word of God to be preached to some but prevents it from being preached to others. As he says elsewhere, "And when we tried to enter into Bithynia the Spirit of Jesus prevented us."[216] And in the Gospels the Savior says, [M859] "To you it has been given to know the mysteries of the kingdom of God, but to others it is in parables, so that seeing they may not see, and hearing they may not hear."[217]

(3) However, if "but thus far I have been prevented" is related to what he says in another passage, "Satan hindered us,"[218] then he is suitably revealing here that he is struggling without ceasing in prayer[219] in order that, when the hindrances of Satan have been overcome, his journey might become successful by the will of God to see those who are in Rome. For he longs for this and does not cease to supplicate in his prayers that he might receive some fruit from them, as from the other Gentiles.

212. Cf. Rom 1.16.
214. Cf. Hab 2.4.
216. Cf. Acts 16.7.
218. 1 Thes 2.18.
213. Cf. Ex 14.31.
215. Cf. Rom 1.17.
217. Lk 8.10.
219. Cf. 10.15.3–4.

It is as if Paul, desirous of great wealth and returning from his many spiritual investments, longs to gather in. He gathers fruit from the Greeks, he gathers some from the barbarians, he gathers some from the wise, and he even collects some from the foolish.[220] Whereas he speaks wisdom to some as to the perfect, to others as to the foolish, he claims to know nothing at all except Christ Jesus and him crucified.[221] Whereas he teaches some out of the law and the prophets, others he convinces by signs and wonders.

(4) Truly Paul bears all these fruits because like a good branch he remains in the true vine, who is Christ. He whom the Father, as the vine grower, frequently prunes, also for that reason bears much fruit;[222] but he prunes him through labors, afflictions, and persecutions. For there are other branches who abide in the vine but do not bear fruit but are withered. From these are the ones which remain in Christ in name but in works and deeds are found unfruitful and withered. They are said to be cut off by the Father and cast into the fire.[223] For the first Adam was a type of vine[224] and the root of the human race which produced certain fruitful branches, such as Seth, Enosh, Enoch, and the rest until Noah, but he produced others which were unfruitful and useless, such as Cain and all the offspring generated from him. Likewise in Christ, who is the last Adam,[225] there are some fruitful branches that are bearing fruit in the true vine, but also others that are withered and should be cut off by the Father, the vine grower.[226]

(5) Note the following as well: the Apostle designates the fruit of good things in the singular, just as he does in another passage, "But the fruit of the Spirit is love, joy, peace";[227] but the works of the flesh which he reproaches he mentions in the plural.[228] Now if someone objects to this observation by citing what is written in the Psalm, "You shall enjoy the labors of your

---

220. Cf. Rom 1.10–11, 13.
221. Cf. 1 Cor 2.2, 6.
222. Cf. Jn 15.1–8; Mt 3.10.
223. Cf. Jn 15.6.
224. Cf. *Comm in Jn* 20.3ff.
225. 1 Cor 15.45. See also *Princ* 4.3.7.
226. Jn 15.1ff.
227. Gal 5.22.
228. Gal 5.19.

fruits,"²²⁹ where fruit is properly designated in the plural, he should realize this: Just as the man who dealt with many pearls but who discovered one [M860] of very great value sold everything and bought that one pearl,²³⁰ in the same way someone who begins with many fruits ought to strive for the one fruit of perfection.²³¹

(6) At this point it must be asked in what sense the Apostle is a debtor to Greeks and barbarians, to the wise and foolish. For what had he received from them which would cause him to be indebted to them? In my opinion he has become a debtor to the various nations because, through the grace of the Holy Spirit, he had received the ability to speak in the tongues of all the nations, as he himself says, "I speak in more tongues than all of you."²³² Accordingly, since a person receives the knowledge of tongues not for his own sake but for the sake of those to whom he is supposed to preach, he becomes a debtor to all those, the knowledge of whose language he has received from God. He becomes a debtor to the wise, however, because he received wisdom hidden in a mystery which he was supposed to speak to the perfect and the wise.²³³ But how is he indebted to the foolish? Because he has received the grace of patience and longsuffering; for it is a gesture of supreme patience to bear with the foolish.

(7) But he has most graciously added in the words which follow, "thus for my part I am eager to proclaim the gospel to you also."²³⁴ He testifies that he is eager, for in another passage he says, "For if I do this of my own will, I have a reward."²³⁵ Surely a person is eager to speak to the wise. But with respect to the foolish we must take into consideration what he says, "but if I am not willing, then a commission has been entrusted to me";²³⁶ and, "for woe to me if I do not preach the gospel."²³⁷

---

229. Ps 128:2.
230. Cf. Mt 13.45–46.
231. Cf. *Princ* 1.6.2; 2.1.1–2; *Comm in Mt* 10.9; *Hom in Ezek* 8.2; *Comm in Cant* 2; *Hom in Jer* 8.6.
232. 1 Cor 14.18.
233. Cf. 1 Cor 2.6–7.
234. Rom 1.15.
235. 1 Cor 9.17.
236. 1 Cor 9.17.
237. 1 Cor 9.16.

14. *For I am not ashamed of the gospel; for it is the power of God for salvation to everyone who believes.*[238] Many reproaches against the gospel arose at the beginning of its proclamation, but Paul had learned patient endurance from the prophets, saying, "Do not be conquered by their reproaches, and do not yield when they revile you."[239] He knew that he had to preach the gospel "not with plausible words of human wisdom, but in the power of the Spirit."[240] In defining what the gospel is, therefore, he declares, "for it is the power of God for salvation to everyone who believes, to the Jew first and also to the Greek." When he says, "It is the power of God for salvation," he seems to be revealing that there is some power of God which is not for salvation but instead for destruction. He knows of course that it is written in the prophet, "And the locust is my great power";[241] and again in the Psalms it says, "Destroy them with your power";[242] and therefore he says here, "the power for salvation." It must be seen, then, whether perhaps it is on account of these different kinds of powers of God that there is talk of the right and left hand of God.[243] In this way the power unto salvation is called his right hand and the power by which he destroys is called his left hand. Because Christ is called the power of God[244] and the gospel also is called the power of God, the following ought to be considered: whether [M861] Christ, as he is many other things, ought also to be understood as the gospel. Indeed perhaps what is called the "eternal gospel"[245] should be interpreted with reference to him.

(2) He says, "to everyone who believes, to the Jew first and to the Greek."[246] The Greeks were the first to assess the entire human race with two designations, saying that every single human was either a Greek or a barbarian. In fact for them the distinction was such that everyone who was not a Greek was regarded as a barbarian. Paul makes use of a much more accurate distinction by naming the Jews first, the Greeks next, and the barbar-

238. Rom 1.16.
239. Is 51.7.
240. 1 Cor 2.4, 13.
241. Jl 2.25.
242. Ps 59.11.
243. Mt 25.33, 41. Cf. *Comm in Mt* 16.4.
244. 1 Cor 1.24.
245. Rv 14:6. Cf. 1.4.1.
246. Rom 1.16.

ians in the last position. For although the Greeks may have named all the rest of humanity living without laws as barbarians (since the Greeks themselves did make use of laws), the Apostle rightly puts the Jews ahead of the Greeks since they began to live under laws before the Greeks.[247] Moreover their laws were promulgated by God, rather than men.

15. *For the righteousness of God is revealed in it from faith to faith.*[248] The righteousness of God is revealed in the gospel through the fact that with respect to salvation no one is excluded whether he should come as a Jew, Greek, or barbarian. For the Savior says equally to all, "Come to me, all you that labor and are burdened."[249] But concerning the words "from faith to faith" we have already said above[250] that the first people who had believed God and his servant Moses[251] were also in the faith; from this faith they now transfer over to the faith of the gospel.[252] But it says this from the testimony of the prophet Habakkuk, "the righteous lives by my faith."[253] Either it means that he who is under the law must believe in the Gospels as well, or that he who is under the Gospels must also believe in the law and the prophets. For a person does not possess complete life who has one but not the other.[254]

16. *For the wrath of God is revealed from heaven against all ungodliness and wickedness of men who by their wickedness suppress the truth. Because what is known of God has been manifested to them, for God has manifested it to them.*[255] In other places we have spoken more fully concerning the wrath of God;[256] however let a few things be said at this time as well. So then, it is said that the wrath of God is now being revealed not against a certain part

---

247. Cf. *Cels* 4.21; 5.42–44; Josephus, *Against Apion* 2.151ff.
248. Rom 1.17. 249. Mt 11.28.
250. Cf. 1.13.1. 251. Ex 14.31.
252. Cf. *Hom in Gn* 10.5; Tertullian, *Against Marcion* 5.13.2.
253. Hab 2.4; Rom 1.17.
254. Cf. 2.13.27; 2.14.11. Schelkle, *Paulus, Lehrer*, p. 47, observes, "This is indeed a Pauline thought, but it is not being expressed by Paul here."
255. Rom 1.18–19.
256. Cf. *Cels* 4.11.6; 4.72 (written later than *Comm in Rom*); *Hom in Lk* 22; *Princ* 2.4.4.

but against all ungodliness and wickedness; however, not in all men but only in those who, to be sure, hold fast to the truth [M862] but suppress it by their wickedness. He says that what is known about God is manifest to them. This shows that there is something about God that may be known and something about him that may not be known. That is why he says the wrath of God is being revealed to those who suppress the truth by their wickedness. What is revealed is brought forth from obscurity and hiddenness into the state of being known. Since therefore it is said here as well that the wrath of God is revealed from heaven not against those who are ignorant of the truth but against those who hold fast to it, although they hold fast to it in a bad way, evidently he is saying that the rationale for and knowledge of the wrath of God are manifested in those who know the truth, even though they suppress it in wickedness.[257] As he declares in what follows, this is interpreted as having been spoken about the wise men of this world and the scholars and the philosophers. Although they knew the truth and righteousness of God, "they did not honor him as God or give thanks to him, but they became bankrupt in their thinking," having turned to idols.[258] And "claiming to be wise, they became fools," for "they exchanged the glory of the incorruptible God for the likeness of the image of man and birds and four-footed animals and reptiles."[259]

(2) With these words the Apostle also makes known the following: That which the wise men of this world have attained in respect to the knowledge of the truth, they have attained as God reveals them. But as long as they strive for vain glory or fawn over ancient errors or become intimidated by fear of the rulers, they themselves become the judges of their own damnation. The truth which they had known by divine revelation they either covered up when they denied the existence of freedom or they rejected through the wickedness of their deeds.[260]

---

257. Cf. *Cels* 3.37; 3.47; 4.30; 6.3; 6.4; 7.4; 7.46–47.
258. Cf. Rom 1.21.
259. Rom 1.22–23.
260. Cf. Roukema, *The Diversity of Laws*, p. 19, "Origen is rather positive about the natural capacity of man to know about the spiritual world and about

BOOK 1, CHAPTER 16 89

(3) Well then, wrath sometimes seems to refer to that power which governs the ministers of punishments and inflicts penalties which govern sinners.[261] I hold the view that this is the meaning of the text which reports that the wrath of God incited David to command Joab to take a census of the people.[262] Moreover both his ministers and associates are also indicated in the passage which says, "He sent against them the wrath of his fury, affliction, and wrath through evil angels."[263] Sometimes even the pangs of conscience are named wrath[264] when we clarify "avengers" and "punishers," as the Apostle also says, "you are storing up wrath for yourself on the day of wrath";[265] and in another passage, "as their thoughts among them mutually accuse or even defend them on the day when God will judge the secrets of men."[266] Moreover the affliction of distress or of a trial is called the wrath of God, [M863] as Job says, "The wrath of the Lord is in my body."[267]

(4) But why is it said that the wrath is now being revealed from heaven? Perhaps in order to distinguish it from another wrath which is not from heaven, as for example, "Their wine is the fury of dragons and the incurable fury of serpents."[268] Or perhaps, because those against whom this word is being directed are said to be sinning not in ignorance but in the knowledge of the truth, for that reason it is said that the punishment is being directed against them from heaven, from where the minister of the punishments receives his authority.[269] But unquestionably, since the spiritual forces of wickedness against whom we engage in combat are said to be in the heavenly regions,[270] it logically follows that, in those persons who are vanquished by these evil beings, wrath is said to be hurled at them from heav-

---

God, but he is more negative about the way in which the philosophers made use of this capacity."
261. Cf. *Cels* 4.72.   262. Cf. 2 Sm 24.1.
263. Ps 78.49.   264. Cf. 2.6.6; *Princ* 2.10.4.
265. Rom 2.5.   266. Rom 2.15–16.
267. Jb 6.4. The LXX reads, "For the arrows of the Lord are in my body, whose wrath drinks my blood." Thus Origen has accurately perceived the sense, but not the wording, of the verse.
268. Dt 32.33 LXX.   269. Cf. 7.1.3.
270. Cf. Eph 6.12.

en. It is just as if we were to say that flaming missiles are being shot at them from there[271] and they are receiving wounds from on high by which they fall into sins. For in reality those who are totally devoid of the truth, as if they have nothing in common with heaven and with the light, are bearing the wrath of their own vices and sinful passions, or of the demons to which they have willingly subjected themselves.

(5) "Against all ungodliness and wickedness of men who suppress the truth by their wickedness." "Ungodliness" refers to sin against God, "wickedness" to sin against men. Therefore he who by his wickedness suppresses the truth sins against God and against men. We are to believe that men have known this truth by means of the natural reasoning capacities which God has implanted into the soul. Enough wisdom has been granted to them that they should recognize what is known of God, that is, what can be perceived about God by way of inference from the creation; from the things which can be seen, his invisible things ought to be recognized.[272] Therefore, by his covenant, the just judgment of God will be just even against those who before the arrival of Christ turned away from the worship of God, although they were able to recognize him, and turned to the adoration of images of men and of animals.[273] To put it briefly and in one compressed definition we could say: To worship anything besides the Father and the Son and the Holy Spirit is a crime of ungodliness.

(6) "For what is known of God has been manifested to them, because God has manifested it to them."[274] We have already said above[275] that what we are able to comprehend by the progression of this world and by reason is "known of God." This is what the Apostle himself indicates when he says that his invisible things can be contemplated through the things which have been made.[276] However the knowledge of his substance and nature must be understood to be a matter that is "unknown of God." In my opinion the kind of proper nature he possesses is

---

271. Cf. Eph 6.16.
272. Cf. 2.9.1.
273. Cf. Rom 1.21–23.
274. Rom 1.19.
275. Cf. 1.16.5.
276. Rom 1.20.

something which is concealed not only from us human beings but from every created being. Now whether at some time our rational natures shall have made such great progress that they may be able to attain to this knowledge too, only God knows. Such a thing appears to me [M864] to be hoped for in the Savior's words, "For no one knows the Son except the Father; and no one knows the Father except the Son and anyone to whom the Son wants to reveal him."[277] For he would not have added, "and anyone to whom the Son wants to reveal him," unless he knew that there are some to whom he wants to reveal these things.[278]

17. *For his invisible things are perceived from the creation of the world, having been understood through what has been made, and his eternal power and deity, so that they might be without excuse; for though they knew God, they did not honor him as God or give thanks, but they became bankrupt in their thinking, and their foolish heart was darkened. For claiming to be wise, they became fools and they exchanged the glory of the incorruptible God for the likeness of the image of corruptible man and birds and four-footed animals and reptiles.*[279] In what has been said above we have already discussed nearly all the details of these verses. For we said[280] that these things, although they pertain to all men in whom natural reason exists, are directed in particular to the wise men of this world and those who are called philosophers, whose job it is in particular to discuss the created things of the world and everything which has been made in it. They use reason to draw conclusions about the things which are not seen from the things which are seen.[281] One should of course recognize that the invisible things which he names here refer to created beings.[282]

(2) The same Apostle also writes about these beings in an-

---

277. Mt 11.27.
278. Cf. *Comm in Jn* 1.16; 20.7.
279. Rom 1.20–23.
280. Cf. 1.16.5.
281. Cf. *Cels* 3.47; 6.4; 7.46.
282. By "invisible things" he evidently means incorporeal spiritual powers, i.e., angels, in contrast to God's invisible uncreated nature. Schelkle, *Paulus, Lehrer,* p. 55, notes that Origen does not tell us how this recognition is supposed to take place. Cf. *Princ* 1.7.1.

other passage, "For through him," i.e., through Jesus Christ, "all things were made, whether things in heaven or on earth, things visible and invisible."[283] And for that reason, in addition to the things which he had called invisible, he adds, "and his eternal power and deity."[284] Therefore, the power of God which is eternal and his deity which is no less eternal are known by inference from the creation. His power is that by which he rules all things, his deity is that by which he fills the universe.[285] On this basis, then, men become without excuse, since although they knew God (since God made himself known), they have not, as is fitting, worshiped God or given thanks, but through their own futile way of thinking, while they seek after forms and images for God, they have destroyed the image of God within themselves.[286] Those who were openly boasting to be in the light of wisdom have fallen into the deep darkness of foolishness. For what is so revolting, so dark, and so gloomy as to turn the glory of God into the bodily and corruptible effigy of a human form, as is the custom of those who worship images; to equate the greatness of the divine majesty with birds and four-footed animals and reptiles?

18. It was assuredly for these reasons that *God most justly handed them over to the desires of their hearts to impurity, [M865] to the mutual degrading of their bodies; they exchanged the truth of God for a lie and worshiped and served created things rather than the Creator, who is blessed forever.*[287] Each detail recorded here may seem to be suitably explained according to the faith of the Church, that the people described here have justly and deservedly earned God's abandonment of them for the reasons previously given for their guilt.[288] The truth which they know by God's revelation they suppress by their wickedness and on account of being abandoned they are handed over to the desires of their

---

283. Col 1.16.
284. As Schelkle, *Paulus, Lehrer,* p. 55 observes, Origen has interpreted ἥ τε ἀΐδιος αὐτοῦ δύναμις, not as being in apposition to ἀόρατα but as a part of a series. This mistaken understanding was repeated by later Fathers.
285. Cf. *Hom in Lv* 5.2; *Princ* 1.2.9; 2.1.2–3.
286. Cf. 1.19.8.   287. Rom 1.24–25.
288. Cf. *Cels* 7.47; *Orat* 29.15.

heart. These were the desires of their heart: that they mutually devote their own bodies to impurity and defilement. And the kind of judgment they used against the veneration of the deity when they transferred the glory of the incorruptible God to disgusting and unworthy forms of men and animals was the same judgment they used in turn against themselves, that rational human beings live after the fashion of irrational beasts.

(2) Nevertheless, let us ask those who deny that the good God is also a just judge[289] what shall they say in response to these things which the Apostle says, namely that God "handed them over to the desires of their heart to impurity, to the degrading of their bodies"? For in this not only will their system, once completely excluded, be forced out, but even our own explanation. For how shall it be just that whoever is handed over—granted that it is on account of their own sins that they are handed over—nonetheless are handed over to lusts and handed over to this, to the devotion of their own bodies to impurities and lusts? For example, anyone who is handed over to the dungeon for punishment cannot be charged with the accusation that he is in darkness. Or, anyone handed over to fire cannot, for this very reason, be blamed for why he is burnt. Likewise in the case of those who are handed over to sinful desires and impurities so that they degrade their bodies, it will not seem fitting for them to be charged when, situated amongst lusts and impurities, they defile their bodies with degradations.

(3) Well then, Marcion and all who spring forth from his school like a brood of vipers shall not dare to touch the solution of these matters, not even with their fingertips,[290] since they have thrown away the Old Testament on account of these sorts of problems, wheresoever they happened to have read such things in it. But what good did it do them? For they are no less strangled by similar problems in the New Testament.[291]

(4) For us, however, who acknowledge one God, good and

---

289. Cf. 2.4.8. Intended are Marcion and his gnostic followers, who are important dialogue partners with Origen throughout the *Commentary*. Origen also directs comments against Marcion while discussing Rom 1.22–28 in *Orat* 29.12–13. Cf. also *Hom in Lv* 11.2; *Princ* 2.5.1ff.
290. Cf. Mt 23.4; Lk 11.46; 16.24. See also 3.7.4; 5.6.3.
291. Cf. *Princ* 2.4.4.

just, of the law and the prophets and the Gospels, the Father of Christ, we make use of the same explanations in both the New and Old Testament.[292] We call upon him who placed in Zion a stone of stumbling and a rock of offense[293] to reveal to us through his own Holy Spirit the explanation of the stumbling block and offense [M866] of the apostolic reading on account of which doubting minds are tripped up.

(5) We frequently find in the Scriptures, and we have often discussed this topic, that man may be said to be spirit, body, and soul.[294] And when it is said, "The flesh desires contrary to the spirit, and the spirit desires contrary to the flesh,"[295] the soul is undoubtedly placed in the middle. Either it gives assent to the desires of the spirit or it is inclined toward the lusts of the flesh. If it joins itself to the flesh it becomes one body with it in its lust and sinful desires;[296] but if it should associate itself with the spirit it shall be one spirit with it. It is after all for this reason that the Lord says in the Scriptures concerning those whose souls had been united completely with the flesh, "My Spirit shall no longer abide in these men, for they are flesh."[297] But concerning those whose soul had united with the spirit the Apostle says, "But you are not in the flesh but in the Spirit."[298]

(6) Moreover, as we find in many scriptural passages, there are angels who are patrons and helpers for both sides, or rather for the two ways.[299] For the devil and his angels and all the evil spirits in the heavenly regions together with all the principalities and powers and rulers of the infernal parts of this world against whom human beings must do battle[300] support the flesh in its lust against the spirit.[301] But on the other hand, all the good angels support the spirit as it struggles against the flesh

---

292. Cf. 2.4.8.   293. Cf. Is 8.14; Rom 9.33.
294. Cf. e.g., 1 Thes 5.23. See also 1.10.2; 1.5.3; 6.1.5; *Princ* 1.8.3; 2.6.5; 2.8.4; 3.4.2; *Comm in Jn* 32.18. Origen's trichotomous understanding of man is more functional than ontological, as scholars have observed. Cf. Heither, *Translatio Religionis*, p. 198; von Balthasar, *Origen: Spirit and Fire*, p. 46.
295. Gal 5.17.   296. Cf. 1 Cor 6.16–17.
297. Gn 6.3.   298. Rom 8.9.
299. Cf. *Princ* 3.3.6; *Cels* 8.34. The doctrine of the "two ways" is first found in *Didache* 1. Its scriptural basis is Mt 7:13–14.
300. Cf. Eph 6.12.   301. Gal 5.17.

BOOK 1, CHAPTER 18

and attempt to summon the human soul, which is intermediate, to itself. The Lord says about these angels, "Their angels see the face of your Father in heaven."[302] The Apostle also speaks about them in Hebrews,[303] "Are they not all ministering spirits sent to serve for the sake of those who are receiving the inheritance of salvation?"[304] The Lord himself also lends his support, inasmuch as he even laid down his own life for his sheep.[305]

(7) But out of both sides' support, the duty of choice is preserved. For the matter is not done by force nor is the soul moved in either of the two directions by compulsion.[306] Otherwise neither blame nor virtue could be ascribed to it, nor would the choice of the good earn a reward or the turning aside to evil merit punishment. Instead the freedom of will is preserved in the soul in all things, so that it may turn to what it wants, just as it is written, "See, I have set before you life and death,"[307] "fire and water."[308] Life, therefore, is Christ,[309] and death refers to the last enemy,[310] the devil. The soul therefore makes its own decision whether it wants to choose life, that is Christ, or to turn aside to death, the devil.[311]

(8) But suppose the soul, while recognizing God, should fail to embrace Christ, its life. Suppose it should not honor him [M867] as God or give thanks, but should become bankrupt in its thinking and exchange the glory of the incorruptible God for the likeness of the image of corruptible man and birds and four-footed animals and reptiles and through all these things,

---

302. Mt 18.10.
303. Origen consistently attributed the authorship of Hebrews to the Apostle Paul. Cf. *Ep* 1.
304. Heb 1.14.   305. Cf. Jn 10.15.
306. Cf. *Orat* 29.15; *Princ* 3.1.1; 3.1.6.
307. Dt 30.15.   308. Sir 15.16–17.
309. Cf. Jn 14.6.   310. Cf. 1 Cor 15.26.
311. Cf. *Comm in Mt* 12.33; *Hom in Nm* 9.7; *Princ* 3.1.6; 3.1.11 and esp. *Dial* 27.9–15: "Let us therefore take up eternal life. Let us take up that which depends upon our decision. God does not give it to us. He sets it before us. 'Behold, I have set life before thy face' [Dt 30.15]. It is in our power to stretch out our hand, to do good works, and to lay hold on life and deposit it in our soul." H. Chadwick and J. E. L. Oulton, eds., *Alexandrian Christianity: Selected Translations of Clement and Origen*, LCC 2 (1954).

should turn aside to the flesh and to those beings which lend support to the desires of the flesh. If that should happen it shall doubtlessly be forsaken and abandoned by those beings which, by their support, were encouraging it to be joined with the spirit. They withdraw from it or hand it over to the desires of its own heart, by which it is united and joined to the flesh. Certainly they shall not call back a soul which is resisting or reluctant to the things which it has avoided and spurned.

(9) If the depiction of this matter still seems unclear, let us make it less obscure and more plain by using an illustration.[312] Let us imagine that there is a certain home in which the soul dwells together with the body and the spirit, as it were with a pair of counselors. In front of the entrance of this home stands piety and all the virtues with her. But on the other side are ungodliness and every sort of excess and lust. They are all waiting for a nod from the soul: Which of these two troops watching before her doors does she want to have let in to herself, which does she want to repel? Suppose the soul, in compliance with the spirit and yielding to the better counselor, summons to herself the troop led by piety and modesty. Will not the other group which has been spurned and repudiated go away? But suppose the soul, yielding to the counsels of the flesh, lets into her home the ungodly lust-squad. Then that whole crowd, led by holiness and piety, over which the soul preferred the counsel of the evils, shall withdraw with righteous indignation and leave the soul to the sinful desires of her own heart. The result will be that she degrade her own bodies among herself. The soul has exchanged the truth of God for a lie and, letting into herself the servants of ungodliness and faithlessness, worships and serves the creature instead of the Creator, who is blessed forever.

(10) It is of course for these reasons that the human soul comes into so hazardous a position at a critical moment like this, but this is not to be discussed in the present passage. So then, it is the lot of those who are zealously devoted to images to degrade their own bodies, and for those who have abandoned the Creator to worship the creation. We, however, worship and

---

312. Cf. 2.1.3.

adore only the Father and the Son and Holy Spirit and no created thing. Just as we do not wander into error in our worship, so we do not sin even in our actions and manner of life, nor do we imitate those who mutually degrade their own bodies, considering what the Apostle says, "Do you not know that your bodies are members of Christ?"[313] and again, "Your body is a temple of the Holy Spirit."[314] As members of Christ and a temple of the Holy Spirit let us preserve our bodies [M868] in all holiness and purity so that they might become worthy not only for angels to enter but indeed also to be a habitation of the Holy Spirit and a dwelling place of the Father and the Son, who said of the one who abides in his commands, "I and the Father will come and make a dwelling place with him."[315]

19. *For this reason God handed them over to degrading passions. For their women exchanged natural use for unnatural. In the same way also the men, giving up the natural use of a woman, were inflamed with their desire for one another, men committing shameless acts with men and receiving in their own persons the wage which was due for their error. And since they did not approve to acknowledge God, God handed them over to a base mind that they might do things that should not be done. They were filled with every kind of iniquity, malice, profligacy, covetousness, full of envy, murder, strife, deceit, spite, they were gossips, slanderers, hateful to God, insolent, haughty, boastful, inventors of evil, disobedient to parents, foolish, disorderly, without affection, without mercy. Although they knew the righteousness of God,*[316] *that those who practice such things deserve to die, not only do they do these things but they also consent to those who practice them. Therefore you have no excuse, O man, all of you who judge; for in passing judgment on another you condemn yourself. For you who judge, do the very same things.*[317]

(2) For the third time we find it formulated by the Apostle, "God handed them over." He gave the following as reasons for the first "handing over": "For though they knew God, they did

313. 1 Cor 6.15.   314. 1 Cor 6.19.
315. Cf. Jn 14.23. See also *Comm in Cant* 2.8.
316. Migne's text adds here, "they did not understand."
317. Rom 1.26–2.1.

not honor him as God or give thanks, but they became bankrupt in their thinking, and they exchanged the glory of the incorruptible God for the likeness of an image of corruptible man and birds and four-footed animals and reptiles." "Therefore," he says, "God handed them over to the desires of their hearts unto impurity, to the degrading of their bodies."[318] He seems to set forth the reason for the second "handing over" when he says, "because they exchanged the truth of God for a lie and worshiped and served created things rather than the Creator." "For this reason," he says, "God handed them over to degrading passions."[319] This second "handing over," however, seems to be responsible for more serious acts of shame. "For their women," he says, "exchanged natural use for unnatural. In the same way also the men."[320] [M869] He seems to give the reasons for the third "handing over" when he says, "And since they did not approve to acknowledge God, God handed them over to a base mind that they might do things that should not be done. They were filled with every kind of iniquity, malice," and the other wicked things which he subsequently enumerates.[321]

(3) The distinctions between these reasons, however, do not appear to me to correspond adequately to the crimes to which each person has been subjected. For why is he who serves the creature handed over to baser acts of shame than he who exchanges the glory of the incorruptible God for the likeness of an image of corruptible man and birds and four-footed animals and reptiles? Or why are those who did not approve to acknowledge God handed over beyond either of these other two as it were to some kind of examination of vices?

(4) It therefore seems to me that all the reasons presented for the individual instances of "handing over" should be amassed together in a unity, as well as the notions of "handing over." Thus we could say, for example: Because certain men exchanged the glory of the incorruptible God for the likeness of an image of man and birds and four-footed animals and reptiles, and because they exchanged the truth of God for a lie and worshiped and served the creature rather than the Creator, and

318. Rom 1.21–24.
319. Rom 1.25–26.
320. Rom 1.26–27.
321. Rom 1.28–29.

because they did not approve to acknowledge God, therefore, on account of all these things, God handed them over to the desires of their hearts unto impurity, to the mutual degrading of their bodies. He also handed them over to degrading passions so that their women exchanged natural use for unnatural. In the same way also the men. Moreover God handed them over to a base mind that they might do what should not be done, these people who were filled with every iniquity, malice, profligacy, and greed, and who were full of envy, murder, strife, deceit, and the other evils which are recorded. And those who had known God's righteousness, that those who practice such things deserve to die, not only do these things but even consent with those who practice them. And therefore, on account of all these evils, they will be without excuse when they judge and condemn others for the crimes they themselves practice. For such a person is making a pronouncement about himself when he punishes another for the things which he himself commits.

(5) I think that [M870] enough has been said above concerning the kinds of "handing over," i.e., the sense in which God is said to hand over those whose deeds and mind he shrinks back from and deserts because it turns away from him and indulges in the vices. I consider it superfluous to repeat these things. Doubtless there are two things which I think are indicated in this passage. It seems each of them point to the other. First, it is certain that if God hands anyone over either to the desires of his own heart or to degrading passions or to a base mind, then immediately a whole crop of crimes arises in the one who has been handed over, as in a worthless and rejected land.[322] Second, if someone, who although he has known God, should not honor him as God or give thanks but should be such as the apostolic discourse describes in detail, it is scarcely to be doubted that the soul of such a person has been forsaken by God and handed over. For it is not possible for God to have a dwelling with these evils or for these evils to proceed from a place where God dwells.

(6) In fact the Apostle seems to have enumerated all the forms of ungodliness collectively under these three heads: the

---

322. Cf. Heb 6.8.

ungodliness of those who worship idols, that of those who serve created things rather than the Creator, and that of those who have not approved to acknowledge God. Under the first head he intends pagans in general; under the second he describes their wise men and philosophers. It is my opinion that under the third head the heretics may be intimated, either those who deny that God is the Creator or those who utter various blasphemies against the Most High.[323] Well then, if, as I have said above, each of these classes of people, represented under these headings, is said to have gone astray in the worship of deity, let us who seem to be in the Church and who hold fast to the right faith pay close attention to ourselves.[324] Let us examine ourselves with all circumspection lest, while set apart from these things in only the name of the true worship, we associate ourselves with these matters and affairs.

(7) For example, it is certain that a man who is filled with iniquity, malice, profligacy, and greed has not approved to acknowledge God and belongs to the number of those whom God has handed over to a base mind. Moreover in the case of those whose women or men, by abandoning their natural use, are inflamed with a passion for unnatural use, it is certain that they are of the number of those who serve created things rather than the Creator and whom God has handed over to degrading passions. Furthermore, when people degrade their own bodies in impurity, they belong to the number of those who have exchanged the glory of the incorruptible God. Except that the one who is already a believer who defiles the temple of God[325] is guilty of a greater sacrilege than a profane man who defiles the temple of idols. [M871]

(8) Obviously the passage in which the Apostle says, "they exchanged the glory of the incorruptible God for the likeness of the image of man," must not be left behind.[326] This text must be understood as exposing not merely those who worship idols, but also as refuting the Anthropomorphites who are in the Church, who claim that the image of God is the bodily form of man. They are unaware that it is written in the book of Genesis

---

323. Cf. Ps 73.8ff. See 2.14.11.
324. Cf. Gal 6.1.
325. Cf. 1 Cor 3.16.
326. Cf. *Hom in Gn* 1.13; *Cels* 7.27.

that man was made in the image of God.³²⁷ Now of which man this text ought to be understood, the Apostle himself explains when he says, "having laid aside the old man with his deeds," and, "having put on the new who has been created according to God."³²⁸ You hear that he says that the new man is created according to God. But in another passage he calls this same new man "the inner man."³²⁹ In fact he identifies the corruptible man, whose image he rejects, as the outer man when he says, "Even though our outer man is being corrupted, our inner man is being renewed."³³⁰ And in order that those who are in error concerning the image of God might know [M872] his meaning still more clearly, let them hear which one the Apostle says is the man who has been created in the image of God. He writes in Colossians, "Do not lie, seeing that you have stripped off your old man with his deeds and have put on the new, who is being renewed in knowledge according to the image of him who created him."³³¹ From these words he plainly shows that it is the inner man, which is being renewed through knowledge, who has been created in the image of God. But those who say that the outer man, that is, the bodily and corruptible man, is in the image of God are, by the Apostle, in company with those who have exchanged the glory of God for the likeness of the image of corruptible man.³³² It was indeed necessary that not even these things be omitted from the explanation of the Apostle's discourse so that even in this section of the Apostle's writing as well as in many other passages, the Anthropomorphites, that is to say, those who say that the bodily form of man is the image of God, may recognize themselves as having been exposed and refuted.

(9) However with this let us now bring the content of the first book to a conclusion.

---

327. Cf. Gn 1.27. See also *Cels* 6.63; *Dial* 11.20–12.14; 15.28–16.11.
328. Col 3.9–10; Eph 4.22, 24. In 5.8.12 the same mixed quotation occurs. Cf. *Hom in Gn* 9.2; *Hom in Ex* 1.5.
329. Rom 7.22. 330. 2 Cor 4.16.
331. Col 3.9–10. 332. Cf. *Hom in Gn* 1.13.

THE SECOND BOOK OF THE *COMMENTARY ON THE EPISTLE OF PAUL TO THE ROMANS*

BUT WE KNOW THAT GOD'S JUDGMENT *on those who do such things is in accordance with truth.*[1] We must expect and believe that God's judgment in accordance with truth is not only on those who do the things which have been enumerated above,[2] but also on all who do anything good or evil in any way. But this passage is evidently making known that the judgment of God alone is in accordance with truth. For there are certain things which are committed where the deed is evil but the spirit is not evil,[3] for instance, if someone unintentionally kills a man. Other things happen where the deed is good, but the spirit is not good, as in the case of anyone who shows mercy not because God commands it but in order that he might be praised by men.[4] There are other actions in which the spirit agrees with the deed, whether good or evil.[5] And because it belongs to God alone to know the hearts of men and to discern the secrets of the mind,[6] for that reason he alone is capable of holding judgment in accordance with truth.

(2) But it is asked whether God seems to hold judgment in accordance with truth towards those whose iniquities have been forgiven through the grace of baptism, or whose sins have been covered through repentance, or to whom sin is not going to be imputed on account of the glory of martyrdom.[7] The truthfulness of the judgment, of course, demands that the bad man receives bad things and the good man good things;[8] and although God's gifts and his free bestowal of them by no means permit us

---

1. Rom 2.2. 2. Rom 1.18–2.1.
3. Cf. *Hom in Lk* 2. 4. Cf. Mt 6.2.
5. Cf. *Comm in Jn* 28.13. 6. Cf. 1 Kgs 8.39. See 4.1.5.
7. Cf. Ps 32.1–2. See also 4.1.20; *Cels* 3.71.
8. Cf. *Princ* 2.5.1.

to be overly inquisitive in this investigation, nevertheless I wish to point out in this instance as well how great the truth of his judgment is. By common acknowledgment a good man ought not be punished, nor should an evil one obtain good things. Therefore, if, for instance, someone has done evil at some time, [M873] it is certain that he was evil at that time when he was doing evil things. However, suppose he, repenting of his past deeds, reforms his mind toward good things, behaves well, speaks well, thinks well, and turns his will toward the good. Is it not clear to you that he who does these things is a good man who deserves to receive good things? In like manner if someone should convert from good to evil, he shall no longer be judged as the good man he was and is no longer, but as the evil man that he is. You see, deeds pass away, whether good or evil.[9] According to their own characteristics, they represent and form the mind of the one who is doing them; and they leave it either good or evil, to be devoted to either punishment or rewards.[10] Accordingly it shall be unjust to punish a good mind for evils committed or to reward an evil mind for good deeds.

(3) In order that what we are saying might become even clearer, let me add the following as well.[11] Let us suppose there is a soul in which dwells ungodliness, unrighteousness, foolishness, excess, and the entire multitude of evils to which it has openly subjected itself as servant and slave. But suppose this soul comes back to itself[12] and opens the door of its mind once again to piety and the virtues. Will not piety, when she has entered, immediately drive ungodliness out of there? In like manner righteousness shall also push out unrighteousness and wisdom shall put foolishness to flight, and to excess sobriety shall do the same. And thus, when the foreign occupants have been expelled from itself, the soul shall offer civil and proper hospitality to the virtues. How then shall it be just to convict a soul that is now filled with virtues, of the things it had committed when it was not yet a friend of the virtues? How will it be just to condemn a pious soul for ungodliness, or a just soul for injus-

---

9. Cf. Epictetus, *Discourses* 2.18.7.
10. Cf. 7.7.4; 8.11.7.
11. Cf. 1.18.9.
12. Cf. Lk 15.17.

tice, or a soul practicing moderation for excess? In this way, therefore, God should be believed to hold judgment in accordance with truth on those whose iniquities have been forgiven and whose sins have been covered.[13]

2. *Do you think, O man, all you who judge those who do such things and do them, that you will escape the judgment of God?*[14] If "everything the law says it speaks to those who are under the law,"[15] then also the things the gospel or the Apostle is now saying are being said not to the rulers of the world or to the kings of the earth but to those who lead and govern the churches, that is to say, to those who judge those who are inside the Church,[16] i.e., to the bishops and elders and deacons. So then, Paul is saying to them that they should not think they will escape the judgment of God if they themselves commit the very things over which they judge and condemn others. It is therefore needful for each one first to judge his own conscience and only then to examine the deeds of the one whom he is judging. Would that this would take place! Then all secret ambition for striving after ecclesiastical offices would immediately be cut off. Would that those [M874] who want to lead the people would consider themselves as persons to be judged rather than as those who are about to pass judgment!

(2) Let no one think then that he can escape God's judgment. As the prophet says, "Where shall I go from your Spirit and where shall I flee from your presence?"[17] And because these things are being spoken especially to those who are presiding over the judgments of the peoples, for that reason it says elsewhere, "Judgment shall begin from the house of God."[18] The Lord says the same thing in another passage, "Among those who draw near me I will show myself holy."[19] This was accomplished in the case of Nadab and Abihu when they offered strange fire, that is, unholy fire, on the divine altars.[20] There-

---

13. Cf. Ps 32.1–2.
14. Rom 2.3.
15. Rom 3.19.
16. Cf. 1 Cor 5:12.
17. Ps 139.7.
18. 1 Pt 4.17.
19. Lv 10.3.
20. Cf. Lv 10.1–2. Cf. Irenaeus, *Against Heresies* 4.26.2.

fore judgment begins with the sons first; for God scourges all whom he receives among the number of his sons.[21] It is my opinion, in fact, that even if someone could escape God's judgment, he ought not desire to. For not to come to God's judgment would mean not to come to correction, to the restoration of health and to that which heals.[22]

3. *Or do you despise the riches of his goodness and forbearance and patience, unaware that God's goodness leads you to repentance?*[23] He who considers what great evils men on earth are committing daily, and, with nearly all turning aside and having together become useless;[24] how they are walking down the broad and spacious road which leads to destruction, having disregarded the narrow road which leads to life,[25] despite the fact that God lets his sun rise daily on all of them and serves them with rain;[26] and if one considers how much blasphemy against God they speak every day and how they stretch out their tongues against heaven;[27] this person is able to understand the riches of God's goodness. What might I say about men's deceits, violence, crime, sacrileges, and wicked actions? Yet in this passage those who, while judging others, themselves commit the things which they punish in others, seem to be put ahead of all these others in wickedness.[28] If then someone despises this goodness of God and his forbearance and patience, he does not realize that it is by means of these that he is being invited to repentance.

(2) Forbearance seems to differ from patience. Those who commit a transgression out of weakness rather than out of deliberate intention are said to be "forborne"; those, however, who, as it were, gloat over their transgressions with an obstinate mind must be said to be "endured with patience." But just as God made everything in measure, weight, and number,[29] so

---

21. Cf. Prv 3.12; Heb 12.6.
22. Notice Origen's purgatorial and remedial understanding of judgment and punishment. See 7.5.10; 8.12.8; *Princ* 2.5.3; 2.10.6; *Hom in Ezek* 1.2.
23. Rom 2.4. 24. Cf. Ps 14.3.
25. Cf. Mt 7.13–14. 26. Cf. Mt 5.45.
27. Cf. Ps 73.9; Jer 9.2. 28. Cf. 1.19.7.
29. Cf. Wis 11.20.

also there is a definite measure of his patience. We must believe that this measure was squandered by those who perished in the flood[30] and by those in Sodom who were devastated by heavenly fire.[31] It is also on this account that it is said of the Amorites, "For the sins of the Amorites are not yet complete until now."[32] [M875] So then, God bears with everyone patiently and awaits each one's repentance; but this should not render us negligent or make us slow to conversion, since there is a definite measure to his patience and forbearance.[33]

4. *But in accordance with your hardness and impenitent heart you are storing up a treasure of wrath for yourself on the day of wrath and revelation of God's righteous judgment, who will repay each one according to his deeds.*[34] It seems that a hard heart is mentioned in the Scriptures when the human mind, like wax which has been hardened by the ice of wickedness, does not receive the seal of the divine image.[35] The same thing is called elsewhere a "fat heart," as when it says, "The heart of this people is fattened."[36] But the opposite of hard is soft, which in the Scriptures is named "a heart of flesh";[37] and the opposite of fat is subtle and thin, which the Apostle calls the spiritual man who examines all things.[38] Consequently, when a person knows what things are good and yet does not do the good, we have to believe that he has contempt for good things through the hardness of his heart. But wherever the subtle spiritual sense of understanding is not welcomed there is fatness of the heart. And just as the heart, made impenitent, "stores up a treasure of wrath for itself on the day of wrath and revelation of God's righteous judgment" when a good work is not done owing to the hardness of

---

30. Cf. Gn 6:5ff.   31. Cf. Gn 18.20ff.
32. Gn 15.16.
33. Notice that the threat of divine punishment always lurks. For Origen this applied both in this age and in the age to come. Cf. *Princ* 3.1.17; *Comm in Mt* 15.11.
34. Rom 2.5–6.
35. Cf. *Hom in Lk* 39; *Hom in Ezek* 13.2.
36. Mt 13.15; cf. Is 6:10 LXX.
37. Ezek 11.19; 36.26. Cf. *Hom in Jer* 18.10; *Hom in Is* 6.5.
38. 1 Cor 2.15.

understanding, so a good man is excluded on account of the fatness of the heart. Now concerning the wrath of God, this has been discussed above[39] and often in other passages,[40] as much as the subject permitted.

(2) But now we must endeavor to ascertain what he says, "you are storing up a treasure of wrath for yourself." It is called a "treasure" where wealth and riches of various kinds are collected. We read of three meanings of this term in the Scriptures. In the Gospel it is said that there is a certain treasure on earth where the Lord forbids treasures to be stored up; there is another treasure in heaven where he commands all the faithful to lay up their wealth;[41] and now here the Apostle speaks of treasures of wrath. Therefore all men collect into one treasure out of these three through the things they do in this world. For it is the unbeliever who, being wicked and by the hardness of his heart and his impenitent heart, lays up his own deeds in the treasure of wrath. Or he may be earthly and think of the earth and speak of the earth.[42] And when his field has brought forth an abundant yield for him, he tears down his barns and builds bigger ones and stores up treasure on earth.[43] The first man is designated as hard, but here the second as foolish. For it is said to him, "You fool! This very night they will demand your soul from you. And the things you have prepared, whose will they be?"[44] There is also the person who is wise and rich in relation to God[45] and who, though he lives on earth, has his citizenship in heaven.[46] Everything [M876] he does is worthy of the kingdom of heaven.[47] Such a person lays up the treasures of his riches in heaven.[48] The possessor and compiler of each treasure can be designated first as someone fleshly, but the second as a soulish man, and the third as spiritual.[49]

(3) But now let us see what the Apostle means here by the

---

39. Cf. 1.16.1.
40. Cf. *Cels* 4.72; *Hom in Lk* 22; *Hom in Jer* 18.
41. Cf. Mt 6.19–20. See also *Hom in Jer* 14.12.
42. Cf. Jn 3.31; 1 Cor 15.47; Phil 3.19.
43. Cf. Lk 12.16–18; Mt 6.19.   44. Lk 12.20.
45. Cf. Lk 12.21.   46. Cf. Phil 3.20.
47. Cf. *Comm in Mt* 10.14.   48. Mt 6.20.
49. Cf. 1 Cor 2.14–15; 3.1.

"day of wrath." This shall be more easily discerned if we make an inquiry into what the rest of Scripture reveals about this day. Therefore we shall furnish examples which might parallel the present passage, and from these it will be shown what the day of wrath is. In the prophet Amos it is written, "Woe to those who desire the day of the Lord! What is the day of the Lord to you? It is darkness, not light; as if a man should flee from the face of a lion, and is met by a bear; or enters into his house and rests his hand against the wall, and a snake bites him. Is not the day of the Lord darkness, not light, and gloom with no brightness?"[50] Moreover Joel says to the priests and to those who serve at the altar, "Shout to the Lord without ceasing, Woe is me, woe is me on the day, because the day of the Lord is near and it shall come like misery from misery."[51] A little bit later, "Blow the trumpet in Zion; proclaim it on my holy mountain! All who dwell upon the earth will be confounded, for the day of the Lord is coming, for near is the day of darkness and gloom, a day of cloud and thick darkness! Like the morning dawn, a people great and powerful is spread upon the mountains. Their like has never been from of old, nor will be again after them in the years of the ages to come. Fire devours in front of them, and behind them a flame burns. Before its face the land will be like the paradise of delights, but behind it a field of desolation, and there is no one to escape it. Their faces are like the appearance of horses, and like riders they will charge. As with the sound of chariots, they will leap on the tops of the mountains."[52] Yet he writes of this same day in everything that follows, up to the passage where he says, "The Lord shall give his voice before the presence of his power, for utterly vast is the multitude of his encampments and powerful are the effects of his words! Therefore the day of the Lord is great, great and very remarkable—who shall be equal to it?"[53] Zephaniah, moreover, says the following, "You will be afraid of the countenance of the Lord God. For the day of the Lord is at hand; the Lord has prepared his own sacrifice, he has consecrated those who have

50. Am 5.18–20.
51. Jl 1.14–15 LXX.
52. Jl 2.1–5 LXX.
53. Jl 2.11 LXX.

been called."⁵⁴ A few words later, "The day of the Lord is near, very near and hastening fast. The sound of the day of the Lord has been appointed bitter and hard and strong. That day will be a day of wrath, a day of distress and difficulty, [M877] a day of bitterness and destruction, a day of darkness and gloom, a day of cloud and fog, a day of trumpet blast and battle cry against the fortified cities and against the lofty battlements. I will afflict men and they shall walk like the blind, because they have sinned against the Lord, and I shall pour out their blood like dust, and their flesh like dung. Neither their gold nor their silver will be able to save them on the day of the Lord's wrath. In the fire of his jealousy the whole earth shall be consumed; for a hurried end he will make of all the inhabitants of the earth."⁵⁵ Isaiah also recounts something similar, "Behold, for the day of the Lord will come, incurable, with wrath and fury, to make the earth a desolation, and to destroy sinners from it."⁵⁶ And after a few words, "For heaven will be set on fire with fury, and the earth will be shaken from its foundations, because of the fury of the wrath of the Lord of Hosts on the day when his fury shall come."⁵⁷ With so many testimonies of this sort gathered together concerning the day of wrath, in my opinion no further exposition is needed for this present passage. For in all these texts the "day of wrath" is plainly declared to be a day of vengeance and judgment.

(4) After all, this is why the Apostle adds to "the day of wrath" "and of revelation." He puts it this way, "on the day of wrath and revelation of God's righteous judgment." In the Gospel it is also made known that everything is going to be revealed when it is said, "Nothing is hidden that will not be disclosed, and nothing covered up that will not be revealed."⁵⁸ Moreover, later in this epistle the Apostle says, "as their thoughts accuse or even defend them on the day when God will judge the secrets of men."⁵⁹ By these words he is showing in particular that the secrets of men are only going to be revealed on

---

54. Zep 1.7 LXX.
55. Zep 1.14–18 LXX.
56. Is 13.9.
57. Is 13.13.
58. Mt 10.26; Lk 12.2.
59. Rom 2.15–16.

the day when God is going to judge. He makes this point even more clearly in the letter to the Corinthians, "Do not pronounce judgment on anything before the time, before the Lord comes, who will bring to light the secrets of darkness and will reveal the purposes of hearts."[60] Surely all of these things are understood as having been said about the same day on which darkness and grief and sorrow are said to come on account of those who shall be in need of remedies of fire, since they have been pierced through with many wounds by their sins.[61] At that time it will be said to the saints, "Come, my people, enter your chambers, and shut your door to hide yourselves for a little while until the fury of my wrath is past."[62] There is no need to make known the extent to which the riches of God's goodness are concealed in these words on account of those who despise his patience and goodness.[63]

(5) Naturally some people will ask why this day, concerning which we have, in the foregoing, deployed the library of the prophets, is appointed at the end of the world, so that all those who have died from the beginning of the world until its end [M878] are reserved for this last day of judgment. The interior causes of this matter are certainly veiled in deep mysteries. And indeed "it is good to conceal the mystery of the king."[64] Nevertheless for the sake of explanation let us say as much as it is possible to commit words to paper. There are many people who depart this life having left behind certain "seeds,"[65] whether of good or of evil, from which the men who live after them will take occasions either for salvation or damnation. For example I would say that they are everyone who have founded depraved schools of philosophers which are estranged from God; or those who have contrived sacrilegious magic, or who have devised erroneous teachings and principles based upon the move-

---

60. 1 Cor 4.5.   61. See 8.11.10.
62. Is 26.20.
63. Cf. Ps 31.19; Rom 2.4. Apparently Origen means that after the divine punishment restoration to grace (for those who cooperate) may follow, but Paul has kept this a secret in the current passage. Cf. 2.4.8.
64. Tb 12.7.
65. Cf. *Comm in Jn* 13.46.

ment of the stars. Among us, of course, there exist authors of heresies and perverse doctrines, their books in print. In addition there are those who have caused schisms in the churches, and scandals and dissension.[66] In contrast to all this, the work of the apostolic writings and the advancement of the entire Church by means of them is both the conversion to God and the transformation of the entire world. The causes of all these things will not be concluded until this world ends, and therefore it would not be a just judgment of God as long as advancement and lapses depend upon these things. The Apostle seems to intimate this when he says, "The sins of some people are manifest and are preceding them to judgment, while they subsequently follow others."[67]

(6) Now whether those who are disembodied or the saints, who are now with Christ, do anything and labor on our behalf in imitation of the angels who attend to the service of our salvation;[68] or, on the other hand, whether even sinners, themselves without bodies, do anything in accordance with the intention of their own mind in no less imitation of the evil angels with whom they are to be cast into the eternal fire, as was indeed said by Christ;[69] let this too be kept among the hidden things of God.[70] They are mysteries which are not to be committed to paper. Let this suffice for the words, "on the day of wrath and revelation."

(7) Now we need to ask about the righteous judgment of God in which he will pay back to each one according to his own works. In the first place let the heretics who claim that the natures of human souls are either good or evil be shut out.[71] Let them hear that God pays back to each one not on account of his nature but on account of his works. In the second place let believers be edified so as to not entertain the thought that, be-

---

66. Cf. Rom 16.17.
67. 1 Tm 5.24.
68. Cf. Heb 1.14.
69. Cf. Mt 25.41.
70. Cf. *Hom in Nm* 26.6; *Hom in Jos* 16.5; *Comm in Cant* 3; *Comm in Jn* 13.58; *Orat* 11.1–2.
71. Cf. Preface of Origen (1); *Princ* 2.9.5; 3.1.6. Elsewhere in the *Commentary* (2.10.2; 4.12.1; 8.8.7; 8.11.2) he identifies Marcion, Basilides, and Valentinus as the representatives of this view.

cause they believe, this alone can suffice for them.[72] On the contrary they should know that God's righteous judgment pays back to each one according to his own works. Obviously, because he says here that there is a righteous judgment of God, so that it will be paid back to each one according to his works,[73] the Gentiles will in nowise seem to be excluded when they themselves do good [M879] and behave correctly. There is a text in Ezekiel, however, which will appear to contradict this idea. For he says, "When the righteous man turns away from his righteousness and commits iniquity in accordance with all the iniquities that the wicked man has done, none of the righteousness that he has done will be remembered in view of his falling away, by which he has fallen; but in the sins he has committed, he will die in them."[74] For they will say, "If none of the righteousness of the righteous man will be remembered when he falls away, how will God pay back each one according to his works?" But let us see whether the divine text itself might find its own solution within itself, if we observe how what he says is written, "When the righteous man turns away from his righteousness." And he is not satisfied merely in saying, "When the man turns away from his righteousness," but he has added, "and commits every iniquity in accordance with all the iniquities that the wicked man has done," by which he seems to introduce in a hidden manner a meaning of this kind: If perchance the righteous man does not commit all the iniquities which the wicked man did, then not all of his righteousness will be removed from memory; but if he commits all the iniquities which the wicked man has done, then and only then would his righteousness be taken away from memory in view of his falling away.[75]

(8) Although the Holy Spirit has concealed these things in the Scriptures because of those who despise the riches of his

---

72. Here and in many passages Origen teaches that justification is by both faith and works and that faith alone is not sufficient for justification. Cf. 2.12.4; 2.13.23; 3.7.12; 8.2.7. In other passages, however, he does speak of justification by faith alone. Cf. 3.9.2–4.
73. Cf. 2.7.6.   74. Ezek 18.24.
75. Cf. *Hom in Ezek* 1.3.

goodness and patience,⁷⁶ nevertheless he has not completely removed them. For not even the treasure hidden in the field is found by all, lest it be easily plundered and perish.⁷⁷ Yet it is found by those who are prudent, who are able to go and sell everything they have and buy that field. Accordingly, these things as well, although they may be hidden in the Scriptures, as it is written, "How great is the multitude of your goodness, O Lord, which you have hidden for those who fear you,"⁷⁸ are nevertheless found by those who, based on what things are hidden in the mystery of the Scriptures, defend the God of the law and of the prophets as being not only just but also good.⁷⁹ Necessity demanded that we bring to light a few of these things which disclose the meaning of the apostolic text when he says, "the righteous judgment of God, who repays according to each one according to his deeds."

5. *To those who by perseverance in good works seek for glory and honor and incorruption, eternal life, while for those who out of contention [M880] and who distrust the truth but comply with wickedness, wrath and fury and affliction and anguish for every soul of the one who does evil, the Jews first and the Greeks; but glory and honor and peace for everyone who does good, for the Jew first and the Greek. For God shows no partiality.*⁸⁰

(2) To those who seek glory and honor and incorruption, he says, God will give eternal life on account of their perseverance in good works, not only to the Jews to whom the oracles of God appear to have been entrusted,⁸¹ but also to the Greeks, because the judgment of God is just, and God is not only God of the Jews but also of the Gentiles.⁸² But to those who, through the contention of mind and perverseness of spirit, do not believe the truth but follow after wickedness, wrath, and indigna-

---

76. Cf. 2.4.4.
77. Cf. Mt 13.44. See also *Comm in Mt* 10.5–6.
78. Ps 31.19.
79. This is aimed once again at Marcion, who denied the goodness of the God of the OT and the justice of the God of the NT. Cf. 1.18.2; *Princ* 2.5.
80. Rom 2.7–11.   81. Cf. Rom 3.2.
82. Cf. Rom 3.29.

tion, affliction and anguish are paid back, not only to the Gentile but also to the Jew, because God shows no partiality. Certainly, this treats the literal meaning, but let us now investigate that which concerns their inner meaning.

(3) He says, "To those who by perseverance in good works." When he says, "perseverance in good works," he is pointing out that certain exertions and struggles are close at hand for those who want to do good works.[83] For as the same Apostle says, "Our struggle is not against flesh and blood, but against the principalities and powers and rulers of this world,"[84] all of which are opposed to good works. This is why perseverance is necessary,[85] for it is written, "By your perseverance you will gain your souls."[86] Now let us see what he means by a good work. In the Gospel the Lord declares of the woman who poured the alabaster jar of ointment upon his head, "A good work has been done to me."[87] By this he is showing that the one who pours out ointment upon the Word of God, that is to say, he who unites works with the Word, accomplishes a good work.[88] For the spoken word becomes fragrant, filled with all the sweetness of the ointment, when it has been adorned with deeds and actions.

(4) Now let us investigate what it means to seek for glory and incorruption. In many passages of Holy Scripture the authors write about glory.[89] For it is said in Exodus concerning Moses that when he was descending from the mountain his face was glorified.[90] When the Apostle explicates this passage in the letter to the Corinthians he says, "Now if the ministry of death, chiseled in letters on stone tablets, happened in glory [M881] so that the sons of Israel could not gaze at Moses' face because of his face's glory, which fades, how much more will the ministry of the Spirit be in glory? For if there is glory in the ministry of condemnation, how much more will the ministry of righteousness abound in glory?"[91] And after a few words he adds, "And all of us, with unveiled faces, observing the glory of

---

83. Cf. 1.18.6; 10.15.3.
84. Eph 6.12.
85. Cf. Heb 10.36.
86. Lk 21.19.
87. Mt 26.7, 10.
88. Cf. *Comm in Cant* 2.2.
89. Cf. *Comm in Jn* 32.26–27.
90. Cf. Ex 34.29.
91. 2 Cor 3.7–9.

the Lord, are being transformed into the same image from glory to glory, as by the Spirit of the Lord."[92] According to the Apostle, then, there is a certain glory which is not glorified,[93] as for example the glory, which was in Moses' face, which is said to have been destroyed.[94] This can be understood as the letter of the law. Although it possesses a certain glory in its commands, it is nevertheless not capable of being glorified. There exists another glory which remains[95] and is glorified in Christ. For when he had ascended the mountain with Peter, James, and John, it is written that he was transformed in glory. It says, "And then Moses and Elijah appeared, speaking with him."[96] This shows that when Jesus was transformed into glory, the glory of the law and the prophets then appeared, so that prophecy and law, illuminated by Christ's glory, could be understood in the Spirit, once the veil of the letter had been taken out of the way.[97]

(5) In fact it is even said in Exodus that the glory of God filled the tabernacle of testimony;[98] and no less again at the dedication of the temple the glory of God descended and filled the house with a dark smoke and clouds,[99] in which, it is scarcely to be doubted, the very presence of God is indicated as having arrived. In these passages, this must be considered to be the glory about which the Apostle is speaking when writing to the Hebrews concerning the Son, "For he is the splendor of his glory and the express image of his substance."[100] In these things it is made clear that the source of glory is the Father himself, from whom the splendor of that glory, the Son, is generated,[101] by participation in whom all creatures are said to have glory, just as it is written about those who are of the resurrection, "there is one glory of the sun, another glory of the moon, another glory of the stars, and star differs from star in glory."[102] Therefore those who seek for the glory of the resurrection and

---

92. 2 Cor 3.18.
93. Cf. 2 Cor 3.10.
94. Cf. 3.11.3.
95. Cf. 2 Cor 3.11.
96. Cf. Mt 17.1–3. See also *Comm in Mt* 12.38.
97. Cf. 2 Cor 3.16.
98. Cf. Ex 40.34.
99. Cf. 1 Kgs 8.10–11; 2 Chr 5.13–14; 7.1–2.
100. Heb 1.3.
101. Cf. *Comm in Jn* 32.28.
102. 1 Cor 15.41.

for honor and incorruption, shall assuredly attain what is written, "The body is sown in dishonor, it will rise in glory. It is sown in corruption, it will rise in incorruption."[103] And so the one who searches for this glory and honor and incorruption through perseverance in good works will attain to eternal life.

(6) But now that we have discussed glory as well as we could, let us see what honor refers to, since those who hasten to eternal life seek not only glory but also honor. It is written, [M882] "When man was in honor he did not understand; he was likened to foolish beasts and became like them."[104] So then, he seeks that honor which he had before he was likened to foolish beasts, that is to say, that honor which he had in Paradise before he transgressed it, the honor by which he earned the right to hear the voice of God, the honor by which he enjoyed the fruits of Paradise and the tree of life.[105] Moreover, what the Apostle says later, "Pay to all what is due them, honor to whom honor is due,"[106] seems to me to refer to this. For this is how I understand the honor which is due to be paid if something owed to justice is paid back and no part of it is conceded to injustice. The same applies to truth, if that which is its own is paid back so that none of its parts are left over for a lie. This is also the case for wisdom and innocence and goodness, if we should pay back what belongs to these things so that we allow nothing that is theirs to be given to foolishness or cunning or malice. For example, if you show favoritism to the stronger party in a court case,[107] or if you should suppress that which is the truth for the sake of a friend, you have not paid back the honor which is due either to justice or truth. Rather you have dishonored justice and made a mockery of the truth. And though Christ is justice and sanctification and truth,[108] you will be like those who struck Christ with their fists and spat in his face and, beating his head with the cane, placed the crown of thorns on his brow.[109] Now in the Gospels we learn what is the honor

---

103. 1 Cor 15.42–43.
104. Ps 49.12, 20. Cf. 3.5.1; *Comm in Jn* 1.20; *Hom in Nm* 26.4.
105. Cf. Gn 2.8ff.   106. Rom 13.7.
107. Cf. Lv 19.15; Sir 4.25–27.
108. Cf. 1 Cor 1.30; Jn 14:6. See also 1.1.3; 3.7.14.
109. Cf. Mt 26.67; 27.29–30; Mk 15.17, 19; Heb 6.6.

owed by man to all the virtues when the Lord says, "so that all may honor the Son just as they honor the Father."[110] That person honors the Father and the Son, then, who shows the proper honor and devotion to wisdom, justice, and truth, and to all things which Christ is said to be.[111] Therefore, it is in this manner that those who are hastening to eternal life seek glory and honor and incorruption.

(7) Now precisely what the term "incorruption" means we shall quickly learn if we investigate what is its opposite. The opposite of incorruption is corruption. Corruption is said to happen in two ways: bodily and spiritually. It happens bodily when that which is written comes to pass, "If anyone corrupts God's temple, God will corrupt him."[112] It takes place in a spiritual sense when that happens which the Apostle no less says, "But I am afraid that as the serpent deceived Eve by its cunning, your understanding will be corrupted from the simplicity of faith in Christ Jesus."[113] So then, when a person remains uncorrupted in body and spirit from the things which we have mentioned above, [M883] he is said to seek incorruption. The goal of this, of course, is that through the incorruption of his outward performance [of the virtues] he may deserve to attain to the incorruption of the resurrection.[114]

(8) But now let us see what is given to those who seek these things. It says, "eternal life." The Savior teaches about this life when he says, "And this is eternal life, that they may know you, the only true God, and Jesus Christ whom you have sent."[115] By these words he makes known that the essence of eternal life consists in the knowledge of God and of Christ Jesus. But how the knowledge of God may be obtained we are taught in the Psalms when it says, "Be still[116] and know that I am God!"[117]

---

110. Jn 5.23. Cf. *Cels* 8.9.
111. Cf. 1 Cor 1.30. See also *Cels* 7.13; 8.10.
112. 1 Cor 3.17.   113. 2 Cor 11.3. Cf. *Hom in Lv* 12.5.
114. Cf. Lk 20.35.   115. Jn 17.3.
116. As Heither in Origenes, *Commentarii*, 1:199 n. 17, indicates, *vacate* translates the LXX σχολάσατε, which means "have leisure," "give one's time to," or "devote oneself to" (*BAGD*, p. 797). Origen intends the strenuous effort of Bible study rather than inactivity.
117. Ps 46.10. Cf. *Cels* 3.37.

6. *But for those who out of contention and who distrust the truth but believe in wickedness, wrath and fury, affliction and anguish.*[118] Those who interpret these words in a simple way believe that it is sufficient to understand this according to what was said above:[119] God pays back to each person according to his works. That is to say, just as he pays back "eternal life" to those who "by perseverance in good works seek glory and incorruption,"[120] so also he will pay back "wrath and fury, affliction and anguish to those who out of contention distrust the truth but comply with wickedness." But anyone who does not think one jot or one tittle[121] is superfluous[122] in the apostolic writings in which Christ speaks[123] will assert that the Apostle has not used these expressions erroneously. He says, "He will pay back eternal life to those who by perseverance in good works seek glory and honor." Yet to those "who out of contention comply with wickedness," he did not say "wrath and fury" so as to be attached to the phrase "he will pay back," as he had said earlier. Instead he says, "wrath and fury, affliction and anguish." From this, anyone who is spiritual and understands what the Spirit would say through Paul would say that the Apostle has written these things not through a lack of skill but rather through divine skill.[124] He is undoubtedly trying to communicate here that to those who, by perseverance in good works, seek glory and incorruption, what must be paid back, namely eternal life, is paid back by God. But the other things are not given by God, i.e., those things which come upon those who, out of contention, distrust the truth but comply with wickedness. For God's gifts are absolutely abiding and worthy of him. But as a consequence of their own deeds for those who practice evil there will be wrath and fury, affliction and anguish, in accordance with what they have treasured up for themselves. For surely just as he had earlier used the words "eternal life" as a direct object, here he would also have used "wrath, fury, affliction, and anguish" as di-

---

118. Rom 2.8–9.
119. Cf. 2.4.7.
120. Rom 2.7.
121. Cf. Mt 5.18.
122. Cf. 1.8; 5.10.18; 9.41.8; *Princ* 4.2.3.
123. Cf. 2 Cor 13.3.
124. Cf. 2 Cor 11.6.

rect objects [M884] had he wanted it to refer to the person of God as the one who pays back.[125]

(2) This distinction is also given expression in other passages of Scripture. For instance in the First Book of Kingdoms the Lord says, "Those who honor me I will honor, and those who despise me shall be despised."[126] In this passage the Lord is clearly revealed to say that those who are to be honored are going to be honored through himself; but of those who are going to be despised he has not referred this to himself but has merely said that they shall be despised. For if God were to pay back evil through himself in the same way that he supplies good things through himself, according to reason he would have said, "And those who despise me I shall despise," just as he said, "Those who honor me I will honor."[127] Moreover, something similar to this seems to be shown by the prophet in another passage where those who enter into fire discover that it has been kindled not by God but by themselves. As Isaiah says, "Go in the light of your fire, and in the flame which you have kindled!"[128]

(3) In order that the explanation of these things might become even clearer, let the following be added.[129] Suppose someone, going against a physician's orders by consuming the juice of rotten food, after the agitation of his body's temperature, incurs a fever or whatever sickness you like. Obviously it is not through the physician but rather through his own want of discipline that this person contracted this pestilential sickness. Suppose, on the other hand, that by observing the physician's orders the man remains in health. In that case, he would be said to possess the gift of health through the physician. It is in this way then that God himself will seem to consequently pay back

---

125. Heither, *Translatio Religionis*, p. 51, observes, "This thought is not expressed by Paul at all, but Origen sees it implied in the unusual and rare linguistic form which at first seems careless and insufficiently thought through."
126. 1 Sm 2.30.   127. 1 Sm 2.30.
128. Is 50.11. Cf. *Princ* 2.10.4; *Hom in Ezek* 3.7.
129. Cf. 3.6.9. For a detailed examination of Origen's interest in medicine, cf. Neuschäfer, *Origenes als Philologe*, pp. 196–202, where the following passages are cited: *Cels* 3.3; 3.22–25; 3.42; 3.61; *Comm in Jn* 1.20; *Hom in Jer* 14.1; *Hom in Lk* 8.1; *Comm in Mt* 13.6; *Hom in Lv* 8.10; 9.8; *Hom in Nm* 17.1; *Comm in Cant* 3; *Princ* 2.10.4.

each person in accordance with his good works; but evil should be understood to come not from God but from the evil juices of the lack of discipline and by the blatant perverseness of one's deeds.[130]

(4) Yet we should not leave undiscussed this very passage, which says, "who out of contention distrust the truth but comply with wickedness." For in these details the Apostle is describing certain weaknesses of the soul for which no one will find a cure unless he first recognizes the causes of the disease. This is why in the Holy Scriptures the sicknesses of the soul are enumerated and the remedies described so that those who subject themselves to the Apostle's instructions, when their own documented weaknesses have been diagnosed, once they are cured they may be able to say, "Bless the Lord, O my soul, who heals all your diseases."[131] One should realize that one of the diseases of the soul, indeed the worst one, is contention. Through it every depraved deed is committed. Through it heresies are born, through it schisms and all scandals in the churches are produced, so long as those "who are prudent among themselves and wise in their own eyes"[132] defend as law whatsoever pleases them.[133] And so it happens that a person is made distrustful [M885] of the truth and compliant with wickedness.

(5) On the other hand, "to distrust" is usually found in the Holy Scriptures with the meaning "not to believe" or "not to comply with." This is how it is used in this passage which, in my opinion, the Latin scholar[134] could have more appropriately translated if he would have said, "who do not obey the truth but obey wickedness." No one then who travels down a road which is alien from the truth is following him who said, "I am the truth."[135] He is distrusting the truth and is disobedient to it if he goes astray not only in deeds but also in his judgments and in the faith. This comes to pass especially out of contention. Moreover, those who oppose wisdom and righteousness and

---

130. Cf. *Hom in Lv* 7.1.
132. Is 5.21.
131. Ps 103.2–3.
133. Cf. *Princ* 4.2.1.
134. Rufinus is evidently speaking here of the translator of the Old Latin, which he is using for the lemmata.
135. Jn 14.6.

sanctification are also distrusting Christ, who is both wisdom and sanctification,[136] just as he is the truth.[137] Not to comply with Christ, who is righteousness,[138] means to comply with wickedness. And without a doubt they are the ones upon whom those things which are written follow, i.e., "wrath and fury, affliction and anguish."

(6) We have already repeatedly said concerning wrath that anyone who is struck in his soul by the awareness of sin is called someone tormented by wrath.[139] A certain swelling up of that wrath and a particular agitation in a specific instance, however, is called fury. For example, if we were to imagine some terrible wound as wrath, we could call the swelling up and distention of it the "fury" of the wound. As for that affliction[140] which is followed by anguish, this is not to be considered to be the same type of affliction, concerning which the Apostle says, "Affliction produces perseverance."[141] For that kind of affliction is not followed by anguish, as the Apostle himself says, "We suffer affliction but we are not in anguish."[142] On the contrary, not only does that affliction of the saints contain no anguish, but it has breadth. For this is what the righteous man declares, "You enlarged me in affliction."[143] The Apostle, being himself conscious of this breadth, writes as well to the Corinthians, "You are not anguished over me but you are anguished in your own affections." And he has added, "Enlarge yourselves as well."[144] This is also the reason why God says concerning his saints, whom he has known to be enlarged and who have spacious and broad rooms in the dwelling place of their hearts, "I shall dwell in them and I shall walk about."[145] Solomon also received this gift from God among the other gifts of wisdom, as it is written,

---

136. 1 Cor 1.30.
137. Cf. Jn 14.6.
138. Cf. 1 Cor 1.30.
139. Cf. 1.16.1; 2.4.1.
140. Cf. *Orat* 30.1.
141. Rom 5.3.
142. 2 Cor 4.8.

143. Ps 4.1. It is impossible to render into English the ambiguous meanings latent in *angustia*/στενοχωρία. Each means not only "anguish" but "constriction."

144. 2 Cor 6.12–13. Cf. 3.8.6.

145. 2 Cor 6.16; Lv 26.12. Cf. *Hom in Lk* 21.6–7; *Comm in Cant* 2.8; *Hom in Gn* 1.13.

"The Lord gave prudence to Solomon and very great wisdom and breadth of heart."[146] God not only dwells in this breadth of heart of his saints, he walks about in it. [M886] But in the hearts of sinners where there are anguished places, since they have given room to the devil[147] to enter in, he does indeed enter, but not in order to indwell and walk about—for these are anguished places—but to lie hidden, as in a cave, for he is a serpent. In this way, then, the unfortunate soul, which has this evil serpent occupying it, grows stiff with a serpentine cold. It contracts and is compressed and is driven into extreme anguish. But that soul which complies with the truth is enlarged and spread out like the heavens. And, illuminated by the rays of the "sun of righteousness,"[148] it becomes a palace of wisdom and truth.

7. But why are wrath and fury *for the Jew first and for the Greek?*[149] Because both glory and honor are themselves first, "For the oracles of God were first entrusted to them."[150] And they themselves say, "Blessed are we, O Israel, for we know what is pleasing to God."[151] For this reason, then, the statement in the Gospel applies here, "That slave who knew the will of his master and did things deserving of punishment will receive a severe beating."[152] This refers to the Jew. "But the one who did not know," the Greek, i.e., the Gentile, "will receive a light beating."[153] For there is a difference between knowing God and knowing God's will. God could be known even by the Gentiles "from the creation of the world through the things that have been made, and through his eternal power and deity."[154] His will, however, is not known except from the law and the prophets.

(2) Since the Apostle puts the Jews first for punishment and reward and places the Greeks after them, it should be investigated whom he wants us to understand by "Jews" and "Greeks."

146. 1 Kgs 4.29.
147. Cf. Eph 4.27.
148. Mal 3.20.
149. Rom 2.9.
150. Cf. Rom 3.2.
151. Bar 4.4.
152. Lk 12.47.
153. Lk 12.48.
154. Rom 1.20.

BOOK 2, CHAPTER 7

If he is calling them Jews who are still under the law and do not yet come to Christ, and he calls the Christians Greeks, i.e., believing Gentiles, then it would seem to go against the idea of the entire mystery.[155] For how could they be called first, about whom it has been said, "Behold the first shall be last,"[156] and to whom he further says, "Behold your house shall be left to you desolate"?[157] Moreover, when the Savior approached the fig tree on which he did not find fruit he said, "Never again will fruit be born from you!"[158] Furthermore, in the womb of Rebecca two peoples were signified, of whom it is said, "the elder shall serve the younger";[159] and it was the younger who receives the blessings of the first born.[160] You will also find innumerable other things in accordance with this in the Scriptures. On the other hand, if he is calling us, i.e., the Christians, Jews, as well as those of every race who have believed, [M887] whom he also calls "Jews in secret,"[161] then it would naturally follow that he would designate as Greeks those Gentiles who have not yet believed.

(3) But how can the Apostle ascribe such a hope to the Gentiles who do not yet believe, when the Church's rule of faith seems to be opposed?[162] This rule establishes that "unless one should be born again of water and the Spirit, he cannot enter the kingdom of heaven."[163] Furthermore, Peter declares of Christ in Acts, "For there is no other name under heaven by which they must be saved."[164] How then does Paul here make the [unbelieving] Gentiles sharers of the glory and honor and peace in the second place after the Jews?[165] But let us see whether perhaps these things, which the goodness and sweetness of God usually hides in the Holy Scriptures, might yield something which is concealed here as well.[166]

(4) As I see it, the Apostle has created three ranks in this pas-

---

155. *Mysterium* refers to the "essential core of revelation"; Heither in Origenes, *Commentarii*, 1:210 n. 21.
156. Mt 20.16; Lk 13.30.   157. Mt 23.38.
158. Mt 21.19. Cf. *Comm in Mt* 16.26.   159. Gn 25.23.
160. Gn 27. Cf. *Hom in Gn* 12.3.   161. Rom 2.29.
162. Cf. 5.1.27.   163. Jn 3.5.
164. Acts 4.12.
165. He means "Jews in secret," i.e., Christians.
166. Cf. Ps 31.19. See also 2.4.8.

sage. First he says of those "who by perseverance in good works seek glory and honor and incorruption" that God pays back to them "eternal life."[167] It is certain that perseverance in doing good exists in those who hold out through the struggles and battles of piety. We have explained above that this has been plainly said of Christians, among whom there are martyrs.[168] This may be proved also by the Lord's words to the disciples, "You will have affliction in this world, and the world shall rejoice but you will grieve."[169] And a little while later he goes on to say, "By your perseverance you will gain your souls."[170] Therefore, to endure oppression in this world and to grieve is the lot of Christians, those who possess eternal life. Would you like to know that no one possesses eternal life except the one who believes in Christ? Then hear the voice of the Savior himself making it very plain in the Gospels, "And this is eternal life, that they may know you, the only true God, and Jesus Christ whom you have sent."[171] Therefore anyone who has not known the Father of our Lord Jesus Christ, the only true God, and his Son Jesus Christ, is a stranger from eternal life.[172] Doubtless this knowledge itself and faith are designated in this passage as eternal life.

(5) The first rank, then, belongs to the Christians, to whom eternal life will be given because they seek glory and honor and incorruption by perseverance in good works. This is assuredly the same eternal life which says, "I am the way and the truth and the life."[173] But in Christ, who is eternal life,[174] is the entire fullness of good things.[175] In the second [M888] rank are placed those who "out of contention distrust the truth but comply with wickedness," to whom "wrath and fury, affliction and

167. Rom 2.7.
168. Cf. 2.5.2.
169. Jn 16.20, 33.
170. Lk 21.19.
171. Jn 17.3.
172. Cf. *Cels* 3.81; 6.68. Under the erroneous assumption that Paul intends in this passage to promise eternal salvation to unbelieving Jews based only on their good works, Schelkle in *Paulus, Lehrer*, p. 77 and "Kirche und Synagoga," p. 301, charges Origen and nearly all the Fathers subsequent to him with doing violence to Paul's words in Rom 2:9–16.
173. Jn 14.6.
174. Cf. Jn 17.3.
175. Cf. Col 1.19.

anguish" threatens, i.e., to every soul which does evil, "to the Jew first and to the Greek." However he promises a repayment for good things to these same people in the third rank and in fact with the same distinction [respecting Jew and Greek] when he says, "But glory and honor and peace for everyone who does good, to the Jew first and to the Greek."[176] As far as I am able to understand, he speaks of the Jews and Gentiles, each of whom are not yet believers.[177] For it can come to pass that the one under the law does not believe in Christ on account of the common prevailing opinion, but nevertheless may accomplish what is good. He may hold fast to justice and love mercy,[178] observe chastity and self control; he may preserve modesty and gentleness and accomplish every good work. Such a person does not have eternal life, since, though he does believe in the only true God, yet he has not believed in his Son Jesus Christ whom God sent;[179] nevertheless the glory of his works and his honor and peace might be imperishable.

(6) But also a Greek, i.e., a Gentile, who, though he does not have the law, is a law to himself, showing the work of the law in his heart[180] and moved by natural reason, as we see is the case in not a few Gentiles, might hold fast to justice or observe chastity or maintain wisdom, moderation, and modesty. I grant that such a man might seem a stranger to eternal life, since he has not believed in Christ, and cannot enter into the kingdom of heaven,[181] for he has not been born again of water and the

176. Rom 2.10.
177. Here Origen assumes a different significance of Jew and Greek than found above.
178. Cf. Mi 6.8.
179. Cf. Jn 17.3.
180. Cf. Rom 2.14. See also 2.4.7.
181. Chadwick, *Early Christian Thought and the Classical Tradition* (Oxford: Clarendon Press, 1966), p. 105, summarizes Origen's stance as follows: "He (hesitantly) denies the saving value before God of good works done before justification, and in no way mitigates the absoluteness of the Christian faith as revelation. There is salvation only in Christ, and all must come, sooner or later, to this realization, in the next world if not in this. So Origen combines an estimate of human nature which is strikingly positive and 'humanist' with a cool reserve towards the good pagan." Cf. W. Fairweather, *Origen and Greek Patristic Theology* (Edinburgh: T. & T. Clark, 1901), p. 178: "[In Origen's thought,] philosophy . . . is no passport to the kingdom of heaven."

Spirit.[182] Nevertheless it seems that from what the Apostle has said here, he cannot completely lose the glory of the good works he has accomplished, and the honor and the peace. For if, as we have discussed above,[183] the Apostle seems to condemn the Gentiles because, though they knew God by natural understanding, they did not honor him as God,[184] why do we not think he can and should commend them as well when, while acknowledging God by their good works, they honor him as God? Consequently, I do not think it can be doubted that the one who had merited condemnation on account of his evil works will be considered worthy of remuneration for his good works, if he indeed had performed good works. For consider what the Apostle says, "For all of us must stand before the judgment seat of Christ, so that each may receive recompense for what he has done in the body, [M889] whether good things or evil.[185]

(7) After all, this is the reason why he adds in this passage "For God shows no partiality."[186] If this still seems doubtful to you, listen to what Peter declares in the Acts of the Apostles when he had entered the home of the Gentile Cornelius, "I truly understand that God shows no partiality, but in every place and among every nation anyone who does his will is acceptable to him."[187] Now it is possible to oppose us with the saying of the Lord in the Gospel, "Everyone who believes in me is not condemned; but he who does not believe is condemned already, because he has not believed in the name of the only-begotten Son of God."[188] But let us see in what sense we who believe in Christ are not condemned, in order that we might know how he who has not believed is already condemned. For are we to think that anyone who believes in Christ and afterwards commits murder or adultery or speaks false testimony or does anything of this sort, which we sometimes see even believers perpetrating, that even then he who has believed in Christ will not be

---

182. Cf. Jn 3.5.
183. Cf. 1.16.1–2, 5.
184. Cf. Rom 1.21.
185. 2 Cor 5.10; cf. Rom 14.10. The same conflation occurs in *Orat* 28.5.
186. Rom 2.11.
187. Acts 10.34–35.
188. Jn 3.18.

condemned for these things? It is certain that all these things will come to judgment. Therefore, the word of the Lord, "he who believes in me will not be condemned," has to be understood in the following sense: Anyone who has believed will not be condemned as an unbeliever and infidel; but he will undoubtedly be condemned for his own actions. So then, he who has not believed has already been condemned because he has not believed. Just as judgment still awaits a believer when he commits some sin in addition, though his faith is kept intact, so also the unbeliever shall not lose the remuneration for the good works he has done, his unbelief notwithstanding.

(8) It is possible that someone wants to interject something very serious and intolerable to say, that anyone who sins should not be regarded as a believer, since, if anyone believes, they do not sin; but if anyone sins, it is proven from this that he does not believe.[189] But I reckon that it is doubtful to no one how harsh this opinion is. For how many can be found on earth who so balance their lives that they transgress at no point whatsoever?[190] Moreover John the apostle plainly criticizes this kind of view in his letter when he says, "If someone says he has no sin he is a liar and the truth is not in him."[191] "But if we confess our sins we have an advocate before the Father, Jesus the righteous, who implores for our sins."[192]

(9) We have discussed the contents of this passage to the best of our ability, taking into consideration as well what the Apostle also says, "Is God the God of Jews only? Is he not the God of Gentiles also? Yes, of Gentiles also."[193] Our purpose [M890] was to explain more clearly why the Apostle places the Jews first and then the Greeks. Yet it should be left to the reader's discretion to test what has been said.[194] We have touched upon many subjects in this discussion so as not to appear to leave anything of the Apostle's meaning undiscussed.

---

189. Cf. *Hom in Nm* 10.1. With regard to the rigorist teaching in view here, H. Windisch, *Taufe und Sünde im ältesten Christentum bis auf Origenes* (Tübingen: J. C. B. Mohr, 1908), p. 480, says that it is difficult to determine whether Origen has Montanists or Novatians in mind.

190. Cf. 5.1.20–21; 5.9.11.   191. Cf. 1 Jn 1.8.
192. Cf. 1 Jn 1.8–9; 2.1–2.   193. Rom 3.29.
194. Cf. 1 Jn 4.1; 1 Thes 5.21. See also 1.4.4 n. 134 and Epilogue (4).

8. *All who have sinned apart from the law will also perish apart from the law, and all who have sinned under the law will be judged by the law. For it is not the hearers of the law who are righteous in God's sight, but the doers of the law who will be justified.*[195] When the Apostle says that those who have sinned apart from the law are going to perish apart from the law, we need to ask whether this ought to be understood only of the law of Moses or also of the law of Christ or even of any human law under which any mortal happens to live, so that a person might be judged according to that law against which he sins. Or does he mean that anyone who is outside only the law of Moses will perish, as one who is outside of law, when he sins, even though he may live under some other law? For even the Apostle Paul himself, when he claims to be, as it were, without law for those who are without law, yet adds, "though I am not completely without law but am under Christ's law."[196] By this he makes known that although he is not under the law of Moses, he is nevertheless under law. But you had better see whether even human laws, as we have called them, should be considered to apply here.

(2) We have to consider whether it is not natural law,[197] which dwells in all men generally, that makes it so that nearly all people commit sin against the law, as he says in what follows, "For when Gentiles, who do not possess the law, do naturally the things of the law, they, though not having the law, are a law to themselves. They show the work of the law is written on their hearts."[198] Unless, instead, we should perhaps say that they are placed beyond the law, who comply neither with written laws nor with their conscience and their own thoughts, which rebuke and convict them.[199]

(3) He says, "Shall all who have sinned under the law be judged by the law?" Undoubtedly he who is under the law of Christ will be judged by the law of Christ, and he who is under the law of Moses by the law of Moses. For he who is under Christ's law should not be considered to be one who is to be

---

195. Rom 2.12–13.
196. 1 Cor 9.21.
197. Cf. 3.6.1.
198. Rom 2.14–15.
199. Cf. Rom 2.15.

BOOK 2, CHAPTER 8   129

judged by the law of Moses, even though he may appear to be subjected to Moses' law. He will not be judged for his failure to receive circumcision or for the fact that he does not observe the Sabbath. For even if he should be considered to be judged according to the law of Moses, he will be judged according to the law that is spiritual;[200] for it is not the hearer of the law but the doer who is justified.[201]

(4) He who has sinned apart from the law seems to have been struck down by a very grave judgment indeed when he is declared to be about to perish. Surely he should be thought worthy of some pity since he does not have the use of the law available to him for assistance.[202] But let us see whether some divine goodness, [M891] which is always hidden to those who fear him,[203] does not lie concealed here again, as I have taught elsewhere.[204] For perhaps on that account, in the Gospels the Lord makes known that he has a greater care for those who are perishing[205] when he says,[206] "The Son of Man came to seek and to save what was lost."[207] He also says, "I was sent only to the lost sheep of the house of Israel."[208] And David says, "I have gone astray like a lost sheep; seek your servant."[209] Moreover in the Gospel the woman finds the mina which was lost after she cleaned the house.[210] And the father rejoices more over the penitent younger son, who "was dead and is alive again, who was lost and has been found,"[211] than over the son who had been neither lost nor found. In my opinion the younger son had just then fled from the natural law. This seems to be indicated when it says he squandered the part of his father's property which had fallen to him by extravagant living.[212] And in the prophet Ezekiel it is charged against the shepherds that they

---

200. Rom 7.14. Cf. 1.10.2.
201. Cf. Rom 2.13; Jas 1.22–25. See also 2.9.1.
202. Cf. Is 8.20.   203. Cf. Ps 31.19.
204. Cf. 2.4.4; 2.4.8; 2.7.3.
205. Here and in what follows, the Latin word can be rendered "to perish" or "to be lost."
206. Cf. *Comm in Jn* 13.20.   207. Lk 19.10.
208. Mt 15.24. Cf. *Cels* 4.17.   209. Ps 119.176.
210. Cf. Lk 15.8. See also 8.6.11.   211. Lk 15.31–32.
212. Cf. Lk 15.12–13.

have not gathered in the weak and have not searched for the perishing.²¹³ And shortly thereafter the Lord himself says, "I myself will seek what has perished."²¹⁴

(5) One should observe however that in all these passages on no occasion is God said to have destroyed anyone. Rather each one experiences destruction of his own accord.²¹⁵ For example in this passage it says, "They shall perish apart from law"; and, "The Son of Man came to seek what had perished,"²¹⁶ not what he had destroyed; and, "to the sheep of the house of Israel that had perished,"²¹⁷ not the sheep which he had destroyed. And when the Lord says, "I protected all those whom you have given me and not one of them has perished,"²¹⁸ notice that he did not say, "I have not destroyed any of them." If, of course, God is anywhere said to destroy, you will discover that this is said with the meaning "to reject." For example when it says, "I shall destroy the wisdom of the wise, and the understanding of the prudent I shall reject."²¹⁹

(6) Now consider whether perhaps what he says, "All who have sinned under the law will be condemned by the law," might be the future judgment, referring to those punishments which are recorded in the law²²⁰ and, by which, judgment was carried out when offenders were to be stoned or handed over to be burned or to flee to a city of refuge or to suffer other such things.²²¹ For indeed those who are under the law are said to be serving the type and shadow of the heavenly things.²²² Perhaps the future judgment will be carried out in a similar manner against those who would become transgressors of the law?

(7) It is evident then that the Scriptures speak of different kinds of laws. If someone has shunned them all to such a degree that even the natural law, which is absent from practically no one, seems to be obliterated and [M892] nullified in him through the hardness or fatness of his heart,²²³ it can seem to

---

213. Cf. Ezek 34.4.
214. Ezek 34.16.
215. Cf. 2.6.1ff.; *Hom in Jer* 18.9.
216. Lk 19.10.
217. Mt 15.24.
218. Jn 17.12.
219. 1 Cor 1.19; cf. Is 29.14.
220. Cf. *Hom in Nm* 28.1–2.
221. Cf. Lv 20.2, 27; 20.14; 21.9; Ex 21.13; Nm 35.11ff.; Jos 20.
222. Cf. Heb 8.5.
223. Cf. 2.4.1.

BOOK 2, CHAPTER 9   131

be said of him that he will perish apart from law.[224] On the other hand, it might be said that the one who lives under law should be judged by the law; for even the Apostle calls everyone who circumcises himself to witness that he is obligated to keep the whole law.[225]

9. *For when Gentiles, who do not have the law, do naturally the things of the law, they, though not having the law, are a law to themselves. They show that the work of the law is written on their hearts, while their own conscience also bears witness to them and their thoughts mutually accuse or even defend them on the day when God will judge the secrets of men according to my gospel through Jesus Christ.*[226] It is certain that the Gentiles who do not have the law are not being said to do naturally the things of the law in respect to the Sabbath days, the new moon celebrations, or the sacrifices written about in the law.[227] For it was not *that* law which is said to be written in the hearts of the Gentiles. The reference is instead to what they are able to perceive by nature,[228] for instance, that they should not commit murder or adultery, they ought not steal, they should not speak falsely, they should honor father and mother, and the like.[229] Possibly it is also written in the hearts of the Gentiles that God is one and the Creator of all things. And yet it seems to me that the things which are said to be written in their heart agree with the evangelical laws, where everything is ascribed to natural justice. For what could be nearer to the natural moral senses than that those things men do not want done to themselves, they should not do to others?[230] Natural law is able to agree with the law of Moses according to the spirit but not according to the letter. For what natural insight shall there be in the command, for instance, that a person should circumcise his infant son on the eighth day;[231] or

224. Rom 2.12.
225. Cf. Gal 5:3.
226. Rom 2.14–16.
227. Cf. Col 2.16.
228. Cf. 3.7.10; *Cels* 1.4–5.
229. Cf. Ex 20.12–16.
230. Cf. Acts 15.20, 29; Tb 4.15; Mt 7.12; Lk 6.31. See also 3.7.6. Tollinton, *Selections from the Commentaries and Homilies of Origen* (London: SPCK, 1929), p. 56, suggests that Origen was influenced by Rabbinic and heathen writers who give this maxim, "the golden rule," in its negative form, whereas the Gospel (Mt 7.12) states it positively.
231. Cf. Gn 17.12; Lv 12.3.

that wool ought not be woven together with linen;[232] or that one must not eat anything with yeast in it during the feast of unleavened bread?[233] At different times I have presented such texts to the Jews[234] and demanded of them that if there is something of benefit in such laws, let them make it known. We know that they usually give only this answer, "This is what has seemed good to the Lawgiver." But we who are aware that all these things must be understood spiritually believe therefore that it is "not the hearers but the doers of the law who will be justified,"[235] but not the law according to the letter, since, because of its unattainableness, it cannot have any doer.[236] Rather it is according to the Spirit, through which means alone is it possible for the law to be fulfilled. This, then, is the work of the law which the Apostle says even the Gentiles are able to fulfill by nature. For when they do the things of the law it seems that God has written the law on their hearts, [M893] "not with ink but with the Spirit of the living God."[237]

(2) Now with respect to the words, "on their hearts," it is not to be thought that the law is said to be written on the bodily organ which is named the heart. For how could the flesh bring forth so much understanding of wisdom or contain such a great reservoir of memory? Rather one should realize that the soul's rational power is normally called the heart.[238]

(3) Certainly the Apostle says that those who have the law written down in their hearts make use of the testimony of the conscience. Consequently it appears necessary to discuss what the Apostle is referring to by "conscience," whether it is something substantially different from the heart or the soul. For it is said elsewhere of the conscience that it condemns and is not condemned, and it judges man but is itself not judged. As John

---

232. Cf. Dt 22.11.
233. Cf. Ex 12.15–20; 23.15. See also 1.10.2; 6.12.2–3; *Hom in Lv* 4.7; *Hom in Lk* 5; *Princ* 4.3.2.
234. Cf. *Cels* 1.45; 1.55; 2.31.   235. Rom 2.13.
236. Cf. 2.8.3.
237. 2 Cor 3.3. Cf. 5.6.3; *Hom in Nm* 10.3. Hanson, *Allegory and Event*, pp. 296 n. 2; 299, cites Clement, *Paedagogus* 3.12.94 and Barnabas 4.7–9 as parallels to Origen's discussion here.
238. Cf. *Princ* 1.1.9; *Cels* 6.69; *Orat* 29.2; *Hom in Jer* 5.15; *Comm in Jn* 2.35.

says, "if our conscience[239] does not condemn us, we have confidence before God."[240] And again Paul himself says in another passage, "this is our boast, the testimony of our conscience."[241] And so I perceive here such great freedom [of conscience] that indeed it is constantly rejoicing and exulting in good works but is never convicted of evil deeds. Instead it rebukes and convicts the soul to which it cleaves.[242] In my opinion the conscience is identical with the spirit, which the Apostle says is with the soul as we have taught above.[243] The conscience functions like a pedagogue to the soul,[244] a guide and companion, as it were, so that it might admonish it concerning better things or correct and convict it of faults.[245]

(4) It is of the conscience that the Apostle can say, "For no one among men knows the things of man, except the spirit of man that is in him."[246] And that is the spirit of the conscience, concerning which he says, "The Spirit himself testifies with our spirit."[247] Perhaps this is also the spirit who is united with the souls of the righteous which have shown themselves to be obedient in all matters, on account of which it is written, "Praise the Lord you spirits and souls of the just."[248] But if a soul becomes disobedient to it and stubborn, it will be divided from it after death and will be separated.[249] This is why, I think, it is said in the Gospel about the evil steward, "the master will divide him, and assign his part[250] with the unbelievers."[251] Perhaps it is the spirit about which it is written, "an incorruptible spirit is in

---

239. The text in 1 John has "heart," not "conscience." Origen reads "conscience" in the citation of this passage also in *Hom in Jer* 16.3.
240. 1 Jn 3.21. 241. 2 Cor 1.12.
242. Cf. 2.8.2; 3.2.9; *Hom in Nm* 20.4.
243. Cf. 1.5.3; 1.10.2; 1.18.5; *Hom in Ezek* 1.16; *Hom in Lv* 2.2.
244. Cf. Gal 4.2.
245. Cf. Wis 12.1–2. See also 7.2.1; *Comm in Mt* 13.26. Sanday & Headlam, *Romans*, p. 60, identify a passage which is closely parallel to Origen's comment here in Epictetus, *Fragment* 97, where the conscience is compared with a παιδαγωγός.
246. 1 Cor 2.11. 247. Rom 8.16.
248. Dn 3:86 LXX. Cf. 7.1.2; *Dial* 6.20–31; 7.9–12; *Comm in Mt* 13.2.
249. Cf. 1.18.5; *Princ* 2.10.7.
250. As Tollinton, *Selections*, p. 58 n. 3, observes, Origen probably means that God will assign a part of the person, i.e., his soul, with the unbelievers.
251. Lk 12.46.

all."[252] In accordance with what we have said above, namely that the spirit is divided and separated from the sinful soul, with the result that it takes its place with the unbelievers, it is likewise possible to apply to this discussion that which is written, "There will be two in the field; one will be taken and one will be left. Two will be at the mill; one will be taken and one will be left."[253] These comments pertain to what is written, "while their conscience bears witness to them." [M894]

10. Now let us consider what follows, *While their thoughts mutually accuse or even defend them on the day when God will judge the secrets of men according to my gospel through Jesus Christ.*[254] Who could doubt that this judgment-trial conducted by God is fair, when accusers, defenders, and witnesses are summoned?[255] We men ought to take the example of this fair trial God carries out as a pattern. We should never think it possible for a fair trial to be held without someone to accuse, someone to defend, and witnesses. It must next be seen how the thoughts will either accuse the soul or defend it, on that day when God will judge the secrets of men. Surely he is not speaking here about thoughts which shall arise at that time but rather those which are now occurring within us.[256] For when we think either good or evil things, certain marks and signs are left behind in our heart as if on wax tablets, both for the good thoughts and for the bad.[257] These marks, which now lie hidden in the breast, are said to be revealed on that day by none other than him who alone is able to know the secrets of men.[258] Our conscience shall also bear witness that the reasons for these signs and marks are not hidden from God. This judgment-trial shall take place according to Paul's gospel, i.e., according to what Paul is declaring[259]

252. Cf. Wis 12.1; Jb 32.8. See also *Cels* 4.37; 7.51.
253. Mt 24.40–41. 254. Rom 2.15b–16.
255. Cf. Rom 2.5.
256. Cf. Sanday & Headlam, *Romans,* p. 62: "Origen with his usual acuteness, sees the difficulty of connecting v. 16 with v. 15 and gives an answer which is substantially right. The 'thoughts' accusing and condemning' are not conceived as rising up at the last day but now."
257. Cf. 9.41.6; *Hom in Jer* 16.10; *Princ* 2.10.4.
258. Cf. 1 Kgs 8.39. See also 2.1.1.
259. Cf. 1.3.5; *Comm in Jn* 1.4.

through Jesus Christ. For "the Father judges no one but has given all judgment to the Son."²⁶⁰

(2) As for Marcion and all who, by different kinds of fictional constructions, introduce the concept of different kinds of natures of souls,²⁶¹ they are confuted in a most clear way in this passage. For it is said by Paul that God judges the secrets of men through Jesus Christ. And it is revealed that each person must be judged not by the privilege of possessing a certain nature, but by his own thoughts, accused or defended by the testimony of his own conscience.²⁶²

11. *But if you call yourself a Jew and rest in the law and boast in God and recognize the will and test what is more useful because you are instructed in the law, and if you are confident that you are a guide to the blind, a light to those who are in darkness, an instructor of the foolish, a teacher of children, having in the law the form of knowledge and truth; you, then, that teach others do not teach yourself. You, who preach against stealing, steal. You, who forbid adultery, commit adultery. You, who abhor idols, rob temples. You, who boast in the law, dishonor God through transgression of the law. "For the name of God is blasphemed among the Gentiles because of you," as it is written.*²⁶³

(2) As we have observed in the writings of the prophets, not only has the person speaking been suddenly changed without notice, but also the person of those to whom or about whom the discourse is addressed.²⁶⁴ For instance, sometimes something is said under the *persona* of the Father, [M895] sometimes of the Son or of the Holy Spirit, and sometimes even something under the *persona* of the prophet or anyone else you like. And indeed, sometimes the message is directed to the nation of Israel, sometimes to foreign nations or to kings or to thousands of others. It seems to me that the Epistle to the Romans has been written in this way too. At various times the role of the one who is speaking is changed, so that sometimes the spiritual Paul is speaking, as is the case in a great number of passages in the

---

260. Jn 5.22. Cf. 7.10.3.
261. Cf. Preface of Origen (1); 2.4.7; 4.12.1; 8.11.2; *Princ* 2.9.5.
262. Cf. 9.41.5; *Hom in Nm* 11.4; 20.4; 24.3.
263. Rom 2.17–24.
264. Cf. *Comm in Jn* 1.46.

letter.²⁶⁵ But at other times the fleshly Paul is speaking, as, for instance, when he says, "I am fleshly, having been sold under sin."²⁶⁶ This shall be made clear when we come to this passage, as the Lord directs. But occasionally a change also takes place of the persons to whom the discourse is being addressed, so that at one moment he is now speaking to the whole church of the Romans, "I thank God through Jesus Christ for all of you, because your faith is proclaimed throughout the whole world";²⁶⁷ but in other passages it is not to the whole church but all who judge others and yet themselves do the things which they condemn in others and are without excuse.²⁶⁸

(3) Here, however, the discourse is addressed neither to the church nor to the one who is passing judgment, where he says, "But if you call yourself a Jew and rest in the law," and the rest up to the passage, "those who are by nature uncircumcised but who perfect the law will judge you that have the letter and circumcision but are a transgressor of the law."²⁶⁹ So then, as in the prophetic writings, the person who wants to understand what is written must direct his attention carefully in order to ascertain the *personae*, i.e., who is speaking, to whom the words are addressed, or about whom the discourse is being made. So also, it seems to me, one must now do here in the Epistle to the Romans.

(4) But now let us see what the Apostle says to him who is called a Jew. First of all it must be observed that he has not said of him, "But if you are a Jew," but rather, "if you call yourself a Jew." This is because to be a Jew and to be called a Jew are not the same thing. For Paul teaches in what follows that he is truly a Jew who has been circumcised "in secret" with the circumcision of the heart,²⁷⁰ who keeps the law "in the Spirit, not the letter," whose "praise is not from men but from God."²⁷¹ But he who has been circumcised "visibly in the flesh,"²⁷² keeping the law in order that he might be seen by men,²⁷³ is not truly a Jew

---

265. Cf. 6.9.2–3.
266. Rom 7.14.
267. Rom 1.8.
268. Cf. Rom 2:1. See also 3.1.3.
269. Rom 2.27.
270. Rom 2.29.
271. Rom 2.29.
272. Rom 2.28.
273. Cf. Mt 23.5.

but is only called a Jew. For it is also concerning them that the Apostle says, "Beware of the mutilation. For it is we who are the circumcision, who serve God in the Spirit."[274] Moreover, John thus speaks in the Apocalypse about certain men "who claim to be Jews but are not."[275] He even declares them to be "from the synagogue of Satan."[276] Now one should know that he who is truly a Jew in secret derives his name from Judah, of whom [M896] it is written, "Judah, your brothers praise you; your hand is on the back of your enemies. Judah is a lion's whelp";[277] and the other things prophesied there about our Lord and Savior.[278]

(5) If then it is clear about the differentiation of *personae* and the question of who is truly a Jew and who is called a Jew but in name only, let us see what the apostolic discourse has to say to this person who boasts that he is a Jew but is not.[279] He says, "You who call yourself a Jew and place your repose entirely in the letter of the law and boast in God that you are his portion[280] and that it has been granted to you to know God's will, and like an expert in the matter of testing things, you boast that you know and discern what is most beneficial and how to make these distinctions, so that you not only know what the good things are, indeed you discern as well what is better and more useful. You are confident too that you can be a guide for the blind. It is scarcely to be doubted that you belong to that lot of leaders, concerning whom the Lord was saying, 'They are blind guides of the blind. And if a blind man leads a blind man, both fall into a pit.'[281]" So then, he is confident that he is a guide for the blind and also a light for those in darkness. Yet the Lord speaks no less to these, "If then the light in you is darkness, how great is that darkness!"[282] In spite of this they are confident that they are instructors of the foolish and teachers of children, as those who have received the form of knowledge and truth from the letter of the law. And because these things are professed but

---

274. Phil 3.2–3.
275. Rv 2.9.
276. Rv 3.9.
277. Gn 49.8–9.
278. Cf. 2.13.36; *Comm in Jn* 1.23; 1.35; *Hom in Jer* 9.1.
279. Cf. Rv 2.9; 3.9.
280. Cf. Dt 2.9; Jer 12.10. Cf. 8.9.6.
281. Mt 15.14.
282. Mt 6.23.

not truly possessed, the Apostle says to them, "You then that teach another do not teach yourself. And you who preach against stealing steal" the coming and presence of Christ, which has shone forth in the whole world. "You who forbid adultery commit adultery" in the synagogue of the people of God by introducing a depraved and adulterous word of doctrine to it; and you join that doctrine to the letter of the law, which is outward, when you should instead read what has been written of the law, "all the glory of the king's daughter is within."[283] You should also note what is no less said of the law by the prophet, "Unless you listen in secret your soul shall weep."[284]

(6) You therefore who forbid adultery, you commit such a grave adultery that you introduce an adulterous understanding to it, of which you read that God said, "I will betroth you to myself in faith and mercy"![285]

(7) "You that abhor idols are robbing temples" by violating the true temple of God, which is Christ Jesus; for you destroyed the temple of God which has been raised up again in three days in those who believe.[286] Furthermore, he who steals from the law and the prophets the word that predicts Christ and conceals it, lest the people should hear and believe, is committing temple robbery and is truly violating the temple of God.

(8) This same person who calls himself a Jew and who boasts in the letter of the law of Moses is also convicted as a transgressor of the law when he does not believe in Christ. For if he believed Moses he would certainly believe in him of whom Moses wrote.[287] [M897] It is on account of such people, then, those who are called Jews but are not,[288] that the name of God is blasphemed among the Gentiles. This is not only because of their most evil deeds but also on account of the base and dispirited understanding they have of the law and the prophets. Moreover they become a laughingstock to the Gentiles themselves when they say, following the letter of the law, "Do not handle, do not taste, do not touch. All these things lead to corruption as the commands and teachings of men."[289]

283. Ps 45.13.
284. Jer 13.17 LXX.
285. Hos 2.20–21.
286. Cf. Jn 2.19.
287. Cf. Jn 5.46.
288. Cf. Rv 2.9; 3.9.
289. Col 2.21–22.

BOOK 2, CHAPTER 11 139

(9) In truth the Apostle is saying these things to the one who is a Jew in name but not in deed. Nevertheless it can also be applied to all people who possess merely the name of religion and piety but in whom works, knowledge, and faith are missing. For this reason we ought to discuss these things with greater concern for ourselves than for those who do not come to faith in Christ, lest anyone among us, who has become a true Jew through faith in Christ and the circumcision given in baptism,[290] and who rests in the law of Christ, should boast too that he has come to know God by having turned away from the error of idols, and that he knows God's will. He even knows how to test what is good and pleasing and perfect,[291] and for that reason he even reaches the point of being a leader and teacher of the Church to illuminate those who are blind in knowledge, to instruct babes in Christ.[292] I speak lest such a person wish to teach others more strictly and, over those whom he teaches, to exact the highest discipline and chastity, he himself should be driven by the vice of excess and greed, and should even burn sometimes with the fires of hidden lust! The Apostle's word here is properly applied to a man of this sort when he says to him, "You, then, that teach others, do not teach yourself. You, who preach against stealing, steal; you, who forbid adultery, commit adultery."

(10) But if, even as it is occasionally accustomed to take place, someone turns financial gifts offered to God and the donations given to the poor into private gain, it is rightly said to him, "You, who abhor idols, rob temples." But even if someone incurs open reproaches and public censure should apprehend him for his greed, unjust judgments, and drunkenness, then God is dishonored by his actions. When it becomes public knowledge that a teacher of the Church is like this, the name of God is blasphemed among the Gentiles. For they are certain that disciples are like their teacher.[293]

(11) But in the third place[294] these same words can also be

---

290. Cf. Col 2.11–12. See also 2.12.4; 2.13.2.
291. Cf. Rom 12.2.   292. Cf. 1 Cor 3.1.
293. Cf. Lk 6.40.
294. Cf. 2.8.9. Heither in Origenes, *Commentarii*, 1:246 n. 40, conveniently summarizes the three interpretations, "According to Origen Paul's words in

applied to the heretics. For they also call themselves Christians, and some of them even profess to keep the law, through which they have been instructed to be teachers [M898] of the blind and instructors of children. They claim to be able to judge what is more useful, which they say has escaped the notice of those who belong to the Church. Yet since they steal the words of God and secretly snatch away their meaning by a perverse interpretation and into the royal apartments they bring to the bride of Christ, the Church, an adulterous understanding of the faith, it is rightly said to them, "You, who preach against stealing, steal. You, who forbid adultery, commit adultery. You, who abhor idols, rob temples," by stealing precious vessels from the temple of God, namely the pearls of the true faith from the Holy Scriptures. Through them as well "the name of God is blasphemed among the Gentiles" as they defile the pure and honored doctrines of the Church with corrupted and disgraceful errors of heretical depravity. For from them have arisen even infanticides, incest, and shameful acts of other similar wickedness, to the discredit of holy religion.[295]

(12) We need to realize, however, that the Apostle is using irony when he addresses these things to the Jews. For it is impossible to believe that those who truly rest in the law and boast in God and test what is more useful could do the things which are enumerated in this passage. The testimony he has cited, i.e., "the name of God is blasphemed among the Gentiles because of you," is of course from Isaiah.[296]

12. *Circumcision indeed is of value if you keep the law; but if you are a transgressor of the law, your circumcision has become uncircumcision. So, if the uncircumcised keeps the righteous requirements[297] of the law, will not his uncircumcision be regarded as circumcision and will not that which is by nature uncircumcision, but who perfects the law,*

Rom 2:17-24 apply 1) to unconverted Jews; 2) to nominal Christians whose way of life does not correspond to their profession; 3) to the heretics who call themselves Christians but spread abroad false doctrine."

295. For the way of life of the heretics see *Hom in Ezek* 3.4; Clement, *Stromateis* 3.2.10 (= FOTC 85:262); for accusations against them see *Cels* 6.27; 6.40.

296. Cf. Is 52.5 LXX.   297. *Iustitias*.

BOOK 2, CHAPTER 12

judge you who, through the letter and circumcision, are a transgressor of the law? For a person is not a Jew who is one outwardly, nor is circumcision something outward in the flesh. Rather, a person is a Jew who is one in secret, and with the circumcision of the heart in the Spirit, not the letter, whose praise is not from men but from God.[298] Which circumcision is said by the Apostle to be of value and in what does this value consist? Which law is useful if it is kept? It seems that these are the questions which must be diligently investigated, so that when we understand these things we might be able to be circumcised ourselves. For if, in fact, circumcision is of value in accordance with the word of the Apostle's word, saying, "circumcision is of value if you keep the law," the Apostle himself teaches in what follows[299] that it is not the outward circumcision in the flesh but rather the circumcision of the heart, which is done by the Spirit and not through the letter, [M899] which receives praise, not from men but from God. And elsewhere he says, "Beware of the mutilation, for we are the circumcision, who serve God by the Spirit and who do not take confidence in the flesh."[300] In my opinion this is the circumcision which the Apostle says is of value if you keep the law, not the law of the letter, whose circumcision you certainly do not receive in the flesh, but the law of the Spirit, according to which you must be circumcised in the heart. "For the letter kills but the Spirit gives life."[301] For even God's law is not described as having been written with ink but by the finger of God,[302] which refers to his Spirit.[303] It was not written on tablets of stone but on the tablets of the heart.[304]

(2) However someone could raise the objection that if the Apostle says that the circumcision of the heart is of value,[305] which is, of course, understood to be none other than the cleansing of the soul and the casting aside of vices, why does he still add that a circumcision of this sort is of value if you keep the law, since it would seem that this circumcision does not

---

298. Rom 2.25–29.
299. Cf. 2.11.4.
300. Phil 3.2–3.
301. 2 Cor 3.6. Cf. 1.10.2.
302. Cf. Ex 31.18; Dt 9.10.
303. Cf. Lk 11.20; Mt 12.28.
304. Cf. 2 Cor 3.3. See also 2.9.1; 5.6.3.
305. Cf. 2.13.18ff.

happen except from the observation of the law? But consider whether perhaps the cutting off of vices and the cessation from evil works signifies circumcision; but to do good and to make what is perfect is to keep the law. For perfection does not exist in the one who merely ceases from evil, but in him who does good. This is what we are plainly instructed in the Psalm when it says, "Turn away from evil." Yet it does not stop there, but goes on to say, "and do good."[306] In a similar manner then the Apostle, since he was steeped in these things, says exactly that circumcision and the casting aside of evil things is of value if you keep the law of good things. For one cannot be perfect if he merely does nothing evil, but only if he does something good. This is also why the circumcision which was carried out in the flesh was not signified without a figure of this meaning we are now explaining. After all, it was given to infants on the eighth day[307] who would not yet have done anything.

(3) Now someone may mention to us what has been set down at the beginning of the Book of Job in praise of him when it says, "And Job was a truthful man without fault, a just worshiper of God who refrained from every evil thing."[308] Why was his refraining from evil listed last, whereas the praise of his good works came first? In my opinion what is indicated in this passage is what frequently takes place, namely that very many people indeed do good; nevertheless they intermingle some evil works as well. Yet there are few like Job who are so truthful and above reproach, who indeed are such just worshipers of God, that by doing all these things they keep themselves from every evil thing.

(4) He says, "but if you are a transgressor of the law," i.e., by failing to do good, as we have explained above, "your circumcision has become uncircumcision." That is to say, even your apparent abstention from evil is reckoned to you as unbelief, since you do not do works of faith and righteousness. For it is not possible to convert someone's fleshly circumcision back to uncircumcision, since obviously the flesh of the foreskin which

---

306. Ps 37.27.
308. Jb 1.1 LXX.
307. Cf. Gn 17:12; Lv 12.3.

has been cut off cannot grow back over. [M900] Therefore it will be understood more fittingly and plainly that if the refraining from evil deeds, which is signified by circumcision, is not accompanied by the works of faith, it must be reckoned as uncleanness. Moreover, if anyone in the Church who is circumcised by means of the grace of baptism should afterwards become a transgressor of Christ's law, his baptismal circumcision shall be reckoned to him as the uncircumcision of unbelief.[309] For it says, "Faith without works is dead";[310] and the lot of the wicked steward is with the unbelievers.[311]

13. *But if the uncircumcision keeps the righteous requirements of the law, will not that which is by nature uncircumcision, but who perfects the law, judge you who, through the letter and circumcision, are a transgressor of the law?*[312] We have said above that the Apostle discusses two kinds of Jews and two kinds of circumcision.[313] Sometimes he mentions the fleshly, sometimes the spiritual, circumcision. In the present passage it seems that he is calling the Gentiles who have come to faith in Christ uncircumcised in their flesh, "the uncircumcision." He compares and contrasts them, as they observe the spiritual law, with the Jews who, through the letter and the circumcision of the flesh, are transgressors of the law and whom he says are going to be judged by those in whom there is no circumcision of the flesh but the observation of the law.

(2) By comparison, however, we can admonish our own people in the Church as well. For instance we might say that the catechumens are the ones who are still uncircumcised, or even Gentiles, and those who are believers by means of the grace of baptism are the circumcised. If a catechumen, then, who has not yet been circumcised by means of the grace of the [baptismal] bath, should observe the law of Christ and keep his commands and righteous requirements, by comparison, is he not judging him who is called a believer but who does not keep

---

309. Cf. 2.11.9; *Hom in Jos* 5.6. 310. Jas 2.26.
311. Cf. Lk 12.46. 312. Rom 2.26–27.
313. Cf. Preface of Origen (8); 2.11.4.

the precepts and law of Christ and who despises the commandments? After all, the Lord himself said, "The queen of the South will rise up at the judgment with the men of this generation and condemn them, because she came from the ends of the earth to listen to the wisdom of Solomon."[314]

(3) These things should be said by us for the purpose of instructing the Church. But consider whether it is possible that he is understood in this passage to concede that it is said that even after the coming of Christ, fleshly circumcision, which was observed from the law, is of some value for those who keep the law?[315] This accords with the fact that at the beginning phase of our faith it was still being observed by believers, as in the Acts of the Apostles it is taught that Peter kept the law respecting the discrimination of foods,[316] as did Paul respecting the sacrifices of purification.[317] Perhaps here also the Apostle seems to have set forth a circumcision of this kind, which he says is of value in this way, if the law should also be kept. But if the law is not kept, this circumcision will be turned into uncircumcision, that is to say, it will be of no value whatsoever. On the contrary, he who seems to profess the observance of the law through his circumcision of the flesh has a more severe judgment, and by transgressing the law he is judged by him who has not in fact received the circumcision of the flesh, [M901] but nevertheless has kept the righteous requirements of the law. Whether this sense ought also be received here, you as the reader must consider since the Apostle himself professes to become a Jew to the Jews, and to become as one without law to those who are without law, and to be all things to all men that he might gain them all.[318] Perhaps it is on that principle that he seems to have here granted to the Jews things which he does not grant to gentile believers when writing Galatians. For he says, "If you let yourselves be circumcised, Christ will be of no value to you."[319]

(4) Circumcision is of no value, then, for those who think that some justification is to be obtained from it, but it is of value

---

314. Mt 12.42.
315. Cf. *Cels* 2.1; *Comm in Jn* 1.7; Clement, *Stromateis* 7.8.53.3.
316. Cf. Acts 10.11ff.   317. Cf. Acts 21.26.
318. Cf. 1 Cor 9.20–22.   319. Gal 5.2.

for those who imagined that certain people were not going to come to Christ if circumcising their sons would be denied them. For at the beginning there were some who were clinging to circumcision with an excessive devotion as an indigenous mark of their own nation. They seemed to be hindered from the faith if that which they could not be without were denied them. Therefore, it seems that the Apostle is saying to men of this sort, so as not to close the door of faith to them, "Circumcision is of value if you keep the law; but if you are a transgressor of the law, your circumcision has become uncircumcision."[320] But, on the other hand, if believing Gentiles were to be compelled to receive circumcision, an injury would seem to be done to faith in Christ and to the proclamation of the word.

(5) But this must also be observed, that when he says, "Circumcision indeed is of value if you keep the law," he has not added, "but if you do not keep the law," as the sequence would have seemed. Rather he says, "but if you are a transgressor of the law." By this he shows that not to keep the law is different from transgressing the law. For not even Paul himself always keeps the law, and yet on no occasion is he a transgressor of the law. Furthermore, in what follows he says, "If the uncircumcised keeps the righteous requirements of the law, will not that which is by nature uncircumcision but who perfects the law condemn you who, through the letter and circumcision, are a transgressor of the law?"[321] He keeps the law, then, who observes it according to the letter; and he transgresses it, who does not keep its spiritual sense.

(6) But the "righteous requirements"[322] of the law are a matter of its moral aspect. For "law" is a general term; righteous requirements are but a part of the law.[323] For the law contains righteous requirements, judgments, commands, formalities,[324] and many other categories like this. If he is not saying that the uncircumcised keeps not law itself, but the righteous requirements of the law, then he is put so far ahead of the circumcised

---

320. Rom 2.25.   321. Rom 2.26–27.
322. Or "righteousnesses." Lat. *iustitiae*.
323. Cf. *Hom in Nm* 11.1; *Hom in Ex* 10.1.
324. Cf. Nm 36.13.

one who transgresses the law that he may even judge [the law]. And he has added well, "who perfects the law." For he who lives according to the letter is said to keep the law; but he who lives according to the Spirit perfects it. The perfection of the law takes place in Christ, who said, "I have not come to destroy the law but to fulfill it."[325] Now to fulfill the law means to perfect the law.[326]

(7) Therefore the fleshly Jew keeps [M902] the law, but the spiritual man and the Jew in secret perfects it. Where the one becomes a transgressor of the law, in contrast the other here becomes a judge of the transgressor. The fleshly Jew becomes a transgressor because the law itself is weak through the flesh. For if it were not weak according to the flesh it would certainly not have been said, "For what was impossible for the law, in that it was weak through the flesh."[327] You shall never find it written, however, that the law was weak through the Spirit. Consequently, "those who are in the flesh cannot please God,"[328] but those who through the Spirit put to death the deeds of the flesh[329] will not only live but will even be judges, not only of men but even of angels.[330] For the praise of the one is from men, but the praise of the other is from God.

[Excursus on Circumcision]

(8) These things should be said by us as an explanation of the Apostle's discourse, which we have determined to discuss. It will not seem to be improper, however, to undertake a general investigation of circumcision itself, since indeed the passage itself has reminded us of it.[331] Let us go back then and make known what is contained in the law and in the other Scriptures about circumcision. We find the first written command to circumcise in Genesis, when to Abraham were given responses

325. Mt 5.17.
326. Cf. 2.11.4; 3.2.8.
327. Rom 8.3.
328. Rom 8.8.
329. Cf. Rom 8.13.
330. Cf. 1 Cor 6.3.
331. This is the beginning of a long and detailed excursus on circumcision, mention of which is made in *Cels* 5.47. For a parallel discussion see *Hom in Gn* 3.4–6. References to Origen's essay on circumcision are found in Ambrose, *Ep* 69; Jerome, *Ep* 36.

in this fashion, "God said to Abraham, 'You shall keep my covenant, you and all your descendants after you throughout their generations. And this is the covenant which I have arranged between me and you and between me and between your descendants after you throughout their generations: every male among you shall be circumcised. And you shall circumcise the flesh of your foreskin, and it shall be a sign of the covenant between me and you. And the boy among you shall be circumcised on the eighth day, every male throughout your generations, the indigenous slave and the one bought with money from any of the sons of those born in a foreign land who is not of your descent. Both the slave born in your house and the one acquired with your money must be circumcised with circumcision. It shall be my covenant over your flesh, an everlasting covenant. And any uncircumcised male who is not circumcised in the flesh of his foreskin on the eighth day, that soul shall be cut off from his race because he has broken my covenant.'"[332] We should not conceal, however, that in other copies the words "on the eighth day" are not found, at least not in this passage.[333]

(9) Further, it is written in Leviticus, "The Lord spoke to Moses, saying: Speak to the sons of Israel, and say to them: If a woman conceives and bears a male offspring, she shall be unclean seven days; according to the days of her cleansing, she shall be unclean. On the eighth day she shall circumcise the flesh of his foreskin. For thirty-three days she will sit in her clean blood."[334] I have cited these testimonies from the law of Moses. But the Savior also says in the Gospel that a man receives circumcision [M903] on the Sabbath day without breaking the law of Moses. He says further that it comes from the fathers and was given before Moses.[335] Influenced by the au-

---

332. Gn 17.9–14.
333. He is referring to the Hebrew text of Gn 17.14. These words are, however, found in the LXX. There are other references to Hebrew readings in 2.13.25; 8.6.2; 8.6.12; 8.8.4; 8.12.5. These passages give clear evidence that Origen consulted Hebrew manuscripts.
334. Lv 12.1–4. For the same erroneous reading of Lv 12:4 see *Hom in Lv* 8.3; *Hom in Lk* 14. Cf. also Ambrose, *Ep* 69. Migne's text corrects this to "unclean blood."
335. Cf. Jn 7.22–23.

thority of Jesus' pronouncement, together with the weight of the legal precept, certain men have been persuaded to be circumcised even after the coming of Jesus, even though they were Gentiles.[336] Indeed others, being frightened by the burden of the precept, fled completely from these laws, in which things like this have been written. In fact they have gone so far as to imagine that these commands do not originate with a good god nor the one whom our Lord and Savior had come to proclaim.[337]

(10) Therefore it seems to me that a detailed examination of these passages is called for, to examine whether there be any benefit in a command of this type, even according to the letter, and whether there be anyone for whom circumcision is beneficial or to what end this benefit is directed, or whether it figuratively indicates something of greater benefit.

(11) Going back then to the testimonies which we have brought forth from the law, let us discuss more attentively whether this kind of command seems to loom over the Jewish nation alone or whether it binds believing Gentiles to the same fate. Therefore, let us consider the oracle which came to Abraham. Whom did he command to keep the covenants of circumcision? It says, "You and all your descendants after you throughout their generations, between me and them that every male among them shall be circumcised. They shall circumcise the flesh of their foreskin, so that it might be a sign of the covenant between me and them. Every male shall be circumcised on the eighth day."[338] Indeed, he openly declares that he wants even those born of foreign parents to be circumcised, that is to say, those who by no means are regarded as Abraham's stock. For he says, "Both the indigenous slave and the one bought with money from all the sons of those born in a foreign land who is not of your descendants must be circumcised with circumcision."[339] On no occasion has he mentioned the proselyte, i.e., the foreigner, but he certainly orders the indigenous slave to be

---

336. Cf. *Hom in Gn* 3.5.
337. A further reference to Marcion and his followers. Cf. *Hom in Lv* 5.1.
338. Gn 17.9–12.   339. Gn 17.12–13.

circumcised, whether born at home in that nation or even the one bought at a price. He does not bind the freedman, the guest, or the foreigner to be circumcised.

(12) Let us now examine even the law found in Leviticus in order to ascertain in what sense God is instructing Moses concerning this command. He says, "Speak to the sons of Israel, and say to them: If a woman conceives and bears a male offspring."[340] After a few things it says, "On the eighth day she shall circumcise the flesh of his foreskin."[341] Notice here as well how Moses is commanded to speak only to the sons of Israel concerning the law of circumcision; there is no mention of those born in a foreign land. For if we believe that what is entered in the law has been written through the divine Spirit, then assuredly nothing can be considered either to have been added or kept silent to no purpose. For this reason it is absolutely critical to observe the distinctions. Sometimes in certain commands it is said, "Speak to the sons of Israel and say to them."[342] But in certain others it is added that not merely the sons of Israel but also the proselytes, that is to say, the foreigners, [M904] are being addressed. In light of the fact that in some passages it is said, "Speak to Aaron!"[343] and elsewhere, "to Aaron's sons";[344] and elsewhere, "Speak to the Levites and say to them",[345] certainly the rest of the sons of Israel are not subject to these laws which have been promulgated for the sons of Aaron, or for the Levites or for Aaron himself. Likewise, in the things commanded to the sons of Israel, where no mention is made of the one born in a foreign land, it must not be considered to have universal validity or to become a universal law when a qualification of the addressee is given. But to demonstrate this let us quote a few testimonies out of many, by which we may establish that the addition or qualification in names like this is essential.

(13) In the first parts of Leviticus a law of this sort is given to the sons of Israel alone. "The Lord says: Speak to the sons of Israel and say to them: When any of you bring gifts to God from

340. Lv 12.2.
342. Nm 6.2.
344. Nm 6.23.
341. Lv 12.3.
343. Ex 8.12.
345. Nm 18.26. Cf. *Hom in Lv* 5.2.

your livestock,"³⁴⁶ and so on. And then again, "The Lord spoke to Moses, saying, Speak to the sons of Israel, saying: When anyone sins unintentionally,"³⁴⁷ and so forth. Can anyone doubt that these commands, and commands of a similar kind, are addressed to the sons of Israel alone? Yet there are other commands given not to them but to Aaron or his sons, as is said in the following, "The Lord spoke to Moses, saying: Command Aaron and his sons, saying: This is the law of the burnt offerings,"³⁴⁸ and so forth. And again, "The Lord spoke to Moses, saying: Speak to Aaron and his sons, saying: This is the law of the sin offering. The sin offering shall be slaughtered before the Lord at the spot where the burnt offering is slaughtered."³⁴⁹ And again to Aaron he says, "Drink no wine or strong drink, neither you nor your sons with you, when you enter the tabernacle of testimony."³⁵⁰ Yet there are other things commanded neither to Aaron nor to the sons of Israel, but instead to the elders of Israel he says in this manner, "Speak to the elders of Israel, saying: Take a male goat from the goats for a sin offering,"³⁵¹ and so forth. Can there be any question that this law is directed only to the elders of the sons of Israel? Moreover the law, no less special, concerning clean and unclean animals appears also to be given to the sons of Israel; for it is written in this way, "The Lord spoke to Moses and Aaron, saying: Speak to the sons of Israel, saying to them: These are the animals that you may eat,"³⁵² and so on. In this manner then we should also understand the things said about circumcision, whether in what has been said to Abraham or in what is contained in Leviticus: no one is bound to the law of circumcision unless he derives his lineage from Abraham or is their indigenous slave or a purchased slave. Now would you like to see that God, whenever he wants, could have expressly made known that those born in a foreign land are bound by one and the same law? Listen then to what is written, "And the Lord said to Moses: [M905] Speak to Aaron and his sons and to all the sons of Israel and say to

346. Lv 1.2.
348. Lv 6.1–2.
350. Lv 10.8–9.
352. Lv 11.1–2.
347. Lv 4.1–2.
349. Lv 6.17–18.
351. Cf. Lv 9.1, 3.

them: If anyone of the sons of Israel or of the foreigners who reside among them eats any blood, I will set my soul against that soul that eats blood, and I will cut it off from his own people. For the soul of all flesh is its blood. And I have given it to you for making atonement for your souls on the altar; for the blood makes atonement for the soul. Therefore I have said to the sons of Israel: No soul among you shall eat blood, nor shall any foreigner who resides among you eat blood."[353]

(14) You see then that the law respecting blood, which was given universally, both to the sons of Israel and to foreigners,[354] is observed by us Gentiles as well who, through Jesus Christ, believe in God. For Scripture customarily calls us proselytes and foreigners when it says, "The foreigner residing among you shall ascend higher and higher above you, while you shall descend lower and lower. He shall be your head and you shall be his tail."[355] This is why the Church of even the Gentiles has received the universal law which safeguards against blood with the sons of Israel. For in those days the blessed council of the apostles, understanding that these things were written in the law in this way, for that reason pronounced dogmas and decrees for the Gentiles, writing that they should not only keep themselves from things sacrificed to idols and from fornication but also from blood and strangled things.[356] But you will perhaps ask whether, just as the observance concerning blood makes clear, so it could be taught concerning things strangled that a universal law has been given both to the sons of Israel and to foreigners, since the statutes of the apostles decreed that the Gentiles are to observe even this. Listen to how carefully it has been safeguarded in the laws of God concerning this as well, "And anyone of the sons of Israel, or of the foreigners who reside among you, whoever hunts down a beast or bird that may be eaten shall pour out its blood and cover it with earth. For the soul of all flesh is its blood."[357] Behold, then, how the Lawgiver takes care to join the foreigners to the sons of Israel,

---

353. Lv 17.1–2, 10–12.
354. Cf. *Hom in Nm* 16.9; *Cels* 8.29–30.
355. Dt 28.43–44.   356. Cf. Acts 15.20, 29.
357. Lv 17.13–14.

through what he wants to be a universal command, but to distinguish whom he wants to observe these matters, through the special precepts he gives.

(15) However among the things we have quoted above from Leviticus, there is mentioned this writing as well, "Anyone of the sons of Israel or of the foreigners who are among them who offers a burnt offering or sacrifice, and does not bring it to the entrance of the tabernacle of testimony to offer it to the Lord, that man shall be cut off from the people."[358] It appears here that the sacrifices have been imposed upon the foreigner as well and therefore Gentiles in the Church are accountable to make burnt offerings. But even the words and syllables of the law, so I would say, must be examined very carefully. For it says, if anyone offers a burnt offering or sacrifice he should bring it to the entrance of the tabernacle of testimony. The law does not [M906] command him to offer it; it merely teaches how one should offer it if, by chance, he does so. For it is certain and cannot be doubted that, while the temple of Jerusalem was standing and the religion entrusted to the fathers was flourishing, many, even from the Gentiles, were coming to the temple to worship and to offer sacrifices. But this could properly happen only as long as the condition of that place remained unimpaired. The reason for this was that it had been commanded to happen in only one place, concerning which he commands here that the victim to be slaughtered should be brought to the entrance of the tabernacle. After all, even the Savior said to those ten lepers whom he had cleansed, "Go and show yourselves to the priest and make the offerings for yourselves as Moses commanded."[359] When one of them had returned to give thanks to the Savior, the Lord said, "Were not ten made clean? Where are the nine? Was no one found to return and give thanks to God except this foreigner?"[360] So then, while the condition of the temple remained intact it was customary for foreigners to offer sacrifices. But now, can that which is impossible for Israel's own worshipers to offer be demanded from foreigners?[361]

358. Lv 17.8–9.
359. Cf. Lk 17.12–14; Mt 8.4. Here Origen conflates the Gospel sources.
360. Lk 17.15–18.
361. Cf. 6.7.11; *Hom in Nm* 7.4; 10.2.

(16) But we have said all these things in order to show what great distinctions exist in the law between the commandments, and to teach in particular about the precept of circumcision, which was imposed upon no one else except those who stem from Abraham's race, their home-born slaves, and those slaves purchased at a price. But free from such laws are those from the Gentiles who, through Christ, believe in God.

(17) For the moment we have explored these things without the support of any allegory, lest we leave an opportunity to those of the circumcision to clamor against the truth, as customarily happens.[362] And yet, they could still heave a deadly javelin at us by protesting that proselytes too were made accountable to circumcision in the law, based on what was written in Exodus in this manner, "But if a proselyte should come to you and should celebrate the Passover to the Lord, you shall circumcise all his males and then he shall draw near to celebrate it and he shall be regarded as a native of the land. No uncircumcised person shall eat of it. There shall be one law for the native and for the foreigner who comes to you."[363] Although the objection may appear to have penetrated, nevertheless the admirable caution of the Lawgiver comes to our aid on all occasions. For consider what he has not said in this passage, namely that the foreigner who comes to you must celebrate the Passover to the Lord and must be circumcised. Rather he is discriminating with extremely careful reserve when he says, "If he should come to you and if he should celebrate the Passover."[364] For it is impossible to doubt in this connection that if someone celebrates the Jewish Passover with the Jews, he ought also to be circumcised. Meanwhile, the caution of the Lawgiver has anticipated one thing, by which those who oppose our interpretation have their weapons blunted. It is moreover something against which they cannot mutter a sound. The Passover which the law commanded is instructed to be carried out in that place which the Lord God had chosen,[365] namely Jerusalem. For in that temple [M907] alone sacrifices are decreed to be offered.[366]

362. For polemic against the literalists, cf. 8.8.8; *Hom in Lv* 16.4; *Hom in Gn* 13.3; *Hom in Nm* 7.2.
363. Ex 12.48–49.
364. Ex 12.48.
365. Dt 16.5–6.
366. Cf. *Cels* 5.44.

Let them therefore first recover the condition of the temple and then let them contend about circumcision. But if every stone which was not demolished did not remain upon another, according to the Savior's pronouncement,[367] their pleading about circumcision is in vain.

(18) So much so is circumcision the native emblem of that nation and no other that nowhere is it related that anyone else has been rebuked on account of it in the historical accounts of the ancients, except the son of Moses, whose mother Zipporah restrained the violence of the angel who was threatening her son's death by circumcising him.[368] Therefore from all these things it is shown that only Israel according to the flesh is accountable to practice circumcision of the flesh. Free from it and foreign to it are the proselyte people who come to him, who ascends and has come higher and higher.[369] But that one is descending and has gone lower and lower; and through the mercy of Christ the former people has become the head and the latter the tail.[370] For the last have become first and the first last.[371] And on this account, "that which is by nature uncircumcision but perfects the law condemns those who, through the letter and circumcision, are transgressors of the law." For it is not that circumcision which is outward in the flesh that purifies the soul, but the circumcision of the heart, which is in secret, purifies the mind and cuts away the stains of the vices.

(19) Up to this point we have spoken to the best of our ability concerning fleshly circumcision. Now let us see what should be thought about it according to the rules of allegorical interpretation, in accordance with him who has said, "the law is spiritual,"[372] and who says of the things which are recounted in the law that they have been spoken in allegory.[373] I am aware that many have spoken and written about this theme;[374] but let me also add what the Lord has given me to that which has been properly composed by others.

---

367. Mt 24.2.
368. Cf. Ex 4.24–25. See also *Cels* 5.48.
369. Cf. Dt 28.43. See also *Comm in Mt* 15.26.
370. Cf. Dt 28.43–44.   371. Cf. Mt 20.16.
372. Rom 7.14.   373. Cf. Gal 4.24.
374. Cf. Clement, *Stromateis* 3.5; Philo, *De Specialibus Legibus* 1.1–11.

BOOK 2, CHAPTER 13

(20) Circumcision means to cut off a certain part of the genital organ through which the succession of the human race and fleshly propagation is served. I judge that, through this, something is indicated in a figurative sense: namely, that if some uncleanness cleaves to the soul by association with the flesh, if someone has covered his soul with a mind that is set on seductive desire, these things ought to be cut off from it. The reason why the cutting is inflicted upon the genital organs and not upon the other bodily parts is to clarify that the vices of this sort do not come to the soul from its own essence but rather by an inborn impulse and by the incentive of the flesh.

(21) That circumcision is given on the eighth day signifies, in my opinion, that a week has been allotted to the present age; but the eighth day contains the mystery of the future age.[375] Consequently, the spiritual circumcision belongs to those who fight for the future age, in that they neither marry nor are given in marriage, but will be like the angels of God.[376] And it belongs to those [M908] who have castrated themselves for the sake of the kingdom of God,[377] and to those whose citizenship while living on earth is found in heaven;[378] it belongs to those who look not to the things which are seen but to what is unseen, and who know that what is seen is temporal, but what is unseen is eternal.[379]

(22) As I have related above, what has been said by others is true,[380] that spiritual circumcision means to cut off and throw away from the heart every unclean thought and all impure passions.[381] But some object to published statements of this kind by referring to what is found written in the book of Ezekiel, where the Lord says, "No son of a foreigner, uncircumcised in heart and uncircumcised in flesh, of all the sons of foreigners who are among the house of Israel, shall enter my sanctuary."[382] Tru-

---

375. Cf. 4.2.4; *Hom in Lv* 8.4; *Hom in Nm* 7.1; 7.4. A. von Harnack, *Der kirchengeschichtliche Ertrag der exegetischen Arbeiten des Origenes*, TU 42 (Leipzig: J. C. Hinrichs, 1919), p. 36 n. 2, finds this passage reminiscent of Barnabas 15.9.
376. Cf. Mt 22.30. 377. Cf. Mt 19.12.
378. Cf. 2 Cor 10.3; Phil 3.20. 379. Cf. 2 Cor 4.18.
380. Cf. 2.13.19 n. 374.
381. Cf. *Hom in Gn* 3.4–5; Clement, *Stromateis*, 3.5.43.3–5 (= FOTC 85:282–83).
382. Ezek 44.9.

ly, the prophetic text plainly makes known two circumcisions in this passage when it says, "uncircumcised in heart and uncircumcised in flesh." From this we are compelled to assign form and kind to both circumcisions, in accordance with the laws of allegorical interpretation. Granted it may still be possible to reproach us for our explanations of the matters we have discussed above. But meanwhile let us at this time track down what figure of the two circumcisions may possibly be contained according to allegory.[383]

(23) Let us see whether they could perhaps refer to the two general sins, in respect to which to be uncircumcised is not advantageous, that is to say, in respect to faith and works. This would mean that the one who does not have faith would be uncircumcised in the heart and the one who does not have works would be uncircumcised in the flesh. For one without the other is condemned, seeing that faith without works is called "dead";[384] and that no one is justified before God by works without faith.[385] Thus I am convinced that the prophetic word shall be properly applied to that people which is made up of believers, to whom it is being said, "No foreigner who is among you in the midst of the house of Israel, who is uncircumcised in heart and uncircumcised in flesh, shall enter my sanctuary."[386] Doubtless this is what the Lord also says in the Gospel, "He who believes in me keeps my commands";[387] and again, "he who hears these words of mine and does them";[388] and likewise, "Why do you say to me, 'Lord, Lord,' and do not do what I say?"[389] You see, then, that everywhere faith is joined with works and works are united with faith. Accordingly, circumcision of the heart means to hold no base and unworthy opinions concerning the faith; circumcision of the flesh means to commit nothing unclean and defiled in our works and actions. For whoever becomes uncircumcised and unclean in one of these areas is prohibited by the utterances of God from entering into the

---

383. Cf. *Hom in Gn* 3.4–6; *Hom in Jer* 5.15.
384. Cf. Jas 2.17, 26.
385. Cf. Rom 3.20; Gal 2.16. See 2.4.7 n. 72.
386. Ezek 44.9.   387. Cf. Jn 14.15, 21, 23.
388. Mt 7.24.   389. Lk 6.46.

sanctuary. Yet even the foreigner who was not allowed to enter according to the literal interpretation of the law, where previously only priests were permitted, now enters into the sanctuary.[390] [M909] Indeed at the present time it is granted even to foreigners to enter, insofar as they are cleansed by the circumcision of faith and deeds.

(24) But suppose someone contends this point with us by calling up the questions discussed above. Suppose he repeats to us the objection that it is written of the foreigner that not only circumcision of the heart is demanded from anyone who wants to enter into the sanctuary but also circumcision of the flesh.[391] I shall direct against this person, who persists in annoying us in this manner, that which the prophet Jeremiah said, "Behold your ears are uncircumcised."[392] Let the one who demands fleshly circumcision show us a perceptible and bodily circumcision of his ears if he can! Yet it is certain that this is absolutely impossible. Forced by necessity, then, he will revert to allegories and will say that the ears are circumcised when, according to the admonitions of Solomon, they do not receive groundless hearsay[393] and when they are stopped up from listening to plans of murder,[394] and when they are hedged in with thorns lest they should receive words of envious detraction.[395] Instead they allow only the word of God and what contributes to edification. So then, the circumcision of the heart would be like that of the ears, which seems to be interpreted generally.

(25) In this manner as well a person is called uncircumcised in lips who would not circumcise blasphemy, scurrility, obscene speech from his mouth;[396] who could place no guard at his mouth and no watch at the door of his lips;[397] who would not even circumcise his mouth from every idle word.[398] Finally, in that place where Moses says to the Lord, "Provide another, Lord, whom you might send; I am slow in speech and my voice is weak,"[399] they themselves claim that the Hebrew copies con-

390. Cf. Nm 18.7.
392. Jer 6.10.
394. Cf. Is 33.15.
396. Cf. Col 3.8; Eph 4.31; 5.4.
398. Cf. Mt 12.36.
391. Ezek 44.9.
393. Cf. Ex 23:1.
395. Cf. Sir 28.28 Vulg.; cf. Ps 15:3.
397. Cf. Ps 141.3.
399. Ex. 4.10, 13.

tain the following, "But I am uncircumcised in lips."[400] But if it is possible for someone to appear uncircumcised in the ears and uncircumcised in the lips in the manner I have described above, why should someone not be called uncircumcised in the foreskin of his flesh in similar fashion, who, in respect to the natural drive of sexual intercourse, immoderately and intemperately wastes his life? On the other hand, if someone makes use of his lawful obligations in an affair of this sort, as much as suffices for the production of offspring, would he not be considered to be circumcised?

(26) Indeed since we are treating the reasoning behind circumcision, it will not seem absurd to add to the discussion the fact that Joshua[401] the son of Nun is reported to have circumcised the sons of Israel for the second time with stone knives by the command of the Lord,[402] which, when looked at literally, seems factually utterly impossible. For in those who have been circumcised once in the flesh of their foreskin, what could be found to remove in a second circumcision? But it is plain that our Jesus, who, after Moses, truly leads the sons of the Israel into the holy land flowing with milk and honey,[403] the promised land,[404] circumcises the people comprised of believers[405] not once but twice.[406] For his first circumcision is where he cuts away from them the worship of idols and the fabrications of philosophical persuasion. But he carries out the second circumcision [M910] when he cuts off the habits and passions of the old man and the vices of the flesh. Then is fulfilled what is written in Joshua son of Nun, "Today I have taken away from you the reproaches of Egypt."[407] For a person carries around the reproaches of Egypt within himself who, though he is in the Church serving as a soldier under our general, Jesus, is nevertheless enslaved to Egyptian customs and barbaric mental inclinations.

---

400. Ex 6.12; 6.30. Origen also speaks of this in *Hom on Gn.* 3.5; the Masoretic Text transmits the two statements in different passages. See NRSV n. *ad loc.*

401. Lat. *Jesus.*
402. Cf. Jos 5.2ff. See also *Hom in Gn* 3.6; *Hom in Jos* 5.5.
403. Jos 5.6. 404. Heb 11.9.
405. Col 3.9. 406. Cf. *Hom in Jos* 1.7.
407. Jos 5.9.

(27) Indeed, Marcion, who is a man who takes no pleasure at all in allegorical interpretation,[408] is completely at a loss in explaining the Apostle's words, "Circumcision is of value." Not even concerning the details which are mentioned was he able to give an account in any respect whatsoever. Indeed, not only was Marcion accustomed to oppose the God of the law who gave circumcision, and to mark him out with a certain derision but *all* the heretics who repudiate the Old Testament, in company with the pagans. They all repeat similar things in opposition to the God of the law, as if they were in a federation committed to detraction. "So be it," they say,[409] "Circumcision may indicate some mystery and may even contain an allegorical figure. Was it then proper that the forms of figures and enigmas of the law be established with pain and danger for the little children, with torments for the infant, tender and still innocent? Did the Lawgiver not have anywhere to put mystical figures except in the mutilation of shameful places? And was the law of the omnipotent and eternal God not able to arrange for a sign of the covenant except in the obscene parts of the bodily members? Is he then a good God who has ordered newborn human beings to be wounded immediately after they first look upon the light of a new day? And if, as it seems to you, he is Creator of soul and body, either he reprimands himself for forming that bodily part superfluously, since he immediately commands it to be sliced off, and he is correcting his own error through the sufferings of these unfortunate wretches; or he is unjustly commanding the removal of something he has made to be a necessary and useful bodily part. Moreover, if it is important to God to lead many people to the worship and practice of his religion, the greatest obstacle springs from circumcision, because everyone turns away from pain and flees from the derisive mockery which results from shameful deformity. Hence circumcision must be considered to be more of a hindrance to religion than an emblem of it." Either pagans opposed to the Lawgiver or heretics make great noises like these and many others similar to them.

---

408. Cf. *Comm in Mt* 15.3.
409. *Esto, aiunt.* Migne reads, *Stoici aiunt,* "The Stoics say."

(28) I think it necessary to respond to both groups, but first to the pagans. No intelligent human being reprimands things in others which he considers honorable and great when practiced among his own people.[410] For among yourselves, O heathen nations, circumcision is deemed as something so great that it may not be entrusted indiscriminately to the common person of low birth but to priests alone and to those among them who have been assigned to higher studies. For example, according to your own superstitions the Egyptians are deemed to be extremely ancient and learned. For nearly all the other nations have borrowed their sacred rites and ceremonies from them.[411] Among them, I say, no one studied either geometry [M911] or astronomy, which are considered of particular importance among them, and assuredly no one tried to pry into the secrets of astrology and horoscopes, than which they reckon nothing more divine, unless he has received circumcision. The priest among them, the soothsayer, or attendant of any of their sacred temples, or as they themselves call them, their prophets: all of them are circumcised.[412] In addition no one learned the priestly literature of the ancient Egyptians, which they call hieroglyphics, except the circumcised. No high priest or seer or mystic among them, no one whom they regard as knowledgeable of the mysteries of heaven (as they suppose) and of the underworld, is confided in unless he has been circumcised. Do you then condemn in us as something disgraceful and obscene what is esteemed among yourselves to be so honorable and great that you believe it possible for the secrets of the heavens and of the regions below the earth to be declared to you only by means of this particular sign? But suppose among you it would be necessary to seek a reason for so many causes of so many of your secret rites which were carried out with the aid of circumcision, and the kind of reason which ought not be despised, lest all your own ceremonies be equally undermined along with it. Why should you not expect that even this is done among us as well? Indeed if you would thumb

---

410. Cf. Philo, *De Specialibus Legibus* 1.2–3.
411. Cf. Herodotus 2.50, 58; Plato, *Timaeus* 21e ff.
412. Cf. *Hom in Jer* 5.14.

BOOK 2, CHAPTER 13   161

through your own histories you will find that not only the priests and religious teachers of the Egyptians practiced circumcision but also the Arabs, Ethiopians, Phoenicians, and others, whose endeavors respecting superstitions of this kind were esteemed all the more honorable because of it.[413]

(29) Enough has been said against the pagans, to whom it was not proper to speak more openly concerning the mysteries of our law. Now our discourse should be directed against those who indeed believe in Christ but do not receive the law and the prophets. Without doubt you confess it to be true what is written in Peter's epistle, "We have been redeemed not at a corruptible price of silver and gold but with the precious blood of the only begotten."[414] If then we have been bought at a price, as Paul also confirms,[415] undoubtedly we were bought from someone whose slaves we were, who also demanded the price he wanted so that he might release from his authority those whom he was holding.[416] Now it was the devil who was holding us, to whom we had been dragged off by our sins.[417] Therefore he demanded the blood of Christ as the price for us. So then, until the blood of Jesus was given, which was so precious that it alone would suffice for the redemption of all, it was necessary for those who were being trained up in the law to offer their own blood for themselves [in the act of circumcision] as a kind of foreshadowing of the future redemption. And therefore for us as those for whom the price of Christ's blood has been furnished, we do not have need to offer a price for ourselves anymore, that is to say, to offer the blood of circumcision. But if it seems criminal to you that the God of the law should command that wounds be inflicted upon infants and that their blood be shed, [M912] you will find fault with what has been done to Christ as well. For he was circumcised on the eighth day,[418] and he also received wounds during his passion and poured out his

---

413. Cf. *Cels* 5.41; 5.48; Philo, *Questions and Answers on Genesis* 3.48; Barnabas 9.6. For the tradition that the Egyptians and other nations practiced circumcision see Herodotus 2.104.
414. Cf. 1 Pt 1.18–19.   415. Cf. 1 Cor 7.23.
416. Cf. 3.7.14; 4.11.4.
417. Cf. *Comm in Mt* 16.8; *Hom in Ex* 6, 9.
418. Cf. Lk 2.21.

own blood with his punishment on the cross. But the fact that, out of horror of circumcision, the entry to religion appears difficult to you, how much more difficult will the entrance into the gospel seem, where a person is commanded to lay down not some insignificant part of his body but his very life?[419]

(30) Moreover, according to you, the examples of the martyrs will hinder men from approaching the faith. On the contrary, is there not greater reason to believe that a religion is reliable which promises nothing indulgent, nothing luxuriant or soft? But even if circumcision contained no figurative meaning other than the ritual, why would it be absurd if the people who were being trained up under God's law were to bear some sign peculiar to themselves to distinguish them from the other nations?[420] And if the cutting off of someone's bodily part appeared to be mandatory, what could be more suitable than to find what appeared obscene and to remove that part whose diminution would not at all impede the body's function?

(31) But they say, "If that bodily member was not necessary, it ought not have been made by the Creator; if it was made as something necessary, it should not be removed." Let us also ask them whether they would call the procreation of children necessary. Doubtless they will respond that it is necessary. Then those who, by their affirmation of continence and virginity, do not attend to the necessary duties of nature shall be reproachable; and everyone is to be compelled to get married, even those who, in accordance with the laws of the Gospel, "have castrated themselves for the sake of the kingdom of God,"[421] even though these people have the authority for this precedent both in many other saints and even in the Lord Jesus himself.

(32) Finally it ought to be said that just as many baptisms were necessary before the baptism of Christ, and many purifications were carried out before the purification through the Holy Spirit, and many sacrifices before the one sacrifice, the spotless lamb, Christ, offered himself to the Father as a sac-

---

419. Cf. Mt 10.39; 16.25.
420. Cf. Josephus, *Antiquities* 1.192; Irenaeus, *Against Heresies* 3.12.14.
421. Mt 19.12.

rifice,[422] so also there was need of many circumcisions until the one circumcision in Christ was imparted to all.[423] The pouring out of the blood of many came first until the redemption of all was accomplished through the blood of the one.[424]

(33) For the present we were able to come up with the above arguments concerning the reasoning behind circumcision. We have said these things, however, with the stipulation that if anyone should speak about these matters in a better and more rational manner, let his arguments be held to rather than mine.[425]

[End of Excursus on Circumcision]

(34) But now that this digression is finished, which was perhaps justifiably somewhat long, let us return to the conclusion of this section of the Apostle's letter. Often it is discussed by the Apostle where he points out through specific examples that men are of dual aspects; the one he usually calls the outer man and the other, the inner man.[426] He says that the one is according to the flesh and the other is according to the Spirit. In my opinion [M913] this is established from what is written in Genesis, where it says that the one was made in the image of God and the other was formed from the mud of the earth.[427] And here he calls the one an outward Jew and the other a Jew in secret.[428]

(35) One should know that both the inner and outer man act differently in some circumstances but act in common in others. For there are certain things which begin in the inner man and extend to the outer man. Yet other things begun by the outer man extend to the inner. What I am saying is as follows. Suppose chastity should begin with the inner man. It will undoubtedly extend to the outer, for it is impossible for some-

---

422. Cf. Heb 9.14; 1 Pt 1.19.
423. Cf. *Princ* 4.3.12; *Hom in Lv* 3.5; *Hom in Nm* 17.1.
424. Cf. Heb 9.12. See also *Cels* 5.48.
425. Cf. 5.8.9.
426. Cf. Rom 7.22; 2 Cor 4.16; Eph 3.16; Col 3.9–10.
427. Cf. Gn 1.27; 2.7. See also 1.19.8.
428. Rom 2.28–29.

one who does not previously commit adultery in his heart to be able to commit adultery with his body.[429] But if chastity begins in the outer man, it does not immediately pass as well into inner self control, as if the one who avoids committing adultery in the body will be free from adultery in his heart. In this way then circumcision of the inner and outer man should be understood according to the laws of allegorical interpretation since the inner man no longer lusts in his heart, nor does the outer man serve lustful desire in the body. So he is called circumcised in the flesh whom the Apostle says is no longer in the flesh but in the Spirit,[430] and who puts to death the deeds of the flesh by means of the Spirit.[431]

(36) Indeed, since anyone who has been circumcised has given some of his flesh up to destruction and has preserved some of it uninjured, in the part which perishes is signified, I suppose, the flesh, about which it is written, "All flesh is grass and all its glory is like the flower of the grass."[432] However I believe that the flesh which is preserved and remains uninjured may contain the figure of that flesh of which it is said, "All flesh shall see the salvation of God."[433] However, it is necessary to have ears which can perceive that which is the flesh which perishes and that which is the flesh which shall see the salvation of God, which remains saved after the laying aside of the flesh of the foreskin when that other falls like the flower of the grass.[434] For he who has understood this shall find the figures of vast mysteries foretold in the reasoning behind circumcision. He will also discover that he who is a Jew in secret and who has been circumcised in the inner man excels and surpasses the one who is a Jew according to the flesh to the same degree that Judah, who is praised by his own brothers and who slept like a lion and arose like the whelp of a lion,[435] excels and surpasses the Judah who was born from the loins of Jacob according to the flesh.

---

429. Cf. Mt 5.28.
431. Cf. Rom 8:13.
433. Is 40.5 LXX; Lk 3.6.
435. Cf. Gn 49.8–9.

430. Rom 8.9.
432. Is 40.6 LXX; 1 Pt 1.24.
434. Cf. *Comm in Mt* 17.29–30, 33.

14. *Then what advantage has the Jew? Or what is the value of circumcision? Much, in every way. For in the first place they were entrusted with the oracles of God. What if some of them did not believe? Has their unbelief nullified the faithfulness of God? By no means! Let* [M914] *God be true but every man a liar; as it is written, "So that you may be justified in your words, and prevail when you are judged."*[436] In this letter Paul, like an arbiter sitting between the Jews and the Greeks, i.e., believing Gentiles,[437] summons and invites both groups to faith in Christ in such a way as to not offend the Jews completely by destroying the Jewish ceremonies nor to cause despair in the Gentiles by affirming the observance of the law and of the letter. And whether he is recalling the promises or the punishments, he apportions the word to each people. For instance when he says, "for those who are contentious and who distrust the truth but believe in wickedness, there will be wrath, fury, and anguish for the entire life of a man who does evil, for the Jew first and for the Greek."[438] This refers to punishments.

(2) But he adds some things which concern the promises: "but glory and honor and peace for everyone who does good, the Jew first and the Greek."[439] He again appears to speak of the Gentiles, "For all who have sinned apart from the law will also perish apart from the law."[440] And again of the circumcised, "and all who have sinned under the law will be judged by the law."[441] But then once again he encourages the Gentiles by saying, "For when Gentiles, who do not have the law, do naturally the things of the law, these, though not having the law, are a law to themselves. They show that the work of the law is written on their hearts,"[442] etc. Then he turns the discourse back to the Jews by saying, "But if you call yourself a Jew and rest in the law" and so on, until the place where he says, "For the name of God is blasphemed among the Gentiles because of you."[443]

(3) However, lest he should have seemed to be too excessive in his rebuking of the Jews, he says, "Circumcision is of value if you keep the law."[444] But again, so as not to encourage those

---

436. Rom 3.1–4.
438. Rom 2.8–9.
440. Rom 2.12.
442. Rom 2.14–15.
444. Rom 2.25.

437. Cf. 2.14.5; 3.1.2–3; 3.2.2.
439. Rom 2.10.
441. Rom 2.12.
443. Rom 2.17–24.

who place too much glory in circumcision, he adds, "But if you are a transgressor of the law, your circumcision has become uncircumcision."[445] Yet in order also to lift up the souls of Gentile believers a little, he adds, "But if the uncircumcised keeps the righteous requirements of the law, will not his uncircumcision be regarded as circumcision?"[446] And then in order to raise up the souls of the Gentiles very robustly that they might recognize themselves as capable of becoming better even than the Jews, if they observe the law more perfectly, he says, "Then that which is by nature uncircumcision but who perfects the law will judge you who, through the letter and circumcision, are a transgressor of the law."[447]

(4) Yes, in fact because he knew that many promises in the law and the prophets evidently came to the Jews, in order that the Gentiles might not despair as those having nothing in common with the recorded promises, he teaches them that [M915] they themselves may become Jews and possess circumcision according to the mystical meaning. That is why he says, "For a person is not a Jew who is one outwardly, nor is circumcision something outward in the flesh. Rather, a person is a Jew who is one in secret, with the circumcision of the heart, in the spirit and not the letter, whose praise is not from men but from God."[448] Yet because in all these things he had made the cause of the Gentiles superior in a measure, as if he is replying to the complaints of those who are of the circumcision group, he sets forth these things contained in the present section, by saying, "Then what advantage has the Jew? Or what is the value of circumcision? Much, in every way."

(5) If, then, he says that a person is not reckoned a Jew who is one outwardly and circumcision which is outward in the flesh is not reckoned as circumcision, but he is a Jew who is one in secret and the circumcision of the heart which takes place in the spirit is the true circumcision, you will say to me: What advantage is there for those Jews who are designated by this name? Or what value is there in bodily circumcision? Lest he should

---

445. Rom 2.25.
446. Rom 2.26.
447. Rom 2.27.
448. Rom 2.28–29.

seem to be a less than fair arbiter⁴⁴⁹ sitting between these two peoples, he tells us what advantage the Jew and circumcision in the flesh possess and he says they have great advantages in every way.

(6) He now adds what great advantages there are. "First," he says, "they were entrusted with the oracles of God." For though now the oracles of God are entrusted even to the Gentiles, at first, he says, they were entrusted to the Jews. But my question is: What does it mean when it is said that the oracles of God were first entrusted to the Jews? Is he saying this concerning both the writings and the books, or concerning the meaning and understanding of the law? For we see many Jews from infancy until old age ever learning but never attaining the knowledge of the truth.⁴⁵⁰ And how shall what is said appear to be true, that they possess some advantage in that to them were first entrusted the oracles of God, in which they understood, "neither what they say nor what they assert"?⁴⁵¹ In fact if, according to Solomon, that man is really called wise who "understands what comes from his own mouth" and who "bears understanding on his lips,"⁴⁵² then these things have to be understood as spoken about Moses, the prophets, and others like them, to whom the oracles of God were entrusted, since it is impossible to doubt that they were Jews and possessed circumcision.

(7) But if one of them was a wise and intelligent hearer and a wonderful counselor, it is said that the Lord removes them from Jerusalem because he was offended by the impieties of the people.⁴⁵³ For Isaiah says the following, "Behold, the Lord, the Lord of hosts, shall remove them from Jerusalem and from Judea," and a little later, "the prophet and the diviner and elder and the captain of fifty and the wonderful counselor and the wise builder [M916] and prudent hearer."⁴⁵⁴ To such persons, then, it must be assumed that the divine oracles were first entrusted. We have to admit then that they possessed a great advantage in every way. There were moreover others like them, as

---

449. Cf. 2.14.1; 3.2.2.
451. 1 Tm 1:7.
453. Is 3.1, 3.

450. Cf. 2 Tm 3.7. See also 8.8.9.
452. Prv 16.23 LXX.
454. Is 3.1–3.

the Apostle has mentioned is written in the books of Kingdoms, "I have reserved for myself seven thousand men who have not bowed their knees to Baal."[455] Furthermore, Christ's apostles themselves and Paul, the chosen vessel,[456] because he came from the Jews and from the circumcision, he too possessed a great advantage in every way over the Gentiles whom he was teaching. For the oracles of God had been entrusted to him.

(8) One should take note of that which he says, "they were entrusted with the oracles of God," that he has not said that their writings were entrusted to them, but the oracles of God. From this, a way is given to us to understand that to those who read and do not understand, and who read and do not believe, the letter alone is entrusted, concerning which the Apostle says, "The letter kills."[457] But the oracles of God are entrusted to those who, by understanding and believing the things Moses has written, believe also in Christ, as the Lord also says, "If you had believed Moses, you would certainly also believe me, for he wrote about me."[458]

(9) But granted that the Jew should have an advantage in their writings, that he should even have some advantage in the oracles of God, does this mean that Gentiles who come to Christ are completely abandoned? Or is there also some respect in which they also might have an advantage? Listen to the Lord as he speaks to the centurion who was a Gentile believer, "Truly I tell you, in no one in Israel have I found such faith."[459] Notice therefore what a great advantage the Gentiles possess when it comes to faith. The Lord speaks of them in another passage as well, "they will come from the east and the west and from the four winds of the earth and will recline with Abraham and Isaac and Jacob in the kingdom of God; but the sons of the kingdom will be thrown into the outer darkness."[460] So then, when it comes to the laws and writings, the Jews possess a great advantage in every way; but when it comes to faith, I would say that, comparatively, the Gentiles have a great advantage in every way.

(10) In the investigation of this subject we must of course

---

455. Rom 11.4; cf. 1 Kgs 19.18.
457. Cf. 2 Cor 3.6.
459. Mt 8.10.
456. Cf. Acts 9.15.
458. Jn 5.46.
460. Cf. Mt 8.11–12; Lk 13.29.

ask whether the oracles of God may be said to have been entrusted first to the Samaritans as well. For it appears that among them as well the law of Moses is preserved. Yet I would say that not even the letter, which is said to kill,[461] has been entrusted to them. For the prophet says of them, "Woe to those who spurn Mount Zion and trust in the mountain of Samaria."[462] By repudiating the prophets, they estrange themselves from the writings of God.[463]

(11) Nor would I say that the oracles of God have been entrusted to the heretics just because the Holy Scriptures seem to be read publicly among them. For they utter unrighteousness from on high,[464] and by their own godlessness they tear asunder the unity of the deity, and they sever the law from the Gospels.[465] [M917] But because they discern nothing spiritual and worthy of God in these writings, I would say that they possess only the letter that kills.[466]

(12) Suppose the Jews are unwilling to accept the opinion of our Apostle which says that the letter of the law kills. Perhaps they think injury is done to the law if it would seem to be spurned according to the letter. Let us then turn back to Moses himself and see how highly he esteemed the letter of the law. When he had received the stone tablets inscribed by the finger of God,[467] he conferred so little honor upon the letter of the law that he threw down the tablets from his own hands and shattered to pieces what had in fact been written by the finger of God.[468] Yet he was not branded as being guilty of impiety because of this act. You see, then, that it is not Paul alone who

---

461. 2 Cor 3.6.   462. Cf. Am 6:1 LXX.
463. Cf. *Hom in Nm* 25.1. De Lange, *Origen and the Jews*, p. 37, informs us in connection with this passage, "The Samaritans were well distributed throughout the cities of Palestine, and in any case Samaria was less than thirty miles from Caesarea. It is not surprising that Origen was interested in their rich and strange tradition; what is surprising is that he does give them any place in his theology; he does not regard them as a separate nation or religion, but seems to see them as a sect of Judaism. This may speak for easy relations between Jews and Samaritans at the time, or for the lack of importance and articulateness of the Samaritans at this period, before the advent of their great theologian, Marqah."
464. Cf. Ps 73.9.   465. Cf. *Princ* 2.4–5.
466. 2 Cor 3.6.   467. Cf. Ex 31.18.
468. Cf. Ex 32.19.

spurns the letter of the law, but well before him Moses had also spurned and rejected and broken up the letters of the law. In so doing he was without doubt even then showing that the glory and power of the law was not contained in the letters but in the Spirit.

(13) Moreover in my opinion the Lord has called the meaning of the law, "the kingdom of God," when he says in the Gospel to the Jews, "The kingdom of God will be taken away from you and given to a people producing its fruit."[469] This kingdom has been taken away from the Jews, among whom only the letters of the law remain, and it has been given to the Gentiles, who could bear the fruit of the Spirit through faith.[470]

(14) If these things are so, why are we so lazy and idle that we do not hasten to accept the oracles of God with simplicity and purity of heart, having rejected all evil,[471] and to receive the sense of Christ from them? All the more should this be the case when we hear that the kingdom of God is in these oracles. Certainly each person who is able should make room for the oracles of God to the best of his ability. He who is capable of and suitable for receiving solid food should receive the oracles of God, which are the wisdom which the Apostle speaks among the perfect.[472] Those who are not yet capable of this should receive the oracles of God, in which they would know nothing more than Christ Jesus and him crucified.[473] Whoever is not capable of this should receive the oracles of God to use milk and not solid food.[474] But if one is even this weak in the faith, let him take the oracles of God in the form of vegetables.[475] All that matters is that we should all know in common that "the oracles of the Lord are pure oracles, silver examined in the fire, purified on the ground seven times."[476] This means that we should preserve the divine oracles by chastity and holiness of the heart and body.

---

469. Mt 21.43.
470. Cf. *Hom in Gn* 9.1; *Cels* 2.5; 4.42; *Hom in Jer* 14.12; *Comm in Mt* 17.7.
471. Cf. Jas 1:21; 1 Pt 2.1.   472. Cf. 1 Cor 3.2; 2.6.
473. Cf. 1 Cor 2.2.
474. Cf. 1 Cor 3.2; Heb 5.12. See also 4.6.4; 9.36.
475. Cf. Rom 14.2.   476. Ps 12.7.

(15) The oracles of God then have been entrusted first to those of whom we have spoken above. But some, as he says, have not believed either in God or in God's oracles. You see that those who do not believe are themselves "according to the flesh," of whom he speaks elsewhere, [M918] "The natural man does not comprehend the things of God's Spirit, for it is foolishness to him."[477] Yet the unbelief of these persons does not make void the faithfulness of God. I understand "faithfulness of God" to mean either that faith by which God has faith in those to whom he entrusts his oracles or that faith by which those who receive the divine oracles from him believe in God. Let us therefore remember that the unbelief of those who do not come to faith or who fall away from it—if, perchance, anyone should ridicule us for doing works of faith, either when we fast, or when we practice mercy, or when we devote ourselves to studies and to the law of God, or even when we endure tortures and martyrdom for Christ's sake—we should always remember that their unbelief does not make void the faithfulness of God which is in us.

(16) What follows after this appears to have been added somewhat out of sequence. For he says, "But let God be true but every man a liar, as it is written, 'So that you may be justified in your words, and prevail when you are judged.'" Nevertheless by bending these words, so to speak, we shall attempt to fit them into their context.

(17) It may be, he says, that certain Jews have not believed; yet concerning their unbelief it must be said that God alone is true while every man is a liar. For even if there is someone who is just, it is nevertheless unavoidable that he would deviate from the truth in something, inasmuch as it is nearly impossible for human nature to stay true in everything. Because every man is a liar, on that account some of the Jews, as lying men, have not believed. For since every man is a liar, it is inevitable that on that day when the Lord will come into judgment with men, he alone will be justified in his words. For his words are true in respect to everyone because they are words of truth. That the

---

477. 1 Cor 2.14.

172   ORIGEN

Lord is coming into judgment with men, the prophet says, "Come and let us hold judgment, says the Lord";[478] and "The Lord himself shall enter into judgment with the elders of the people";[479] and again, "You must remember, we also shall be judged, says the Lord."[480] The Apostle introduces these things, paying attention to the objection which he posed to himself in another passage, where he says, "But if our unrighteousness serves to confirm the righteousness of God."[481] We shall examine this latter text when we come to it.[482]

(18) But now let us see what the following words mean, "Let God be true but every man a liar." This is how it stands in the Greek copies. Those in Latin read "May God be true" rather than "Let God be true." In the first place, then, it ought to be recognized that it does not say "Let God be true" in the imperative mood. For it is ridiculous to think that God can be commanded to be true. Rather, just as we say, "Let your will be done [M919] on earth as it is in heaven";[483] or, again, as we say, "Let there be peace by your power,"[484] not commanding but wishing, or rather proclaiming and being certain that it is impossible for peace to take place except by the power of God. So also here, it should be interpreted as a phrase of proclamation, "Let God be true," as a way of saying, God is true, "but every man is a liar."

(19) It should also be realized that the phrase "every man is a liar" is taken from the 115th Psalm where it says, "I said in my alarm, Every man is a liar."[485] We hope it will not seem burdensome to the readers if we briefly explain the contents of the Psalm from which he takes this testimony, for the purpose of shedding more light on the Apostle's meaning. The prophet seems to me to be setting forth some such meaning as this, "Although there are many systems of doctrine among men," he says, "and many who philosophize in their investigation of truth and although faith in God was supposed to have precedence in

478. Is 1.18. 479. Is 3.14.
480. Is 43.26 LXX. 481. Rom 3.5.
482. Cf. 3.1.
483. Mt 6.10. Cf. *Orat* 24.5; *Hom in Cant* 1.3.
484. Ps 122.7. Under debate in this passage are the words *sit* ("may") and *fiat* ("let").
485. Ps 116.11.

all these investigations, some who sought without having first believed have not found. But because I believed before I began the search, for that reason I found what I was searching for. Not only did I find it but I spoke about it and I declared to the nations the truth which I had found. Yet I did not become carried away in my own wisdom when I found the truth, nor did I become puffed up in my knowledge.[486] Instead, all the more I was humbled, since I knew and understood that it is God who teaches man knowledge.[487] Then I considered how much and what sort of things men have said concerning truth, whether amongst philosophers or amongst the heathen. I pondered the fact that in saying so much and with very great effort, they have found nothing, since they did not first believe before they began the search. When I considered all these things, both their utterances and writings, I became alarmed in my mind, that is to say, I was struck with amazement in my heart that all the books of the philosophers, which appeared to have been composed with magnificent and very brilliant rhetoric, stood so far away from the truth. In the alarm and amazement of my mind, I said, 'Every man is a liar.' But I, the one to whom God had made known these things, was not ungrateful. Instead I pondered and sought in myself what I might repay to the Lord in compensation for this knowledge of the truth which the Lord manifested to me.[488] I understood, of course, that the eternal nature and ruler of all things stands in need of nothing.[489] Consequently I found one thing only which was fitting for me to offer God, namely, that I should believe that it is never possible for him to receive anything from a man, but only to give. Therefore, I said, 'I must take the cup of salvation,'[490] just as if one were responding to him who says, 'Are you able to drink the cup that I am about to drink?'[491] and he were to say, 'I am able, Lord.' In this way, then, he says, 'I must take up the cup of your passion freely and with my whole will,' and I say as well, 'May I preserve the grace of your cup, that is, of your passion,

486. Cf. 1 Cor 8.1. 487. Cf. Ps 94.10–11.
488. Cf. Ps 116.2; Ps 94.10.
489. Cf. Acts 17.25. See also *Hom in Nm* 23.2; Clement, *Stromateis* 5.11.75.
490. Ps 116.13. 491. Mt 20.22.

until the end. May I do this not in my own strength, [M920] but by calling upon the name of the Lord. For a death which is sustained on account of piety and truth is precious in your sight.'[492]" It is in this manner then that the words of the Apostle, "every man is a liar," must be received. They refer either to the one who without faith trusts in the letter of the law or to him who boasts in any old dogmas and writings.

(20) But it may be objected to us: If every man is a liar, then Paul himself will be a liar, since he is a man. But David, who said these things, because he was a man, he himself will be a liar, if every man is a liar. And what he says, that every man is a liar, will be false, since he necessarily pronounces himself a liar together with the rest of men. And if he is a liar, then undoubtedly what is said by the liar shall not be true, that every man is a liar. It seems, then, that his discourse has run into a syllogism which they call a conundrum,[493] that is to say, an insubstantial syllogism which is also called unsound.[494]

(21) But if we turn back to the inner meaning of Scripture we shall find that all prophets and apostles are among those to whom the word of God comes, as it is written, "and the word of the Lord came to this or that prophet." But the Lord declares in the Gospel that those to whom the word of God comes are not men but gods. For he says the following, "If he calls them 'gods' to whom the word of God came—and the Scripture cannot be annulled."[495] Therefore since the word of God came both to David as a prophet and to Paul as an apostle, doubtless they were not men but gods, to whom the word of God has come. Accordingly, since they were not men but gods, what he declares concerning the rest of men to whom the word of God has not come, namely, that every man is a liar, is true.

(22) What follows has clearly been taken from the Fiftieth Psalm, "so that you may be justified in your words and prevail

---

492. Cf. Ps 116.13, 15. Cf. *Mart* 28–29.

493. *Aporus.* Heither in Origenes, *Commentarii*, 1:322 n. 71, explains, "This is a technical term of contemporary logic referring to a statement which cancels itself out."

494. *Insubstantivus.* This unusual word occurs in *Princ* 1.2.2.

495. Jn 10.35; cf. Ps 82.6. See also *Comm in Jn* 20.27.

when you are judged."⁴⁹⁶ The complete sense in this Psalm is put in this fashion, "Against you alone have I sinned, and done what is evil in your sight, so that you are justified in your words and prevail when you are judged."⁴⁹⁷ Since it would require a long digression to go over the Psalm from its beginning, for the sake of brevity let us investigate only what we have quoted, the words taken from the middle of the Psalm, the initial explanation of which appears to be difficult. For if we follow the historical reference written in the title of the Psalm, we find it reported that when Uriah the Hittite had been slain, David took his wife.⁴⁹⁸ Why then does he say, "Against you alone have I sinned," when he had certainly sinned not only against Uriah and against his relatives but also against Bathsheba and all her household? For it was against her that he seemed to inflict the stain of adultery. What needs to be recognized here is that the content of the Psalm does not always follow the history of its title, as anyone who observes many of the Psalms will find to be the case. For instance I could cite the title of the Seventeenth Psalm, "Unto the end. [Mg21] By David, servant of the Lord. The words of this song were spoken on the day the Lord liberated him from the hand of all his enemies and from the hand of Saul, and he said. . . ."⁴⁹⁹ The content of the Psalm, however, is completely different from what is contained in the title. For what foundations of the mountains trembled, or when did the earth quake, when David was fighting against his enemies?⁵⁰⁰ Or where is it mentioned that thick darkness was under the feet of the Lord?⁵⁰¹ Where is it made known that he mounted cherubim and flew on the wings of the winds?⁵⁰² Or where is nearly anything else which fails to harmonize with the history of every type of title?

(23) Therefore, in this same manner, even in the Fiftieth Psalm it should be seen that there is no correspondence to history unless, perchance, the mention of the woman in the title may have been made figuratively so that under this designation

496. Ps 51.4.
498. 2 Sm 11.26–27.
500. Ps 18.7.
502. Ps 18.10.

497. Ps 51.4.
499. Ps 18.1.
501. Ps 18.11.

some other type of woman should be understood. Perhaps she is the sort described as being strong, who made double garments for her husband;[503] or perhaps we are to think of the opposite sort of woman, those who are said to have turned Solomon's heart away with the result that he built pagan altars and idols.[504] Taken allegorically in this way the women are certainly not to be understood as stemming from divine wisdom but from that which is contrary to the divine wisdom, namely, from the sects which are estranged from God.[505] The wife of Uriah the Hittite, a foreigner to Israel, can be understood in this way.[506] While standing above, David watched her washing her own impurities in the waters and wanting to wash away her own filth. And he desired her and took her.[507] But because it was not the Lord's will for sects which are estranged from the truth of God to be led into the house of David, his first birth and first fruit is extinguished in order that the second offspring would be born as a wise king from a foreign mother.[508] But to pursue these figures and enigmatic matters takes much time. [M922] Nevertheless let us briefly follow up what is relevant to the subject.

(24) David says that it is the case that there is much subtlety among the varieties of the sects. And the question of which of them possesses an understanding in accordance with God and which are foreign from God in their treatments and disputations of the wise, is a matter which can be known and determined by no one except God, who alone understands the wise in their craftiness.[509] That is why David says, "Against you alone have I sinned and done what is evil in your sight,"[510] since all the others, that is to say, natural men, are incapable of judging me, who am spiritual, although I have gone astray. The reason for this is that "the spiritual man judges all things, but he himself is judged by no one."[511] But Paul, being a spiritual man, says additionally, "It is the Lord who judges me."[512] And David,

---

503. Cf. Prv 31.10, 22 LXX.
505. Cf. *Hom in Nm* 20.3.
507. 2 Sm 11.2–4.
509. Cf. Jb 5.13; 1 Cor 3.19.
511. 1 Cor 2.15.

504. Cf. 1 Kgs 11.1–8.
506. Cf. 2 Sm 11.3.
508. Cf. 2 Sm 12.18, 24.
510. Ps 51.4.
512. 1 Cor 4.4.

aware that the Lord alone judges both the spiritual man and the prophet, therefore says, "Against you alone have I sinned," by whom alone I can be judged.[513] For the human court cannot judge the spiritual.[514] Moreover what follows tends to this understanding, "So that you may be justified in your words and prevail when you are judged." For God is judged in the disputations of the wise, when some think one way about God, but others think differently in various details. Therefore he prevails over those who make judgments about him when he himself reveals his own verdict to all who are in error, both how and in what manner he ought to be believed in and worshiped.

(25) But the length created for the second book is enough. For indeed, while it is regrettable to pass over any points brought up that call for clarification, I do not know how we extricate ourselves from the brevity, which, provided the meaning is evident, we greatly desire to preserve, keeping in mind the fastidiousness of the reader.

513. Cf. *Hom in Ex* 11.5.
514. Cf. 1 Cor 4.3.

THE THIRD BOOK OF THE *COMMENTARY ON THE EPISTLE OF PAUL TO THE ROMANS*

BUT IF OUR UNRIGHTEOUSNESS CONFIRMS *the righteousness of God, what shall we say? That God is unjust to inflict wrath? I am speaking according to man. By no means! For then how shall God judge the world? For if in my falsehood God's truth has abounded to his glory, why am I still being condemned as a sinner, and not, as some people blaspheme us by saying that we say, Let us do evil so that good may come? Their damnation is deserved.*[1]

(2) Through nearly the entire text of this epistle composed by the Apostle Paul, it will perhaps seem that the sequence of thought[2] is quite incoherent. One moment his words are directed against the Gentiles, the next instant they judge in their favor and against the Jews, then at another moment something about the Jews or even in favor of the Jews is asserted. And some of them he considers worthy of praise, others he disparages.[3]

(3) The diversity of subject matter and meanings will be thought to lead him outside the boundaries of the case at hand, as for example when he uses the exclamation, "May God be true but every man a liar";[4] or even what he subsequently adds when he says, "But if our unrighteousness confirms the righteousness of God," and so on. The result is that he seems to slip from one digression into another. But we who believe him who says, "He has made us competent to be ministers of the new

---

1. Rom 3.5–8.
2. *Ordo dicendi.* Heither in Origenes, *Commentarii*, 2:30 n. 1, notes that this term expresses the Greek word, ἀκολουθία, "logical train of thought," one of the requirements of good literature according to ancient rhetorical standards. See Preface of Origen (1); 1.13.2; 6.9.9; Neuschäfer, *Origenes als Philologe*, pp. 244–46.
3. Cf. 2.14.1; 3.2.2; 3.9.1; 8.1.2; 8.6.9; 8.10.2; 10.8.2; 10.11.2.
4. Rom 3.4.

covenant, not of the letter but of the Spirit,"⁵ find that his meaning is far loftier than the method of human craft is credited to possess.⁶ For through the entire text of this epistle [M923] he wants to show either how salvation came to those who lived according to the law before the coming of Christ or how, on the basis of Israel's unbelief, salvation would be bestowed upon the Gentiles through the coming of the Savior.⁷ Furthermore he wants to show that not all Gentiles entirely come to salvation but only those who have believed; nor is the entire nation of Israel rejected but a remnant of believers are being saved.⁸ This is why, as I have said, the sequence of thought seems confused, as he pursues the different interests of the believers and unbelievers of both sides. In such matters he is inevitably forced to turn his words even to God in order to teach that the judgments of God in all these various cases of reception and rejection are true and just⁹ but that, among men, much lying abounds. That is why he says, "May God be true but every man a liar, as it is written, "in order that you may be justified in your words and prevail when you are judged."¹⁰ We have spoken above about these matters above as well as we could.¹¹

(4) Therefore, seeing now that it would be possible to make the very pertinent objection to him that if, in order for God to be true, every man must necessarily be a liar, and if the righteousness of God is confirmed through the unrighteousness of men, God, who brings wrath upon men, will appear unjust. For it would seem to be through human unrighteousness that his own righteousness is proven. For if our, that is human, unrighteousness confirms the righteousness of God, then humanity will not seem to really deserve punishment, since it is through human beings that God's righteousness is regarded as clearer and more commendable. By no means, he says, may we inter-

---

5. 2 Cor 3.6. 6. Cf. 2.6.1; 5.1.4.
7. Cf. Rom 11.11.
8. Cf. Rom 9.27. For similar thematic summaries of Romans, see Preface of Origen (8) and 9.1.1.
9. Cf. Ps 19.9; Dn 3.27. 10. Rom 3.4.
11. Cf. 2.14.16ff.

pret it so that God seems unjust when he brings wrath against men. For how will he who judges the world be considered unjust, since the term itself, "judgment," shows that he does nothing without judgment? It is established that where there is judgment there is justice. For both "judge" and "judgment" are named from "justice."[12]

(5) If, therefore, he says, when they lie that we assert that "the truth of God abounded in my lie, then I am unnecessarily condemned as a sinner." But this will be seen all the more in that which they blaspheme us, he says, where we seem to be saying that if God's truth is revealed all the more in the lying of men, and if his righteousness is vindicated through the unrighteousness of men, "then let us do evil that good may come" from the evils; and let us tell lies so that the truthfulness of God might shine forth from our lying. They fabricate these things as they blaspheme us, that such things should seem to be said and follow as the logical inference of our very declarations. The logic of the doctrine of those of us who understand God to be a just and true judge does not in any way accept this account.

(6) It is certainly important to know that even in some Greek copies the following is found, "Is God unjust who inflicts wrath against men?"[13] What we have already said seems [M924] to agree more with this sense. But it seems that it should be understood according to that which we find in the Latin copies[14] and in some of the Greek ones, "Is God unjust who inflicts wrath? I am speaking according to man. By no means!" That which is said, "God is unjust who inflicts wrath," because of the

---

12. In this section and in what follows, indeed in the whole *Commentary*, it needs to be remembered that *iustitia/iniustitia* can be translated as justice/injustice or righteousness/unrighteousness, just as *iustus/iniustus* can mean just/unjust or righteous/unrighteous. Both senses should be kept in mind where these words and their verbal forms occur.

13. Rom 3.5. Heither in Origenes, *Commentarii*, 2:36 n. 8, calls attention to the fact that Origen often "allows equal validity to two variant readings without deciding on which is more correct." This shows his respect for Church tradition.

14. Bammel, *Römerbrieftext*, p. 204, suggests that Rufinus has added this report about the Latin manuscripts to Origen's original authentic discussion about Greek variants. The two text forms are also mentioned in the Greek papyrus excerpts.

fact that "our unrighteousness confirms the righteousness of God," is being said not according to God nor according to God's wisdom but according to man and according to what is said, "Every man is a liar."[15] We have said these things treating only as far as the sequence of his discourse and the coherence of the statements, so that the very separating of the words might give us a broader path for understanding.

(7) But now let us ascertain what meaning is contained in these words, according to the apostolic rank. Every discipline rests upon things which are proper to it and things which are adverse, that is to say, opposites.[16] For instance, medical science professes the knowledge not only of health, but also of illness. Though it strives after health, nevertheless it cannot ignore what relates to illness. Likewise wisdom is based upon the knowledge of good and evil;[17] moderation consists in knowing what things ought to be chosen and what ought to be shunned; and fortitude is not ignorant of those things which pertain to fear. So also in righteousness, it is necessary for it to know the aspects of unrighteousness. Therefore, if we want to know what righteousness is, it is essential for us to know what unrighteousness is; and when we have arrived at a complete knowledge of unrighteousness, on that basis we shall recognize what righteousness is as well; for when it becomes clear what is unjust, as a consequence, what is just will become visible as well. And because righteousness is in God, whose nature is inaccessible to human perception, but unrighteousness dwells in us men, in fact in all rational creatures, from our unrighteousness, which is known to us, the righteousness of God, which is, as it were, inaccessible and incomprehensible to us, is recognized and confirmed and produced as if from the opposition of opposites.[18]

(8) Therefore the Apostle Paul reproaches the ignorance of those who raise the unreasonable objection, supposing that

---

15. Cf. Rom 3.4.
16. Cf. *Comm in Jn* 2.20; Aristotle, *Nicomachean Ethics* 5.1.4–5, 1129a.
17. Cf. *Hom in Jer* 8.2.
18. Cf. *Hom in Gn* 1.10; Gregory Thaumaturgus, *Address of Thanksgiving to Origen* 9 (= FOTC 98:110–12).

God, who brings wrath upon men, is unjust since his righteousness is confirmed by our unrighteousness. What these people are ignoring is that these things happen not by means of our sins but as a consequence of logic itself, just as opposites may be proven from their opposites. This is why the Apostle says it this way, "But if our unrighteousness confirms the righteousness of God, what shall we say? That God is unjust to inflict wrath? I speak according to man. By no means! For then how shall God judge the world?" So then, God is not proven to be unjust in this if even the logic of a discipline proves contraries from contraries, and confirms righteousness from unrighteousness.

(9) But with complete rational consistency righteousness is rightly and deservedly hostile to and opposed to unrighteousness, just as [M925] life is hostile to and opposed to death and light to darkness. And therefore it is said that God, in whom there is righteousness, inflicts wrath upon men, in whom unrighteousness dwells. For these things are naturally opposed to each other. How indeed shall God, who opposes injustice, appear to be unjust? It is for this reason, perhaps, that the Apostle has not said that we unjust *men* confirm the righteousness of God, but he says, "if our *unrighteousness* confirms the righteousness of God," in order to show that God is not against men but righteousness is against unrighteousness. But wrath is brought against men because they have given room to unrighteousness in themselves. Consequently God, who is righteousness, shall not seem unjust when he vents his anger against unrighteousness. For it would not befit him to be favorable toward it. But this wrath too reaches unto men who have offered themselves as servants of the unrighteousness with which God is angry.[19] For in no one can both unrighteousness and righteousness subsist. But just as righteousness is the disposition of a just and upright work, which disposition is found first of all in God and then also in those who imitate him, so also unrighteousness is the disposition of an unjust and depraved work, which is detect-

---

19. As Heither in Origenes, *Commentarii*, 2:40 n. 11, indicates, Origen is now explaining the reading "against men," which Rufinus did not receive in the lemma but only mentioned as a variant.

BOOK 3, CHAPTER 1

ed first of all in the devil, then also in those who want to imitate him. And therefore it is deservedly recorded that wrath is inflicted against them,[20] although the righteousness of God might seem to become visible from their unrighteousness, as from an opposite. For just as they received within themselves a disposition for unjust and depraved works, so were they much more capable of receiving a disposition for just and upright works.

(10) It is therefore justly said that wrath from God is brought upon all men. For those in whom wrath does not have a place are no longer men but ought to be called "supermen." Perhaps it is on this account that the Apostle Paul likewise declares concerning all men, "For we were by nature sons of wrath just as the rest."[21] For he did not say, "we were sons of wrath," but he said additionally, "we were by nature sons of wrath, just as the rest." For all men have become by nature sons of wrath from what they were, namely gods and sons of the Most High,[22] and consequently they are called men.[23]

(11) For consider very carefully how he says, "I said: You are gods and sons of the Most High," and he added "all."[24] This addition has connected together the entire human race under this title. After all, in what follows it says, "But you die as men."[25] Whence also the following is written in Genesis, "And God reconsidered that he had made man upon the earth; and he regretted it in his heart and God said: I should destroy man, whom I have made, from the face of the earth."[26] In my opinion this was said not only respecting the destruction of the flood but even something else was prophesied in this concerning the

---

20. Cf. Rom 1.18.   21. Eph 2.3.
22. Cf. Jn 10.35; Ps 82.6.
23. Cf. 2.14.21; *Comm in Jn* 8.33; 32.18; *Hom in Ex* 6.5; *Hom in Ezek* 1.7. Some scholars see here a veiled reference to Origen's doctrine of the pre-existence of souls and their fall and subsequent punishment in being assigned to bodies. The discussion that follows, however, does not support this. Bammel, *Römerbrieftext*, p. 52, makes the following observation concerning this doctrine: "Origen expressed himself more cautiously in the *Romans Commentary* than in the much earlier writing *De Principiis*, and in the meantime transferred the chief stress of his own interests."
24. Ps 82.6.   25. Ps 82.7.
26. Gn 6:6–7.

future, in the form of a mystery. The words, "I should destroy man," should be interpreted in the sense in which God says through the prophet, "Behold I am destroying your iniquities like a cloud,"[27] so that it may be seen that God destroys man in respect to what is human, [M926] in order that afterward he can make him into a god at that time when God shall be all in all.[28] It is possible to apply what is said in Genesis to this interpretation, "The time of every man has come into my sight."[29] This utterance should not only be considered to have been spoken concerning the time of the flood back then but also concerning the mystery of baptism. For as the apostle Peter says, just as at that time Noah was saved out of the flood, so also now by means of a similar figure those who believe shall be saved through baptism.[30]

(12) And so it is possible to understand what he says, that "the time of every men has come,"[31] in reference to salvation. Thus, through the grace of baptism those who believe would be understood to be changed from men into a higher order, when the day of the resurrection arrives, when each of the saints shall be like the angels of God.[32] These things have been stated as they occurred to us as an explanation of that which is written, "Is God unjust who brings wrath" either "against men?" as we have said is read in some of the copies, or, as we have it, "I am speaking according to man. By no means!"[33]

(13) Moreover he says next, "For then how does God judge the world?" In this passage "world" refers to the men who are in this world, just as elsewhere we read that "the whole world lies under the evil one."[34] He is certainly showing that all men who dwell in this world are under evil.

(14) Next let us now see the meaning of the statement, "For if the truth of God abounded in my falsehood to his glory." In

---

27. Is 44.22.
28. Cf. 1 Cor 15.28. Cf. *Hom in Lv* 9.11.
29. Gn 6:14: LXX 6:13.   30. Cf. 1 Pt 3.20–21.
31. Gn 6.14.   32. Cf. Mt 22.30. See also *Princ* 1.8.
33. Notice that both textual variants are accepted and explained. Cf. 3.1.6 n. 13.
34. 1 Jn 5.19.

this world there are many kinds of religions and a multitude of philosophical sects. There are many systems of doctrine handed down through erroneous assertions and composed with lying arguments. Although it is by a false use of the word "wisdom" that their authors are named, these men are nevertheless in possession of no scanty or negligible authority. From their place of privilege, errors have been received instead of truth and they occupy nearly the entire world with deceptive opinions respecting religion, "so that even the elect, if one can say it, would be led astray."[35] By the coming of the truth of God and his wisdom and his Word he has exposed and confuted every falsehood and he has undercut all the assertions of false teachings by faith in the truth. For this reason the truth of God abounded in every falsehood which had been first asserted by men, by exposing the clandestine imitations and by handing down the simple truth of the faith in each individual doctrine. And in this manner the Apostle says that the truth of God abounded in the falsehood of men.[36]

(15) But in order that what we are saying might become even more plain, let us offer other things for the sake of example. There used to be a doctrine among men which declared that the highest good is pleasure and in this doctrine it was consequently asserted that providence does not exist. For indeed, if we are not to base our lives upon laws then we must upon inclination.[37] These doctrines were spread about with elegant and richly adorned speech and with extremely brilliant arguments in innumerable books.[38] [M927] But now consider how he who defends God's truth and who is a philosopher according to Christ, who is the truth of God and the wisdom of God,[39] how he teaches men that the highest good is eternal life. Moreover, this is eternal life, that men might know the only one true God and his Son Jesus Christ.[40] And consider how he asserts with

---

35. Cf. Mt 24.24. 36. Cf. 1.14.19.
37. *Voluntate*. Migne's text corrects this to *voluptate*, "pleasure."
38. He has Epicurean philosophy in view here. Cf. *Cels* 1.21; 3.75; 7.63.
39. Cf. 1 Cor 1.24; Jn 14.6.
40. Cf. Jn 17.3. See also *Princ* 2.11.1ff.; 2.11.7; 3.6.1; *Cels* 3.37; Clement, *Stromateis* 4.22.136.5; 7.13.83.3–4.

complete confidence the doctrine of God's providence which says, "Are not two sparrows sold for a penny? And yet not one of them falls to the ground apart from the will of the Father";[41] and that, "He commands his sun to rise upon the good and the evil, and he sends rain on the just and the unjust."[42] In these specific matters, as those dogmas of false knowledge are put to silence, the truth of God is abounding in the falsehood of men.

(16) There are others who say that there are three kinds of good: one respecting the soul, another respecting bodies, and a third external to these. They assert that the highest good consists in handling each of these in a profitable manner.[43] These thinkers, in delimiting the providence of God, contend that it reaches to the sphere of the moon but that it certainly does not descend further below, that is to say, to men.[44]

(17) Moreover there are others who would claim that nothing invisible and incorporeal exists, but they assign everything which exists to bodies. On this basis they claim that God, the Father of all things, is a body. Yet the consequence of their own logic, where it is agreed that every body is corruptible, has undoubtedly forced them, if they maintain that God is a body, to admit that he is corruptible. Because of this logical difficulty they have turned to a verbal artifice and have said that he is indeed of a corruptible nature, but he has not been corrupted because there is nothing superior to him by which he could be corrupted or destroyed.[45]

(18) There are innumerable other fictitious productions of men composed with dialectical reasoning and with fraudulent sophisms. But when the truth of God conquers each one of them by means of churchmen and those who have been instructed in the divine wisdom and when it refutes the snares of these arguments, the truth of God is said to abound in the

---

41. Mt 10.29.
42. Mt 5.45. Cf. *Princ* 2.11.5; 3.2.7; *Cels* 6.71; 8.70.
43. The Peripatetics are intended.
44. Cf. *Hom in Gn* 14.3; *Cels* 3.75. In a related passage, Heine in Origen, *Homilies on Genesis and Exodus*, p. 199 n. 26, refers to Cicero, *De natura deorum* 1.18.45; Lucretius, *De rerum natura* 2.646–51; 3.18–24.
45. These are Stoic views. Cf. *Cels* 1.21; 3.75; 4.14; *Comm in Jn* 13.21. See H. Chadwick, "Origen, Celsus, and the Stoa," *JThS* 48 (1947): p. 35.

falsehood of men, and not only to abound but to abound "to his glory." In my opinion this is to be understood in the following manner: Suppose a teacher of the Church gives instruction to certain simple hearers not yet occupied with false doctrines and, concerning each one of these, explains to them the rationale of divine truth. In [false] instruction of this sort, the truth of God shall seem to abound. But if the discourse is given to those who resist the truth and who contradict words of sound doctrine[46] and, while trying to contradict it, they find themselves confuted and proven wrong, so that when the darkness of their errors has been forsaken they come to the light of the truth, then not only will the truth of God abound, but it will abound to God's glory. For God is glorified through the one who, having been set free from the error of falsehood, has beheld the light of the truth.

(19) The one who [M928] has understood these things in this manner will certainly not utter the foolish objection set forth in the following words, "Why am I still condemned as a sinner?" On the contrary he will understand that he is to be deservedly condemned if he remains in the falsehood of men. And, in accordance with what we have explained above, the one who, when convicted by the truth of God, realizes that he has gone astray and, once he has turned from error, glorifies the true God by his recognition of the truth, does not commit blasphemy against those who proclaim the truth, when they say, for instance, "Let us do evil that good might come." For he knows that the damnation of the one blaspheming by such a word is just. One should also observe that he has stated that those who declare the truth of God are not so much "slandered," which applies to men, but "blasphemed," which pertains to God.

2. *Then what advantage do we have? For we have charged that all Jews and Greeks are under sin, as it is written, "There is no one who is righteous; there is no one who has understanding, there is no one who seeks God. All have turned aside, together they have become worthless;*

---

46. Cf. 2 Tm 3.8; Ti 1.9.

there is no one who does goodness, there is not even one. Their throat is open grave; they use their tongues to deceive. The venom of vipers is under their lips. Their mouths are full of cursing and bitterness. Their feet are swift to shed blood; contrition and misfortune are in their paths, and the way of peace they have not known. There is no fear of God before their eyes."[47]

(2) We have already declared[48] that in this letter Paul always tempers and balances his discourse as a kind of arbiter between those who had believed from the circumcision and those who believed from the Gentiles, so that sometimes he seems to accuse the one group of certain things, sometimes the other group. Next he openly encourages specific groups with the sure hope in the promise. Therefore, he had seemed to say above that if the uncircumcised should keep the righteous requirements of the law, then he will condemn him who, with his circumcision, is a transgressor of the law.[49] For this reason, wanting next to encourage those whom he had humbled, he added, "Then what advantage has the Jew? Or what is the value of circumcision? Much in every way. For in the first place they were entrusted with the oracles of God."[50] After these things, since he had suitably followed up these things with others, he now goes on and says, "Then what advantage do we have? For we have charged that all Jews and Greeks are under sin." But if all are under sin, consequently there shall be no grounds for the self-exaltation of one group against the other since both come to salvation not on the basis of their own righteousness but on the basis of God's mercy.[51]

(3) Therefore he accused certain Greeks, i.e., the Gentiles, of being under sin when he says, "For claiming to be wise, they became fools and exchanged the glory of the incorruptible God for the likeness of the image of corruptible man and birds and four-footed animals and reptiles. Therefore God handed them over [M929] to a base mind,"[52] and so forth. But he accuses the Jews when he says, "But if you call yourself a Jew and

---

47. Rom 3.9–18.
49. Cf. Rom 2.26–27.
51. Cf. Ti 3.5.

48. Cf. 2.14.1; 2.14.5; 3.1.2–3.
50. Rom 3.1–2.
52. Rom 1.22–23, 28.

rest in the law,"⁵³ and so on, to which he adds, "You then who teach others do not teach yourself. You who preach against stealing steal,"⁵⁴ etc. By means of these things, then, he says, "For we have charged that all Jews and Greeks are under sin." But after these things, as is his custom, he wants to affirm what he had said from the Holy Scriptures. Simultaneously he sets an example for teachers of the Church, that they too should set forth the things which are spoken to the people not as matters adopted as private opinions but as matters fortified by the divine testimonies. For if such a great kind of apostle does not believe that the authority of his own words is able to suffice unless he shows that what he is saying is written in the law and the prophets, how much more should we, who are very insignificant by comparison, observe this custom, so that when we teach we should set forth not our own thoughts but those of the Holy Spirit?

(4) We also consider it necessary to remind the reader that in some of the Latin manuscripts, the testimonies which follow are found in order and in their entirety in the Thirteenth Psalm. However in nearly all the Greek manuscripts no more is written in the Thirteenth Psalm than up to that versicle, "there is none who does good, not even one."⁵⁵

(5) Moreover what the Apostle says, "As it is written: There is no one who is righteous, there is no one who has understanding, there is no one who seeks God," is not found in the psalm with the same words, but some [words] are changed, some are introduced, and others are left out. Because if it is very attentively observed, apostolic authority is given by all scholars,⁵⁶ I suppose, to this, that when there is need to make use of scriptural testimonies, we should aim to take more from the sense than the words.⁵⁷ For you will find this done frequently in the Gospels as well.

(6) In the Thirteenth Psalm, then, the following is written, "The Lord looked down from heaven upon the sons of men to

---

53. Rom 2.17.
54. Rom 2.21.
55. Ps 14.3.
56. Cf. 5.8.7; 7.18.7; 8.8.4; 10.8.4–5.
57. Cf. *Comm in Mt* 11.11; 16.14.

see if there is an understanding person who seeks God."[58] But also in the Fifty-second Psalm it says this, "God looked down from heaven upon the sons of men to see if there is an understanding person who seeks God."[59] And clearly the identical sense is preserved in what the Apostle has stated, "There is no one who understands, there is no one who seeks God." And I think that what he said, "There is no one who is righteous," he has also taken from what is written, "There is no one who does goodness, not even one."[60] There, although the wording seems to be changed, nevertheless one and the same sense is preserved. But what is said in what follows, "Their throat is an open grave, they use their tongues to deceive,"[61] you will discover in the Fifth Psalm. After this he says, "The venom of vipers is under [M930] their lips," which I think is also taken from some psalm[62] with changed wording as we have said above. But what follows, "Their mouths are full of cursing and bitterness"[63] is clearly taken from the Ninth Psalm. Next, you will find, "Their feet are swift to shed blood" either in Isaiah or in the Proverbs.[64] But I do not quite recall[65] where "Contrition and misfortune are in their paths, and the way of peace they have not known" is written, but I suspect it can be found in one of the prophets.[66] "There is no fear of God before their eyes" is written in the Psalms.[67] Evidently he wanted to gather all these testimonies in order to show that what he is charging, namely that "all Jews and Greeks are under sin," is being declared not so much as his own opinion but as the thought of the Holy Scripture.

(7) But let us investigate the meaning of this, to be "under sin." For his words seem to involve all men without exception, whether Jew or Gentile. But another statement of his suggests itself to us, where he says, "But where there is no law, there is no transgression."[68] Now it is plain that among the Jews there is the

---

58. Ps 14.2.
60. Ps 14.3.
62. Cf. Ps 140.3.
64. Is 59.7; Prv 1.16.
66. Cf. Is 59.7–8.
68. Rom 4.15.

59. Ps 53:2.
61. Ps 5.9.
63. Ps 10.7.
65. Cf. 8.8.3; 9.42.2.
67. Ps 36.1.

law of Moses, whereas among the Gentiles, he asserts, there is the law of nature which convicts the offender by the testimony of his conscience.[69] Well then, where do we look for a man in whom there is no law and who therefore does not seem to be in the transgression of sin? For even Paul says of himself, "But I was once alive without law."[70] And when did Paul live without law, who says moreover concerning himself, "[I was] circumcised on the eighth day, a Hebrew born of Hebrews"?[71] How then will it be true that he had lived at one time without law, this man who, eight days after his own birth, received the sign of circumcision from the law?

(8) Whence it is certain that a man comes under law at the time when he reaches the age when he can choose and discern what the law is.[72] He does not receive the yoke of any external law before he begins to have the strength of the internal natural law. After all, in the text where he said, "But I was once alive without law," he adds, "but when the commandment came, sin revived,"[73] in which he shows that in childhood, before anyone has the capacity to distinguish between good and evil, one is said to be without law.[74] Even if he sins, the sin is not imputed to him since there is no law in him.[75] But when he receives the capacity for distinguishing between good and evil, it is said that the law has come to him and has given commandments to him. But when the power of the commandment is within, i.e., the accusing conscience, it is said that sin, which formerly was dead in him, has revived. From this time on, then, if someone should submit himself to the law of Moses so that he observes it according to the letter, he becomes [M931] an outward Jew. But if he follows it according to the Spirit, he becomes a Jew in secret.[76]

(9) This has been said on behalf of what was stated, "For we have charged that all Jews and Greeks are under sin." It is obvious that "all" should be understood as having been said concerning those about whom it is an established fact that they are

---

69. Cf. Rom 2.15. Cf. 2.8.2; 2.9.1.
71. Phil 3.5.
73. Rom 7.9.
75. Cf. Rom 5.13.
70. Rom 7.9.
72. Cf. 3.6.1.
74. Cf. 4.1.17; 6.8.3.
76. Cf. Rom 2.28–29.

being instructed not to sin, whether by natural or written law. For we shall interpret this concerning the Gentiles brought under sin in the same way as we have said above, when they will have begun to do naturally the things of the law and are a law to themselves, when they are accused by their conscience in those matters which they seem to do contrary to the law.[77] Therefore those who call the law of nature, "the law of God," but who designate written law as the "adopted law,"[78] have, it seems to me, perceived these matters in a logical manner.[79] For if Paul had been speaking of written law, that is, of the law of Moses, when he said, "But sin is not imputed when there is no law,"[80] then sin would not have been imputed to Cain or to those who died in the flood or to those who were consumed by fire in Sodom.[81] But since we see that not only have sins been imputed to these people but that revenge was given to them, it is shown from this that Paul is speaking of natural law, which, with the exception of the first period of childhood, exists in all men.[82] And thus he was quite justified in saying, "For we have charged that all Jews and Greeks are under sin." This is also why, to my way of thinking, it was not contrary to reason for certain sages to have stipulated that every type of mortal receives the ability to discern right and wrong when he arrives at the age when natural law enters his life. It is evil that gets aroused first of all, but afterward it is gradually driven out by means of instruction, education, and exhortation; and it passes over to virtue.[83] For it seems to me that Paul as well has perceived what is in accord with these things in that which he says, "But when the commandment came, sin revived."[84] In fact the Savior too, when he says in the Gospels, "If I would not have come and spoken to them, they would have no sin; but now they have no excuse for their sin,"[85] will seem to have spoken according to this

77. Cf. Rom 2.14–15.
78. *Positione legem* = θέσει νόμον. For θέσει cf. Philo, *Allegorical Interpretation* 3.
79. Cf. *Cels* 5.37.   80. Rom 5.13.
81. Cf. 4.4.4.
82. Cf. *Comm in Mt* 13.16 (= ANF 10:484): "No passion is incident to the little children who have not yet attained to full possession of reason."
83. Cf. *Cels* 4.64; *Comm in Mt* 17.33; *Hom in Ex* 4.8.
84. Rom 7.9. Cf. 5.1.26; 6.8.3; *Cels* 3.62.
85. Jn 15.22.

understanding, that by the power with which he is said to fill the world,[86] he comes to each man and speaks in his heart and teaches him discretion of good and evil.[87]

(10) So then, this is why Paul says that it is written, "There is no one who is righteous, no one who has understanding, there is no one who seeks God; all have turned away, together they have become worthless," just as the prophet says elsewhere, "No one living will be justified in your sight."[88] This may perhaps appear contrary to other Scriptures which bear witness to many persons, partially righteous to such a degree that it could even be said to Jerusalem in reference to the Sodomites, "Sodom has been justified because of you."[89] But consider very carefully the caution of Holy Scripture, that it has not said, "Sodom has been justified," but it says, [M932] "because you [Jerusalem] are committing many wicked deeds and what you are doing is of such a nature that you surpass everyone in the magnitude of your sins, in comparison with your crimes, now even Sodom should be justified."[90]

(11) So then, in what he has said here, "No one living will be justified in your sight," he did not mean for this to be understood in the sense that no one living will be justified, but "in your sight," that is to say, no one will be justified in God's sight. For however just someone may be, however holy he may be, not only among men but even among the higher and more eminent creatures, it is certain that in comparison with God he cannot be justified.[91] For even in the Apocalypse of John when the sealed book is brought into the presence of the Ancient of Days[92] and someone who is able to open it is sought from every tribe, tongue, and people, no one was found except the lamb from the tribe of Judah, who was justified in the sight of God. And he alone deserved to open the book, for he alone is the one "who opens and no one closes; he closes and no one

---

86. Cf. Jer 23.24; Wis 1.7. See also *Comm in Jn* 6.39; *Cels* 4.5; 5.12; *Hom in Lv* 5.2.
87. Cf. *Comm in Jn* 1.37; 2.15; *Princ* 1.3.6.
88. Ps 143.2. 89. Ezek 16.51–52.
90. Cf. Ezek 16.51–52.
91. Cf. *Hom in Lk* 2.3–4; *Comm in Jn* 2.17.
92. Cf. Dn 7.9, 13; Rv 5.

opens."[93] Therefore our Savior alone, the Lord Jesus Christ, is justified in the sight of the Father, since "whatever the Father does, even that the Son does likewise."[94] But every creature is justified in comparison with inferiors.[95] Thus we might say, for example, that in comparison with the rest of the people, Miriam, the sister of Moses, was just; and again, in comparison with Miriam, Aaron was just; and again, compared with Aaron, Moses was just. But blessed is he who is called just in comparison with better things and not in comparison with what is worse, as was Sodom, which is recorded to have been justified in comparison with Jerusalem.[96]

(12) For this reason I am apprehensive, because of us who seem to be in the Church of God and who apply ourselves to his law and who are in devoted service to the precepts of the Gospel, some unbelievers might be found who ought to be justified. For example, I would say that if we are enslaved to lust and impurity, whereas the pagan, who is a stranger to faith in Christ, preserves chastity, then that pagan is justified because of us. Similarly, if we are overwhelmed by greed, rapacity, arrogance, and other evils of this sort, but a pagan and those who do not know the law of God abstain from all these things, then they will be justified because of us and we shall be condemned in comparison with them. Indeed we need to exert ourselves harder so that just as we surpass the pagans in faith, so also we may outdo them in actions and deeds. Otherwise our evils may become another's goods, and their moderation may convict our immoderation.

(13) Yet it is possible to explain in still another way what he has said, "There is no one who is righteous," or what he said, "no one living will be justified in your sight."[97] For as long as a person lives in the body, he cannot be justified or declared righteous, but when he departs from the body and leaves the struggle of this life, as the Scripture also says, [M933] "Do not pronounce a man happy before death since you do not know

---

93. Rv 3.7.
94. Jn 5.19.
95. Cf. *Hom in Ezek* 9.3; *Hom in Jer* 8.7.
96. Cf. Ezek 16.51–52.
97. Ps 143.2.

what his end shall be";[98] and again as Ecclesiastes says, "And I praised all the dead, who have already died, more than the living, who are still alive; but better than both is the one who has not yet been born."[99] Moreover, you have still another scriptural statement which says that whoever is least in the kingdom of God is greater than the one who is in the body, even if it be John himself, than whom there was no one greater among those born of women.[100]

(14) Therefore "there is no one who is righteous." He says additionally, "there is no one who has understanding." And in truth, seeing that the Apostle himself claims to know in part and to understand in part,[101] who will there be who would be called "one who has understanding"? For to whatever extent one does understand, he shall appear to understand as in a mirror and in a riddle;[102] since it is only after the laying aside of the earthly body that a man is preserved to understand face to face.[103] For the present time, however, it is indeed as the Scripture says, "A corruptible body weighs down the soul, and this earthy tent depresses the thoughtful mind,"[104] from which it follows that "there is no one who has understanding" and "no one who seeks God." For as long as we are occupied with the troubles of the body and we seek things which pertain to men, we cannot seek God or be mindful of the things which pertain to God.[105]

3. *All have turned aside, together they have become worthless.*[106] It seems to me that no one could be said to have turned aside except one who, at one time, stood on the right path. From this observation it is clear that the original work of the rational nature which was made by God had been upright[107] and was set on the right path as a gift of its Creator. But because he turned away from this to the wayward road of sin, he is now justly said

---

98. Sir 11.28; Wis 2.17; Jb 23.8; Mt 12.45; Lk 11.26.
99. Eccl 4.2–3.   100. Cf. Mt 11.11.
101. Cf. 1 Cor 13.9.   102. Cf. 1 Cor 13.12.
103. Cf. *Mart* 47.   104. Wis 9.15. Cf. 6.3.8.
105. Cf. 1 Cor 7.32–33. See also *Hom in Nm* 23.11.
106. Rom 3.12.   107. Cf. Eccl 7.29.

to have turned aside.[108] There is, for example, the case of the first man, Adam, who turned aside from the right road in Paradise, by the seductive deception of the serpent, to the wrong and tortuous paths of mortal life. Consequently then, all who come into this world in succession from Adam have turned aside and together with him have become worthless. I think it is also on this account that the Lord gives the command in the Gospels that when we have done everything which we have been instructed to do, we should nevertheless remember what we are and we should say, "We are worthless servants, we have done what we ought to have done!"[109] For as long as someone does only what he ought, that is to say, what has been commanded him, he is a worthless servant; but if you should add to what has been commanded then you will no longer be a worthless servant but it will be said to you, "Well done, good and faithful servant!"[110] Now just what that is which may be added to the things commanded and made to surpass obligation, the Apostle Paul tells us, "Now concerning virgins, I do not have a command of the Lord: but I give counsel as one who has attained mercy from God."[111] This work goes beyond the command.[112] Therefore whoever has fulfilled the commands and adds to them this as well, that he preserves the state of virginity, he is no longer [M934] a worthless servant but will be called a good and faithful one. Moreover there is the command that those who proclaim the gospel should earn their living from the gospel. Yet Paul says, "I have made use of none of these things."[113] On that account he was not a worthless servant but a faithful and wise one.[114]

(2) Therefore, "All have turned aside, together they have become worthless." To this he has added, "There is no one who does goodness, there is not even one." This is a severe judgment which could be alleged only with difficulty. For how does it appear to possibly be that no one at all, not even one single person among the Jews and among the Greeks, can be found

---

108. Cf. *Comm in Jn* 13.37; *Princ* 2.9.2.
109. Lk 17.10.
110. Mt 25.21.
111. 1 Cor 7.25.
112. Cf. 10.14.7.
113. 1 Cor 9.14–15.
114. Cf. Mt 24.45.

who does goodness? Are we thus to believe that there has been no one who has received a guest at some time or who has given bread to a hungry man or has clothed a naked person[115] or has rescued the innocent from the hands of the mighty[116] or has carried out some other kind of good work? It does not seem to me that the Apostle Paul wanted to make such an incredible assertion. But in my opinion when he denies that anyone has done goodness, we should understand him in the following way: Suppose, for instance, someone should lay the foundations of a house and construct one or two walls, maybe even bring in some of the building material. Will he be said to have built the house, even though he seems to have worked on the house? On the contrary a man is said to have made a house who completely builds each individual section of the entire structure. It is in this way, I think, that the Apostle is saying here that no one has done goodness: He means that no one has brought it to perfection and entire completion. But if we ask, who is truly good and who has done perfect goodness, we shall find only him who says, "I am the good shepherd," and again, "The good shepherd lays down his life for his sheep."[117]

(3) After these things he, citing from the Fifth Psalm as we said above,[118] says, "their throat is an open grave."[119] By these words he is describing the various sins of the human race, as it seems to me. Every grave covers the defilement of a dead corpse. The Lord also spoke of this in the Gospel concerning the scribes and Pharisees, that they were white-washed graves which indeed outwardly appear beautiful to men but within are filled with every defilement.[120] But Paul seems to be indicating in this passage some greater crime in those concerning whom he is writing. For he calls them not covered or concealed, but open graves. For they are called closed graves who are prevented from sinning openly and bringing forth their crimes into the public by even a small amount of decency. But they are called open graves who publicly display their defilement and

---

115. Cf. Is 58.7; Mt 25.35–36; Tb 1.17.
116. Cf. Ps 72.14; Jb 29.12. 117. Jn 10.11.
118. Cf. 3.2.6. 119. Ps 5.9.
120. Mt 23.27.

impurities. In such persons the constant repetition and practice of wicked deeds, which is the ultimate of evils, has removed from them even the sense of shame of their crimes. Thus, no longer do they open their mouths and express the word of God, the living word,[121] but instead they open [M935] their throats and express the dead word, the word of the devil, not from the heart but from the grave.[122] Whenever you see someone with a lascivious mouth uttering shameless words, or expressing insults and abuses with an arrogant and frenzied mouth, do not hesitate to say of such a person, "his throat is an open grave." "For out of the abundance of the heart the mouth speaks."[123]

(4) To these things is added, "They use their tongues to deceive." Deceit is when one speaks one thing with the tongue and ponders something else in his heart.[124] I do not know if even those who are righteous and chosen may remain immune from this fault. I do think, however, that one person may be more prone to this fault, another less prone, but no one is cleansed from it to the point of perfection except he alone, of whom it is written, "He committed no sin and no deceit was found in his mouth."[125] For even if someone may be found who is careful and cautious, he can perhaps guard himself in more serious matters; but when would you find anyone who does not offend in this matter either out of timidity or negligence? Sometimes through forgetfulness things which were supposed to be attended to are neglected, and lest the fault should become known, excuses are made as if the matters had actually been done. For this reason Peter as well, knowing that these various forms of deceit exist, writes in his epistle, saying, "therefore laying aside all deceit and pretense and envy and slander, like newborn infants long for the rational milk which is without deceit so that by it you might grow into salvation."[126]

---

121. Heb 4.12.
122. Cf. *Comm in Cant* 3.
123. Mt 12.34.
124. Cf. Achilles' words in Homer's *Iliad* 9:312, "Hateful to me as the gates of hell is that man who hides one thing in his heart and speaks another." See also Sir 12.16.
125. Is 53.9; 1 Pt 2.22.
126. 1 Pt 2.1–2.

4. *The venom of vipers is under their lips.*[127] The serpent's bite kills the body by its venom; the bite of a venomous word kills the soul by its deceit. This can happen through those who deceive men by the invention of false accusations; it can also occur through those who deceive the souls of the simple with heretical doctrine, infected by the devil's poison.

(2) "Their mouths are full of cursing and bitterness."[128] He has not said that the lips are full of the venom of vipers. For though it is possible to find very many people with that vice, most do not use the poison of that venom fully and completely. However, the mouth of exceedingly many is filled with cursing and bitterness. For who exists whose mouth is so pure that habit does not provoke him to cursing, I do not mean against those who are deserving of being cursed, but even against those whom the Lord has not cursed,[129] that is to say, against righteous and innocent men? This flaw of human frailty is common and habitual, especially towards inferiors and those in subjection, so much so that they no longer consider this kind of name-calling to be cursing. That is why it is said that their mouths are full and that cursing flows out incessantly, as it were, from the full vessel of the mouth. To this, however, bitterness is also joined because it is produced from the gall of anger. For the tongue is incited to curse by means of anger and rage. And that is why the same Apostle says, "Bless [M936] and do not curse!"[130] and elsewhere, "that no root of bitterness should spring up and cause trouble."[131]

(3) In what follows he adds, "Their feet are swift to shed blood."[132] It will perhaps appear that this crime cannot be applied to many of those concerning whom he has said, "For we have charged that all Jews and Greeks are under sin." Unless perchance we should understand that it is not so much *physically* that the blood of those whose bodies are slain is shed, but also those who separate the soul from God by any stumbling block whatsoever are called "men of blood." For just as a man is

---

127. Rom 3.13.
128. Rom 3.14.
129. Cf. Nm 23.8.
130. Rom 12.14.
131. Heb 12.15; cf. Dt 29.17.
132. Rom 3.15.

called a murderer who separates the body from the soul, through which it is vivified, how much more truly should he be called a murderer who separates the soul from the true life, which is God?[133] But know that the "feet" in this passage are those concerning which the prophet says, "My feet had almost slipped";[134] that is to say, it refers to the plan by which we direct the path of our life.[135]

5. *Contrition and misfortune are in their paths, and the way of peace they have not known.*[136] He is not speaking here of that contrition by which the sinner's spirit is afflicted because of penitence, of which it is said in the Psalms, "God does not despise a humble and contrite heart."[137] Rather he is speaking of that contrition by which sinners are said to destroy the yoke of the Lord and cast it from their necks.[138] Likewise "misfortune" or, as another reading says, "misery" must be taken to refer to the man who has become miserable and unfortunate, who "while he was in honor did not understand" but "became like the foolish beasts and has become like them."[139]

(2) "And the way of peace they have not known."[140] Our peace is Christ.[141] The way of peace, then, is the way of Christ. But even if we take it to mean that sinners, while continually prodded on into the battles against the vices, do not know the way of peace, we shall understand correctly. For the prophet says to the Lord, "There is great peace for those who love your name, and there is no stumbling block for them.[142] Furthermore, that people which was led out of Egypt advanced along the way of peace in order to come to the promised land and dwell in Jerusalem, which is interpreted "Vision of Peace."[143] As

---

133. Cf. 6.6.7; *Dial* 25.13–18.
134. Ps 73.2.
135. Cf. 8.5.5–7.
136. Rom 3.16–17.
137. Ps 51.17.
138. Cf. Jer 2.20; 5.5.
139. Ps 49.12, 20. See also 2.5.6.
140. Rom 3.17.
141. Cf. Eph 2.14.
142. Ps 119.165.

143. Cf. 10.14.6; *Comm in Cant* 2.1; *Hom in Jos* 21.2; *Hom in Jer* 9.2 (= FOTC 97:87). Lawson in Origen, *The Song of Songs: Commentary and Homilies*, ACW 26 (1956), p. 330 n. 23, notes that *visio pacis* = ὅρασις εἰρήνης was a popular etymology of the name Jerusalem. See Philo, *On Dreams* 2.38.250; Clement, *Stromateis* 1.5.29.4.

BOOK 3, CHAPTER 5

the prophet also says, "His place has been established in peace and his dwelling is in Zion."[144] Now whoever strives for a dwelling in the heavenly Jerusalem knows the way of peace more fully as he ascends to the holy city of the living God.[145]

(3) After these things he adds, "There is no fear of God before their eyes."[146] If there is anyone who always contemplates the fear of God and who seeks to know what is pleasing or displeasing to him, of such a person it is said that the fear of God is before his eyes. But he must be experienced and diligently trained in the law of the Lord,[147] lest he greatly fear where fear would not be necessary.[148] The fear of God, then, should always be placed before the eyes, not the fleshly eyes—for nothing visible or bodily is intended here—but he is speaking about the eyes of the mind, [M937] with which both the understanding and instruction of the fear of God are discerned, by means of which, as we said above, one may understand what is to be feared and what is not to be feared. Whoever fears God has no fear of the authorities of this age. But why am I speaking about the authorities of this age? He fears neither the powers and authorities nor the rulers of this world nor the spiritual forces of wickedness in the heavenly realms.[149] And in order that we might reinforce this by the authority of Paul himself, listen to what he says of the human authorities. "Do you wish," he says, "to have no fear of authority? Then do what is good, and you will receive praise from it."[150] The prophet says as well, "The Lord is my helper, I shall not be afraid of what man might do to me."[151] But it seems to me that the prophet also had in mind the hostile spiritual authorities when he says, "There are many warring against me from on high, they shall fear through the day";[152] and again, "Though an army encamps against me, my heart shall not fear."[153] There is a need, then, both noble and magnificent, always to have the fear of God before the eyes of

---

144. Ps 76.2.
145. Cf. Heb 12.22. See also *Cels* 7.29.
146. Rom 3.18.   147. Cf. Ps 94.12.
148. Cf. Ps 14.5; 53.5.   149. Cf. Eph 6.12.
150. Rom 13.3.   151. Ps 118.6; Heb 13.6.
152. Ps 56.3–4.   153. Ps 27.3.

the heart, that fear which filled the shoot which arose from the root of Jesse, the flower which grew from his root, concerning whom it is said, "And the Spirit filled him with the fear of God."[154] But the fear of God renders a man perfect and he lacks nothing to such a degree that the prophet says, "those who fear him shall lack nothing."[155]

(4) We have arranged these things according to our ability in each of the individual matters taken up by Paul, as it seemed appropriate to the matters about which he wrote, "For we have charged that all Jews and Greeks are under sin." In my opinion this ought to be understood not in the sense that every human being is proven guilty of all these crimes, but rather, one person is charged in one matter, another in another; yet this is such that in everyone the whole universe is filled with vices.

6. *Now we know that whatever the law says, it says to those who are under the law, so that every mouth may be shut, and the whole world may be subjected to God. Therefore no flesh will be justified in the sight of God by works of the law. For through law comes the knowledge of sin.*[156] We have previously said in the preface that the Apostle was going to be discussing several kinds of law in this epistle,[157] the distinction and discrimination of which could potentially confuse the reader's mind unless it were considered in individual passages. Consequently in the present passage as well, which says, "We know that whatever the law says, it says to those who are under the law," we need to examine carefully which law he means is spoken to those who are under the law, and through which it says to them that it strips them of every excuse so that they are not able to find any excuse for their own sins. For this is what he says, "so that every mouth may be shut, and the whole world may be subjected to God." Now suppose we want to understand this of the law [M938] of Moses which, it is scarcely to be doubted, speaks only to those whom it obligated to be circumcised at birth and whom it instructed. How shall it

---

154. Is 11.1, 3.   155. Ps 34.10.
156. Rom 3.19–20.
157. Cf. Preface of Origen (8); 3.7.5; 4.4.5; 5.1.24; 5.6.2–4; 5.10.9; 6.8.2; 6.9.2; 7.1.1; 7.19.7.

appear consistent that through this law, which governs one nation only in its stipulations, every mouth is shut and through it the whole world is held accountable to God? For what are we to believe? That all the Gentiles and the whole world share this law in common? Moreover, how is it said that the knowledge of sin comes through the law of Moses when very many individuals may be found who knew their sin even before the law of Moses existed?[158] Cain, after all, when he had sinned, said the following, "My sin is too great that I may be forgiven."[159] Moreover the patriarchs, when they had gone down to Joseph in Egypt and were incited by him by means of a feigned accusation, say to one another, "We are in sins on account of our brother; for we saw the distress of his soul when he pleaded with us, but we did not listen to him. That is why this affliction has come upon us."[160] But Job too, who is acknowledged to have lived before the law,[161] says the following, "If I have sinned unintentionally, if I have hidden my sin, or if I have been intimidated before the multitude of people to declare my fault."[162] All these individuals are plainly shown to have recognized their sin. Consequently it is concluded from this that the Apostle Paul is not speaking about the law of Moses, that "the law speaks to those who are under the law," but instead about natural law, which is written in men's hearts. Whatever this law says, then, it says to those who are under the law. Those who are at the time of life at which they have already received the ability to distinguish good and evil are under this law. But those whose minds have not yet reached the point of discretion are "without law," according to what Paul also says, "I was once alive without law."[163] The Apostle will appear to have spoken reasonably, in accordance with natural law, that every mouth should be shut and the whole world will be accountable to the judgment of God. For there is no one who does not have experience of this law, which is naturally innate within men, both Jews and Gentiles. Therefore the statement, "God might be justified in his

---

158. Cf. 6.8.3.
160. Gn 42.21.
162. Jb 31.33–34 LXX.

159. Gn 4.13 LXX.
161. Cf. *Cels* 6.43.
163. Rom 7.9.

words and prevail when he is judged," also appears to have been reasonably said.[164]

(2) For instance, we say that if it is investigated what has God bestowed upon a person and what a person has done with what he has received from God, God will seem to enter judgment with men. One finds that God has in fact given to man every disposition and every drive by which he can press forward and advance toward virtue. Over and above the power of reason God has ensured that man should know what he ought to do and what he ought to avoid.[165] One finds then that God has supplied these things universally to all men.[166] But if a man who has received these things has disdained to advance upon the road of virtue, this man, to whom nothing was lacking from God, [M939] is found to be lacking in what is given to him by God. Deservedly, then, God is said to prevail in such a judgment and to be justified in his words.[167]

(3) This natural law then speaks to all who are under the law. From its precepts it appears to me that little children alone are exempt, for whom the judgment of right and wrong does not yet exist. Now whether those who, for whatever reason, are mentally incompetent ought to be joined to these as well is a question which needs to be investigated. Apart from these exceptions, however, no human being, it seems to me, escapes this law.

(4) What now needs to be considered is whether this law binds not only human beings but also angels and every rational creature of whatever sort. For if law has been rightly defined by wise men as that which says what one ought to do and which forbids what one ought not to do,[168] how will such a law not seem to have also been ingrafted into the higher heavenly orders? Surely they also have instruction that certain things must be observed and certain things are to be avoided. And unless they were bound by this law, Holy Scripture would never have said about them, "Even angels who did not keep their original

---

164. Cf. Rom 3.4; Ps 51.4. See also 2.14.17.
165. Cf. *Comm in Jn* 2.15.   166. Cf. 1.16.5.
167. Cf. Rom 3.4.
168. Cf. 6.8.7; Clement, *Stromateis* 1.25.166.5 (= FOTC 85:146); Philo, *On Rewards and Punishments* 55; *On Joseph* 29.

state, but left their proper dwelling, God has kept bound in eternal chains in deepest darkness in Tartarus for the judgment of the great day."[169] Therefore it is confirmed that they possess this law. Having failed to keep it, they suffered these things which the Scripture has testified above. Moreover, when Paul says, "Do you not know that we will judge angels?"[170] of what else is he expressing knowledge than of the fact that these too, whom he declares should be brought before the judgment, stand under law?[171]

(5) We have said above that God is about to enter into judgment with men.[172] Suppose someone should object to us that we seem to be saying that God himself is under law. Listen to what great caution is found in this connection in the letters of the Apostle, who relates that Christ is not under the law but is the fulfillment of law.[173] And just as he himself is the righteousness through which all become righteous;[174] and he is the truth through which all stand firm in the truth; and he himself is the life through which all live;[175] so also he himself is the law through which all are under law.[176] He comes to the judgment, then, not as one who is under law but as one who *is* law.[177] But I think that even those who are already perfect and, by being united with the Lord, have become one spirit with him[178] are themselves not under law but are *themselves* law. This is precisely what this same Apostle says in another place, "The law has not been laid down for the just."[179] Meanwhile "whatever the law says, it says to those who are under the law so that every mouth may be shut," in the sense in which we have spoken above, "so that the whole world might be subjected," or, as we read in other manuscripts, "may be held accountable to God," which also agrees more with the Greek copies.[180]

---

169. Jude 6.
170. 1 Cor 6.3.
171. Cf. 5.1.29; *Cels* 7.68; *Hom in Ezek* 4.1.
172. Rom 3.4.
173. Rom 10.4.
174. Cf. 1 Cor 1.30.
175. Cf. Jn 14.6.
176. Cf. Mi 4.2.
177. Cf. *Comm in Jn* 2.15.
178. Cf. 1 Cor 6.17.
179. 1 Tm 1.9.
180. Rufinus has cited *subditus*, "subjected," in the lemma but *obnoxius*, "accountable" = ὑπόδικος agrees more with Origen's comments. From this point on, however, he cites the latter reading. Heither in Origenes, *Commentarii*, 2:91 n. 43, says it is not clear if Origen knew of a variant to ὑπόδικος.

(6) Now let us ascertain what the Apostle has designated as "the whole world" in this context. Should it be supposed that by "the whole [M940] world" the earthly region here ought to be understood in the sense that even trees, stones, grass, seeds, and chaff, which are all in this world, are equally being designated?[181] To be sure each of these things seem to be a part of the world, but I don't think anyone so foolish can be found who could make such an assertion. It remains then that he is calling every living rational creature "the whole world." And just as everything which is irrational is excluded from this meaning, so it seems to me that no rational creature is excluded from this condition. The whole world then becomes accountable to God because he has ingrafted the natural law into them all. In another passage he speaks of these beings as well, "For at the name of Jesus every knee will bow of beings in heaven and on earth and under the earth."[182] Assuredly if the whole world would do this, then it will seem to have fulfilled the law; but if it does not do this, it will seem to be accountable to the law, and through the law, logically, also to God.

(7) But suppose it would seem to anyone that this saying concerns only human beings because he might say that natural law dwells within them[183] and of them alone he interprets what is written, "so that every mouth may be shut, and the whole world may be held accountable to God." Such an interpreter takes advantage of what is said in the subsequent words which read, "Because by works of the law shall no flesh be justified." For this statement certainly would seem to have been spoken only of those who are placed in flesh. However those who want instead to defend the former interpretation will carefully observe the sense in which the Apostle has said, "no flesh is justified by works of the law." For *works* of the law concern those who are in the flesh, but the *meaning* of the law pertains to those who are in the spirit, that is to say, to higher orders of heavenly offices. "By works of the law, therefore, shall no flesh be justified in his sight," should be understood, in my opinion,

---

181. Cf. 1.9.4–5; 3.1.13.
183. Cf. Rom 2.14–15.

182. Phil 2.10.

that nothing that is flesh and that lives according to the flesh can be justified by the law of God.[184] Just as the same Apostle says elsewhere, "Those who are in the flesh cannot please God,"[185] and again in another passage, "For the wisdom of the flesh is hostile to God; for it is not subjected to God's law—indeed it cannot be."[186] The prophet also says, "All flesh is grass";[187] and in the Gospel it is written, "It is the Spirit that gives life; the flesh profits nothing."[188] It is based upon such things, then, that he says that from the law of God "no flesh will be justified before him."[189]

(8) Moreover you should not casually pass over the added words, "before him," as I have already frequently warned,[190] since to be justified before God is different from being justified before men. That is to say, in comparison with other men, one man can be deemed just if he has lived relatively free from faults; but in comparison with God, not only is a man not justified, but as even Job says, "But the stars are not pure before him."[191] They are certainly [M941] pure to us, that is, in comparison with men they are deemed pure and holy; but they are not able to be pure in comparison with God.[192]

(9) "Through the law," he says, "comes the knowledge of sin." Let us see how the knowledge of sin comes through the law. While we learn[193] through the law what is to be done and what is to be avoided, at the same time we acquire the knowledge both of what sin is and what it is not. Then it is not the

---

184. Cf. 3.2.11.
185. Rom 8.8.
186. Rom 8.7.
187. Is 40.6.
188. Jn 6.63.
189. Sanday & Headlam, *Romans*, p. 148, cite this passage as an example of "how little Origen had grasped some points in St. Paul's thought." Cf. Wiles, *Divine Apostle*, p. 29, "This line of interpretation clearly weakens the apparent absoluteness of Paul's attack upon the law." On the other hand, Schelkle, *Paulus, Lehrer*, p. 105, insists that Origen's interpretation here, although it is not Paul's immediate intention, "is nevertheless biblical."
190. Cf. 3.2.10–13.
191. Jb 25.5.
192. Cf. *Princ* 1.7.2. Origen viewed the stars as rational, changeable beings which became unclean through their own sloth, although in *Comm in Jn* 1.40 he asks whether Job (25:5) might be speaking hyperbolically.
193. Hammond Bammel's text reads *dicimus*, "we say," but she notes that the reading *discimus*, "we learn," is possibly correct.

case, as the heretics accuse the God of the law, that the law is a bad root and a bad tree[194] through which the knowledge of sin comes.[195] For he has not said, "*from* the law comes the knowledge of sin," but, "*through* the law," so that you might know that sin did not arise from it but is known through it. Suppose, for instance, we were to say: Through the art of medicine is given the knowledge of sickness.[196] You don't think, do you, that medical science will be deemed to be the cause of sickness just because by means of it the nature of sickness is recognized? But just as it is indisputable that medical science is a good thing since it offers understanding of illness by which the one who wills can avoid illness, so also the law is good, through which means sin is detected and known.[197] In my opinion such an explanation preserves as well the coherence of the explanation we set forth above[198] concerning that which was written, "For we have charged that all Jews and Greeks are under sin, just as it is written, 'There is no one who is righteous, there is no one who has understanding or who seeks God.'"[199]

7. *But now apart from law the righteousness of God has been disclosed, attested by the law and the prophets. But the righteousness of God is through faith in Jesus Christ for all who believe. For there is no distinction. For all have sinned and lack the glory of God, justified freely through his grace, through the redemption that is in Christ Jesus.*[200]

(2) In the above discussion[201] we asserted that not about the law of Moses was it said, "Whatever the law says, it speaks to those who are under the law."[202] Now someone will think that this was asserted in violation of the text rather than said truly,

---

194. Cf. Mt 7.18; 12.33; Lk 6.43.
195. This again appears to be directed against Marcion and his followers, though Schelkle, "Kirche und Synagoge," p. 82, thinks that Mani and Manichean Gnosticism are Origen's targets. Cf. 4.4.3; 5.6.2; *Princ* 2.5.4; Clement, *Stromateis* 2.34.4; 4.3.9.6.
196. Cf. 2.6.3.
197. Cf. Clement, *Stromateis* 1.27.171.1 (= FOTC 85:148f.).
198. Cf. 3.2.7.   199. Rom 3.9–11.
200. Rom 3.21–24.   201. Cf. 3.6.1.
202. Rom 3.19.

since he now sees that the term "law" refers not to the law of nature but to that of Moses. He would say that in the present passage the Apostle declares that the righteousness of God is disclosed through the law, and not only through the law but also through the prophets, so that without any ambiguity what is written should be understood as having been said about the law of Moses, from which law the righteousness of God is disclosed through faith in Jesus Christ to all who believe, whether they come from the Jews or from the Gentiles. These are justified, however, not by works but by the grace of God, through the redemption accomplished for them by Jesus Christ himself.[203] This much he would say, he who would charge that the Apostle's meaning, in these passages we have interpreted above, has been violently twisted by us.

(3) Nevertheless we can assert the following with consistency: Those who assert these things think that we can find no basis in the Apostle's words, which we have explained, [M942] on which to support our claim that he has not recorded these things about the law of Moses but about natural law. Yet in just the same way not even they are able to find any way how what has been spoken above could seem to refer to the Law of Moses rather than to that of nature. And, therefore, just as for them the foregoing will not hold up because the things said later appear to be certain, so not even for us can the interpretation of the first passage be disturbed just because what follows does not seem to run along the same path.

(4) What then? Shall we say that the Apostle is writing things that are mutually contradictory? That would be a claim of a most distinguished commentator indeed![204] This usually happens to people who break apart the one single doctrine of faith into the diverse interpretations of the sects. They investigate only those testimonies in the Holy Scriptures by which their own doctrines are established. But the explanations of those thoughts of the Holy Scripture which run contrary to their

---

203. Cf. Ti 3.5.
204. Referring to this passage Tollinton, *Selections*, p. xviii, writes, "Could Paul contradict himself? Origen has only scorn for such a desperate assertion."

views is something they do not touch, not even with their fingertips,[205] as the saying goes.[206] But the one who compiles the meaning of the sacred volumes faithfully and completely is responsible to show how the things in Scripture which appear contradictory are not truly contradictory.[207] We shall therefore attempt to show even in the present passage how his subsequent statement is not inconsistent with my former explanation.

(5) We have often said, and we clearly demarcated this point in the Preface,[208] that the Apostle mentions many kinds of law in this epistle in such a way that when he passes from one kind to another it is scarcely possible for this to be detected except by a reader who is sufficiently attentive. Up above he had said that through law comes the knowledge of sin. But now he has sensed that it is possible for someone to respond to him: Well then, if the knowledge of sin comes from natural law, the knowledge of righteousness can come from it as well, following the example of the medical arts which we gave above, that in the same way that, by means of medical science, illness is known and health is attained, so also if the knowledge of sin can come through the law of nature, the knowledge of righteousness can come by the same means.[209] When he had seen, then, that this could be raised as an objection, he joins to the words he had previously said, "For through law comes the knowledge of sin," the following, "But now apart from law, the righteousness of God has been disclosed."[210] What he is saying, then, is this: It is not the case that, just as the knowledge of sin comes through the law, so also the disclosure of God's righteousness comes through law. But God's righteousness is disclosed apart from law. For the law of nature was able to reveal the nature of sin and bring to light the knowledge of sin; but the righteousness of God surpasses and rises above whatever the human mind can scrutinize by natural senses alone. For the mind does not suf-

205. Mt 23.4; Lk 11.46; cf. Lk 16.24.
206. Cf. 1.18.3; 5.6.3.
207. Cf. *Philocalia* 6 = *Comm in Mt* 5.9.
208. Preface of Origen (8); 3.6.1.   209. Cf. 3.6.9.
210. Rom 3.21.

fice, not so much for every kind of human righteousness, but for grasping the righteousness of God and the judgments which descend from it, concerning which it is said that they are the great deep.[211] For the righteousness of God and his judgments are so profound that the Apostle says, "How unsearchable are the judgments of God."[212]

(6) Moreover, wisdom also speaks this way to men, as if [M943] the righteousness of God cannot be known by the impulses of nature alone but must be sought through the study of doctrine; and for this reason it says, "Learn righteousness, you who judge the earth!"[213] Wherefore the law of nature will be of no help whatsoever for knowing God's righteousness, though it appears to understand something about human righteousness. For that law is indeed able to perceive what is just among men, as, for example, that what someone does not want to suffer himself, he should not do to his neighbor.[214] But is it able to perceive naturally that righteousness which says, "Beware of practicing your righteousness before men," and, "do not let your left hand know what your right hand is doing"?[215] These and just things of a similar nature are things which the law of nature cannot declare, and therefore the Apostle says, "But now, apart from the law," sc. "of nature," "the righteousness of God has been disclosed,"[216] having the attestation of the law of Moses and of the prophets, in whom the Holy Spirit had recorded many things about God's righteousness through figures and enigmas.[217]

(7) I don't want you to be surprised that the single term "law," which is found twice in the very same passage, should signify different things. We find this to be customary in the Scripture even in other passages like here, "Do you not say, 'Four months more, then comes the harvest?' Lift up your eyes and

---

211. Cf. Ps 36.6.   212. Rom 11.33.
213. Wis 1.1; Ps 2.10.
214. Cf. Tb 4.15; Mt 7.12; Lk 6.31; Acts 15.29, Western text. See also 2.9.1 n. 230.
215. Mt 6.1, 3.   216. Rom 3.21.
217. Melanchthon calls Origen's interpretation in this section "childish, foolish and inept"; in *Commentary on Romans (1540)*, trans. F. Kramer (St Louis: Concordia, 1992), p. 14.

see the fields, that they are already white for harvest."[218] Does not the word "harvest," which is named twice in this passage, refer in the first instance to the material harvest but in the second instance to the spiritual? Again in the Gospel when the Savior says to the Samaritan woman, "Give me a drink,"[219] and after her response, he goes on to say to her, "If you knew who it is who says to you: Give me a drink, you would certainly have asked him and he would have given you living water."[220] And then he says additionally to her, "All who drink of this water shall thirst again; but whoever drinks from the water which I give him shall never thirst again."[221] Do you see how both "to drink" and "water" are understood at one time in a material sense, at another in a spiritual sense, in one and the same passage? Something similar is found in the passage where the man who was blind from birth is cured.[222] After this, the Savior says, "For judgment I have come into this world so that those who do not see might see and those who see may become blind."[223] Here as well are not the words "to see" and "not to see" understood at one time in a bodily sense, at another spiritually? So then in the present passage as well, when the Apostle says that the righteousness of God is disclosed apart from law, the law of nature is understood; but when he says, "attested by the law and the prophets" he is referring to the law of Moses.

(8) But if you still think that what we have said is not yet complete, we shall add the following as well. Suppose it seems to anyone that it is one and the same law about which he says, "But now, apart from law, the righteousness of God has been disclosed," which is also that law about which he says, "attested by the law and the prophets." Well then, if God's righteousness has been disclosed apart from law, then it does not receive attestation from the law; but if it does receive attestation [M944] from the law, then it has not been disclosed apart from the law. Because these phrases are inseparable and cannot be severed on any rational grounds, then the righteousness of God must

218. Jn 4.35.
219. Jn 4.7.
220. Jn 4.10.
221. Jn 4.13–14.
222. Cf. Jn 9.1ff.
223. Jn 9.39.

be said to be disclosed by Christ Jesus, who attests to it, not in the law of nature, which is undoubtedly small and scanty, but in the law of Moses, not the law of Moses according to the letter but according to the Spirit, of which the same Apostle says, "For the law is spiritual."[224] But it is likewise attested in the prophets through him who spoke in them, the Spirit of God.

(9) There is moreover a noteworthy distinction made by the Apostle in relation to this expression, if one observes very carefully. It is customary in Greek to place ἄρθρα before nouns. Among us these might be called articles. Thus whenever Paul wants to designate the law of Moses, he customarily places an article before it; but when he wants natural law to be understood, he designates "law" without the article.[225] And so in this passage where he says, "But now, apart from law, the righteousness of God has been disclosed," "law" does not have an article; but in what follows where he says, "attested by *the* law and the prophets," in this second passage he has cited law with an article.

(10) If then the matter about the diverse meanings of the term "law" has become sufficiently clear, let us now see which righteousness is supposed to be disclosed apart from natural law. The Apostle Paul himself says elsewhere of Christ that "he has become for us wisdom from God and righteousness and holiness and redemption."[226] This righteousness of God, therefore, which is Christ, is indeed disclosed apart from the natural law, but not apart from the law of Moses or the prophets. For the law testifies to it just as he himself says, "You search the Scriptures, and they are those which offer testimony about me."[227] For the natural law can indeed supply explanations and give understanding, as we have said,[228] either of the things which equity de-

---

224. Rom 7.14.
225. Sanday & Headlam, *Romans*, p. 58, treat Origen's observation sympathetically and comment, "though it holds good generally, does not cover all the cases." As Wiles, *Divine Apostle*, p. 51, has pointed out, however, Origen has never claimed that this is an invariable rule. Origen draws attention to other significant uses of the definite article in *Hom in Lk* 35.7; *Comm in Jn* 2.2; 6.7; *Comm in Mt* 11.5.
226. 1 Cor 1.30.   227. Jn 5.39.
228. Cf. 2.9.1.

mands to be done among men or by its perception that God exists. But who can perceive from nature alone that Christ is the Son of God? It is therefore apart from this law that the righteousness of God, which is Christ,[229] has been disclosed, attested by the law of Moses and the prophets.

(11) But before we hasten to what comes next, it seems that even this observation ought not be omitted: he has put "knowledge" in relation to sin but "disclosure" in respect to righteousness. "For everything which is disclosed is light."[230] And if what is disclosed is light, sin, which is not light, is not disclosed but is known. It is in this way I understand the following passage, "Nothing is concealed which will not be disclosed, nothing is covered which will not be revealed."[231] But let us return to our theme.

(12) The law and the prophets then are witnesses of the righteousness of God; this righteousness is disclosed through faith in Jesus Christ to all who believe, among whom there is no distinction whether they believe as Jews or as Gentiles.[232] Notice, however, that [M945] he does not put down to faith alone the single cause of the disclosure of the righteousness of God, but he associates with it both the law and the prophets. The reason for this is that faith alone, apart from the law and the prophets, does not disclose the righteousness of God nor, on the other hand, do the law and the prophets disclose it apart from faith. Thus the one is rooted in the other so that perfection comes from both.[233]

(13) He says there is no distinction between Jews and Greeks since it is certain that all equally have come under sin, as became clear above.[234] And he says that now the righteousness of God, which is supported by testimonies in the law and the prophets, has also been given equally to all through faith in Je-

---

229. 1 Cor 1:30.   230. Eph 5.14.
231. Mt 10.26; Lk 8.17. For this form of the quote see 2.4.4; *Hom in Jer* 16.10; *Comm in Mt* 14.9.
232. Cf. 1.15.
233. This again appears to be directed against Marcion. Cf. 2.4.7. See Introduction (17). For the theme of the unity of the Testaments see 2.14.
234. Cf. 3.2.3.

BOOK 3, CHAPTER 7

sus Christ. But because all had come under sin, doubtless they were likewise estranged from the glory of God because they were able neither to receive it in any respect whatsoever nor to merit it. For how would a sinner dare to give glory to God, to whom the prophet says, "But God has said to the sinner: Why do you recite my righteous requirements?"[235] And again another Scripture says, "Praise is unseemly in the mouth of a sinner."[236] Therefore the righteousness of God through faith in Jesus Christ reaches to all who believe, whether they are Jews or Greeks. It justifies those who have been cleansed from their past crimes and makes them capable of receiving the glory of God; and it supplies this glory not for the sake of their merits nor for the sake of works, but freely to those who believe.[237]

(14) "Through the redemption," he says, "which is in Christ Jesus."[238] Let us look carefully at the meaning of "redemption which is in Christ Jesus." The term "redemption" refers to that which is given to enemies for those whom they are keeping in captivity, in order that they might restore them to their original freedom.[239] Captives conquered by sin, as if by war, were being held fast, then, by the enemies of the human race. The Son of God came, who "has become for us" not only "wisdom from God and righteousness and holiness" but also "redemption."[240] He gave himself as the redemption price,[241] that is to say, he handed himself over to the enemies and, what is more, poured out his own blood to those thirsting for it;[242] and this is the redemption accomplished for those who believe, just as Peter also writes in his epistle when he says, "You were redeemed not with perishable silver or gold, but with the precious blood of the only begotten Son of God."[243] Perhaps even Solomon was describing this under a mystery when he said, "The redemption price of a man's soul is his own wealth."[244] For if you ask what the wealth of the soul is, you will discover that its wealth is wisdom, righteousness, and holiness. But the Apostle says that

---

235. Ps 50.16.
237. Cf. 1.3.3.
239. Cf. *Comm in Jn* 1.34.
241. 1 Tm 2.6.
243. 1 Pt 1.18–19.

236. Sir 15.9.
238. Rom 3.24.
240. 1 Cor 1.30.
242. Cf. 2.13.29; 4.11.4.
244. Prv 13.8.

Christ is all these things.[245] Christ then is the soul's wealth and therefore he himself is the soul's redemption price.[246] For material wealth ought to be regarded as the ruin of the soul rather than its redemption price, unless it should be converted into good works and becomes righteousness and mercy and is transformed from material wealth into the wealth of the soul. [M946]

8. *Whom God pre-determined*[247] *as a propitiation through faith in his blood, as a manifestation of his righteousness, through the remission of previously committed sins, in the forbearance of God, as a manifestation of his righteousness in this time, that he himself might be just in justifying him who is from faith in Jesus Christ.*[248] Although the holy Apostle has taught us many things about our Lord and Savior Jesus Christ which are to be marveled at, things which are spoken about him through a mystery, in this passage he has brought forth something even more admirable which I do not think is easy to find in other passages of Scripture. For above he had said that Christ had given his very self as the redemption price[249] for the entire human race so that he might redeem those who were being held in the captivity of their sins,[250] when "apart from God he tastes death for everyone."[251] Now he has added something even more profound and says, "God pre-determined him as a propitiation through faith in his blood."[252] This means of course that through the sacrifice of himself[253] he would make God propitious to men and through this he would manifest his own righteousness as he forgives them their past sins, which they had contracted by serving the worst tyrants at the time when God was tolerating and allowing this to be done. God allowed this so that afterwards, i.e., at this time, he would manifest his own

---

245. 1 Cor 1.30. Cf. 1.1.3; 2.5.6.   246. Cf. *Hom in Lv* 9.7; *Cels* 7.21.
247. *Proposuit.* Because Origen sees temporal significance in this word, I translate it so. Cf. 3.8.9.
248. Rom 3.25–26.   249. Cf. Rom 3.24; 1 Tm 2.6.
250. Cf. 3.7.14.
251. Heb 2.9. For this reading see 5.7.6. Origen knew of both readings: χωρὶς θεοῦ and χάριτι θεοῦ. Cf. *Comm in Jn* 1.35.
252. Cf. *Hom in Lv* 9.5; 9.10.
253. Cf. Heb 9.26.

righteousness. For at the consummation of the age,²⁵⁴ at the end of time, God disclosed his own righteousness and, for the redemption price, gave him whom he made a propitiator. If perchance he would have sent the propitiator earlier, he would not have made propitiation unto God for so many of the human race as was accomplished at this time, when the world now appears to be filled with men.²⁵⁵ For God is just, and the one who is just could not justify the unjust; for that reason he wanted there to be the mediation of a propitiator so that those who were not able to be justified through their own works might be justified through faith in him. These things had to be said first, as much as pertains to the explanation of his discourse, in order that the apostolic reading might become clearer.

(2) But now, in keeping with our custom, let us endeavor to ascertain what the inner meaning of the apostolic discourse may contain. First of all, in what manner was it said, "Whom God predetermined as a propitiatory," or propitiator,²⁵⁶ "through faith in his blood"? It is certain that in nearly every passage, the Apostle's meaning flows from the treasure chambers of the law and the prophets. Let us inquire then where he may have found the term "propitiatory" and from which passage he may have taken this word. I recall that in Exodus the Lord was speaking to Moses and was instructing him in what he was supposed to do. First he orders an ark to be made along with carrying poles and rings through the sides of the ark.²⁵⁷ After this he says, "And you shall make a propitiatory of pure gold; two cubits and a half shall be its length, and one cubit and a half its width. And you shall make two golden cherubim out of hammered work, [M947] and you shall place them over the two ends of the propitiatory, one cherub at the one end, and the other cherub at

---

254. Cf. Heb 9.26.   255. Cf. *Cels* 2.30.
256. *Propitiatorium sive propitiatorem.* Notice that the lemma reads "propitiation." Heither in Origenes, *Commentarii,* 2:114 n. 59, helps to clarify this: In Rom 3:25 Paul uses the term, ἱλαστήριον, the LXX designation for the cover of the Ark of the Covenant, i.e., the mercy seat. [cf. Ex 25.17] It is a substantival adjective and means "that which propitiates," but here in the accusative case it can mean "the one who propitiates." This is why Rufinus translates *propitiatorium sive propitiatorem.*
257. Cf. Ex 25.10ff.

the other end of the propitiatory. And you shall make the two cherubim from its two ends, spreading out their wings and overshadowing the propitiatory, facing one another. The faces of the cherubim will be over the propitiatory. You shall put the propitiatory on the top of the ark; and in the ark you shall put the testimonies that I shall give you. There I will become known to you, and from above the propitiatory, from between the two cherubim that are on the ark of the covenant, I will speak to you according to all which I will command you for the sons of Israel."[258] It seemingly appears that the Apostle found the word "propitiatory" in this passage and now has recorded it in his own writings, of which our current discourse is speaking. It also seems that this propitiatory which had been written about in Exodus referred to nothing other than the Savior and Lord since it says, "God pre-determined him as a propitiatory through faith."

(3) Indeed, it is worth the trouble to investigate the manner in which that object, described in Exodus as having been made of pure gold, has become the form and figure of the true propitiatory.[259] First of all, one must consider in which places the gold which is employed in the work is called "pure gold" and in which places it is recorded merely as "gold" without any adjective. After observing many passages, what I think I have detected is this: wherever it is called "gold" with the addition of the word "pure," he indicates that holy and pure soul of Jesus which "committed no sin nor was deceit found in his mouth."[260] This is congruent also with the measure of length and width of the propitiatory, though it may be hard to explain these matters and to fit all the details which are recorded about the propitiatory to that holy soul.

(4) Let us first observe that it says that the length of the propitiatory was neither merely two cubits, which is the number customarily applied to bodies which must be united and created, nor a full three cubits, a number that customarily exceeds the title of "creature" and which is reserved for incorporeal nature. It says therefore that the length of the propitiatory is two cubits and a half and it is one and a half in width. But if it is

---

258. Ex 25.17–22. 259. Cf. *Comm in Jn* 1.33.
260. Is 53.9; 1 Pt 2.22. Cf. *Comm in Cant* 2.

proper to be bold in such matters, in view of the fact that the same Apostle says about Christ that, "he is the mediator between God and men,"[261] it seems to me that this soul is intermediate between God and men.[262] It may be indeed less than the nature of the Trinity, since it measures somewhat less [than three]; but nevertheless, though it may be lower, it is not on that account mingled with the number two, which is reserved for things consigned to bodies, without the exceptional and preeminent excellence of its own powers. For this is shown in that it designates its measure [M948] as being somewhat more than two but less than three [cubits]. Yet also its increased width is said to be one and a half cubits, departing indeed from its single and unique status,[263] yet not completely sinking down to the number two, which is sometimes appointed even for unclean things. For although he had taken on the flesh of our nature, it was nevertheless conceived by an undefiled virgin and formed by the chaste operation of the Holy Spirit.[264] For that reason then the Apostle, when discussing the mediator, indicated this by a plain distinction by saying, "the mediator between God and men, the man Christ Jesus";[265] by which he was obviously teaching that "mediator" must be referred not to Christ's deity but to his humanity, i.e., his soul.[266] Both its length and width are therefore recorded. The length signifies that which pertains to God and is associated with the Trinity; the width signifies that he abides among men who customarily go along the wide and spacious road;[267] and therefore he is rightly called by the name of "mediator," since, as we have said, this holy soul was a certain mid-point between the divinity of the Trinity and the frailty of humanity.[268]

(5) It can therefore be understood as the propitiatory in accordance with what we have said above. Over it two cherubim are said to have been placed, one on one end and one on the other end.[269] What figure then should be understood to be contained in the two cherubim? For "cherubim," when translated

---

261. 1 Tm 2.5.
263. Cf. *Hom in Nm* 21.2.
265. 1 Tm 2.5.
267. Cf. Mt 7.13.
269. Cf. Ex 25.18–19.

262. Cf. *Princ* 2.6.3; *Cels* 3.34.
264. Cf. 5.9.10; 6.12.4.
266. Cf. 1.6.2 n. 185.
268. Cf. *Hom in Gn* 2.5; *Princ* 2.6.3.

into our language, means "the fullness of knowledge."[270] Where then would we say there is a fullness of knowledge if not in him of whom the Apostle says, "In whom are hidden the treasures of wisdom and knowledge"?[271] Surely the Apostle is saying these things about the Word of God. Moreover, he writes similar things about the Holy Spirit when he says, "But God has revealed it to us through his Spirit; for the Spirit searches all things, even the deep things of God."[272] Therefore he signifies, as I think, that the Word of God, who is the only begotten Son, and his Holy Spirit always dwell in the propitiatory, that is, in the soul of Jesus, and that is what the two cherubim placed over the propitiatory indicate.[273] Moreover, notice that he has not said "one cherub at the right end and the other cherub at the left end," but it says, "one cherub at one end and the other cherub at the other end"[274] in order to show that in the propitiatory, that is in the soul of Jesus, there was nothing evil.[275]

(6) But these two cherubim are winged creatures; and not only are they furnished with wings but they even have their wings spread out. If one of the saints has merited the right to possess the supreme attestation from God, it is said that God is with him, as is said to Joshua[276] son of Nun, "And God was with him just as he was [M949] with his servant Moses."[277] But if anywhere God promises an even greater reward, it is when God says, "I shall be among them and I shall walk among them."[278] Now among men you will find no soul this blessed and this exalted except that one alone in which the Word of God and the Holy Spirit find such a great breadth and such a great volume that they are said not only to indwell [that soul] but to spread forth their wings and sometimes even fly about,[279] according to

---

270. Cf. *Hom in Nm* 5.3; 10.3; *Hom in Ezek* 1.15; *Comm in Cant* 2; Origen's allegorical exegesis in this section draws heavily on Philo, (*On Moses* 2; *Questions and Answers on Exodus* 2.62). In effect, Origen has applied Philo's allegories to the subject of the Trinity. Cf. Clement, *Stromateis* 5.6.35.6.

271. Col 2.3.
272. 1 Cor 2.10.
273. Ex 28.18.
274. Ex 25.19.
275. *Sinistrum* means both "left" and "evil." The Greek εὐώνυμος, "well-named" is itself a euphemism and expresses what is unlucky.
276. *Jesus.*
277. Jos 1.5; 6.27.
278. Lv 26.12. See also 2.6.6.
279. Cf. Is 6.2.

a new institution of the mystery.[280] Both cherubim are also said to be facing each other over this blessed soul, by which fact an understanding of divinity, united and harmonious with [the soul], is infused by the Son of God and the Holy Spirit.

(7) Now, where is this soul placed which has been filled with God and in which all the fullness of deity has been pleased to dwell?[281] It says, "over the ark of the covenant."[282] The ark of the covenant can be understood of his holy flesh in which this blessed soul is placed, possessing within itself the testimonies[283] of God which are understood as matters of Christ prophesied in times past by the divine testimonies as to what sufferings he would endure in the flesh. The heavenly powers can also be understood as the ark. They too are capable of containing the Word of God and the Holy Spirit; but the soul of Jesus is placed before them, and by his mediation, as it were, they receive the divinely bestowed grace.[284]

(8) After these things he says, "And I shall become known to you from that place, and I shall speak to you from above the propitiatory."[285] This applies not only to Moses but to any saint who is a servant of God. God does not become known from another place nor is he known from any other location except from that propitiatory, which we have expounded above, and from the midst of the cherubim. For Habakkuk the prophet indicates this as well when he says, "In the midst of the two living creatures you will be known; when the years draw near, you will be known, when the time has come you will be manifested."[286] "For no one knows the Father except the Son, and him to whom the Son wants to reveal him."[287] Moreover Paul says, "God revealed it to us through his Spirit."[288] For that reason, then, he says, "I shall become known to you from that place and I shall speak to you from above the propitiatory between the two cherubim which are above the ark of the covenant."[289]

---

280. Cf. *Princ* 1.3.4; 4.3.14.
281. Cf. Col 1.19; 2.9.
282. Ex 25.21; *arca testamenti*.
283. *Testimonia*.
284. A different interpretation is given in *Hom in Nm* 10.3.
285. Ex 25.22. Cf. Philo, *Questions and Answers on Exodus* 2.67.
286. Hab 3.2 LXX.
287. Mt 11.27.
288. 1 Cor 2.10.
289. Ex 25.22.

(9) Now I think that these matters which we have taken from Exodus have been appropriately explained so that the sense might become clearer of how the Apostle adopts the term "propitiatory" in the passage presently under discussion, when he says, "Whom God pre-determined as a propitiatory through faith." His expression, "pre-determined" is better understood as said of the soul of Jesus than about his deity. For "pre-determine" means "previously to determine," which means that it was prior. For what is, is "determined"; what not yet is, is "pre-determined."[290] It was therefore not fitting to say of him who always was, i.e., the Word of God, that he has been pre-determined. [M950] It does not seem unsuitable, however, to say this of his soul which is, to be sure, inseparable from the Word of God, but nevertheless has been created and is posterior to his uniquely begotten deity.[291] It will not seem inappropriate to be said of this soul that before it was, it was pre-determined and preordained that it would be a propitiatory.

(10) Therefore since, in accordance with what we have explained above, God "pre-determined" Jesus Christ "as a propitiatory through faith in his blood," it seems necessary to inquire from the divine laws which propitiation is accomplished by means of blood so that from this we might be able to deduce how a propitiation has also been accomplished through the blood of Jesus. It is written in Leviticus, after [regulations concerning] the priestly sacrifice, "If the whole congregation of Israel errs unintentionally and the word escapes the notice of the assembly, and they do any one of the things that by the Lord's commandments ought not to be done, and they transgress and the sin they have committed becomes known to them, the assembly shall offer a bull of the herd as a sin offering";[292] and a few words later, "The anointed priest shall bring some of the blood of the bull into the tabernacle of testimony";[293] and again after a few words, "He shall do with the bull just as is done with the bull of sin offering; and the priest shall make propitiation for them, and they shall be forgiven."[294] So then, it is by means

---

290. Cf. 1.5.1.
292. Lv 4.13–14.
294. Lv 4.20.

291. Cf. *Princ* 2.6.3; *Cels* 6.47.
293. Lv 4.16.

of blood that the priest makes re-propitiation for the entire assembly so that they may be forgiven.

(11) Let us now examine each of the designations recorded of the Savior, and let us carefully ponder what it is that is being depicted in his individual titles. You will thus find that indeed in him all the fullness of deity was pleased to dwell in bodily form.[295] He is also the propitiatory and priest and sacrifice which is offered for the people.[296] Now of the propitiatory enough has already been said. But of the priesthood both David, in the Psalms, and the Apostle Paul, in Hebrews, plainly write.[297] That he would also be a sacrifice John testifies when he says, "This is the lamb of God who takes away the sin of the world."[298] In accordance with this, then, that he is a sacrifice, propitiation is effected by the shedding of his own blood for the forgiveness of past sins. And this propitiation comes to every believer by way of faith. For unless he were to grant the forgiveness of past sins, the propitiation could not be proven to have been accomplished. But since forgiveness of sins is being bestowed, it is certain that a propitiation has been performed by the shedding of his sacred blood. "For without the shedding of blood," as the Apostle says, "there is no forgiveness" of sins.[299]

(12) But lest it appear to you that Paul alone has dared to use the term "propitiation" in reference to Christ, listen to how John speaks with an understanding concordant to this when he says, "My little children, I am writing these things to you so that you may not sin, [M951] and if anyone does sin, we have an advocate with the Father, Jesus Christ the righteous; and he is the propitiation for our sins, not for ours only but also for the whole world."[300] With one and the same understanding, then, the apostles designate Christ as the propitiatory, or propitiation, or, as is frequently found in the Latin manuscripts, propitiator. There is however no difference whether "propitiator" or "propitiation" or even "appeasement" is recorded, since in

---

295. Cf. Col 1.19; 2.9.
296. Cf. *Comm in Jn* 1.35; *Comm in Cant* 1.
297. Cf. Ps 110.4; Heb 2.17.   298. Jn 1.29.
299. Heb 9.22.
300. 1 Jn 2.1–2. Cf. *Comm in Jn* 1.22.

Greek it is always expressed by one and the same word. Unless it should seem to some that "propitiation" is understood of his divine substance whereas "propitiator" is understood when he fulfills his services among men.

(13) But what John has said, namely that he is "the appeasement" or propitiation "for our sins, and not only for ours but also for the whole world,"[301] appears to have introduced even greater mysteries for us. For he is making known that Jesus is the propitiator not only of believers and the faithful but also of the whole world; yet not first of the world and then of us, but first of us and only then of the whole world. For although the entire creation is awaiting the grace of the redeemer,[302] nevertheless each one shall come to salvation in its own order.[303] This, I think, is indicated as well in Leviticus when sacrifices of re-propitiation are commanded to be offered through the high priest.[304] Yet in these instructions the order of the sacrifices is not set forth in a confused manner. Rather it is certainly said in the first place which propitiation and what sort of sacrifice should be offered when the priest has sinned;[305] second, it tells us what sort of sacrificial victims are pleasing to God when the entire congregation transgresses out of ignorance;[306] third, it is recorded by which ordinance the ruler must be cleansed when he has sinned;[307] fourth, it is explained what rite exists for the expiation of the individual soul who sins.[308] By a mystical understanding, each of these things, through certain specific ordinances, modes, and reasons, depict the future propitiation of Christ, which was not only for our sins but also for the whole world.[309] But whoever has been illuminated by the Holy Spirit must consider these things in accordance with that revelation which is said to have been made known to Moses on the mountain.[310]

(14) Through the re-propitiation by Christ's blood, then,

---

301. 1 Jn 2.2.
302. Cf. Rom 8.9.
303. Cf. 1 Cor 15.23.
304. Cf. Lv 4.20.
305. Lv 4.3ff.
306. Lv 4.13ff.
307. Lv 4.22ff.
308. Lv 4.27ff.
309. 1 Jn 2.2. Cf. *Hom in Lv* 1.2; *Comm in Jn* 1.3.
310. Ex 25.9, 40; 26.30; Heb 8.5.

comes the forgiveness of past sins, in God's forbearance, as a manifestation of his own righteousness. It is "God's forbearance" when a sinner is not at once punished when he sins, but instead, in accordance with what the same Apostle has said, is led by God's patience to repentance;[311] and in this God is said to manifest his own righteousness. However it says well in addition, "at this time"; for in the present age God's righteousness comes with forbearance, but in the future age it will come with retribution. For God has deemed it just to commit the present age to forbearance and patience, since the future age [M952] has been appointed for judgment. For if he were to punish the sinner in this present time, he would not seem just to call forth again to judgment the one whom he had already punished. But if he shows forbearance and exercises patience in the present age he will rightly be a just judge in the future.[312] So then he justifies him who is of faith; just as has also been written about Abraham, that "Abraham believed God and it was reckoned to him for righteousness."[313] Now if Abraham believed and was justified by faith, doubtless it will be logical that even now whoever believes in God through faith in Jesus Christ would be justified with the believer Abraham.[314]

9. *Where then is your boasting? It is excluded. Through what law? Through that of works? No, but through the law of faith. For we hold that a man is justified through faith without works of the law.*[315] Once again, we often remind those who desire to give careful attention to the things Paul has written to observe tenaciously that distinction about which we have spoken above, namely, how [Paul] (always in a discreet manner) now assails the circumcision group, now the uncircumcision, that is, the Jews and Gentiles, respectively.[316] For if a trifling bit should escape the reader's attention, immediately the extremely narrow path to understanding will be thrown into disorder.

(2) Therefore, the Apostle had made known above what ad-

---

311. Cf. Rom 2.4.
313. Gn 15.6; Rom 4.3; Gal 3.6; Jas 2.23.
314. Cf. Gal 3.9.
316. Cf. 2.14.1–3; 3.2.2; 3.1.2–3.
312. Cf. *Hom in Lv* 11.2; 14.4.
315. Rom 3.27–28.

vantage the Jew possessed and what value there was in circumcision and he had taught that the oracles of God were first entrusted to them.[317] And by these words he had seemed to be eliciting boasting from [the Jews], with which they were accustomed to raise themselves up against the Gentiles. On the other hand, in what followed he had countered that the righteousness of God through faith in Jesus Christ is for all who believe that there is no distinction, but all have sinned, both Jews and Greeks, and lack the glory of God and are justified through the grace and redemption which is in Christ Jesus. He himself is the propitiatory through faith, and all who are of faith are justified by him.[318] In this current passage, the Apostle, as if establishing the conclusion of his previous arguments, now says, "Where then is your boasting? It is excluded. Through what law? That of works? No, but through the law of faith. For we hold that a man is justified through faith without works of law." He is saying that the justification of faith alone suffices, so that the one who only believes is justified, even if he has not accomplished a single work.[319]

(3) It is incumbent upon us, therefore, as those who are attempting to defend the harmoniousness of the Apostle's writings and to establish that they are entirely consistent in their arrangement,[320] that we should ask: Who has been justified by faith alone[321] without works of the law? Thus, in my opinion, that thief who was crucified with Christ should suffice for a suitable example. He called out to him from the cross, "Lord Jesus, remember me when you come into your kingdom!"[322] In the Gospels nothing else is recorded [M953] about his good works, but for the sake of this faith alone Jesus said to him, "Truly I say to you: Today you will be with me in paradise."[323] If it seems appropriate, let us now apply the words of the Apostle Paul to the

---

317. Cf. Rom 3.1–2.   318. Cf. Rom 3.22–26.
319. Cf. 3.9.3–4; 4.1.18. See Introduction (18).
320. Cf. 3.7.4.
321. *Sola fide.* C. E. B. Cranfield, *A Critical and Exegetical Commentary on the Epistle to the Romans*, 2 vols. (Edinburgh: T. & T. Clark, 1975, 1985), 1:221 n. 3, notes the similarity between Origen's words and Luther's well known translation of Rom 3:28: *allein durch den Glauben*, "through faith alone."
322. Lk 23.42. Cf. 4.1.16.   323. Lk 23.43.

case of this thief and say to the Jews, "Where then is your boasting?" Certainly it is excluded, but excluded not through the law of works but through the law of faith. For through faith this thief was justified without works of the law, since the Lord did not require in addition to this that he should first accomplish works, nor did he wait for him to perform some works when he had believed. But by his confession alone the one who was about to begin his journey to paradise received him as a justified traveling companion with himself.

(4) Moreover there is the case of that woman concerning whom it is mentioned in the Gospel according to Luke, "When she learned that Jesus was reclining in the Pharisee's house, she brought a jar of ointment. And standing behind him at his feet and weeping, she bathed his feet with her tears and dried them with the hair of her head. And she was kissing his feet and anointing them with the ointment. Now when the Pharisee who had invited him saw it, he said to himself, 'If this man were a prophet, he would certainly have known who and what kind of woman this is who is touching his feet—that she is a sinner.'"[324] But Jesus told him that parable of the five hundred and the fifty denarii. It was on the basis of no work of the law but for the sake of faith alone that he said to her, "Your sins are forgiven you";[325] and again, "Your faith has saved you. Go in peace."[326] Furthermore in many passages of the Gospel we read that the Savior has used this phrase to say that the faith of the believer is the cause of his salvation.[327] From all of these things he is making clear that the Apostle is correct to hold that a man is justified through faith without works of law. But perhaps someone who hears these things should become lax and negligent in doing good, if in fact faith alone suffices for him to be justified. To this person we shall say that if anyone acts unjustly after justification, it is scarcely to be doubted that he has rejected the grace of justification.[328] For a person does not receive the forgiveness of sins in order that he should once again imagine that

---

324. Lk 7.37–39.   325. Lk 7.48.
326. Lk 7.50.
327. Cf. e.g. Mt 9.22; Mk 5.34; 10.52; Lk 8.48; 17.19; 18.42.
328. Cf. Gal 2.21. See also *Hom in Jos* 5.6.

he has been given a license to sin; for the remission is not given for future crimes, but only past ones.[329]

(5) Now then let us return to our theme. A human being is justified through faith; the works of the law contribute nothing to his being justified. But where there is no faith which justifies the believer, even if one possesses works from the law, nevertheless because they have not been built upon the foundation of faith,[330] although they might appear to be good things, nevertheless they are not able to justify the one doing them, because from them faith is absent, which is the sign of those who are justified by God.[331] This is what we have said above,[332] "Abraham believed God and it was reckoned to him for righteousness."[333] So much so is this the case that according to Paul the one who is justified through the grace of faith says, "For the grace [M954] of God which was given to me was not without effect."[334] Therefore all boasting which comes from the works of the law is excluded.

(6) In order that what we are saying might become even clearer, we shall cite an example from those which are recorded in the Gospel. "A Pharisee and a tax collector went up to the temple of God. And the Pharisee," it says, "standing in the middle, was saying, God, I thank you that I am not like other men: thieves, the unjust, adulterers, or like this tax collector. I fast twice a week; I give a tenth of everything I possess,"[335] and so on. Very possibly the Pharisee was speaking the truth when he said these things; yet in the Lord's opinion this man, who was corrupted by the vice of ostentatious boasting, did not go down from the temple a justified man. Such boasting then, which was coming from the works of the law, is excluded, because it does not embrace the humility of the cross of Christ. Listen to what one says who boasts in the cross, "May I never boast except in the cross of my Lord Jesus Christ, through whom the world has been crucified to me, and I to the world."[336] You see that the

---

329. Cf. Rom 3.25.
330. Cf. Col 1.23; 2 Tm 2.19. See also *Hom in Jos* 4.3; *Comm in Mt* 16.9.
331. Cf. Rom 4.11. See also 2.7.3; 2.7.6; *Hom in Nm* 12.4; *Hom in Ezek* 13.2.
332. Cf. 3.8.14.   333. Rom 4.3.
334. 1 Cor 15.10.   335. Lk 18.10–12, 14.
336. Gal 6.14.

Apostle does not boast about his own righteousness nor about chastity nor about wisdom nor about his other virtues and deeds, but he declares with the utmost openness and says, "Let him who boasts, boast in the Lord."

(7) And so, Judaic boasting is excluded, not through the law of works but through the law of faith, which is in Christ Jesus, in whose cross the Apostle boasts. For who will legitimately boast about his own chastity when he reads what is written, "anyone who has looked at a woman to lust after her has already committed adultery with her in his heart"?[337] This is why the prophet also says, "How will someone boast that his heart is pure?"[338] Or who will boast about his wisdom when he observes that it is written, "The world through wisdom did not know God; and therefore God was pleased through the foolishness of what was preached to save those who believe,"[339] and again, "God chose the foolish things of the world to confound the wise"?[340] And who will boast about his own righteousness when he hears God saying through the prophet, "all your righteousness is like the rag of a menstruous woman."[341] The only just boasting then is based upon faith in the cross of Christ, which excludes all boasting that derives from the works of the law.[342]

(8) We have said these things because the Apostle has stated, as if in the language of an investigator, "Where then is your boasting?" And to this question he has given himself the answer, "It is excluded." And again, as though he were interrogating, he says, "Through what law? That of works?" And he responds to himself, "No, but through the law of faith. For we hold that a man is justified through faith without works of the law." We have already spoken about these matters above. But he again makes mention of two laws even in this present passage. [M955] He says the "law of works" and the "law of faith." You who read should consider whether this expression ought to be applied to the law of Moses and the natural law, or to the law of the letter and the law of the Spirit; for the law of the letter kills

---

337. Mt 5.28.
338. Prv 20.9.
339. 1 Cor 1.21.
340. 1 Cor 1.27.
341. Is 64.6.
342. 1 Cor 1.31. See Introduction (19).

and works death,[343] but the law of the Spirit of life sets free from the law of sin and death.[344] He therefore appropriately adds in what follows:

> 10. *Or is God the God of Jews only? Is he not the God of Gentiles also? Yes, of Gentiles also. Since God is one who will justify the circumcision from faith and the uncircumcision through faith.*[345] Certainly, those who want there to be one God of the Jews and another God of the Gentiles, that is to say, one God of the law and another God of the Gospels,[346] will be hard-pressed and constrained to give an adequate reply to the Apostle Paul, abundantly satisfying his thought. He says that not only is there only one God of the Jews and Gentiles, but he says additionally that he is the very same one who justifies the circumcision from faith and the uncircumcision through faith. Now if they want to interpret circumcision here allegorically in order to claim that [Paul] is designating the saints and the spiritual as the circumcision, they shall immediately meet with an obstacle in the words which follow. For if he has designated the circumcision to be the saints, or, as they designate them, the "pneumatics," the logical inference would be that he would designate the uncircumcision to be sinners, whom they call "natural men." How then shall it be congruent that the good God should justify spiritual and natural men equally? Consequently, the Apostle's words present these interpreters[347] with an inextricable knot. To us, however, the explanation will be plain and easy: We claim that the circumcision refers to Jewish believers, and the uncircumcision, no less, refers to those who have been called to faith from the Gentiles. For the very same God justifies members of both peoples who believe, and this is based not upon the privilege of circumcision or uncircumcision but in consideration of faith alone.[348]

---

343. Cf. 2 Cor 3.6; Rom 7.13.   344. Cf. Rom 8.2.
345. Rom 3.29–30.
346. Intended is Marcion. Cf. 2.14.11; 3.11.2; 4.7.4; *Comm in Jn* 13.17.
347. A comparison with *Cels* 5.61 shows that the followers of Valentinus are intended here. Notice that Origen condemns the allegorical interpretation as an artifice of the heretics and defends the literal understanding.
348. Cf. 3.9.2 n. 319.

BOOK 3, CHAPTER 10

(2) There remains a difference of one syllable, by which the Apostle seems to make a differentiation of meaning, which we should not casually pass over. He says that God justifies the circumcision *from* faith and not *through* faith; but the uncircumcision *through* faith and not *from* faith. That alteration of prepositions, it seems to me, was not uttered by him purposelessly. For we find in other passages of [Paul] that [prepositions] are not used arbitrarily but in a carefully considered fashion, and the necessary difference of this distinction is preserved. For instance, when speaking of God he says, "Because all things are from him and through him and in him."[349] And again in another passage he says, "For as the woman is from the man, so also the man is through the woman, but all things are from God."[350] What he writes to the Corinthians is similar, "Now to one a word of wisdom is given through the Spirit, [M956] to another a word of knowledge according to the same Spirit, to another faith in the same Spirit."[351] But Paul is not the only apostle who maintains distinctions in the use of prepositions, but John does this as well. When, for example, he says of the Word of God that "all things were made through him,"[352] he testifies that life was not made *through* him but *in* him. For he says, "What was made is life in him."[353]

(3) Now since it would be too much to explain all the passages we have just now produced as examples, let us briefly summarize the sense of them as well as we can. When "from him" is said, something originative seems to be indicated under the token of this preposition. But when "through him" is said, the intelligence of a secondary cause, that is to say, one which is after the principal cause, is designated.[354] For instance we might cite what [Paul] says, "All things are from him and through him and in him."[355] "From him" means the initial creation of all things and that the things which exist received their beginning "from God." "Through him" signifies that the things which were previously made are being ruled and superintend-

---

349. Rom 11.36.
350. 1 Cor 11.12.
351. 1 Cor 12.8–9.
352. Jn 1.1–3.
353. Jn 1.3–4.
354. Cf. *Comm in Jn* 2.10; 1.18; Philo, *On the Cherubim* 35.125–126.
355. Rom 11.36.

ed "through" him from whom they derive the beginning of their existence. "In him" means that those who have now been reformed and corrected stand firm "in" his perfection. So then just as these things contain differences of the most pregnant meaning, these things are taught: We are said to possess "from God" the fact that we exist; that we are being superintended and ruled is designated to come to pass "through him"; and that we stand firm in the summit of perfection is said to take place "in him."[356]

(4) Moreover it is possible to observe such a distinction in the present passage as well. It is noted that the circumcision who are justified, as it were, in the first place and first in order, need to be justified *from* faith and not *through* faith. The uncircumcision, however, because they are drawn to justification in the second place, are said to need to be justified not *from* faith but *through* faith. I think that in this verse that differentiation we mentioned above, "For just as the woman is from the man, so also the man comes through the woman,"[357] is being designated in a stronger degree. For in the first place it is the man *from* whom the woman descends, not *through* the man.[358] In the second place, however, the man comes through the woman, because the woman seems to serve in some manner as a helper to the man, her source. This is why the man is said to be born through the woman and not from the woman.

(5) But perhaps someone may respond to our interpretation about the woman and the man and object that the Apostle has said about Christ, "He was made from a woman, made under the law,"[359] and he did not say, "made through a woman." The following, I think, should be said in response to this. Of every human being it will indeed be fitting to say that he has been made through a woman, since indeed he received his origin from a man before he was born through a woman. Christ, however, who has not assumed the origin of his flesh from a man's seed, [M957] is rightly said to have been made "from a woman."[360] For to her, i.e., to the woman, the principal origin

---

356. Cf. 8.13.10; *Cels* 6.65.
358. Cf. 1 Cor 11.8.
360. Gal 4.4.

357. 1 Cor 11.12.
359. Gal 4.4.

of his flesh is itself ascribed; and so the Apostle rightly records that he was made not through a woman but "from a woman."³⁶¹ One and the same God therefore will justify the circumcision from faith and the uncircumcision through faith. Now suppose someone with even more curiosity asks: Through whom are those who are justified from faith justified? and again: From whom are those who are justified through faith justified? Although it is possible to see excessive curiosity in this, nevertheless we can respond appropriately: Those who are justified from faith, since the beginning was received from faith, need to be perfected through the fulfillment of good works; and those who are justified through faith, having begun with good works, receive the summit of perfection through faith. Thus both elements, being rooted in each other, need to be brought to perfection. It is for this very reason, I believe, that the Apostle has set down immediately in what follows:

11. *Do we then make void the law through faith? By no means! Instead we establish the law.*³⁶² Because in what was recorded above it seemed that everything referred entirely to faith, he alleges against himself the case which could be put forward by another and says: If a man is justified through faith and not from works of the law, and if God justifies the circumcision from faith and the uncircumcision through faith, are you then, O Paul, setting aside the law of Moses through faith? Yet he responds to himself against this objection and says, "By no means! On the contrary we establish the law," that is to say, we confirm it. Now it is worth the trouble to see in what sense [Paul] is declaring that the law is confirmed. Prior to this he had said that a man is not justified by works of the law.³⁶³ In the Gospels the Savior says, "Moses wrote about me."³⁶⁴ Whoever then does not believe in Christ, of whom Moses wrote in the law, sets aside the law; but he who believes in the Christ, of whom Moses writes, confirms the law through the faith by which he believes in Christ.

(2) Now we say that faith in the Father and the Son and the

---

361. 1 Cor 11.8. See also 5.1.13; *Cels* 1.70.
362. Rom 3.31.   363. Cf. Rom 3.20, 28.
364. Jn 5.46.

Holy Spirit is complete, full, and perfect. It acknowledges nothing inconsistent, discordant, or foreign in the Trinity. For Marcion, who claims that there is one God of the law and another who is the Father of Christ, neither establishes nor confirms the law through his own faith,[365] but he sets it aside. Ebion does this too.[366] In fact all who introduce any corruption into the catholic faith do this. I might appropriately add that everyone who, while believing in Christ, behaves well and keeps himself from every stain of sin confirms the law of God by living uprightly; but the one who plunges headfirst into sinful vices and without any restraining halter of repentance is stained by the constant repetition of evil deeds, this man, even if he may seem to believe in Christ, does not establish the law through his own faith but instead sets aside [M958] the law.

(3) By no means, however, should it appear that we are passing over that objection which someone can advance, saying that the Apostle seems to be writing mutually contradictory statements. For in the present passage he claims that he does not set aside the law but confirms it. But in Second Corinthians he writes the following, "Now if the ministry of death, chiseled in letters on stone tablets, came in glory so that the sons of Israel could not gaze at Moses' face because of the glory of his face, which is set aside, how much more will the ministry of the Spirit not be in glory?"[367] And a little bit later he says, "For if what is set aside came through glory, the permanent in glory is much more!"[368] It can be claimed then that, "the glory of Moses' face, which is set aside," and what he says, "for if what is set aside comes through glory," seem to contradict that thought where [Paul] declares, "We do not set aside the law through faith but we establish and confirm it."

(4) But consider whether we can resolve what is intended in the following manner. It is not the same thing to say, "we set aside the law," and, "the law is set aside." Thus in the present passage Paul is declaring that he himself does not set aside the

---

365. Cf. 3.10.1.
366. Cf. *Cels* 2.1; 5.61; 5.65; *Hom in Lk* 17.4 (= FOTC 94:72).
367. 2 Cor 3.7–8.
368. 2 Cor 3.11.

law. For even if the law is set aside through the glory which surpasses it,³⁶⁹ it is not set aside through Paul or through any other saint. This is also why the Lord was saying, "I have not come to destroy the law but to fulfill it."³⁷⁰ No saint then, not even the Lord himself, sets aside the law, but its temporal and transient glory is set aside and surpassed by the eternal and abiding glory. Consider then how carefully and with what sharp-sightedness the apostolic writings need to be read! He has not said, "For what was made glorious has not been glorified," and then reverted to silence—otherwise it would have been deemed a false statement; for how could that which is glorious not be glorified? But he has said additionally, "on account of the glory which surpasses it."³⁷¹ He wanted to show that the glory of Moses, that is to say, the glory of the law, is not set aside by some individual. But, as we have said, in comparison with the greater glory which is in Christ, the glory which is in the law is covered over and obscured. This is why he says, "For if what is set aside came through glory, the permanent in glory is much more."³⁷² That which is Christ's is permanent, he says; that which is of Moses is set aside; but set aside not through a human being but in comparison with the surpassing glory, as we have said; since indeed "the law was our pedagogue unto Christ"³⁷³ until the fullness of times should come.³⁷⁴ Just as we say that the task of a pedagogue is necessary only as long as the one who is under the pedagogue is little,³⁷⁵ and the duty of the pedagogue is set aside and becomes unnecessary when the one who was under the pedagogue reaches maturity; thus in the same way we shall say that [M959] the task of the law is set aside now that the fullness of time has arrived.³⁷⁶ And the son, who at one time differed in no respect from a slave,³⁷⁷ has become an heir of the father's property. But learn his custom with this word in other passages as well, that these things which the Apostle designates as things to be set aside should be under-

369. 2 Cor 3.10.
371. 2 Cor 3.10.
373. Gal 3.24.
375. Cf. Gal 4.1.
377. Cf. Gal 4.1.

370. Mt 5.17.
372. 2 Cor 3.11.
374. Cf. Gal 4.4.
376. Cf. Gal 4.4.

stood in this way, where he says, "We know in part and we prophesy in part. But when the perfect comes, the things which were in part must be set aside."[378] In that passage it is said that both Paul's knowledge and prophecy are set aside, yet no harm is done to his gift of apostolic grace. We should understand, of course, that in comparison with the perfect, that which is imperfect is superfluous and insignificant.

(5) So then in the expression under discussion, Paul certainly does not set aside the law but confirms it. But when the glory of Christ would be revealed, it silences and exposes and shows that the glory which appeared in Moses and by which he was glorified is not to be reckoned as glorious by the comparison in which [Christ's glory] surpasses it.[379] This is precisely [M960] what is said elsewhere, "He must increase but I must decrease";[380] and as Paul himself says, "But when I became a man I set aside the things of childhood."[381] He shows this also by the comparison with the pedagogue, whose task is set aside and comes to an end when the child reaches the age of maturity.[382] Therefore the Apostle has spoken with marvelous reserve, "Do we then set aside the law through faith? By no means!" He did not say: Is the law then set aside through faith, but, "do we then set aside the law?" Then in what follows, "No, but we establish the law." For even if the law is set aside, it is set aside not through the faith but through the all-surpassing glory.[383] Not only is the law not set aside through the faith, it is established and confirmed through the apostles.[384] For these very apostles are proclaiming that the Christ has now come, whom the law and the prophets predicted was going to come; and it is assuredly a confirmation of prophecy and of the law when what was predicted is shown to be fulfilled.

378. 1 Cor 13.9–10.
379. Cf. 2 Cor 3.10.
380. Jn 3.30.
381. 1 Cor 13.11.
382. Cf. Gal 3.24–25.
383. Cf. 2 Cor 3.10.
384. Cf. *Comm in Jn* 13.17.

THE FOURTH BOOK OF THE *COMMENTARY ON THE EPISTLE OF PAUL TO THE ROMANS*

WHAT THEN ARE WE TO SAY *Abraham found, our father according to the flesh? For if Abraham was justified by works, he has something to boast about, but not before God. For what does the Scripture say? "Abraham believed God, and it was reckoned to him as righteousness." Now to one who works, wages are not imputed as a gift but as something due; but to one who does not work but believes in him who justifies the ungodly, his faith is reckoned as righteousness. So also David speaks of the blessedness of the man to whom God credits righteousness apart from works: "Blessed are those whose iniquities are forgiven and whose sins are covered. Blessed is the man against whom the Lord will not impute sin."*[1]

(2) Up above [Paul] had set forth two kinds of laws, one of which he called the law of works and the other the law of faith. He says that through the law of faith the boasting of those who boast in the works of the law is excluded;[2] moreover he has declared that a man is justified by faith apart from works of the law.[3] Fittingly he now produces the example of Abraham in order that these matters may be affirmed from the Scriptures. He says, "If Abraham was justified by works, he has something to boast about, but not before God." He certainly discusses this not without dialectical logic. For suppose anyone who is justified by works does not have anything to boast about before God. But it is certain that Abraham does have a ground for boasting before God. Therefore it follows that Abraham has been justified not by works but by faith since he necessarily has a ground for boasting before God.[4] For this is what the Scrip-

---

1. Rom 4.1–8.   2. Cf. Rom 3.27.
3. Cf. Rom 3.28.
4. The argumentation has the form of a classical syllogism, as defined in Aristotle's *Analytica Priora*. Bammel, "Justification in Augustine and Origen," p.

ture declares, "Abraham believed God, and it was reckoned to him as righteousness."[5] But if God reckoned it to him as righteousness, it can hardly be doubted that his faith is also his ground of boasting before God. This is also why the Apostle adds his own assertion to this testimony, which he had taken from the book of Genesis, and says, "Now to one who works, wages are not imputed as a gift but as something due; but to one who does not work but believes in him who justifies the ungodly, his faith is reckoned as righteousness."

(3) Through this entire passage, then, the Apostle clearly makes known that there are two kinds of justification, one of which he designates as by works and the other by faith. He says that the one which is by works has a boast, but in itself and not before God. The one which is by faith, on the other hand, has a boast before God, as before the one who examines men's hearts[6] and knows who believes in secret and who does not believe. Therefore it is deservedly said that such a person has a boast before God alone, who sees his disposition of faith which is in secret.[7] However, it can come to pass for the person who hopes for the justification by works that his works may be approved by men as well. For whatever has been done by work and by hand is openly visible and can be seen with the eyes. And if faith is in secret yet works are openly visible, then it will be appropriate to include that which is written, "The secret things belong to the Lord your God, but what is manifested is for you and your sons."[8]

(4) In addition it will be appropriate to apply to these things [M961] that which is written, "The just shall live by my faith."[9] We shall fittingly say then that for those who are circumcised according to the inner man and who are Jews in secret in the spirit, not in the letter, their praise and boasting is not before men

---

224, discusses Origen's analysis of Paul's argument here. She observes that Origen's second premises, i.e., that Abraham has glory before God, is not present in Paul's text, but has been added by Origen. Cf. 4.1.5.
    5. Gn 15.6.   6. 1 Sm 16.7.
    7. Cf. Mt 6.4, 6, 18.   8. Dt 29.28 LXX.
    9. Hab 2.4 LXX; Rom 1.17; Heb 10.38. The LXX of Hab 2:4 differs from the MT by replacing the third person pronoun "his faith" by the first person "my faith." Paul retains neither pronoun in his citations of this passage.

BOOK 4, CHAPTER 1

but before God.[10] But as for those who are justified by works, since their works are openly visible and manifest, their boasting can be either before all the saints and the righteous, who receive authority from God for passing judgment upon visible human works, or even before angels and the other authorities of the heavenly powers who are certainly able to glorify the one whose works they have approved.[11]

(5) But since it is for God alone to know the secrets of the heart,[12] he perceives clearly whether any disposition of faith dwells in an individual; and therefore the one who is justified by faith has a boast before God alone, who alone is the observer of the secrets of faith. Therefore, he says, even Abraham, if he was justified by works, indeed has a boast coming from the works, but not that [boast] which is before God alone. But it is certain that Abraham has a boast before God alone. The inference then is that he was justified not by works but by faith.

(6) Now you should not imagine that if someone has such faith, by which, having been justified, he may have a boast before God, that he would be able at the same time to have unrighteousness with it as well.[13] For there is no common ground between faith and infidelity; there is no communion of righteousness with wickedness, just as light can have no fellowship with darkness.[14] For if "he who believes that Jesus is the Christ has been born of God"[15] and "he who has been born of God does not sin,"[16] it is plain that he who believes in Jesus Christ does not sin; and that if he sins, it is certain that he does not believe in him. Therefore the proof of true faith is that sin is not being committed, just as, on the contrary, where sin is being committed, there you have proof of unbelief.[17] For this reason then it is also said of Abraham in another passage of Scripture that he was justified by the works of faith.[18] For it is certain that he who truly believes works the work of faith and righteousness

---

10. Rom 2.29.
11. Cf. 1.9.4; *Mart* 18.
12. Cf. 1 Kgs 8.39; Acts 1.24. Cf. 2.1.1.
13. Cf. 4.7.6.
14. Cf. 2 Cor 6.14–15. See also *Comm in Jn* 19.21.
15. 1 Jn 5.1.
16. 1 Jn 3.9; 5.18.
17. Cf. 2.7.8; *Comm in Jn* 19.23.
18. Cf. Jas 2.21–22.

and of complete goodness and becomes capable of both kinds of boasting: both that which is in secret before God as well as that which is openly visible and is not only before God.

(7) Having explained these things to the best of my powers, it would not seem right for me to pass over the observation that Paul has referred to Abraham as "our father according to the flesh." Yet it seems that Abraham is the father of the Gentiles according to faith and not according to the flesh. For it is, of course, possible for the Apostle to call Abraham his father according to the flesh, seeing that Paul also descends from the Israelite race [M962] according to the flesh. Those who come from Ishmael and those who descend from Keturah's sons likewise can name Abraham their father according to the flesh.[19] But the rest of the Gentiles will call him a father in the spirit and not in the flesh; unless we choose, when caught in such narrow places, to turn to the breadth of allegorical interpretation, where the "father according to the flesh" can be taken to be him who would transmit the primary elements of fleshly doctrine, that is to say, of the law according to the letter, and who would stand out as a teacher of primary instruction in the divine law. That indeed teachers may be called fathers is something even the Apostle Paul says, "In Christ Jesus I became your father through the gospel."[20] But you who are reading ought to gather for yourself testimonies from the divine books pertaining to this.[21]

(8) In what follows is added, "Abraham believed God and it was reckoned to him as righteousness." This sentence is taken from the book of Genesis, from that passage where not Abraham but Abram[22] says to the Lord, "Because you have given me no offspring, this slave born in my house is to be my heir. And the Lord said to him, 'He shall not be your heir; no one but your very own issue shall be your heir.' He brought him outside and said to him, 'Look toward heaven and count the stars, if

---

19. Cf. Gn 25.1ff.
20. 1 Cor 4:15. Cf. 4.2.8–9.
21. The reader is often addressed in this way: cf. 1.4.4; 2.7.9; 4.2.9; 5.8.9; 5.9.11; 7.5.6; 7.5.7; 7.12.7; 8.10.3; 10.42.1.
22. Cf. 4.2.11.

you are able to count them.' And he said to him, 'So shall your descendants be.' And he believed God, and it was reckoned to him as righteousness."[23]

(9) We have extensively quoted these passages from the book of Genesis as an example, so that we might come to understand what was the cause of this justification. It must be very acutely examined to determine whether it is said that "his faith was reckoned as righteousness" merely on account of the fact that he believed that a son was going to be given him, and that from him offspring were going to be produced like the multitude of the stars; or was it on account of this and everything [else] which he had already believed beforehand? For it ought not be supposed that without faith he would have departed from his own homeland and from his own father's relatives and have gone to a land which God had showed him.[24] Nor was faith absent when Lot separated from him and the Lord said to him, "Raise your eyes and look from this place where you are standing, and look to the north and south and to the west and to the east; for all this land that you see I will give to you and to your descendants forever."[25] And who is going to say that when Abraham went and dwelled among the oaks of Mamre in Hebron and built there an altar to the Lord, it was done without faith?[26] Furthermore, was it not also a work of faith when Melchizedek blessed Abraham and said, "Blessed be Abraham by God Most High, who created heaven and earth; and blessed be God Most High, who has delivered his enemies into his hands"?[27] [M963]

(10) From all these episodes it is inferred that Abraham possessed faith in each individual [instance] but only in part. However, in that story where it is said, "his faith was reckoned to him as righteousness,"[28] his faith should be declared perfect. For just as the Apostle says that knowledge and prophecy are in part, but, in contrast, says that they are perfect when he writes, "For we know in part, and we prophesy in part; but when the

23. Gn 15.3–6. Cf. 4.2.10; *Hom in Gn* 3.3.
24. Gn 12.1ff.   25. Gn 13.14–15.
26. Cf. Gn 13.18.   27. Gn 14.19–20 LXX.
28. Rom 4.3, 5, 9; Gn 15.6.

perfect comes, the things which are in part will be set aside,"[29] in the same way we can understand that faith is sometimes in part and sometimes perfect.

(11) But in order that what we are saying might be fortified by still other testimonies of Holy Scripture, listen to the Apostles speaking to the Lord in the Gospel, "Lord, increase our faith!"[30] Are they not plainly showing by this that they indeed have faith but the kind which was in need of increase? Moreover the Apostle Paul himself, when he says, "If I have all faith so as to remove mountains,"[31] when he says "all" he is teaching that the whole is the composite of the parts. For "all" can not be predicated where there is no diversity in quantity and quality.[32] It would seem, then, even in the present passage that, even though Abraham is great, faith preceded through individual instances, some of which we have recorded above. Now in this occurrence his entire faith was gathered together and was thus reckoned to him as righteousness.

(12) Now you may of course already be pondering whether it might be possible to say about all the other virtues the same thing that was said about faith, i.e., that it was reckoned to him as righteousness.[33] For instance, could someone's mercy be reckoned for righteousness, or wisdom or knowledge or gentleness or humility?[34] Or would faith be reckoned to every believer as righteousness? When I have recourse to the Scriptures, I do not find that faith is reckoned to every believer as righteousness. After all, it is written of the sons of Israel, "They believed in God and in his servant Moses";[35] however it is not added that it was reckoned to them as righteousness, as was written about Abraham. This leads me to believe that in their case they did not possess the perfection of faith, collected together from many parts into one whole, which deserved to be reckoned as righteousness, as we taught to be the case for Abraham.

---

29. 1 Cor 13.9–10.
30. Lk 17.5.
31. 1 Cor 13.2.
32. Cf. 4.6.4; *Comm in Jn* 32.15.
33. Rom 4.3, 5, 9; Gn 15.6.
34. Cf. Ps 106.31, where it says that Phineas's zeal was reckoned to him as righteousness.
35. Ex 14.31.

(13) What he says, "Now to the one who works, wages are not imputed as a gift but as something due. But to one who believes in him who justifies the ungodly, faith is reckoned as righteousness," seems as if to declare that in faith there is the gift of the one who justifies; in works, however, there is the righteousness of the one who repays.

(14) But when I consider the majesty of this passage in which he says that to the one who works it is repaid as something due, I can hardly convince myself that there could be any work which would demand from God repayment as something due. For even the fact that we are able to do anything at all, to think and to speak, [M964] we do through his gift and generosity.[36] What debt will he have to pay back to us, seeing that his capital came first? Therefore, we must consider whether perhaps the words, "Now to one who works, wages shall be imputed as something due," should instead be understood of the debt which is due for evil works.

(15) For you will find frequently in the divine books that sins are called debts, just as the Lord himself taught us to say in prayer, "Forgive us our debts as we forgive our debtors";[37] and again when the Lord says, "There were two debtors to a certain householder, one had a debt of five hundred denarii and the other fifty."[38] And he himself interpreted this to refer to sins.[39] Perhaps then in this passage as well the Apostle has treated the wages of a work which is repaid as a debt in this same sense which we have just described above concerning those who work in the same manner as Cain, who worked the ground,[40] and just as it says in another passage, "Depart from me, workers of iniquity!"[41] Surely the due punishment for the wages of iniquity is paid out to them. This is also why the same Apostle says in another passage, "The wages of sin is death."[42] And he did not go on to say in similar fashion: but the wages of righteousness is eternal life. Instead he says, "But the gift of God is eternal

---

36. For Origen's view that our natural endowments are gifts of grace, cf. 4.5.2; 10.38. See Introduction (15).
37. Mt 6.12.
38. Lk 7.41–42.
39. Cf. Lk 7.47.
40. Gn 4.2.
41. Mt 7.23; Lk 13.27.
42. Rom 6.23.

life,"[43] in order [not only] to teach that the wages, which are assuredly comparable with a debt and a reward, are a repayment of punishment and death, but to establish eternal life in grace alone. According to this sense, I think we ought to interpret as referring to evil works that which is written in the Gospel, "With the same measure you use, it will be measured out to you."[44] For upon his own grace God has not placed measures, since it is written, "For God does not give the Spirit according to measure."[45]

(16) If these things are reckoned to have been discussed correctly, it seems that the matters closely linked must indeed be understood such that to the one who does evil works, rewards are paid back according to the debt of sin; but to the one "who believes in him who justifies the ungodly, faith is reckoned as righteousness"—if we remembered well what was said above[46] when we showed that faith cannot be reckoned as righteousness to one who believes in part, but only to him who believes completely and perfectly. This kind of faith would justify even one who had been ungodly, so that he would no longer be ungodly, [not] as was that thief who was hanging on the cross blaspheming,[47] but he should be like the one who was confessing and was saying, "Lord Jesus, remember me when you come into your kingdom."[48]

(17) After these words, as if confirming his previous statement, "But to the one who does not work but believes in him who justifies the ungodly, faith is reckoned as righteousness," he adopts the testimony of the Psalms and says, "So also David speaks of the blessedness of the man to whom God credits righteousness [M965] apart from works: 'Blessed are those whose iniquities are forgiven, and whose sins are covered; blessed is the man against whom the Lord will not impute sin.'" For he sees that in these words it can be consequently proved that righteousness is reckoned to a person apart from works. This is why it seems to me that the Apostle understood that ei-

---

43. Rom 6.23.
45. Jn 3.34.
47. Lk 23.39.
44. Mt 7.2; Lk 6.38.
46. Cf. 4.1.10–12.
48. Lk 23.42. Cf. 3.9.3.

ther righteousness or unrighteousness must dwell in a person who has cognizance, through being old enough to distinguish good and evil.[49] If this is so, no soul can be found without one of the two dwelling in it; and it is certain that if that [soul] should desist from evil, it would then be found in the good. But that soul is not in evil "whose iniquities are forgiven and whose sins are covered and against whom the Lord will not impute sin." It is therefore logical that it is in the good.

(18) So then in connection with the forgiveness of iniquities and the covering of sins and [the fact] that the Lord does not impute sins, the Apostle fittingly says that only on the basis that he believes in him who justifies the ungodly, righteousness would be reckoned to a man, even if he has not yet produced works of righteousness.[50] For faith which believes in the one who justifies is the beginning of being justified by God. And this faith, when it has been justified, is firmly embedded in the soil of the soul like a root that has received rain, so that when it begins to be cultivated by God's law, branches arise from it, which bring forth the fruit of works. The root of righteousness, therefore, does not grow out of the works, but rather the fruit of works grows out of the root of righteousness, that root, of course, of righteousness which God also credits even apart from works.[51]

(19) In my opinion this is the reason David gave that beginning to the Thirty-first Psalm, which he superscribed, "The Understanding of David." He was warning in the very superscription that a deeper understanding ought to be sought in the things he was about to say, "Blessed are those whose iniquities are forgiven."[52] We spoke of these matters to the best of our ability when we spoke about the Psalms in order.[53]

(20) The distinction of the order of these [phrases] is striking to us. He has said firstly, "Blessed are those whose iniquities are forgiven"; secondly, "whose sins are covered"; and thirdly,

---

49. Cf. 3.2.8; *Comm in Jn* 20.13.
50. Cf. 3.9.2 n. 319.
51. Cf. 3.9.2–4. See Introduction (20).
52. Ps 32.1.
53. The passage does not survive. Cf. 4.11.6.

"to whom the Lord will not impute sin."[54] Consider whether perhaps it is possible for this order to be recognized in one and the same soul. Thus, because the starting point of a soul's conversion is to abandon evil, on account of its doing so it would merit the forgiveness of iniquities. But when it begins to do good, as if covering over each of the evils it had previously committed with later good actions and introducing a quantity of goods more numerous than the evils which had existed, it may be said to cover its sins. But when a [soul] would forthwith reach perfection so that every root of evil is completely cut off from it to the point that no trace of evil can be found in it, [M966] at that point the summit of blessedness is promised to the one to whom the Lord would be able to impute no sin. There is clearly a difference between iniquity and sin. "Iniquity" is used of those matters which are committed against the law. This explains why the Greek language calls iniquity ἀνομία, that is, "what is committed contrary to[55] law." On the other hand, a matter can be called "sin" if it is wrongfully committed, contrary to what nature teaches or what the conscience convicts us of.[56]

2. *Is this blessedness, then, for the circumcised, or also for the uncircumcised? For we say, Faith was reckoned to Abraham as righteousness. How then was it reckoned? Was it when he was circumcised or when he was uncircumcised? It was not when he was circumcised but when uncircumcised. He received the sign of circumcision as a seal of the righteousness of faith which he had while he was still uncircumcised, so that he might be the father of all who believe without being circumcised, so that it might be reckoned to them as righteousness, and the father of the circumcised who are not only circumcised but who also follow the footsteps of the faith that our father Abraham had before he was circumcised.*[57]

(2) He had said above that "Abraham believed God and it was reckoned to him as righteousness."[58] He then showed,

---

54. Cf. 2.1.2.
55. Migne, "apart from."
56. Cf. Clement, *Paedagogus* 1.13 (= ANF 2:235), "Everything that is contrary to right reason is sin."
57. Rom 4.9–12.
58. Rom 4.3.

based on what was written in the Thirty-first Psalm, what blessedness a faith of this sort possesses, that to the one who believes, the Lord does not reckon sin.[59] Therefore Paul now presents a question so that, through its response and the sequence of events itself, it might be taught that the blessedness of Abraham's justification was not granted after he had been circumcised but while he was still uncircumcised. But if Abraham was justified by faith while he was still uncircumcised, then everyone else who believes God, even if one is uncircumcised, can be justified through faith; and that blessedness can apply to him as well, which says, "Blessed is the one to whom the Lord will not impute sin."[60] In this way Paul shows that it is not to just anyone that the Lord does not impute sin, but because of his faith he will not reckon sins against the one who has believed. For just as faith has been reckoned to Abraham as righteousness, so also sins, it is scarcely to be doubted, are not imputed to any believer when faith is reckoned as righteousness. For he is not speaking of righteous men when he says that faith is reckoned to them as righteousness. For if that was assumed here, just what grace will seem reckoned for righteousness to the righteous man? Surely [Paul] is saying instead that faith is reckoned as righteousness for the one who did not have righteousness before he had this faith. It is that man, assuredly, who is blessed, whose righteousness God credits apart from works, and to whom sin is not imputed, to whom even iniquities have been forgiven, and previous sins have been covered.

(3) At the same time, however, [Paul] is teaching us to look more attentively at the text [M967] since he wants these things written about Abraham, that "faith was reckoned to him as righteousness," to be studied by us very carefully: when it was reckoned, where, and what sequence of time can be deduced from what was written, whether he was still uncircumcised when these things were said of him or whether he had already been circumcised. And he says, "How then was his faith reckoned to him as righteousness? Was it while he was circumcised or when he was uncircumcised?" For if it had happened at the time

---

59. Rom 4.6–8; Ps 32.1–2.   60. Rom 4.8; Ps 32.2.

when he was already circumcised, it would certainly seem that the uncircumcised are excluded from the grace of his faith. But now he shows that faith was reckoned as righteousness while he was still uncircumcised, and on this account he declares that, since Abraham was justified through faith while he was uncircumcised, doubtless he will deservedly be called the leader and father of all who believe through uncircumcision. Yet because [Abraham] received circumcision after he had faith, a faith which occurred during his uncircumcision, [Paul] consequently sets forth the reason circumcision would have been given to him: It was to be a sign of his faith which he had while uncircumcised, so that through this he might become the father even of those who are born into circumcision, but only if they should attain to that faith which justified Abraham while he was uncircumcised. He becomes therefore a father of both peoples. Through faith he is a father of those who are uncircumcised; through the flesh, of those who are circumcised.

(4) And after he was circumcised, he first becomes the father of Isaac,[61] and with him the beginning of the number eight[62] was entered upon, that is to say, the first mysteries of the eighth day are consecrated in him and from that point on Abraham's lineage begins to run through a twofold mystery. For just as faith is understood to be of one nature and the righteousness reckoned to him through faith of another, so also his lineage was of one sort when he was uncircumcised, and of another sort after he received circumcision. For in my opinion the uncircumcised are those stones from which God is said to be able to raise up sons of Abraham.[63] In them as well that which is written is fulfilled, "In you shall all the tribes of the earth be blessed."[64]

(5) But let us repeat again what he says, "And he received the sign of circumcision as a seal of the righteousness of faith which he had while he was still uncircumcised," and let us contemplate Paul's profound wisdom in these words. For perhaps to some he appears to be saying the same word twice, [M968]

---

61. Gn 21.2–4.
62. Cf. 2.13.21; *Hom in Lv* 8.4.
63. Cf. Mt 3.9; Lk 3.8.
64. Gn 12.3. Cf. 4.5.9.

namely "sign" and "seal." But to me there appears to be a great difference in meaning between these words. For something is called a sign when, through that which appears, something else is indicated. For example the Lord says in the Gospel, "This generation asks for a sign, but no sign will be given to it except the sign of the prophet Jonah. For just as Jonah was three days and three nights in the belly of the sea monster, so also for three days and three nights the Son of Man must be in the heart of the earth."[65] This, then, is the sign: where Jonah was seen, Christ was recognized. Similarly it is said about the Lord himself in the Gospel, "Behold, he is destined for the falling and the rising of many, and to be a sign that will be spoken against."[66] For the sign under which Christ had come was spoken against because one thing was seen in him, and something else was recognized. Flesh was perceived, and God was believed.

(6) In this way then Abraham too received a sign. And that it *was* a sign, it says in what follows, "circumcision," a circumcision which was the "seal of the faith which he had" before he was circumcised. [Paul] has done well, then, in calling circumcision a sign for Abraham, because one thing was seen in it and another thing was recognized. And he shows that even then that fleshly circumcision was a sign of spiritual circumcision which is received not in the flesh but in the heart.[67]

(7) But in my opinion what he has called a seal ought to be understood in the following way: Something is called a seal when a protective guard is placed upon some object which is to be protected for a time and which no one else is allowed to unseal except the one who impressed it. As the Apostle explains, therefore, through that seal is indicated both the righteousness of faith which Abraham deserved to receive when he was uncircumcised, and also his being the father of many nations.[68] We believe that it is to be unsealed only at the time when the fullness of the Gentiles comes in and all Israel will be saved.[69] For at that time what the Apostle says will come to pass, for Abra-

---

65. Mt 12.39–40.   66. Lk 2.34.
67. Cf. Rom 2.29. See also Origen's Excursus on Circumcision in 2.13.20–22.
68. Rom 4.11, 17; Gn 17.5.   69. Cf. Rom 11.25–26.

ham to be the father not only of the Gentiles but also of the circumcision through faith.

(8) Let us discuss this matter about the sign and the seal even more explicitly. A sign, as we have said, is where something is indicated through that which is seen. A seal, on the other hand, is where something which is closed up for a time and is not open to view. In this way it is possible to understand that the mysteries which were foreshadowed in the law and in the patriarchs were of such a kind that they were to be both indicated in signs and guarded with seals.[70] Because what was to be indicated by signs was in those who were gentile believers, it is said that Abraham had received a sign. Yet he is said to have received a seal because these things were to be guarded and covered for those who were of the circumcision who were not going to believe. [M969] The seal will undoubtedly be designated[71] at that time when, in the last days after the fullness of the Gentiles comes in, as we have said, all Israel will be saved.[72] After all, that is the reason Abraham is justified by faith earlier, while he was still uncircumcised, and afterwards is circumcised, so that he might first be shown as one who was going to be the father of many nations and afterwards of those who were going to believe from the circumcision. For it is not those who are born from Abraham according to the flesh who should be called Abraham's sons, unless they also possess the faith and works of Abraham.[73] After all, it was for this reason as well that the Lord says in the Gospel to the Jews who were boasting to be sons of Abraham, "If you were Abraham's sons, you would do the works of Abraham."[74]

(9) But do you also want to be instructed from the Old Testament that one is called a son but not of the one from whose fleshly seed he descends, but of the one whose deeds and works he imitates? Listen to what Daniel says to one of the elders whom he convicts of adultery, "[You are] an offspring of Canaan and not of Judah; beauty has seduced you and lust has

---

70. Cf. Rv 5.1. Cf. *Comm in Mt* 12.3; *Comm in Jn* 5.6.
71. Migne, "opened."   72. Cf. Rom 11.25–26.
73. Cf. Rom 9.7–8.   74. Jn 8.39.

turned your heart away."⁷⁵ You see that the one who had descended in a fleshly manner from the race of Judah is denied to be Judah's son, but is obviously a son of Canaan, whose deeds and works he was following. So also in this way those who derive their race from the seed of Abraham according to the flesh are not called Abraham's sons if they do not possess his faith. After all, the prophet also speaks in this way to them, "Your father was an Amorite and your mother a Hittite."⁷⁶ Assuredly not the bond of race but the imitation of their moral behavior united [the Israelites] to these nations.

(10) "So that he might be the father of all who believe without being circumcised that it might be reckoned to them as righteousness, and the father of the circumcised who are not only of the circumcision, but who also are of those who follow the footsteps of the faith that our father Abraham had before he was circumcised." Here he plainly declares, as we said above, that what is demanded from members of both peoples is not the lineage of the flesh but the noble quality of faith. But we have already spoken extensively about the mystery of circumcision above;⁷⁷ and also in many other places which, because of the time and subject, seemed appropriate, we have expounded this.⁷⁸

(11) Not even this ought to escape the notice of the attentive reader who does not pass over a single jot or tittle of the law,⁷⁹ that the Apostle said, "His faith was reckoned to Abraham as righteousness." However at the time when it was written of him that he believed God and it was reckoned to him as righteousness he was not yet called Abraham, but his name was Abram.⁸⁰ For, as the Apostle explains, up to this point he was still uncircumcised. Concerning this, to some there will perhaps seem to be an error contained in the manuscripts, since it

---

75. Dn 13.56 LXX.
76. Ezek 16.3.
77. Cf. 2.13.8–33; 4.1.8ff.
78. Cf. *Hom in Gn* 3; *Hom in Jer* 5.
79. Cf. Mt 5.18.
80. Until Gn 17 the Scripture speaks of Abram. In Rom 4:3 however Paul quotes Gn 15:6 yet calls him Abraham. Erasmus, CWE 56:107 says of Origen's observation here, "I certainly praise the man's diligence, and am ashamed of my own slackness."

would have been quite easy to write "Abraham" instead of "Abram." Yet because this [M970] is more of an uncertain guess than a solid proof, we should respond briefly that, in consideration of God's pronouncement which said, "Your name shall no longer be Abram but Abraham,"[81] the Apostle has named him [Abraham] here, not as it was written in the passage in Genesis, but as God had declared concerning him. For it is appropriate at a later time to note that which is divinely ordained.

(12) If anyone might take into consideration the strong desire of our mind they will be able to comprehend these matters which have been presented to the best of our ability in reference to passages which are both lofty and difficult. If, however, someone wants to point out weaknesses in my interpretation, I beg pardon and readily yield to anyone who is able to discuss and explain these passages better. Now, however, we redirect our step to the matters which follow, even if it be at a slow pace.

3. *For the promise to Abraham and his descendants that they would be heirs of the world did not come through the law but through the righteousness of faith.*[82] In this passage it seems to me that the Apostle is contending about the law of Moses and affirming that the promise which was made to Abraham, that he himself or his descendants would receive the world, i.e., the entire earth, as an inheritance, was not established from the law of Moses. For before Moses even existed as a legislator, it says, "The Lord appeared to Abraham and said to him, 'Go from your country and your kindred and your father's house to the land that I will show you. And I will make of you a great nation, and I will bless you, and make your name great, and you will be blessed. And I will bless those who bless you, and those who curse you I will curse; and in you all the tribes of the earth shall be blessed.'"[83] Therefore, what it says, "in you all the tribes of the earth shall be blessed," is that he becomes an heir of the entire world. Obviously the promise which came to Abraham preceded the obser-

---

81. Gn 17.5.   82. Rom 4.13.
83. Gn 12.1–3; cf. Acts 7.2–3.

vation of the law commanded through Moses. So then the promise to Abraham and his descendants that he would be heir of the world is not from the law but through the righteousness of faith. What is the righteousness of faith? It is written about above, as we have now frequently said,[84] "Abraham believed God and it was reckoned to him as righteousness."[85] This is not undeserved; for whereas the observance of the law merely evades punishment, the merit of faith awaits the hope of the promise. Precept is laid on slaves, but faith is sought by friends.[86]

(2) Yet even if Paul should be understood to be saying these things about natural law, in accordance with what we have explained above,[87] this will not contradict the arguments given above. For however much the law of nature may offer testimony about good and evil according to the judgment of conscience,[88] nevertheless it cannot be put on the same level as the law of faith, by which Abraham believed God and merited to be justified and to be named a friend of God.[89] [M971]

4. *For if it is those who are of the law who are to be the heirs, faith is null and the promise is void. For the law works wrath; but where there is no law, neither is there transgression.*[90] If, he says, the promise given to Abraham that he would be heir of the world was not from the law but through faith,[91] which was reckoned to him as righteousness,[92] it will doubtless follow that all who hope that God will reckon righteousness to them should hope for this not through the law but through faith. And in order that he might show this more plainly, he added: If those who are of the law will be heirs of that promise which Abraham merited through faith, then the fact that Abraham was justified by faith will be rendered null and void, since assuredly, if the future inheritance were from the law, Abraham would also have been required first to fulfill the law and in this way to merit the inheritance of righteousness. And in order to show that this in no way

84. Cf. 3.8.14; 3.9.5; 4.1.2, 8–9; 4.2.2.
85. Rom 4.3; Gn 15.6.
86. Cf. Jn 15.15.
87. Cf. 2.8.2; 2.9.1; 3.6.2–4; 3.7.5.
88. Cf. Rom 2.15.
89. Cf. Jas 2.23.
90. Rom 4.14–15.
91. Cf. Rom 4.13.
92. Cf. Rom 4.3.

could be the case, he says that "the law works wrath." Where there is wrath, there is no inheritance; and he has added, "But where there is no law, neither is there transgression."

(2) But let us back up a bit and see of which law these things are spoken. Indeed, up above where he says, "For if those who are of the law are heirs, faith is null and the promise is void," it is possible that this refers to both the law of Moses and natural law. For it is certain that if the inheritance is given from the law of Moses, then what is written would be nullified, that Abraham had merited it by his readiness to believe. And, on the other hand, if the sense is transferred to natural law, then this can be said: If the natural law could have sufficed for faith, it would seem that what has been said to Abraham, "Depart from your land and your kindred and your father's house and go to the land that I will show you,"[93] was unnecessary. For why would he depart from his own land and from his own house if the natural law were sufficient for him? Certainly he could have possessed and kept this law while he was in his own land. But now, as if that law was insufficient, he is commanded to follow the law of faith,[94] without which neither he nor his offspring could become heirs of the world nor could he be called a friend of God.[95] In this way, then, what he says, "For if those who are of the law are heirs, faith is null and the promise is void," once separated from each law, concerns only the law of faith.[96]

(3) But now in this place where it says, "For the law works wrath," it should be carefully examined as to which law this discourse seems to concern. The same for that which follows, "For where there is no law, neither is there transgression." Before a fuller explanation is sought from us, we should briefly give an answer to those charges which the heretics are accustomed to allege concerning this passage.[97] For they say, "See how the Apostle says that the law of Moses works wrath! But where that law does not exist, there will be no transgression." [M972] Let us demand of them: Supposing that where there is a law, there

93. Gn 12.1. 94. Cf. Rom 3.27.
95. Cf. Jas 2.23. 96. Cf. Rom 3.27.
97. I.e., the Marcionites. Cf. 3.6.9; 5.6.2.

BOOK 4, CHAPTER 4   255

will also be transgression of the law when it is violated, then also where there is faith, there will be transgression through the violation of faith. For if one becomes a transgressor who turns away from the law, doubtless also he is a transgressor who turns away from faith. And if the law is to blame for that transgression [committed] under the law, then faith should also be believed to be to blame for a transgression [committed] under faith. But if it is absurd to say that faith is to blame when someone becomes a transgressor of the faith (although if that person had not come to faith, he would not have become a transgressor of the faith), so also it shall be absurd to attribute the transgression of the law to the fact that a person has taken upon himself the observance of the law.

(4) Moreover, we will add this: What will they say to us about those who became transgressors before the law of Moses? For if no transgressor existed before Moses, then no one was condemned and no one was punished. What will they say of the residents of Sodom? What about those who were condemned in the flood? What about Cain? What of Adam himself? And what will they answer concerning Eve, of whom the Apostle says, "The woman was seduced and became a transgressor"?[98] If there is no transgression without the law of Moses, why are Adam and Eve called transgressors by the Apostle?[99]

(5) But in fact, as we have already frequently said above,[100] the Apostle introduces different laws in this epistle. One moment he is discoursing about the law of Moses, the next moment he mentions the law of faith, as when he says, "Where then is your boasting? It is excluded. Through what law? That of works? No, but through the law of faith."[101] Moreover he brings in other laws as well, about which he says, "For I delight in the law of God according to the inner man, but I see in my members another law at war with the law of my mind, leading

---

98. 1 Tm 2.14.
99. For the theme of sin before the law of Moses, cf. 3.2.9; 3.6.1; 4.4.4f.; 5.1.23; 5.6.2; 6.8.3.
100. Cf. Preface of Origen (8); 3.7.5; 5.1.24; 5.6.2–4; 5.10.9; 6.8.2; 6.9.2; 7.1.1; 7.19.7.
101. Rom 3.27.

me captive to the law of sin."[102] In this way he passes from one law to another, so that it is scarcely possible to understand and follow him unless the mind is watchful and alert.

(6) One must consider, then, whether perhaps the law which is in our members and leads us captive to the law of sin is not the same law which the Apostle says works wrath. For there can be no doubt that it works wrath on one whom it had led captive to the law of sin.[103] However where that law does not exist, it is certain that there will be no transgression [of it]. In fact, those who are under that law will not be heirs.

(7) But if someone wants to mention the law of Moses and say that it works wrath, he could assert this on this one, perhaps only, point, that it orders the one who sins against it to be stoned immediately or be destroyed with fire[104] or whatever other punishment is decreed in the law against sinners. Thus the penalty itself which is inflicted against the sinner from the law may now appear to be called by the Apostle "wrath."[105] [M973] And similarly regarding transgression in this passage he does not generally include everything termed "transgression," but only those of the one who sinned while under the law. Thus the offence of one who sinned, though forbidden by law, would seem more serious than of one who was not warned by any law.[106]

(8) Moreover one should observe that the Apostle has not said: Where there is law, there is also transgression; but instead he says, "However, where there is no law, neither is there transgression." He shows by this that indeed there could be no transgression at all unless law existed; yet it is not the case that if there is law, in every case there will also be transgression. For it could be that a law may exist but no transgression. It is, however, not possible for there to be transgression where there is no law. For even if we should consider the law of Moses, not necessarily everyone who lived under the law of Moses became transgressors. Otherwise we seem to implicate the prophets together

---

102. Rom 7.22–23.   103. Rom 7.23.
104. Cf. Lv 20.2, 27; Dt 13.11; 17.5; Lv 20.14; 21.9.
105. For "wrath" as punishment cf. 1.16.1; 4.11.6.
106. Cf. 6.8.10.

with all the righteous; unless perhaps anyone should say that all the righteous and all the prophets had lived not so much under the law as under faith, whereas the sinners and the unrighteous were bound with the fetters of the law, as the Apostle also says, "The law is laid down not for the righteous but for the unrighteous and disobedient, for the godless and sinners, for the criminal and profane, for those who kill their father or mother, for murderers, fornicators, homosexual offenders, slave traders, liars, perjurers, and whatever else is contrary to the sound teaching."[107]

(9) But if the law was laid down for such people, will not those persons seem to you to be much better off, of whom it is said, "For when Gentiles, who do not possess the law, do naturally the things of the law, these, though not having this law, are a law to themselves. They show that the work of the law is written on their hearts, as their conscience also bears witness to them"?[108] If it is fitting, let us set before our eyes two men, for example, who have not lain with men as with women.[109] One of them, prohibited by a precept of the law probably would have committed the act had his fear not held him. The other, by a judgment of his own mind, refused even to permit his thoughts to consent to this sort of defiling activity. Do you not much more prefer that man who, although not deterred by the threat of a law, kept himself unstained from contamination of this kind of disgraceful conduct?[110] If an examination were conducted of the other sins, the same thing [would prove true].[111]

(10) Therefore, whether the law of Moses or even the law in our members[112] is understood and works wrath, those who are of this law cannot be heirs, but [only] those who are of the law of faith,[113] that faith by which Abraham was justified.[114] But perhaps someone should ask: How could it seem that those who are under the law of Moses are not also under the law of faith, seeing that it is written in Exodus, "But the people believed

---

107. 1 Tm 1.9–10. 108. Rom 2.14–15.
109. Lv 18.22.
110. Cf. 9.28.4; Clement, *Stromateis* 4.18.113.6.
111. Cf. *Cels* 7.63. 112. Cf. Rom 7.23.
113. Cf. Rom 3.27. 114. Cf. Rom 4.3.

[M974] in God and in his servant Moses"?[115] And the Lord says in the Gospel, "If you believed Moses, you would assuredly believe also in me, for he wrote about me."[116]

(11) For it will seem that just as he said about himself, "He who believes in me believes also in him who sent me,"[117] so also he is saying of Moses, "If you believed Moses, you would assuredly believe also in me." To this we shall respond: What was said in the desert, "The people believed in God and in his servant Moses,"[118] is a narrative in which it is made known that through the ministry of Moses, where he carried out signs and miracles, the people believed in God.[119] But in that passage in which he says, "If you believed Moses, you would assuredly believe also in me,"[120] he exposes the unbelief of those who, as long as they do not believe in [Christ], show that they do not even believe the writings of Moses in which is contained, through prophetic discourse, that concerning the coming of Christ. But when he says, "Whoever believes in me believes in the one who sent me,"[121] he is lifting up the hope of believers to God the Father so that just as a person knows that when he has seen the Son he has seen both him and the Father,[122] so he should know that when he believes in the Son he has believed in both him and the Father.

5. For this reason it is by faith, in order that the promise according to grace may be firm to all his descendants, not only to him who is of the law but also to him who is of the faith of Abraham, who is the father of all of us, as it is written, "I have made you the father of many nations"—in the presence of the God in whom he believed, who gives life to the dead and calls things that are not as things that are.[123] Up above he made a distinction between wages and grace, saying that wages are a matter of debt whereas grace is a favor, not for a debt but for kindness.[124] In the present passage as well, then, since he wants to show that God gives the inheritance of the

---

115. Ex 14.31.
116. Jn 5.46.
117. Jn 12.44.
118. Ex 14.31.
119. Cf. 4.1.12.
120. Jn 5.46.
121. Jn 12.44.
122. Cf. Jn 14.9.
123. Rom 4.16–17.
124. Cf. Rom 4.4–5.

promises not as something due but through grace, he says that the inheritance from God is granted to those who believe, not as the debt of a wage but as a gift of faith.

(2) For, to give an example, just as I might say that we exist, this cannot be understood to mean that we exist as a wage for our works. Plainly it is a gift of God that we exist; it is the grace of the Creator who willed us to exist.[125] In this way as well, if we receive the inheritance of God's promises, it is the wage of divine grace and not of any debt or work.

(3) Now it may perhaps appear that what is said to be "of faith" is not by grace since, if a person must first offer his faith, grace thus has to be merited from God. But listen to what the same Apostle teaches elsewhere about this as well. For in the passage where he lists the gifts of the Spirit,[126] which he says are given to believers according to the measure of their faith,[127] he asserts that the gift of faith as well is granted along with the other gifts through the Holy Spirit. For after many words he speaks of it in this way, [M975] "To another faith is given by the same Spirit,"[128] in order to show that even faith is given through grace.[129] Moreover elsewhere the same Apostle teaches this when he says, "Because it has been granted to you from God not only that you believe in Christ but also that you should suffer on his behalf."[130] You find this also pointed out in the Gospels, where the Apostles, once understanding that faith, which is only human, cannot be perfected unless that which comes from God should be added to it, say to the Savior, "Increase our faith!"[131]

(4) From all of which it is most clearly proven what the Apostle says here, "For this reason it is by faith, in order that the promise according to grace may be firm," because even the very faith by which we seem to believe in God is confirmed in us as a gift of grace. This is the grace which, like a great treasure, one deserves to find if one is blessed.[132] Noah found it, and

---

125. Cf. 4.1.14; 10.38.
127. Cf. Rom 12.3, 6.
129. Cf. 9.3.7.
130. Phil 1.29. Cf. *Comm in Jn* 20.32.
132. Cf. Mt 13.44; Prv 3.13–14.

126. 1 Cor 12.8ff.
128. 1 Cor 12.9.

131. Lk 17.5.

for that reason it is written of him, "But Noah found grace in the sight of the Lord God."[133] Moses had also found this grace; for this reason he was saying to God, "If I have found grace in your sight."[134] Yet we find some saints who have found grace not only in the sight of the Lord God but also in the sight of men. After all, it is written of the blessed Joseph, "And Joseph found grace in the sight of his lord."[135] But even that grace which is found in the sight of men is granted by God's generosity. For so it is written about this same Joseph, "And the Lord was with Joseph and poured out his mercy upon him and gave grace to him in the sight of the chief jailor."[136]

(5) Still more is recorded in the Holy Scriptures about this sort of grace concerning the blessed Esther. For it says, "Esther continued to find grace before all who saw her."[137] And the Scripture a little bit after this says, "Esther found grace beyond all the other virgins, and the king placed the queen's crown upon her."[138] We have taken these things into consideration from the Holy Scriptures—in my opinion not inappropriately—to reinforce what has been said by the Apostle, where he discusses faith and grace. He says, therefore, "For this reason it is by faith, in order that the promise according to grace may be firm."

(6) Moreover what he says must be noted, "For this reason it is by faith, in order that the promise according to grace may be firm." It is as if he wanted to show that if the promise were from the law and not of grace, it would not have been firm; but now for this reason it is firm because it is not from the law but through grace. The sort of thing he wants to be understood here, in my opinion, is that the things of the law are outside of us whereas the things which come through grace are held within us. For instance, what was written in the law was written with pen and ink on parchments or papyrus paper; but what comes down from grace has been transcribed [M976] in our hearts by the Spirit of God. This is precisely what this same Apostle, who

---

133. Gn 6.8.
134. Ex 33.13.
135. Gn 39.4.
136. Gn 39.21 LXX.
137. Est 2.15.
138. Est 2.17. Cf. 9.2.4.

was a minister of this grace,[139] makes clear in other passages, "You are our letter, written not with ink but with the Spirit of the living God, not on stone tablets, but on the tablets of hearts made of flesh."[140] On this account, it seems to me, he says that the things which come through grace are even more firm than the things which come from the law: because the latter are outside of us, whereas the former are within us; the latter consist of fragile material and thus can easily be rubbed off; the former things, however, are inscribed by the Spirit of God and, having been impressed in the depths of the soul, preserve their firmness forever. Thus, with such letters of promise, the soul, which offers its faith in God like prepared wax, is inscribed so that the grace of God can be written upon it in a fitting manner. It is faith of this sort, then, which is reckoned as the righteousness which is receptive of heavenly grace.[141] This comes to pass for Abraham's offspring, not merely for the one who is of the law, but also for the one who is of faith. For the succession from Abraham which is by faith is much more noble than that of the flesh, seeing that it is recorded that he was justified by faith and not by the flesh. For if succession is to be granted not by faith but by descent [from Abraham], it would then be logical that Ishmael's posterity[142] and those who descended from Keturah[143] would be led into the mysteries of the promises.[144] But this is assuredly not admitted. On the contrary, only the posterity who are of law and faith are introduced.

(7) Yet it should not escape our notice that the Apostle's expression in this passage has been brought forth in a somewhat vacillating and ambiguous manner. For he has said, "In order that the promise might be firm to all his descendants, not only to him who is of the law, but also to him who is of faith." If this is interpreted as if he said that some descendants are of the law and others are of faith, so that the promised inheritance may be expected by both groups of descendants, then [Paul] is found to be contradicting what he wrote earlier when he said,

---

139. Cf. Eph 3.7; 2 Cor 8.19.
141. Cf. 4.5.3; 9.3.7.
143. Gn 25.1ff.
140. 2 Cor 3.2–3.
142. Gn 25.12ff.
144. Cf. 4.1.7.

"For it is not those who are of the law who are heirs."[145] Elsewhere he says, "For we hold that a man is justified through faith without works of the law";[146] and again, "For if those who are of the law are heirs, faith is null."[147] For indeed if a man is justified by faith apart from works of the law[148] and those who are of the law are not made heirs,[149] how will what he says in this passage, that the promise is firm through grace, not only to the descendant who is of the law but also to him who is of faith, not seem a contradiction? And when above he seems to have repulsed those who are of the law, how is it then that here he puts them on the same level with those whom he says hope for grace by faith? But what he says, "to all his descendants, not only to him who is of the law but also to him who is of faith," seems here to indicate *natural* law, as we have already frequently said.[150] And he asserts that the promise is firm, not merely for those who come from the natural law, but for those who, from faith, would add to the natural law [M977] the faith which our father Abraham had. Thus he does not seem to indicate that there are two peoples—one of faith and one of the law—but one and the same people who please God not only from the natural law, which all men use, but also from faith, of which Abraham is the author. He is, of course, in this way showing that if anyone should hold to absolutely everything which the law of nature teaches and the awareness of sin accuses him in no respect whatsoever, nevertheless, if he does not also have the grace of faith, he is not able to be justified. For it is faith which is reckoned as righteousness.[151]

(8) And in this manner the intended distinction renders the meaning more plain and those elements which are supposedly contradictory will be discovered to be harmonious and in agreement with one another. Concerning the varieties of "laws," we have already pointed out many times, and it is un-

---

145. Rom 4.14.
146. Rom 3.28.
147. Rom 4.14.
148. Rom 3.28.
149. Rom 4.14.
150. Cf. 2.8.2; 3.6.1; 4.3.2; 4.4.2.
151. Cf. 2.7.4–6; 3.9.5. See also Clement, *Stromateis* 1.7.38.1–2 (= FOTC 85:49–50), "So whatever good actions they perform today will be of no benefit to them after life's close, unless they have faith."

necessary to discuss these things again,¹⁵² that the Apostle, particularly in this epistle, often alters the course of the discussion suddenly and without notice, going from one kind of law to another.

(9) Now it is well that he did not say of Abraham, "the father of all," but instead he says, "the father of us all." That is to say, not of those of us who descend from the law, but of those of us who succeed him from faith and law. And because he is a father of all such people, he deservedly has put down in what follows the opinion about the divine promise when he says, "As it is written, 'I have appointed you a father of many nations'¹⁵³—in the presence of the God in whom he believed." If then he is promised to become a father of many nations, he is not undeservedly called the father, both of those who come from the Gentiles and of those who come from the circumcision. The Apostle rightly added out of his own interpretation, "in the presence of the God in whom he believed."¹⁵⁴ That is to say, he has been appointed to be the father of many nations in the presence of the same God in whom he believed, whose promises he possesses, and from whom he receives the seal of faith in circumcision. How then can the circumcision group defend the claim that Abraham is their *own* father when God himself, who also gave circumcision, appointed him to be the father of many nations? Now if someone wants to apply this to the offspring of Ishmael or Keturah, what is written opposes him, "in you all the tribes of the earth will be blessed."¹⁵⁵ This is also what the Lord¹⁵⁶ was saying in the Gospel, "For God is able to raise up sons of Abraham from these stones."¹⁵⁷

(10) Yet he has added in what follows, "who gives life to the dead and calls the things that are not as things that are."¹⁵⁸ We understand "dead" here with respect to the sin of the soul, since it says, "the soul which sins shall die."¹⁵⁹ For just as the

---

152. Cf. 3.6.1.   153. Gn 17.5.
154. Cf. Rom 4.11, 13, 17.   155. Gn 12.3. Cf. 4.1.7; 4.5.6.
156. These words of John the Baptist are attributed to "the Savior" in *Comm in Jn* 13.58. Migne's text corrects the current text to read "John."
157. Mt 3.9; Lk 3.8. Cf. 4.2.4.   158. Rom 4.17.
159. Ezek 18.4, 20. Cf. 6.6.4; *Dial* 25.13–15.

senses perish at bodily death and the body no longer takes in either the sense of sight, hearing, smell, taste, or touch, so also is it that anyone who has ruined the spiritual senses[160] in the soul neither sees God nor hears the words [M978] of God nor takes in the sweet fragrance of Christ[161] nor tastes the good word of God[162] nor do his hands handle anything concerning the word of life.[163] Men of this sort are deservedly called "dead." The coming of Christ found us in this condition, but he gave us life by his grace, as the same Apostle also says elsewhere, "And when we were dead in our transgressions and sins, he raised us up together with him."[164] Do you want this to be established for you from the prophetic Scriptures as well, namely that all who worship idols and put confidence in them are dead?[165] Listen to what David says, "The images of the nations are silver and gold, the works of human hands. They have mouths, but do not speak; they have eyes, but will not see; they have ears, but will not hear";[166] and a little later it says, "Those who make them will become like them, and all who trust in them."[167] You see, those who worship these things and who trust in them are dead and like images.

(11) Let us examine more diligently whether, perchance, just as those who worship idols and trust in them are said to become like them, in the same way those who worship the true God and trust in him will also become like him. This is perhaps the case, in that, when it was proposed that he become the image and likeness of God,[168] that man was indeed made in the image of God in the beginning, but the likeness was postponed so that he might first trust in God and thus become like him and might himself hear that everyone who trusts in him becomes like him.[169]

---

160. Cf. *Comm in Jn* 20.43; *Princ* 1.1.9; *Cels* 7.34.
161. Cf. 2 Cor 2.15.
162. Cf. Heb 6.5.
163. Cf. 1 Jn 1.1.
164. Eph 2.5; cf. 2.1.
165. Cf. *Hom in Lk* 22.
166. Ps 115.4–6.
167. Ps 115.8.
168. Cf. Gn 1.26–27.
169. H. J. Vogt, *Das Kirchenverständnis des Origenes,* Bonner Beiträge zur Kirchengeschichte, vol. 4 (Cologne: Böhlau Verlag, 1974), p. 342, observes some evolution in Origen's thought by comparing this passage with *Princ* 3.6.1, where Origen states that the perfection of the likeness is achieved by the exer-

(12) We have joined these things to what we have discussed about the different kinds of death as a sort of digression, in order that the means by which God gives life to the dead might become more apparent. But let us also consider what he says in what follows and see how it should be interpreted. "And he calls the things that are not as things that are." Elsewhere[170] we have repeatedly explained that God alone says, "I am who I am."[171] God's essence is one and exists always. If someone should join himself to it, he becomes one spirit with it, and through him who always is, even he himself will be said to be. However the one who is far from him and assumes no participation in him is not even said to be, just as we Gentiles were before we came to the knowledge of the divine truth.[172] And this is why it says that God "calls the things that are not as things that are." For among those who are, that is to say, among those who have a participation in him who is, are numbered Abraham, Isaac, Jacob, and the rest of the saints.[173] But if the Gentiles, by believing, come to the faith of Abraham, the Apostle has suitably declared that God has called "the things that are not as things that are."

(13) Yet the following can also be observed: In this passage the Apostle seems lavish in God's praises and has recorded the beginning of his initial creation with admiration, [M979] when God made the universe to exist from nothing and called the things that were not, by the virtue of his power, as things that are and that do exist. And nothing was difficult for him in the process of creating, to such an extent that although nothing was existing, everything, suddenly summoned, came into existence as if they had always existed.[174]

---

cise of man's own diligent effort and the fulfillment of the necessary works. He concludes, "We can recognize here a development within Origen from a more philosophical point of view, emphasizing the individual achievement of the human being, to a more religious and Christian standpoint, which takes seriously the sinfulness of man." Cf. *Cels* 4.30; Clement, *Stromateis* 2.22.131.6; *Paedagogus* 1.12.98.2–3.

170. Cf. *Princ* 1.3.6; *Comm in Jn* 2.13.
171. Ex 3.14.   172. Cf. *2 Clement* 1.8.
173. Cf. *Comm in Mt* 17.36.
174. For creation *ex nihilo*, see *Princ* 1.3.3; 2.1.5; *Comm in Jn* 1.17.

(14) But suppose someone should counter us with the Apostle's discourse which he wrote to the Corinthians, where he says, "God chose what is despised in the world, things that are not, to set aside the things that are, so that no flesh might boast in the presence of God."[175] [Our objector] may say that this passage is not consistent, that it is said that the things which exist are set aside while those which do not exist are chosen. To this we would say that in that passage he has said that those "who are" are one group, but it is another group that is in this section in the letter to the Romans. For to the Corinthians he made clear that he was speaking of those things which he had earlier enumerated. For just above this he said, "For consider your calling, brothers: Not many of you were wise according to the flesh, not many were powerful, not many were of noble birth. But God chose what is foolish in the world to confound the wise; God chose what is weak in the world to confound the strong."[176] So then he is saying that God had chosen what is foolish in the world, i.e., the Gentiles, to confound the wise, no doubt the Jews; he chose what is weak in the world to confound the strong. In the very same manner he also speaks in this passage of the things which are not, in order to set aside the things which are, and he indicates that the Gentiles are those who are not, and the Jews are those who are. That is to say, the [Jews] who were under the law but were not fulfilling the law were to be set aside. And those who were not under the law were to be brought in and joined by merit of their believing in Abraham's faith. But he says, "to confound the wise," not because they were truly wise—in any case God would never have confounded those who are wise according to God's wisdom—instead he is speaking of those who consider themselves to be wise but are not. As [Paul] says in another passage, "Where is the wise man? Where is the scribe? Where is the debater of this age? Has not God made foolish the wisdom of this world?"[177] So then he confounds those who are wise in this manner by choosing in a similar way the foolish, not because they were foolish and they

---

175. 1 Cor 1.28–29. 176. 1 Cor 1.26–27.
177. 1 Cor 1.20.

lacked intelligence, but in the sense of that which is said, "Let him who wants to be wise become a fool in this world, that he might be wise before God, because the wisdom of this world is foolishness before God."[178]

6. *Who against hope believed in hope that he would become the father of many nations, according to what was said, "So shall your descendants be."* [M980] *He did not weaken in faith. He considered his own body already dead since he was about a hundred years old, and Sarah's womb dead. No distrust made him waver concerning the promise of God, but he grew strong in faith, giving glory to God, being fully convinced that God is able to do what he has promised. Therefore it was reckoned to him as righteousness.*[179]

(2) It seems to me that what the Apostle said, "against hope," refers to what Abraham is recorded in Genesis as having said to the Lord, "'O Lord and Ruler, what will you give me? But I am being dismissed without sons; here is the son of Masech my slave woman, Eliezer of Damascus.' And Abraham said, 'Because you have given me no offspring, this slave born in my house is to be my heir.'"[180] From these words it is, of course, understood that Abraham had given up hope that he would conceive sons. But in my opinion that it said, "he believed in hope," refers to the hope, given to him again. He deduced this from what is written, "And the word of the Lord came to him, saying, 'This man shall not be your heir; but your very own issue shall be your heir.' He brought him outside and said to him, 'Look toward heaven and count the stars, if you are able to count them.' And he said to him, 'So shall your descendants be.' And he believed God; and it was reckoned to him as righteousness."[181] From these words, then, both the initial hopelessness and the subsequent hope given to him by the promises of God are made known. Because he believed in him, what the Apostle now sets forth is written about him, "It was reckoned to him as righteousness."[182]

178. 1 Cor 3.18–19.
180. Gn 15.2–3.
182. Gn 15.6; Rom 4.22.

179. Rom 4.18–22.
181. Gn 15.4–6.

(3) Fittingly and in accordance with his normal practice, the Apostle, when treating the subject of faith, joins hope to it, because he knows that hope cleaves inseparably to faith, just as he teaches the same in the letter to the Hebrews[183] when he says, "But faith is the substance of things hoped for, the proof of things not seen."[184] And again in this very letter to the Romans he says later on, "By hope we have been saved. But hope which is seen is not hope. For who sees that for which he also hopes? But if we hope for what we do not see, we wait for it with patience."[185] But if, "by hope we have been saved," this is the same as what he says elsewhere, "Through faith we have been saved";[186] and, "Your faith has saved you";[187] and, "According to your faith let it be done to you."[188] Surely this is being said to those who, by believing in Jesus, have borne the hope that they can be healed by him. But Abraham "against hope believed in hope," so also all who are sons of Abraham by faith against hope believe in hope [M981] in every detail of what they believe, whether it concerns the resurrection of the dead or the inheritance of the kingdom of heaven. For these things, as far as it concerns human nature, seem to be contrary to hope; but as far as the power of God is concerned in hope they are believed according to the precedent set by Abraham for believers, that whatsoever God has promised, he is able also to do; but only if faith, hope, and love abide in those who believe.[189] I consider faith to be the first beginnings and the very foundations of salvation; hope is certainly the progress and increase of the building; however love is the perfection and culmination of the entire work. That is why love is said to be greater than everything else.[190]

(4) Thus Abraham "against hope believed in hope that he would become the father of many nations," which in the future would be like the stars of heaven, not only in terms of the great-

---

183. For Origen's attribution of Hebrews to Paul, see 1.18.6.
184. Heb 11.1.   185. Rom 8.24–25.
186. Eph 2.8.
187. Mk 10.52; Lk 17.19; 18.42; cf. Mt 9.22.
188. Mt 9.29; cf. Mt 8.13.   189. Cf. 1 Cor 13.13.
190. 1 Cor 13.13.

ness of number but also in splendor. He believed firmly in the one who gave the promise and "did not weaken in faith." It seems to me that he says, "he did not weaken in faith" in order to show that there does exist a certain kind of weakness in faith. Now if there is weakness, doubtless there is also soundness, as he points out elsewhere when he says, "Rebuke them sharply that they might become sound in the faith."[191] Blessed then is the one who is not weak in the faith. But if someone is weak, the Apostle describes the cure for him when he says, "Receive the one who is weak in faith but not for the purpose of quarreling over opinions. For some believe in eating anything, while the weak should eat vegetables."[192] He is assuredly pointing out that the vegetables of the Word are to be supplied to the one who is weak in faith, lest the complete doctrinal teaching of the faith should be forced upon those who are in doubt about it and who are, as it were, ill. Faith is called sound, however, when it is perfect and when it lacks nothing; this is what believes that a person can eat all things,[193] that is to say, which can grasp all things.[194] The person who possesses this ability is called spiritual and he judges all things[195] and can be made to stumble by no expression whatsoever. It becomes apparent from this that there is a certain increase and progress in the faith. Some possess a small share of faith, others a large share, still others have all faith. This is also the reason the Apostle was saying, "If I have all faith so that I may move mountains."[196] Moreover, in the Gospels the disciples call out to the Lord like those in whom a complete faith does not yet dwell, "Increase our faith!"[197]

(5) Consider, if you will, whether we could not also understand the increase of love [in the believer] in a manner similar to the way we have spoken about faith, such that we might also say of love, in the same way [Paul] said, "If I have all faith,"[198] "If I have all love." That person has all love who possesses everything which belongs to love, just as the Apostle says, "Love is patient; love is kind; love is not haughty or envious or vain; it does

---

191. Ti 1.13.
192. Rom 14.1–2.
193. Rom 14.2.
194. Cf. 2.14.14; 9.36.
195. Cf. 1 Cor 2.15.
196. 1 Cor 13.2.
197. Lk 17.5. Cf. 4.1.10–11.
198. 1 Cor 13.2.

not act inconsiderately. It is not [M982] irritable; it bears all things, believes all things, hopes all things, endures all things," and the other similar things.[199] If someone should possess these things, it seems right to me to say that he has all love, a love which doubtless consists of these individual aspects enumerated by the Apostle above. Likewise it can be said about mercy and piety and the other virtues as well, in my opinion. And perhaps it is possible to be said in each instance, just as it was said about faith, that, "faith was reckoned as righteousness,"[200] so also of love, that love was reckoned to him as righteousness, or the same of piety or mercy.[201]

(6) Let us now look at what follows. "And he did not weaken in faith. He considered his own body dead, since he was nearly one hundred years old, and Sarah's womb dead; no distrust made him waver concerning the promise of God, but he grew strong in faith." As far as the simple understanding is concerned, he sets forth a plain account that Abraham, when he heard that God had promised him an offspring, did not look to the defunct strength of his one hundred year old body from which he could not possibly hope for a descendant. Instead, looking to the power of the one who made the promise, he believed that nothing is difficult in whatever the Almighty was promising. It says, "But he gave glory to God," in that he perceived that it was the gift of God alone when the laws of human fecundity had ceased to function. Rightly then he gave glory to God, because he had been abandoned by the help of nature. These things seem to have been discussed sufficiently, as I have said, as much as concerns the simple understanding [of the passage].

(7) However someone may object to us: How can it be said that Abraham had a dead body at the age of one hundred years? For after he gave birth to Isaac and after Sarah had died, who had conceived [Isaac] at the age of ninety[202] and lived to be one hundred twenty-seven years old,[203] and even after Isaac took Rebecca for a wife when he was forty,[204] after all this it is

199. 1 Cor 13.4–5, 7.
201. Cf. 4.1.12.
203. Cf. Gn 23.1.
200. Rom 4.9, 22.
202. Cf. Gn 17.17.
204. Cf. Gn 25.20.

written, "Going further, Abraham took a wife, whose name was Keturah. She bore him Zimran, Jokshan, Medan, Median, Ishbak, and Shuah."[205] How could his body be dead, seeing that he grew much older than he was at that time and was able to take a wife and beget six more children?[206] In order that we might remove such objections in a fitting way let us shift the explanation of [Abraham's] dead body[207] to say that Abraham was not dead with the infirmity of old age but in accordance with that power which the saints have at work, first of all, in themselves, and which they also admonish others to possess by saying, "Put to death your members which are earthly!"[208] For I consider it to be absurd that we should fail to believe that this good which Paul possessed in himself—seeing that [Paul] would not command to others what he himself [M983] did not do[209]—that this good which Paul possessed, I say, Abraham did not possess, so great a patriarch that the Apostle even calls him his own father.[210] In [Abraham] as well, then, there was this mortification of the members. He was not enticed by luxury; he did not burn with lust like those of whom Paul says, "It is better to marry than to burn."[211] This same good was also in Sarah; and therefore it is written about her, "womanish things had ceased to function in Sarah."[212] For in her there was none of that feminine lasciviousness or the dissoluteness of incontinence, nor were either of them carried off unwillingly into the enjoyment of lustful desires. On the contrary when they hear of such a hope of posterity and that the glory of their own offspring would be equal to heaven and its stars,[213] when they hear these things, they do not think about their own goods, about the grace of continence, about the mortification of their members, but instead they regard all these things which contributed to their own gain as loss in order that they might gain Christ.[214]

(8) But perhaps you think that I have erred in that I speak of

---

205. Gn 25.1–2.
206. Cf. *Hom in Gn* 11.1.
207. Cf. *Comm in Mt* 14.2.
208. Col 3.5.
209. Cf. 1 Cor 7.29. Origen seems to suggest that Paul may have been married. Cf. 1.1.3; Eusebius, *Ecclesiastical History* 3.30.1.
210. Rom 4.1.
211. 1 Cor 7.9.
212. Cf. Gn 18.11.
213. Cf. Gn 15.5.
214. Cf. Phil 3.7–8.

Christ when I ought to be speaking of Abraham's posterity and his seed.[215] We have not erred, but we are speaking with the Apostle. For he himself interprets these things as having been spoken about Christ when he says, "It is written, 'I shall give this land to you and to your seed.' He has not said, 'and to your seeds,' as to many, but, 'to your seed,' as to one, who is Christ."[216] You see, then, how the Apostle is teaching us that the Lord has spoken in this way to Abraham in order that he might perceive that Christ was to be understood in his seed.[217] And I think that it is for this reason that the Apostle goes on to say and says, "giving glory to God." For Abraham would not have been able to give glory to God concerning the birth of Isaac as much as he could give glory to God if he understood that Christ was going to be born from his own body, which was already dead and purged from vices.

(9) But you also, if you mortify your members which are earthly,[218] if you, casting off all the passion of lust, keep your body dead and liable to none of these vices, you as well can produce the best fruits from it:[219] You can produce an Isaac,[220] that is, joy; and this is the first fruit of the Spirit.[221] Your seed and your works can ascend to heaven and become works of light and be compared to the splendor and brilliance of the stars, so that when the day of resurrection arrives, you will stand out in brightness as one star differs from another star.[222] I will say still more:[223] If you become so pure in mind, so holy in body, and so spotless in your deeds, you can even produce Christ himself according to him who was saying, "My little children, for whom I am again in the pain of childbirth until Christ is formed in you."[224] And just as the Lord himself says concerning himself, "Whoever should do the will of my father in heaven, he is my brother and sister and mother."[225] Who then shall be a mother

---

215. *Semen* means "seed," "offspring," or "descendant."
216. Gal 3.16; Gn 13.15.
217. Cf. 7.19.4–5; *Hom in Gn* 6.2; 9.2.
218. Cf. Col 3.5.
219. Cf. *Hom in Gn* 8.10.
220. Cf. *Hom in Gn* 7.1.
221. Gal 5.22.
222. Cf. 1 Cor 15.41.
223. Cf. *Hom in Gn* 6.3; *Hom in Jos* 22.4.
224. Gal 4.19.
225. Mt 12.50.

of Jesus if not the one whose womb is dead in this way, so that [M984] only then she might afterward bring forth sons of chastity, like the woman about whom the Apostle says, "Yet she will be saved through childbearing, provided they continue in faith and chastity"?[226] On this account as well, I believe, Paul has fittingly added, "And it was reckoned to him as righteousness." For how could righteousness fail to be reckoned to a man who was holding fast to perfection not only in his faith but in all his other virtues as well?

7. *But it was not written for his sake alone that it was reckoned to him as righteousness, but for ours also, to whom it will be reckoned, to us who believe in him who raised Jesus our Lord from the dead, who was handed over on account of our trespasses and was raised on account of our justification.*[227] In this passage what he says, "for his sake alone" ought to be understood as referring to him. Likewise what he says, "but for ours also," refers to us. For obviously Moses did not write these words, "Abraham believed God, and it was reckoned to him as righteousness,"[228] so that Abraham might read them, seeing that Abraham had died long before, but in order that we might make progress in the faith by this kind of reading, understanding that if we believe God in the manner that [Abraham] believed, faith will also be reckoned to us as righteousness, "to those who believe in him who raised Jesus our Lord from the dead."

(2) By all means, in this passage I would like to examine why it is that when the Apostle designates the God in whom we believe and in whom Abraham believed, he has not said: to those who believe in God, the Most High, or: to those who believe in him who made heaven and earth, or: in him who made the angels and the other powers of heavenly glory. Instead he says, "who raised the Lord Jesus from the dead." Let us inquire, then, why, in comparison with Abraham's faith, that title concerning the Lord's resurrection is adopted.

(3) Had Abraham actually believed in him who raised the

---

226. 1 Tm 2.15. 227. Rom 4.23–25.
228. Gn 15.6; Rom 4.3.

Lord Jesus from the dead? After all, Jesus had at that time not yet been raised from the dead. I would like to examine, then, what may have occurred to Paul when he made the promise to us that, just as faith was reckoned as righteousness to Abraham, the believer, so also it will be reckoned to us who believe in him who raised our Lord Jesus from the dead. Keeping with the insignificance of my understanding, I notice that raising our Lord Jesus from the dead is more magnificent among the praises of God than the making of heaven and earth, the creating of angels, and the establishment of the heavenly powers. For the latter had to do with making what did not exist; the former, however, to restore what had perished.[229] The latter was to establish what was not yet destroyed; the former to re-establish what was already destroyed. Finally, the latter was fulfilled by a command; the former by suffering. The figure and representation of this great and marvelous [M985] mystery was anticipated in Abraham's faith. For when he was commanded to sacrifice his only son,[230] he believed that God was able to raise him even from the dead;[231] he believed as well that this matter would not only be accomplished at that time for Isaac but that the full truth of the mystery would be reserved for his seed, who is Christ.[232] This, after all, is the reason he offered his only son with joy, because he was contemplating in him, not the destruction of posterity but the restoration of the world and the renovation of the entire creation which has been re-established through the resurrection of the Lord. This is why the Lord says of him, "Abraham your father rejoiced to see my day, and he saw it and was glad."[233] Therefore in this way the comparison made between the faith of Abraham and of those who believe in him who raised the Lord Jesus seems to be well made; for what Abraham believed as a matter of the future is believed by us as accomplished.[234]

(4) At the same time, however, something displeasing to the heretics[235] is revealed to be true, that the God in whom Abra-

---

229. Cf. Lk 15.8; 19.10; Mt 15.24. See also 2.8.4.
230. Cf. Gn 22.2.   231. Heb 11.17, 19.
232. Cf. Gal 3.16.   233. Jn 8.56.
234. Cf. *Hom in Gn* 8:2.
235. He means the Marcionites. Cf. 3.10.1; 2.14.11; 3.11.2; *Princ* 2.4.

ham believed and who reckoned his faith as righteousness[236] is the same God who also raised the Lord Jesus from the dead. No room is left for the interpretation that there is one God of the law, but that the Father of the Lord Jesus Christ is another.

(5) Yet we still need to examine why the Apostle should make a most prominent mention of Christ's resurrection in connection with our faith, seeing that there are a great number of things which Christ is said to be. For he is called wisdom, power, righteousness, the Word, the truth, and the life.[237] Elsewhere the same Apostle says, "God raised us up with Christ and seated us with him in the heavenly places."[238] He is therefore reminding us that if you believe that he has raised Christ from the dead,[239] believe also that he has raised you yourselves likewise with him. And if you believe that he sat down at the right hand of the Father in heaven,[240] believe as well that you yourselves have been placed together with him no longer in earthly regions but in heavenly.[241] And if you believe that you have died together with Christ, believe also that you will live together with him. And if you believe that Christ has died to sin and lives to God, you also ought to be dead to sin and live to God.[242] This is precisely what he declares with apostolic authority when he says, "But if you have been resurrected with Christ, seek the things that are above, where Christ is, seated at the right hand of God. Set your minds on the things that are above, not on things that are on earth."[243] For those who do these things are showing themselves to be believers in him who raised our Lord Jesus from the dead; and to such persons faith will truly be reckoned as righteousness.

(6) For it is not possible that righteousness can be reckoned to a person who has any unrighteousness dwelling in him, even if he believes in him who raised the Lord Jesus from the dead.[244] For righteousness cannot have anything in common with unrighteousness; [M986] just as light cannot with dark-

---

236. Cf. Rom 4.3.
237. Cf. 1 Cor 1.24; 1.30; Jn 1.1; 14.6.
238. Eph 2.6.
239. Cf. Rom 6.4; Col 2.12.
240. Heb 1.3.
241. Eph 1.20.
242. Cf. Rom 6.8–11. See also 5.8.11.
243. Col 3.1–2.
244. Cf. 4.1.6.

ness, nor life with death.[245] So also then certainly to those who believe in Christ but do not lay aside the old man with his unrighteous deeds,[246] faith cannot be reckoned as righteousness. Moreover, in a similar way, we can say that just as righteousness cannot be reckoned to an unrighteous man, neither can chastity be reckoned to an unchaste one, nor justice to an unjust one, nor generosity to a greedy one, nor piety to an impious one, so long as he does not lay aside the old garments of the vices and "put on the new man who was created according to God and is being renewed in the knowledge of God according to the image of him who created him."[247]

(7) For it is on this account as well that he adds to this in what follows and goes on to say of the Lord Jesus, "who was handed over on account of our sins and was raised on account of our justification." He wanted to show that even *we* must abhor and reject the things on account of which Christ was handed over. For if we believe he was handed over on account of our sins, why do we not regard every sin as hostile and injurious to us, seeing that it is recorded to be on account of these sins that our redeemer was handed over to death? For if any fellowship or friendship should again occur between us and sin, we are showing that we have no regard for the death of Christ Jesus, since we are embracing and following the things which he fought against and conquered. The Apostle, bringing all this together at once, has designated the garment of the old man as if a body of sin, which he urges those who believe in him who raised the Lord Jesus from the dead to strip off, in order that, by rejecting the garment of unrighteousness, they might put on the Lord Jesus,[248] which is the true garment of righteousness, so that faith would be deservedly reckoned as righteousness to those who believe.

(8) "Therefore he was handed over on account of our sins and resurrected on account of our justification." For if we have been raised together with Christ,[249] who is righteousness,[250] if

---

245. Cf. 2 Cor 6.14.
246. Cf. Col 3.9.
247. Col 3.9–10.
248. Cf. Col 3.9–10; Rom 13.14.
249. Col 3.1.
250. Cf. 1 Cor 1.30.

we walk in the newness of life,[251] if we live in accordance with righteousness, then to us Christ has been raised for our justification. But if we have not yet laid aside the old man with his deeds,[252] but we live in unrighteousness, I dare say that to us Christ has not yet been resurrected for justification nor has he been handed over on account of our sins.[253] For if I believe this, how can I love that for which he endured death? If I believe these things, that he rose for my justification, how can unrighteousness be pleasing to me? Therefore Christ justifies only those who have received the new life in the pattern of his resurrection and who reject the old garments of unrighteousness and iniquity as if they were the cause of death.[254]

(9) But I would like to examine whether it was only for this one thing he said, [M987] "Abraham believed God and it was reckoned to him as righteousness,"[255] that the Apostle says that these things were written, not for Abraham's sake alone but also for ours. Do you think that of all the things said about Abraham, this single statement was written not only for his sake but also for ours? Or does it not seem that certain other things have been written, not for his sake alone but also for ours? Indeed, is not everything which is said about him said not for his sake alone but also for us?[256] And not only regarding Abraham, but consider whether perchance the things said about Isaac should be accepted in the same way as well, so that what was written about him has in view not only him but also us. It is similar for what was written about Jacob and the other patriarchs. For what reason could there seem to be that what was indeed written about Abraham could be said to pertain to us, but, although similar in form, not what was said about Isaac and Jacob and Judah and Joseph and the others? Now if no reason will appear for why what is said of one patriarch ought to be received but not also what is said about the others, then it will be logical that, concerning everything that has been written, not only for the sake of those who were living at the time but also for our sake, they have been written.

251. Rom 6.4.
253. Cf. 8.2.8.
255. Rom 4.3; Gn 15.6.
252. Cf. Col 3.9.
254. Cf. 2.13.23.
256. Cf. *Hom in Ex* 2.1.

(10) What especially persuades me to think this way is the discourse in the Gospel in which our Lord and Savior, to those who said to him, "Abraham is our father," answered, "If you were Abraham's seed, you would assuredly do the works of Abraham. But now you are seeking to kill me, a man who has spoken the truth to you which I heard from my Father. This Abraham did not do."[257] By these words he is clearly showing that those who do the works of Abraham are sons of Abraham, and what was written about Abraham was written for their sake. Now here it belongs to the wise man who has been enlightened by God to consider and to discern how every single work which is written about Abraham might seem to be fulfilled in themselves.[258] For instance it was said to him, "Depart from your land and your kindred and your father's house and go to the land that I will show you."[259] [It should be seen how] the one who wants to be manifested as descending from Abraham's seed by his works needs to comply with these things, since they are obviously written not for [Abraham's] sake alone but also for those "who believe in him who raised our Lord Jesus from the dead." When he has fulfilled these things [it should be seen how] he ought also to hope for what is said in addition, namely, "And I will make you into a great nation and I will bless you and I will make your name great, and you will be blessed. And I will bless those who bless you and those who curse you I will curse; and in you all the tribes of the earth will be blessed."[260] And again when the Scripture says, "So Abraham went in accordance with the things [M988] the Lord had told him,"[261] it should be seen how this too has been written not only for Abraham's sake but also on account of us, in order that we might walk in accordance with everything the Lord has spoken. But it should also been seen how the things which are similarly written about Isaac and the others might pertain to us. Now is not the time, however, for us to bring forward everything and to discuss in detail the manner in which the things said and done in the Holy Scriptures concerning Abraham and the other saints may

257. Jn 8.39–40.
259. Gn 12.1.
261. Gn 12.4.

258. Cf. *Comm in Jn* 20.10.
260. Gn 12.2–3.

be fulfilled in us who believe in the one in whom Abraham believed. Instead we have, to the extent that the requirements of the present work allow, opened up a road in which anyone who longs to train himself in the Holy Scriptures may more extensively proceed. Up to this point my discourse has examined the question of the rationale of his faith which was reckoned as righteousness, the observance of the various kinds of law, and the diverse kinds of uncircumcision and circumcision. Now let us see how those who have been justified by faith and not by works are instructed by the Apostle.

8. *Therefore, having been justified by faith, let us have peace with God through our Lord Jesus Christ, through whom we also have an access through faith to this grace in which we stand; and we boast in the hope of the glory of God.*[262] By these words he is very openly inviting the one who has grasped what it means to be justified by faith and not by works to "the peace of God which surpasses all understanding,"[263] in which the sum of perfection consists. But in order that we might ascertain the Apostle's meaning with greater care, let us examine what the word "peace" means in itself, as well as that "peace" which is through our Lord Jesus Christ. "Peace" is said where no one is in disagreement, no one quarrels, where nothing hostile and nothing barbaric is being done. So then, we who were once God's enemies by following that enemy and tyrant, the devil, now most assuredly have peace with God,[264] if we have thrown down the devil's arms and have taken up the sign of Christ and the banner of his cross.[265] But this takes place through our Lord Jesus Christ who reconciled us to God through the sacrifice of his own blood, as it is written, "When we were God's enemies we were reconciled through the blood of his cross."[266] Elsewhere Paul has added to these things by saying, "We make our appeal on Christ's behalf: Be reconciled to God!"[267] If then someone has peace with God and is reconciled through the blood of Christ, he no longer

---

262. Rom 5.1–2. 263. Phil 4.7.
264. Rom 5.1.
265. For the same military metaphor see 5.1.10; 5.1.31; 5.3.7.
266. Cf. Rom 5.10; Col 1.20. 267. 2 Cor 5.20.

partakes of the things which are hateful to God.[268] Now do you want to hear what those things are which are hateful to God? Paul himself teaches you when he says, "The wisdom of the flesh is hateful to God, for it is not subjected to the law of God."[269] And so, if you are wise in a fleshly manner, [M989] or if you expose your life to the lusts of the flesh and release the floods of luxury, or if you interpret the law with a fleshly understanding and not spiritually and then defend this understanding with assertions which are rooted in a human method of investigation rather than through spiritual grace and a more profound understanding, then you have become God's enemy through the wisdom of the flesh.[270]

(2) Not only Paul writes such things in his letters. Listen also to James, the brother of the Lord, testifying in similar fashion when he says, "Whoever wants to be a friend of this world makes himself an enemy of God."[271] Moreover John testifies to the same things, "Little children, do not love the world or the things in the world, because everything which is in the world, both the lust of the flesh and the lust of the eyes, are not from God."[272] Therefore the person in whom these things exist cannot have peace with God. On the contrary he awakens those hostilities which Christ came to destroy. This is precisely what the Apostle says elsewhere about Christ, "He himself is our peace, who made the two one by destroying the dividing wall of separation, the hostility. He nullified in his flesh the law of commands with its ordinances, that he might form the two into one new man in himself, making peace."[273] But if Christ came to destroy the hostility and to make peace and to reconcile to God those of us who were divided by the barrier of evil which we had constructed by our practice of sin, then, after that barrier of sin has been removed, whoever is turned back again to sin, no doubt he restores the hostility and rebuilds the wall of separation and, by this means, destroys the work of Christ and makes void the cross of his suffering.

---

268. Cf. 4.12.3.
270. Cf. 4.12.5.
272. 1 Jn 2.15–16.

269. Rom 8.7. Cf. 6.12.7.
271. Jas 4.4.
273. Eph 2.14–15.

(3) But as for us, "having been justified by faith let us have peace with God through our Lord Jesus Christ." Let us have peace so that the flesh will no longer struggle against the spirit[274] nor the law of the members strive against the law of God.[275] Among us may it not be "Yes and no,"[276] but may we all say one thing, may we think the same things, may there be no dissension within ourselves nor outside with one another.[277] And then we have peace with God through our Lord Jesus Christ. One thing must be recognized with complete certainty: No one in whom an evil vice exists can have peace. For as long as one is constantly thinking of ways to harm his neighbor, as long as one is always searching for means of doing injury, his mind is never at peace.

(4) Now if you should ask me: How can a righteous man have peace when he is being attacked by the devil and is enduring wars of temptations? I would say that this man has peace more than everyone else.[278] For behold how carefully the Apostle writes. He has not said, "Therefore having been justified by faith let us have peace" and then silence. Rather he adds, [M990] "let us have peace with God," knowing that war against the devil establishes peace with God. We enter more into peace with God at that time when we are persevering in warlike hostility against the devil and when we struggle furiously against vices of the flesh. After all, in this manner the apostle James says, "Resist the devil and he will flee from you; come near to God and he will come near to you."[279] Thus you can see that he thought that one will be near to God at that very moment when he is resisting the devil.

(5) "Therefore let us have peace with God through our Lord Jesus Christ." And he has added, "through whom we also have an access into this grace in which we stand." How we may have access to grace through our Lord Jesus Christ the Savior himself states, "I am the door, and no one comes to the Father except through me."[280] We have access to grace through him,

---

274. Cf. Gal 5.17.
276. 2 Cor 1.18.
278. Cf. *Hom in Nm* 9.2.
280. Jn 10.9; 14.6.

275. Cf. Rom 7.23.
277. Cf. 1 Cor 1.10; Phil 2.2.
279. Jas 4.7–8.

then, because he is the door. But let us see what sort of door he is in order that we might understand what sort of people they ought to be who would enter through it and have access to grace. The door is truth,[281] and through the door of truth liars cannot enter. Again, the door is also righteousness,[282] and through the door of righteousness the unrighteous do not pass. The door says, "Learn from me because I am gentle and humble in heart."[283] Through the door of humility and gentleness, then, neither the wrathful nor the arrogant may enter. Consequently if there is someone who, in accordance with the Apostle's word, wants to have access through our Lord Jesus Christ to the grace of the Lord in which Paul and those who are like him claim to stand, he must be purged from all these things we have recorded above. Otherwise this door will not allow those who are doing things alien to it to enter through it. Instead it closes at once and does not allow those who are dissimilar to it to pass through.

(6) Doubtless this is what happened to those five foolish virgins who, since they did not bring the oil of good works in their vessels,[284] found the door closed when they came too late.[285] For these foolish souls were unable to enter through the door of wisdom and have access to grace. Rightly however does the Apostle Paul claim to stand in grace, who also has said elsewhere, "I have worked harder than all the others, but not I but the grace of God with me."[286] Therefore if there be another who would work harder, who boasts in his weaknesses,[287] who is often occupied with dangers, "dangers at sea, dangers from rivers, dangers from thieves, dangers from false brothers,"[288] and amidst all these things should stand constant in faith, he will likewise be said to stand in grace.

(7) Let us further consider what it is that follows: "And we boast in the hope of the glory of God." What troubles me is why he did not claim to boast in the glory of God, but "in the hope

---

281. Cf. Jn 14.6.
282. Cf. 1 Cor 1.30.
283. Mt 11.29.
284. For oil of good works cf. 2.5.3; *Hom in Lv* 13:2; *Hom in Cant* 2.2.
285. Cf. Mt 25.1–12.
286. 1 Cor 15.10.
287. Cf. 2 Cor 12.9.
288. 2 Cor 11.26.

of the glory [M991] of God." Indeed, something seems to be missing from this expression such that there ought to be supplied: the hope "of seeing" the glory of God. Through these things he is teaching us what he himself says elsewhere, that "the things hoped for are eternal, but the things seen are temporal."[289] For Moses is said to have seen the glory of God; it is also said that the people saw the glory of the God of Israel at the dedication of the Lord's house.[290]

(8) But of this kind of glory which can be seen, Paul, who was well acquainted with the mysteries of God, has dared to proclaim that even this glory which appeared on Moses' face shall be set aside.[291] That glory which is hoped for, however, of which it says, "in the hope of the glory of God," is never set aside. For it is of such a quality that the same Apostle says of it while speaking of Christ, "He is the brightness of his glory and the exact imprint of his substance."[292] Those who bear the hope of seeing this glory, then, are the ones of whom it has been said, "Blessed are the pure in heart, for they will see God."[293] At that time when pain and sadness and sighing flee[294] and when things which are now seen in a mirror and in a riddle are set aside, those things which are face to face remain.[295]

(9) Now perhaps it will seem possible to someone in opposition to object to our explanation that the Apostle himself says, "But we who, with unveiled face, beholding the glory of the Lord, shall be reformed into the same image from glory to glory as from the spirit of the Lord."[296] Our objector will say: Why does he still bear the hope of glory when he claims that he is already beholding the Lord's glory with an unveiled face and is being reformed from glory into glory? Consider whether we can resolve this objection in the following manner. The Apostle, it seems to me, depicts different kinds of glories. There was one glory revealed through the ministry of Moses, concerning

289. 2 Cor 4.18.
290. Cf. Ex 40.34; Lv 9.23; Nm 17.7; 1 Kgs 8.11; 2 Chr 5.14; 7.3. See also 2.5.4–5; *Comm in Jn* 32.26ff.
291. Cf. 2 Cor 3.7.
292. Heb 1.3.
293. Mt 5.8.
294. Cf. Is 35.10; 51.11; Rv 21.4.
295. Cf. 1 Cor 13.12. Cf. 3.2.14.
296. 2 Cor 3.18.

which we have already spoken above.²⁹⁷ Another glory was furnished at the coming of the Savior in the flesh, concerning which John also speaks in the Gospel, "And we have seen his glory, the glory as of an only-begotten of the Father, full of grace and truth."²⁹⁸ We cannot say of this glory that it is the one which is to be hoped for, for the apostles claim to have seen it; and that sentence is true which says, "For who sees what he also hopes for?"²⁹⁹ In point of fact that glory which is to be hoped for, concerning which in the present passage the Apostle is claiming to boast, "in the hope of the glory of God," can be understood to refer to that glory of which the Savior speaks in the Gospel, "When the Son of Man comes in the glory of the Father and of the holy angels."³⁰⁰ But he said "of the Father and the holy angels" not in order to say that there is one glory of God the Father and of the angels [M992] but to show, it seems to me, that those glories which were entrusted either to our predecessors through Moses or to us through the coming of Christ in the flesh were not for angels but for men; for they were administered to men, and were measured in proportion to men's ability to receive them. However that glory with which the Son of Man is about to come for the judgment of the world³⁰¹ shall be as much as the Father's glory, which would be able to be grasped only by angels. Now if there have been certain saints capable of grasping that glory, doubtless they will be the ones of whom it is said that "they will be like the angels of God."³⁰² Thus it appears to be correctly spoken concerning the future glory which is to be hoped for, that "the Son of Man will come in the glory of the Father and of the holy angels,"³⁰³ i.e., in the glory which earthly men are not yet worthy to grasp, but only the holy angels. For God dispenses the various magnitudes of glories in accordance with the capacity of minds.

(10) But no one can believe in or grasp that glory which in the Gospels the apostles claim to have seen, the glory "as of an only-begotten of the Father, full of grace and truth,"³⁰⁴ unless

297. Cf. 2.5.4ff.
298. Jn 1.14.
299. Rom 8.24.
300. Lk 9.26.
301. Cf. Mt 25.31.
302. Mt 22.30.
303. Lk 9.26.
304. Jn 1.14.

he has taken hold of the way of understanding from that glory which was administered through Moses in the law.[305] He also testifies, who was saying to Nathaniel, "We have found him of whom Moses and the prophets wrote, Jesus of Nazareth,"[306] in which he plainly shows that the [apostles], enlightened by the law and the prophets,[307] saw the light of his glory which was as of an only-begotten from the Father. In a similar way as well, what the Apostle has said, "Beholding the Lord's glory with unveiled face we shall be transformed into the same image from glory unto glory as from the spirit of the Lord,"[308] should be understood such that whoever contemplates that glory of the only-begotten with an unveiled face, i.e., with a complete understanding of the faith, will steer the acuteness of their mind, by the same image in which he goes from the law to the Gospels and to the coming of the Savior in the flesh, when the gaze of the heart is enlightened by faith,[309] to the [Lord's] second coming in glory. Such a person will be transformed from the present glory to that of the future glory which is hoped for. In my opinion this is why no one is able to deserve to become receptive to that future glory unless he should already undertake a certain use and exercise of it here, according to what the Apostle says, by looking intently in a mirror and in a riddle.[310] So that, by means of the example of continuous meditation, which the one placed in the flesh makes of the divine glory, becoming more prepared to receive his true glory, he might be transformed through the power of the Holy Spirit.

9. *And not only that, but we also boast in afflictions, knowing that affliction produces patience, and patience produces approved character, and approved character produces hope; and surely hope does not confound, because God's love [M993] has been shed abroad into our hearts through the Holy Spirit who has been given to us.*[311] The very first words in this section contain a certain ambiguity, for in what comes next there is nothing to which what he said, "not

305. Cf. 2 Cor 3.7.
307. Cf. 1.13.1; 1.15.1.
309. Cf. Eph 1.18.
311. Rom 5.3–5.

306. Jn 1.45.
308. 2 Cor 3.18.
310. 1 Cor 13.12.

only that" might be referred.[312] Consider then whether we can resolve the ambiguity of this expression in the following manner. Above [Paul] has taught that there are many things exhibited to us through the Lord Jesus Christ, as when he says that we are justified from faith through our Lord Jesus Christ and through him we have access into this grace; through him as well we boast in the hope of the glory of God.[313] In my opinion, "not only that" should be referred to all these things which have just been said. That is: We have through our Lord Jesus Christ not only these things which I have just said, but also the fact that we boast in our afflictions. For whereas others are saddened during affliction, we boast in afflictions, having been strengthened by the power of his grace. For we have learned a new discipline by his instruction, namely that we should obtain the good of patience through afflictions, and when we possess this good of patience, we shall be judged as having approved character; and when we have been approved through the patience of many afflictions, we may hope for a future reward from God. This hope, because it is certain and real, does not confound those who possess it. For the love of God which is greater than everything[314] follows faith and hope, and not only fills our mind but also abounds and is shed abroad into our hearts in view of the fact that it is not sought by us by human skill, but is flooded through the grace of the Holy Spirit. Let these things be explanations according to the sequence of the discourse itself, or "letter," for this disclosure of the Apostle's eloquence. Now let us examine what the interior meaning contains.

(2) First let us look at what [Paul] has said about boasting: "We boast in our afflictions." Discussion about boasting in the Scriptures is sometimes stated in a praiseworthy manner, sometimes in a blameworthy manner. For example, when Jeremiah says, "Thus says the Lord: Let not the wise man boast in his own wisdom, nor the strong man boast in his strength, nor the wealthy boast in his wealth; but let him who boasts, boast in this, that he understands and knows me, that I am the Lord

312. Cf. 1.9.6; 4.12.5.
313. Cf. Rom 5.1–2.
314. Cf. 1 Cor 13.13.

who practices mercy, judgment, and righteousness upon the earth,"³¹⁵ in one and the same passage he depicts boasting both in a praiseworthy and a blameworthy sense. For he says that if anyone boasts in his own wisdom, strength, or [M994] wealth, he is boasting in a blameworthy manner. But if a person boasts in the Lord, who is to be known, and in the understanding of his judgments, mercy, and righteousness, he boasts in a praiseworthy manner. Since then the discourse may refer to either sense, we need to ask in what does proper boasting consist and in what does less proper boasting consist. We will only be able to know this if we grasp the essence of things with discrimination.

(3) What we are saying is this: Everything which exists or is done is either good or evil or indifferent. Although a discussion of these matters ought to be conducted more in depth, nevertheless let us set forth what is sufficient for the present passage. It is certain that things are strictly called "good" which pertain to the virtues of the spirit; and only those things are to be defined as "evil" which tend to evilness and which are done contrary to God's law. Other things, however, are indifferent,³¹⁶ that is to say, they are to be designated neither good nor evil, as are wealth, physical beauty, strength, height, and those things which serve the needs of the body. If, then, someone is unfamiliar with the differentiation of this diversity and boasts in those things which neither are truly good nor pertain to the virtue of his spirit, he is boasting in a blameworthy manner.

(4) Paul, however, who was extremely experienced in these matters, when he had said, "we boast in our afflictions," lest he be thought to be boasting in things indifferent and neutral, immediately gives the grounds for this and declares that his own boasting in afflictions pertains to the virtues of his spirit. For

---

315. Jer 9.22–24. Cf. *Hom in Jer* 11.4; 17.5.
316. *Indifferentia* = ἀδιάφορα. Cf. Epictetus, *Discourses* 2.9.15, "For who among us is not already able to discourse, according to the rules of art, upon good and evil?—That some things are good, some evil, and others indifferent; the good include the virtues and all things appertaining; the evil comprise the contrary; and the indifferent include riches, health, reputation." Trans. T. W. Higginson (Roslyn, N.Y.: Walter J. Black, 1944), p. 108. Cf. *Hom in Jer* 12.8; *Cels* 4.45; 5.64; 6.54.

he says the following: The "affliction," for the sake of which I boast, "produces patience, and patience produces approved character, and approved character hope; and hope does not confound, because the love of God has been shed abroad into our hearts through the Holy Spirit." By these statements he is teaching that boasting in one's afflictions may ascend, by means of the virtues which accompany them, up to the summit of the Holy Spirit, just as he says elsewhere, "Let him who boasts, boast in the Lord."[317] It is not proper to boast, then, in one's own wisdom or strength or wealth, but in God alone.

(5) But you may perhaps say: Does not wisdom also pertain to the virtues of the spirit? Why is it deemed blameworthy to boast in wisdom? Yet notice how cautious is Scripture's discourse, which seems unpolished and coarse. It has not said, "Let not the wise boast in wisdom" and then silence, but it says, "Let not the wise man boast in his own wisdom."[318] For whoever boasts in his own and not in God's wisdom boasts in a blameworthy manner.[319] As the prophet also says, "Woe to those who are wise among [M995] themselves and learned in their own sight."[320]

(6) So then it is the wisdom of God to know God and to understand his mercy and his judgment and righteousness which he practices upon the earth, wherefore whoever boasts in these things should boast in the Lord. Human wisdom, however, cannot know and understand God nor can it understand his judgments and mercy and his righteousness which he practices on the earth. It is therefore an indifferent matter and is neutral. For it can happen that someone who is learned in human wisdom may be better prepared to attain to the understanding of divine wisdom and, having been trained in the human kind, he may become more receptive for the divine. In a similar manner, whoever will also make use of the other things which we said are neutral, mere strength or wealth (which are neutral), that is to say, as long as anyone is neither strong in God's work nor rich in showing mercy to the poor, he should not boast in his

---

317. 1 Cor 1.31.
318. Jer 9.23.
319. Cf. *Comm in Mt* 10.19.
320. Is 5.21.

strength or wealth. But if those neutral things are converted into virtues of the spirit and to the fruit of good works, they become worthy of boasting, just as, on the other hand, if they should be changed into evil works so that someone uses his wealth to oppress the poor or uses his strength to throw down the weak, they are no longer neutral but are reckoned as evils. This is why they are called indifferent and neutral according to their own nature because, when attached to evil works, they can be called evil, and, when joined to good works, they can be designated as good.[321] But people who call things good without tending toward either of these two [senses] must be believed to be unskilled and ignorant of rational definitions and classifications. At any rate, it is in an improper sense[322] that we call a builder "wise" and designate a sea captain, architect, and weaving woman as "wise."

(7) In the present section the Apostle says, "Affliction produces patience." If then it is established that patience is one of the virtues of the spirit, doubtless the affliction which brings forth the virtues of the spirit must be designated neither as evil nor as indifferent but as good. Patience is so much to be regarded as a virtue of the spirit, as we said above, that he says that through patience comes the approval of our character, and through approved character hope is given. Certainly then [hope], because it is grounded in God who is the father of all virtues, does not confound the one who hopes. For together with hope, [approved character] possesses the fullness of love, which is united in the first place with the Spirit, because "love is greater than everything."[323]

(8) Now suppose someone should raise the objection to us and say that affliction is to be classified as neutral and indifferent, since we find that even the evil and the godless suffer afflic-

---

321. Cf. *Cels* 4.45.
322. *Abusive.* Heither in Origenes, *Commentarii*, 2:272 n. 47, notes, "The linguistic distinction of rhetoric is presupposed here. A thing is named, appropriately or inappropriately, with the same expression. In Greek καταχρηστικῶς is contrasted with κυρίως; Latin *abusive* with *proprie*. This distinction plays a big role in Origen's exegesis." Cf. 10.5.5; *Princ* 1.2.13; *Comm in Mt* 15.10; *Comm in Cant* Prologue (2).
323. 1 Cor 13.13.

tion. And assuredly their afflictions cannot be reckoned as a virtue of the spirit, seeing that they are suffering affliction on account of their own evil deeds. Consider whether we can respond to this objection in the following way: "Affliction" in the strict sense applies to the saints, but the affliction of the godless and the unrighteous is called a "scourge." After all, in the Psalms it says this: "Many are the afflictions of the righteous."[324] Of the others, however, it says, "Many are the scourges of the sinner."[325] Perhaps for this reason as well affliction and distress[326] pertain to saints [M996] because they are the ones who travel the "narrow and constricted road"[327] and therefore they are said to suffer affliction.[328] In my opinion the apostles also understood this in the Lord, who is the true road[329] upon which the saints travel, when they said, "Master, the crowds are pressing about you and are constricting you."[330]

(9) We ought to accept as the afflictions of the righteous, then, not only those which come externally from matters which we have called above indifferent and neutral, for example, from losses or illnesses or any bodily torment; but also from the fact that while at rest they afflict and exhaust themselves[331] by resisting their own desires, by harnessing their lust, by keeping unbounded liberty in check, and by dashing to the ground everything else which is opposed to the good of self-control. This is in accordance with the one who said, "I punish my body and subject it to servitude, so that after preaching to others I myself should not be rejected."[332] And so the affliction of the righteous cannot be called indifferent but is clearly good, by which the good of virtue is fulfilled. The unrighteous, however, even if they suffer affliction, which we have already said are called by Scripture scourges,[333] do nothing in these scourges and corrections according to the spirit's virtue. They do nothing for patience, nor do they hope for approved character through any

---

324. Ps 34.19.
325. Ps 32.10.
326. *Angustia.*
327. Mt 7.13–14; *angustam viam.*
328. Cf. *Mart* 42.
329. Cf. Jn 14.6.
330. Lk 8.45.
331. Cf. Clement, *Quis dives salvetur* 25.3–6.
332. 1 Cor 9.27.
333. Cf. *Hom in Jer* 19.8.

patience. Therefore the Scripture desires that in such people these things not be called afflictions, which lead to good, but instead scourges, even though in an improper sense[334] you may sometimes run across the term "affliction" said concerning the unrighteous as well.

(10) But in order that you might understand that the affliction of the righteous does not constrain the spirit's virtue but instead expands it,[335] listen to how Paul, when writing to the Corinthians, distinguishes these things, for so he says, "In every way we suffer affliction but we are not constrained; we are struck down but not destroyed."[336] You see that he claims to suffer affliction not in one way but in every way; that is, he is afflicted both in those things which come to pass from without, i.e., things done to him by others, and also in the things which he himself bears within himself for the sake of the self-control of his body and his endeavors for the highest instruction. And therefore he says, "In every way we suffer affliction but we are not constrained."[337] For one who is expanded by the virtues cannot be constrained. And what we are saying will become even clearer in the following manner: Paul himself writes in what follows, "I know how to live humbly, and I know what it is to have plenty. In any and all circumstances I have been taught both to be well-fed and to be hungry, both to have plenty and to be in need."[338] If then what he said above is true, "In every way we suffer affliction,"[339] then it is certain that it is made known that when he is in need, he is afflicted, and when he has plenty he is no less afflicted. When in need he is afflicted because he is lacking something; when he has plenty, however, because he is restraining himself lest he should be softened through abundance or incompetently manage those things which seem to abound. The same applies when he is hungry and when he is well-fed, and when he endures persecutions and when he has rest. And in this way the one who [M997] is afflicted in everything shall rightly boast in his afflictions. It cannot

---

334. See 4.9.6.
336. 2 Cor 4.8–9.
338. Phil 4.12.
335. Cf. 2.6.6; *Orat* 30.1.
337. 2 Cor 4.8.
339. 2 Cor 4.8.

be doubted that from such afflictions is produced patience which, when made worthy of approval, gives birth to hope. Hope, when united with love, will bring the person into union with the Holy Spirit.

(11) But what he has said, "The love of God has been shed abroad into our hearts," needs to be carefully pondered. Into whose hearts is the love of God shed abroad? I think that it is in those who no longer have the spirit of slavery to fall back into fear,[340] but also those in whom "perfect love casts out fear."[341] Moreover the Spirit of adoption is given to them who call out in their hearts, Abba, Father.[342] Therefore it is not into the heart of just anyone into which "the love of God is shed abroad through the Holy Spirit,"[343] but only into that of the perfect man, thus, the kind of man Paul was.

(12) But it seems that I must consider whether here that love which, he says, "is shed abroad into our hearts through the Holy Spirit," is that by which we love God or with which we are loved *by* God. Now if, indeed, that love by which we love God is to be understood here, the statement needs no confirmation. But if that love by which we are being loved by God is instead to be understood here, since he said, "the love of God is poured out into our hearts," it is certain that he is putting down love as the highest and greatest gift of the Holy Spirit so that, just as the gift was first received from God, through this [gift], by which we are loved by God, we are able to love God himself.[344] For Paul himself names it "the Spirit of love,"[345] and God is called love,[346] and Christ is designated "the Son of love."[347] Now if "the Spirit of love" and "the Son of love" and "the God of love" are found, it is certain that both the Son and the Holy Spirit are to be understood as springing from the one fountain of paternal deity. From the fullness of the Spirit, the fullness of love is infused into the hearts of the saints in order to receive participation in the divine nature, as the apostle Peter has taught,[348] so that through this gift of the Holy Spirit, the word

---

340. Cf. Rom 8.15.
342. Cf. Rom 8.15.
344. Cf. 1 Jn 4.19.
346. 1 Jn 4.8.
348. Cf. 2 Pt 1.4.

341. 1 Jn 4.18.
343. Rom 5.5.
345. 2 Tim 1.7.
347. Cf. Col 1.13.

which the Lord said might be fulfilled, "As you, Father, are in me and I am in you, may they also be one in us."[349] This is, of course, to be sharers of the divine nature by the fullness of love furnished through the Holy Spirit.

10. *For Christ, while we were still weak, at the set time, died for the ungodly. For rarely will anyone die for the just—though perhaps for the good someone might dare to die.*[350] Wanting to demonstrate more fully the excellent qualities of the love which he had said was shed abroad in our hearts through the Holy Spirit,[351] for reasons we should have understood, he explains, teaching us that Christ died not for the godly but for [M998] the ungodly. For we were ungodly before we were converted to God, and it was assuredly before we believed that Christ took upon himself his death for us. It is beyond doubt that he would not have done this unless he was filled with an overwhelming love for us beyond measure, both our Lord Jesus Christ himself, in his dying for the ungodly, and God the Father, in his handing over his only begotten for the redemption of the ungodly.[352] For since it is rare that anyone would die for the just and each person hesitates to undergo death even if the death is a just cause, then how great is he and how enormous must we judge to be the love for us of him who, at the time when he suffered, did not run away from enduring death for the ungodly and the unjust? This is certainly a sign of his supreme divine goodness. For unless he had come forth from that substance[353] and had been the Son of that Father, of whom it was said, "No one is good except one, God the Father,"[354] he would assuredly not have been able to show forth so much goodness to us.[355] Therefore, because he himself is recognized to be good from the sign which points to so much goodness, perhaps one might dare to die for this good man. Certainly when anyone has become thoroughly acquainted with how great is Christ's goodness toward him and how great is his love, shed abroad in his heart, he will desire not

---

349. Jn 17.21.
350. Rom 5.6–7. Jerome uses the Greek text of this section in his *Ep* 121.7.
351. Cf. Rom 5.5.   352. Cf. Rom 8.32.
353. Cf. 7.13.9.   354. Mk 10.18; Lk 18.19.
355. Cf. *Comm in Mt* 15.10.

only to die for this good man but even to die bravely.[356] We often see this fulfilled in fact and deed when they, into whose hearts the love of Christ has been abundantly shed, offer themselves, even of their own free will and with complete boldness, to those who persecute them. They confess the name of Christ in the presence of the angels and men[357] while the world listens since they dare not only to suffer mistreatment for his name, but even to undergo death for this good man, which one seldom does for the just. For so great is the love of this life that even when just cause for death is at hand, hardly anyone receives death patiently. But a cause for death appears just when the law of nature imposes it. And even though it may be just to own up to our mortal condition, nevertheless the [human] spirit does not gladly accept submitting to the laws of nature. Therefore "rarely will anyone die for the just." But for the *good* someone might dare to die, and die boldly, especially when he has come to understand that while we were still ungodly and weak, at that time, he first died for us. And how could one who has realized that these things were first offered to him by the [good man], not repay to him the death which he himself paid out for the wicked?

(2) Moreover the error is exposed of those who imagined that this passage is to be interpreted in the way they allege, that what [Paul] says, "For rarely will anyone die for the just," ought to be understood of the god of the law, whom they affirm is just but not good as well.[358] They would however affirm that Christ is good, [M999] as if being the son of a good Father. But what will they do about the fact that we find many martyrs even under the law? They ought to read the books of Maccabees, where a blessed mother endured martyrdom with complete constancy together with her seven sons.[359] Indeed not only do they patiently accept martyrdom, but they also pour out invectives against a tyrant. Then let the [heretics] consider whether what they say is true, that "rarely does anyone die for the just." Let

---

356. Cf. 8.6.10. 357. Cf. Mt 10.32; Lk 12.8.
358. I.e., the Marcionites. Cf. 1.18.2–4; *Princ* 2.5.1.
359. Cf. 2 Mc 7.1–42. Cf. *Mart* 22–27.

them see the three youths who, with all confidence, were together hurled into the blazing furnace of fire[360] for the sake of the freedom of faith. *Then* let them say, "rarely does anyone die for the just." Only the death endured with boldness is a death for God; hardly any other kind of death is submitted to patiently, even if it should be just and should come down by a law of human making.[361]

11. *But God shows his own love in us because if, while we were still sinners, Christ died for us, how much more then, now, having been justified by his blood, will we be saved through him from the wrath.*[362] Since he had said above that "Christ, at the set time, died for those who were still ungodly,"[363] now he wants to show from this the greatness of God's love for men. For if it was so great for the ungodly and sinners that he gave his only Son for their salvation,[364] how much more bountiful and widespread shall it be toward those who have been converted and atoned and, as he himself says, redeemed by his own blood?[365]

(2) In my opinion, for Paul this variety of words is not superfluous, that sometimes he calls those for whom Christ died "the weak," sometimes "the ungodly," and sometimes "sinners." And even though he confesses that he is unskilled in speech,[366] nevertheless I do not believe that he has alternated in this [terminology] through any lack of skill, but rather through profound knowledge.[367] For in these three terms every class of sin is collected. A person, being ignorant of God, is led into every evil and is called "ungodly." Another, while knowing God and wanting to keep the commandment, is conquered by the frailty of the flesh and becomes ensnared by the allurements of the present life and is called "weak." Or a person may knowingly and willingly despise the commandment and hate the correction of God and cast his words behind him[368] and is named "sinner." And so Paul, who, as we have said, confesses that he is un-

---

360. Cf. Dn 3.20ff.
362. Rom 5.8–9.
364. Cf. Rom 8.32; Jn 3.16.
366. Cf. 2 Cor 11.6.
368. Cf. Ps 50.17.

361. Cf. Jerome, *Ep* 121.7.5.
363. Rom 5.6.
365. Cf. Rom 5.9; Eph 1.7.
367. Cf. 7.6.1.

trained in speech,[369] has comprehended by this threefold diversity of expressions all those for whom Christ is being proclaimed to have died.

(3) Now if sometimes even those who are under the law and who seem to worship God are called "ungodly" in the Holy Scriptures, [M1000] it is because they, having abandoned the God of their fathers, worship the gods of the nations.[370] Now when Paul, although he elsewhere says, "We who are Jews by nature and not gentile sinners,"[371] numbers himself among the sinners,[372] this is [but] the excellence of his humility.[373] For he is imitating the one who, "though he committed no sin was made sin for us,"[374] and who, though he was God, lived among men.[375]

(4) "But God shows his own love in us." "He shows" means here, "he reinforces," or "he makes attractive," in proportion to the kindness he has exhibited. For the fact that "Christ died for us while we were still sinners" gives us hope that through him he will much more save us, who have now been purged of sin and justified from the wrath which threatens sinners. And he who so loved strangers and enemies that he gave up his only Son for us unto death,[376] how much more will he present those who have become his own and who have been reconciled to himself to eternal salvation. Now the question of how Christ died for us and in what way he, since he is the lamb of God, would take away the sin of the world[377] and bear our weaknesses[378] and suffer pain on our behalf, has been frequently discussed by us in other passages.[379] There we have cited instances reported in secular histories, that even among the heathen several individuals are regarded to have averted plagues, storms, and similar things by devoting themselves to death, or to have delivered their own homeland or nation from the de-

369. Cf. 2 Cor 11.6.
370. Cf. Jgs 2.12; 2 Chr 7.22; 24.18, 24; 28.6.
371. Gal 2.15; I Tim 1.15.   372. Rom 5.8.
373. Cf. 1.1.1; 6.9.12.   374. 2 Cor 5.21.
375. Cf. Bar 3.36, 38; Phil 2.7.   376. Cf. Rom 8.32; Jn 3.16.
377. Cf. Jn 1.29.   378. Cf. Is 53.4; Mt 8.17.
379. Cf. *Comm in Jn* 6.53ff.; 28.19; *Cels* 1.31 (dated later than the *Commentary*).

struction of a threatening scourge.[380] To what extent these recorded events are actually true, or what significance they may have if they are true, God alone knows. However, none of those concerning whom these stories are told, not even in *fiction*, is presented as having absolved the sins of the whole world—except Jesus alone, who, "though he was in the form of God, thought it not robbery to be equal with God, but he emptied himself."[381] And having taken the form of a slave, in accordance with the Father's will, he offered himself as a sacrifice for the whole world[382] by handing over his own blood to the ruler of this world.[383] This was in accordance with the wisdom which "none of the rulers of this world understood; for if they would have understood, they would not have crucified the Lord of majesty";[384] nor would that blood after which they thirsted[385] have quenched, not so much their thirst as their power; nor would it have destroyed their kingdom;[386] nor would what the Lord said in the Gospel have befallen them: "Behold, now the ruler of this world has been condemned";[387] and, "Behold, I was seeing Satan falling like lightning from heaven."[388]

(5) "Much more surely then," he says, [M1001] "having now been justified by his blood will we be saved from wrath through him." Indeed, above he had said, "Therefore having been

---

380. Two such pagan examples are given in CWE 70:303 nn. 20–21: Codrus, legendary king of Athens, sacrificed his own life to save his country, in fulfillment of a prophecy made about him which said that the Dorian invasion would be successful if his life were spared. Also Marcus Curtius was said to have leapt while on horseback into a chasm which opened in the Forum to save his country. This too was in fulfillment of an oracle's prophecy. One calls to mind as well Iphigenia, daughter of Agamemnon, who was sacrificed at Aulis to avert the bad weather that was delaying the Greek fleet *en route* to Troy. Also, Alcestis was willing to die in the place of her husband, Admetus, King of Pherae in Thessaly. Finally, Origen was familiar with Josephus, who offered his own life in exchange for the Jews of Jerusalem; *War of the Jews* 9.4. Cf. *1 Clement* 55.55.

381. Phil 2.6–7.

382. Cf. 1 Jn 2.2. For Origen's view of the atonement, see Fairweather, *Origen and Greek Patristic Theology*, p. 187f., "Although Origen did not develop the conception of the vicarious character of Christ's sacrifice, as was subsequently done by Anselm, he undoubtedly took this view of it." See also *Comm in Mt* 13.8.

383. Cf. 2.13.29.
384. 1 Cor 2.7–8.
385. Cf. 3.7.14.
386. Cf. *Comm in Mt* 16:8.
387. Jn 16.11.
388. Lk 10.18.

justified by faith let us have peace with God."[389] Now he says, "Much more now, having been justified by his blood will we be saved from wrath through him." By this he is showing that neither does our faith justify us apart from the blood of Christ nor does the blood of Christ justify us apart from our faith. Of the two, however, the blood of Christ justifies us much more than our faith. And for this reason: It seems to me that, although he plainly said above, "having been justified by faith,"[390] here he adds, "how much more then, now, having been justified by his blood"; in order to teach that even if our faith saves us from the coming wrath, and even if our works of righteousness save us,[391] nevertheless beyond all these things it is much more the blood of Christ that will save us from the coming wrath.

(6) How the wrath of God should be understood has been sufficiently discussed by us in the exposition of the Second Psalm,[392] as well as how what was written can be fulfilled, "Let us be saved by fleeing from the coming wrath,"[393] indeed by fleeing wrath in such a way that it does not lay hold of us as we pursue righteousness, piety, faith, love, patience, gentleness,[394] and other similar things.[395] And thus wrath is that to which each one is handed over in proportion to the measure and merit of sins.[396] According to what is written in the Seventy-seventh Psalm, however, God does not kindle all this wrath.[397] For who could endure it if the Lord kindled all his wrath against sinners? After all, very dreadful is that which is foretold in the Song of Moses, where he says, "A fire is kindled by my fury, it will burn to the depths of the infernal regions; it will devour the earth and its increase, it will set on fire the foundations of the mountains."[398] Behold then, for that fire which is kindled from the wrath or fury of the Lord devours the earth and the depths of the infernal regions and consumes the works of the

---

389. Rom 5.1. 390. Rom 5.1.
391. Cf. 1 Thes 1.10; Jas 2.21.
392. Cf. 4.1.19. The greater part of Origen's *Commentary on the Psalms* is no longer extant. On the theme "wrath" see 1.16.1; 2.4.1.
393. Cf. Mt 3.7; Lk 3.7; 1 Thes 1.10.   394. Cf. 1 Tm 6.11.
395. Cf. *Hom in Lk* 22.7.   396. Cf. 4.4.7.
397. Cf. Ps 78.38.   398. Dt 32.22.

earth. It even sets on fire not the heights of the mountains but their foundations, that is to say, not the profound souls or the heavenly minds, but those which have been cast to the ground or the earth, or even submerged in the earth's depths, in the same way as are the foundations of the mountains. It was necessary to discuss the wrath of God a little bit at this point so that it might be recognized more clearly from what evils the blood of Christ has rescued us.

12. *For if while we were enemies, we were reconciled to God through the death of his Son, much more surely, having been reconciled, will we be saved by his life. Not only that, but we even boast in God through our Lord [M1002] Jesus Christ, through whom we have now received reconciliation.*[399] When he says, "when we were enemies, we were reconciled to God," he plainly shows that there is no substance which, in accordance with Marcion's or Valentinus's definition, is naturally hostile to God.[400] Otherwise, if it were hostile by nature and not by its will, it would assuredly not receive reconciliation. But when some enemy becomes a friend, it is certain that so long as he does the works which God does not love, he is God's enemy. And each person becomes as bad and as detestable an enemy of God as much as he multiplies deeds which merit enmity. So then there are certain degrees and grades, distinguished according to the quality and quantity of the sins committed among those who are God's enemies.

(2) This is the reason he who sinned beyond all others is recorded by Paul as the last enemy to be destroyed.[401] Conversely, it is certain that those who have been reconciled through the death of his Son are deemed to be friends. Thus someone is a friend in the way Moses was called a friend of God,[402] and also those to whom the Savior said, "No longer do I call you slaves but friends."[403] I believe however that in heaven there are certain others who are even more intimate friends of God, whether

---

399. Rom 5.10–11.
400. Cf. Preface of Origen (1); 2.4.7; 2.10.2; 8.11.2; *Princ* 3.1.8; *Hom in Jer* 2.12; 10.5; *Comm in Jn* 2.7.
401. 1 Cor 15.26.   402. Cf. Ex 33.11.
403. Jn 15.15.

those who always look upon the face of God[404] or those who are always standing in the presence of the Most High.[405] Just as we said above that there exists a certain ultimate enemy,[406] so also here certain ones are called God's ultimate friends because of the merits of their virtues.

(3) Since then these things are so, I do not know whether the one who is still abiding in those works which God hates and for the sake of which there are hostilities between God and men, may be deservedly said to be reconciled to God through the blood of Christ. For how can he who does the things of an enemy be reconciled? But of himself and of those like him Paul deservedly says, "When we were God's enemies we were reconciled to God through the blood[407] of his Son." Where such a reconciliation has occurred, where not the word of a suppliant but the blood of a mediator has removed the hostilities between God and men, how great is the disgrace for us to return again to the state of hostility and do the things which he hates, the one whom no one, other than the shedding of his holy blood, reconciled for us.

(4) But when writing to the Ephesians Paul recounts in even more detail the matter of reconciliation and hostility and the shedding of Christ's blood, which can more easily open up the passage from the present section, provided we join the former with the latter. Hence he says in this way, "Therefore, remember that at one time you who are Gentiles in the flesh, called 'the uncircumcision' [M1003] by that which is called 'the circumcision,' done in the flesh by human hands since you were at that time without Christ, being aliens from the commonwealth of Israel, and strangers to his covenants of promise, having no hope and being without God in the world. But now in Christ Jesus, you who once were far off have been brought near by the blood of Christ. For he is our peace; he has made both groups into one and has broken down the middle wall of the enclosure, the hostility in his own flesh, making void the law

---

404. Cf. Mt 18.10.
405. Cf. Dn 7.10; Tb 12.15; Lk 1.19.
406. Cf. 1 Cor 15.26.
407. Concerning the reading "blood" see Bammel, *Römerbrieftext*, p. 331.

with its commandments and ordinances, that he might create in himself one new man in place of the two, thus making peace, and might reconcile both groups to God in one body through the cross, thus putting to death that hostility through himself. So he came and proclaimed peace to you who were far off and peace to those who were near; for through him both of us have an access in one Spirit to the Father."[408] Notice especially in these words that Christ has broken down the middle wall of the enclosure in his flesh, that is, the hostility;[409] and that he reconciled both groups to God in one body through the cross;[410] and that in the cross he put to death the hostility. It seems to me that it was not without reason that Paul put down the word "hostility" twice in this passage. First he said that Christ broke down the hostility in his flesh. The second time he says he put it to death at the cross.[411] For it seems to me that he breaks down the [hostility] in those who are still carrying on the struggle against sin and who fight against it with all their might; but he puts it to death in those who no longer admit any sin whatsoever, but all their members are entirely dead to sin.[412] Among them was he who was saying, "I have been crucified with Christ and it is no longer I who live but Christ lives in me."[413] But Christ also killed the hostility in his own flesh in this way when, by his endurance of death, he gave men an example which teaches us to resist sins even to the point of death.[414] Not until then, when the hostility has been destroyed in his flesh, did he reconcile [M1004] men to God through his blood, provided that they keep the covenant of reconciliation inviolate by sinning no longer.

(5) Consequently, his death inflicted death to the hostility which was between us and God. This was the beginning of reconciliation. His resurrection and life, however, conferred salvation to believers, as the Apostle says elsewhere about Christ, "For in that which he died, he died to sin once and for all; but what he lives he lives to God."[415] He is said to have died to sin,

---

408. Eph 2.11–18.
409. Eph 2.14.
410. Eph 2.16.
411. Eph 2.14, 16.
412. Cf. Col 3.5.
413. Gal 2.19–20.
414. Cf. Heb 12.4.
415. Rom 6.10.

[but] not his own, for he committed no sin,[416] but he died to sin itself, that is, like one who inflicted death upon sin itself by his own death.[417] He is said to live to God, just as we too should live not for ourselves or for our own will but for God[418] so that, in this way, we can be saved in his life according to him who said, "But it is no longer I who live but it is Christ who lives in me."[419] But just as above he recorded, "But not only that but we boast in God," and then added nothing further to the words "but not only that,"[420] in a similar way, just as above, it should be understood to be said of those matters which were understood above. That is, not only, "when we were enemies, we were reconciled to God through the death of his Son," and not only, "we shall be saved by his life," but also, "we now boast in God through our Lord Jesus Christ, through whom we have received reconciliation." But it is not without reason that he added the word "now" when he could say, "through whom we have received reconciliation." But he did this to show that boasting about the knowledge of God and the reformation of our lives and the correction of our errors is granted to us not only in the future but even in the present. As the Apostle says in another passage, "having hope both for the present life and the future,"[421] The present because [our life] is more virtuous and free from faults; the future, because it is eternal.

416. Cf. 1 Pt 2.22.
417. Cf. Heb 2.14.
418. Cf. 2 Cor 5.15; Rom 6.11.
419. Gal 2.20.
420. Cf. 1.9.6; 4.9.1.
421. 1 Tm 4.8.

THE FIFTH BOOK OF THE *COMMENTARY ON THE EPISTLE OF PAUL TO THE ROMANS*

THEREFORE, JUST AS SIN *came into this world through one man, and death through sin, and so death passed through to all men in that[1] all have sinned. For sin was in the world until the law. But sin is not imputed when there is no law. Yet death exercised dominion from Adam to Moses, in those who sinned[2] in the likeness of Adam's transgression, who is a type of that which[3] was to come.*[4]

(2) After he taught the difference between faith and law[5] and between those who are justified through faith and those who cannot hope through the law for the promises that had been made to the fathers,[6] and since he has uncovered the secrets of the concealed mystery[7] that "while we were God's enemies, we were reconciled through the death of his Son,"[8] he now explains coherently the reasons why we were enemies and why this reconciliation required the death of the Son of God. His purpose is that, by considering what great things Jesus has given us, or rather [M1005] how much he suffered on our behalf, we might be held by a faith more deeply rooted in him and by an inseparable love.[9] Although it is not revealed to us in every possible respect, nevertheless he does intimate a reason

---

1. *In quo.* Possibly "in which" or "in whom" or "because." Elsewhere (*Comm in Jn* 20.39) Origen interprets the ἐφ' ᾧ of Rom 5.12 causally, i.e., "because" or "in that." In the present section he is somewhat ambivalent. He seems to allow the interpretation of *in quo* as a relative clause, i.e., "in whom," namely in Adam. See 5.1.3 and 5.1.14 below. However nowhere does Origen develop the concept of guilt inherited or imputed from Adam, as taught by Augustine and Ambrosiaster in the subsequent doctrine of original sin.

2. Origen's text of Rom 5.14 did not have καί and μή, though he was aware of this reading. See 5.1.37.

3. Or "of him who was to come." *Futuri* can be masculine or neuter.

4. Rom 5.12–14. 5. Cf. Rom 3.27ff. See 3.9.1ff.
6. Cf. Rom 4.13ff. See 4.3.1ff.; 6.12.9. 7. Cf. Rom 16.25; Col 1.26.
8. Rom 5.10. Cf. 4.8.1ff.; 4.12.1ff. 9. Cf. Rom 8.35ff.

for yet another mystery when he says, "Therefore, just as death came into this world through the one," etc. But before we come to the explanation of this entire section, a few things need to be said about something that appears to be an incoherence and a defect of his style.[10]

(3) For when it is said, "Therefore just as," it would seem necessary that some kind of completion should be added so that it be said: so also this or that. This is what he writes in several other passages, for example when he says, "For just as in Adam all die, so also in Christ all were made alive."[11] Here, however, when he said, "Just as sin came into this world through one man, and death through sin, and so it[12] passed through to all men," he did not complete [his thought] to say, for example: so also righteousness came into this world through one man and life through righteousness, and so life passed through to all men, in which[13] all have been made alive. For the sense of purposive style seemed to demand this, agreeing with what he himself says in other passages. For there is no great difference between this and what he says elsewhere, "For just as in Adam all die,"[14] and what he says here, "Therefore just as sin came into the world through one man and death through sin, and so it passed through to all men, in whom[15] all have sinned." Moreover, what he has said, "so in Christ all will be made alive,"[16] does not differ at all from that sense which above we said lacked style and was left to the reader's understanding.

(4) But it seems to me that Paul, who says, "Our competence is from God, who has made us suitable to be ministers of the new covenant,"[17] and who also says, "Or do you desire proof that Christ is speaking in me?"[18] has not missed these things through a failure in his eloquence.[19] On the contrary he has an-

---

10. For the theme of Paul's linguistic incompleteness see Preface of Origen (1); 1.9.6; 1.13.1; 4.8.7; 4.9.1; 4.12.5; 6.3.2; 7.18.2.

11. 1 Cor 15.22.

12. On the omission of "death" here and three sentences later see Bammel, *Römerbrieftext*, pp. 332–333.

13. *In qua*, which refers to *vita* (life) or *iustitia* (righteousness). This construction corresponds to *in quo* above (see 5.1.1 n. 1).

14. 1 Cor 15.22. 15. See 5.1.1 n. 1.
16. 1 Cor 15.22. 17. 2 Cor 3.5–6.
18. 2 Cor 13.3. 19. Cf. 2.6.1; 3.1.3.

ticipated something useful where, even if the things which we said were lacking style and which need to be supplied ought to be understood here, however, on account of certain negligent people who perhaps could become slack, should they hear that just as death passed through to all men through sin, so also life will pass through to all men through Christ, [Paul] took care that these matters ought not be spoken of openly and publicly.[20] At the same time he was also showing that even though righteousness will come into this world through one man and, through righteousness, life will also pass through to all men, nevertheless this does not happen at once in the present, nor does it come to pass to those who are idle. [M1006] On the contrary it occurs to those who, by a great deal of effort and sweat, are able to ask for what is not seen, knock on that which is closed, and seek what is hidden.[21]

(5) After all, even in the passage which we brought in on account of the similarity of its sayings, namely, "For just as in Adam all die," he has not said: so also in Christ all have been made alive, or: all are being made alive, but instead, "all will be made alive."[22] He wanted to show by this that the present time is one of effort and work, in which merits may be procured through good conduct. The future, on the other hand, is the time when those who die together with Christ in the present life will be made alive,[23] as the Apostle says elsewhere, "For if we die together, we shall also live together."[24] For this reason in the present passage as well he pretends not to develop and complete his discourse with things which seem to be understood through sense and coherence.[25]

(6) Someone else will perhaps say: What seems to be lacking in the things we said above, according to the order of his style, is brought back in later passages, though a bit tardy, where he says, "But it is not the case that just as the gift so the trespass. For if the many died through the trespass of the one, much more surely has the grace of God and the gift in the grace of the one man, Jesus Christ, abounded for very many."[26] With

20. Cf. 5.1.7.
22. 1 Cor 15.22.
24. 2 Tm 2.11; cf. Rom 6.8.
26. Rom 5.15.
21. Cf. Mt 7.7–8.
23. Cf. 5.10.3.
25. Cf. 5.1.3.

these words he would have declared that what seemed to have been lacking above is completed. What he would have said there, that sin[27] had passed through to all men, is not much different from what he says here, that the gift and the grace of Jesus Christ abounded for very many. This is so because "all" men may be understood to mean "very many" men, and it does not seem absurd to take "very many" to mean "all," especially since in what follows he says so explicitly, "Just as the trespass of the one led to condemnation for all men, so also the righteousness of the one leads to the justification of life for all men."[28] And in order that he might show still more plainly that "all men" and "many men" mean one and the same thing, he added to these things, "For just as by the one man's disobedience the many were made sinners, so also by the obedience of the one the many will be made righteous."[29] Thus those whom he had above designated as "all men" he has called here "many" with the exact same meaning.[30]

(7) Except that someone could say that the Apostle, wanting to mix up and confound what he had revealed above, lest, as we said, [31] he should soften and weaken his hearers,[32] those whom he had earlier called "all,"[33] here he designated "very many"[34] in order that the "all" be referred only to those who have attained to the gift of Christ's grace, who are, however, not few but very many.[35] For it is a custom of the Apostle Paul, when he is disclosing anything about the kindness of God in his ineffable goodness,[36] in turn to roughen up, as it were, at least in some measure because of certain negligent hearers, what he said and to put some fear [M1007] into those who are remiss, just as when, while discussing with the Corinthians about the end of all things, he says, "For just as in Adam all die, so also in Christ all will be made alive";[37] and a little bit later, "Then the end when he hands over the kingdom to God the Father,"[38] and

---

27. On the reading "sin" see Bammel, *Römerbrieftext*, p. 333.
28. Rom 5.18.
29. Rom 5.19.
30. Cf. 5.4.2.
31. Cf. 5.1.4.
32. Cf. 5.2.6.
33. Rom 5.12, 18.
34. Rom 5.15.
35. Cf. Rom 5.15.
36. Cf. 2.4.8.
37. 1 Cor 15.22.
38. 1 Cor 15.24.

so forth. Afraid for them, lest any of them, "despising the riches of God's goodness and patience and forbearance by their own hard and impenitent heart, should store up wrath for themselves on the day of the righteous judgment of God,"[39] he added just after what he had said about the end, "Do not be deceived! Bad company ruins good morals. Wake up as you should,[40] and do not sin! For some people are ignorant of God. I say this to confound you."[41] Paul is thus acting as a wise steward of the word.[42] And when he comes to the passages in which he has to speak about God's goodness, he expresses these things in a somewhat concealed and obscure way for the sake of certain lazy people lest, perchance, as we have said, "they despise the riches of his goodness and patience and forbearance and store up for themselves wrath on the day of wrath,"[43] into which all people who have stored up deeds of this kind for themselves must of necessity face, even though you have seen what may happen after these things.[44]

(8) But what he says, "But sin was in this world until the law, but sin is not imputed when there is no law," this seems to show that until the law came, that is to say, until Christ came,[45] "who takes away the sin of the world,"[46] sin existed. But sin obviously cannot be imputed where there is no law which convicts the sinner. "But death reigned," which had entered through sin, "until Moses," that is, continually while the law abided "over those who sinned in the likeness of Adam's sin," through whom death itself had gained an entrance. Adam was a "type of that which was to come," not in his being a transgressor but in the following sense: Just as death had entered through him, so through the last Adam life has entered this world;[47] and just as, through him, condemnation comes to all men, so also through Christ

39. Rom 2.4–5.
40. *Iuste*. Migne, *iusti*.
41. 1 Cor 15.33–34.
42. Cf. Lk 12.42.
43. Rom 2.4–5. Cf. 5.1.4.
44. Origen seems to be alluding to his belief that Paul promises a universal restoration of all creatures, which is conditional on their cooperation with God's grace. Paul conceals this doctrine about God's goodness, Origen thinks, to keep people from presuming upon it, falling away, and being re-sentenced to punishment. Cf. 2.2.2; 2.3.2; 5.2.6.
45. Cf. 5.1.34; *Comm in Jn* 20.39.
46. Jn 1.29.
47. Cf. Rom 5.17; 1 Cor 15.22, 45.

justification comes to all men.[48] Let these things be said concerning the content of the Apostle's words.

(9) Let us now also see what the inner meaning might contain. First of all I believe that it must be warned that, particularly in these passages with which we are presently engaged, [M1008] it seems to me that the Apostle Paul is saying these things in a fashion as if being some faithful and wise steward.[49] He is being led by a powerful king, his lord, into the royal treasuries, and various large apartments are being shown to him.[50] The rooms have different entrances which are not clearly marked.[51] Thus, as an entrance is shown to him through one door and an exit shown through another, yet sometimes from different entrances he may be led into a central chamber, as we often see in lofty palaces on earth as well. To this faithful steward who is being led around is shown a storeroom of the king's silver; and another treasure chamber containing the gold, plus the precious stones, pearls, and various necklaces; and even the place for the royal purple, as well as another of diadems. Even the queen's chambers are pointed out to him, spread out in many different rooms. Yet none of these individual things is disclosed to him all at once or completely, with the doors wide open, but only part-way opened. Thus, though he does indeed recognize his lord's treasures and the royal wealth, yet he does not become thoroughly and perfectly acquainted with every individual thing.

(10) But later on that servant, who is considered so faithful that his lord and king made known to him the greatness of his own wealth, is sent out to recruit an army for the king. He himself is to do the recruiting and test the soldiers. Because he is

---

48. Rom 5.18. Cf. 5.1.38; 5.2.6; 5.2.7–8; *Cels* 6.36; Irenaeus, *Against Heresies* 3.19.6.
49. Cf. Lk 12.42.
50. Cf. Is 39.2.
51. Cf. 6.7.16. In his *Paraphrase on Romans*, CWE 42:13, Erasmus praised both the elegance and truthfulness of Origen's comparison. One point of the parable is to illustrate the difficulties of Paul's speech. For example, the different entrances and exits to the inner chambers can indicate Paul's custom of using a single word to designate different things, e.g., "law," "Jew," "death," etc. Cf. Heither, *Translatio Religionis*, p. 108.

faithful, he will endure the necessity of making known in part what he has seen, in order to summon more men to military service and to assemble a larger army for his king. Yet because he is wise and recognizes the necessity to conceal the mystery of the king,⁵² he will use only certain tokens and indications rather than detailed reports, so that, though the king's power is not concealed, yet the arrangement of the layout and the adornment and the condition of the palace remains a secret.⁵³

(11) In this manner, then, as I have said, it seems to me that the Apostle Paul does this with his words not only because, as he says concerning himself, he knows in part and understands in part,⁵⁴ but also for our sake. For we are not even able to grasp the things he knows in part. Thus he carefully weighs his speech and the chambers of each mystery he touches on and slightly opens to us in only one or two words. Sometimes when he has entered through one door, he departs through another. Sometimes having entered from one door, he dashes into another room so that if you search for him at that entrance by which he went in, you may not find him exit.⁵⁵

(12) Well then, since we have first arranged these things in our minds concerning the things Paul is writing, [M1009] let us now turn, to the best of our ability, to the matters at hand which need to be investigated and considered. First let us ascertain how "sin came into this world through one man and death through sin." Someone may perhaps ask whether it was not in fact the woman who sinned before Adam,⁵⁶ since it is said of her, "having been seduced she became a transgressor",⁵⁷ and whether, moreover, the serpent had sinned before her. For it

---

52. Cf. Tb 12.7, 11.
53. Cf. 7.16.2 for a continuation of the palace analogy. Origen uses a similar metaphor in his *Comm in Ps*, excerpts of which are preserved in the *Philocalia* 2.3.
54. Cf. 1 Cor 13.9, 12.
55. Cf. Tollinton, *Selections*, p. 76 n. 2, on this passage: "Origen's comment on this characteristic passage of St. Paul shows real insight. The many ideas, the abrupt changes, the hints of thoughts not developed, the lack of order and control, are all in keeping with Origen's suggestive and appropriate figure."
56. Cf. *Cels* 6.43; *Orat* 29.18; *Comm in Cant* 2.3.
57. 1 Tm 2.14.

sinned when it said to the woman, "What is this God has said, that you must not eat from any tree in paradise?"[58] It sinned again when, since God had said, "On whatever day you eat of it you will surely die,"[59] it said to the woman, "You will not surely die; but God knew that on whatever day you eat of it your eyes will be opened from that time and you will be like gods, knowing good and evil."[60] Well then, if the woman sinned before Adam, and the serpent sinned before the woman, and in another passage the Apostle says, "Adam was not seduced, but the woman was seduced,"[61] how can it seem that sin entered through one man and not rather through one woman? For the beginning of sin was from the woman,[62] and before the woman from the serpent,[63] or from the devil, of whom it is said in the Gospel, "He was a murderer from the beginning."[64]

(13) But observe that the Apostle has held fast to the order of nature in these things. And for this reason, because he was speaking about the sin from which death had passed through to all men, he did not ascribe to the woman the succession of human posterity which succumbed to this death coming from sin but to the man.[65] For people do not attribute posterity to the woman but the man, as the Apostle himself says elsewhere, "For the man is not from the woman, but the woman from the man"; and again, "For just as the woman is from the man, so also the man is" not *from* the woman but "*through* the woman."[66] Therefore the mortal posterity and physical descent are reckoned to the man, as if the source, and not to the woman.[67]

(14) But in order that what we are saying might become clearer, let us add the following as well. The same Apostle writes as follows to the Hebrews, "Moreover Levi, who received tithes, paid tithes. For he was still in the loins of his father Abraham when Melchizedek met him as he was returning from the slaughter of the kings."[68] If then Levi, who is born in the fourth

---

58. Gn 3.1.
60. Gn 3.4–5.
62. Sir 25.24.
64. Jn 8.44.
66. 1 Cor 11.8, 12.
68. Heb 7.9–10; cf. 7.1.

59. Gn 2.17.
61. 1 Tm 2.14.
63. Cf. *Comm in Jn* 20.26.
65. Cf. 3.3.1; 5.1.35.
67. Cf. 3.10.5; *Hom in Lv* 8.3.

generation after Abraham, is declared as having been in the loins of Abraham, how much more were all men, those who are born and have been born in this world, in Adam's loins [M1010] when he was still in paradise.⁶⁹ And all men who were with him, or rather in him, were expelled from paradise when he was himself driven out from there;⁷⁰ and through him the death which had come to him from the transgression consequently passed through to them as well, who were dwelling in his loins; and therefore the Apostle rightly says, "For as in Adam all die, so also in Christ all will be made alive."⁷¹ So then it is neither from the serpent who had sinned before the woman, nor from the woman who had become a transgressor before the man,⁷² but through Adam, from whom all mortals derive their origin, that sin is said to have entered, and through sin, death.

(15) But it is certainly one man through whom sin entered, and through sin, death, the one whom the Apostle himself calls elsewhere, "The first was of the earth, earthly," but the second one was "heavenly."⁷³ This is the passage where he encourages us to bear the image of the heavenly after casting off the image of the earthly;⁷⁴ that is to say, by living according to the Word of God we are to be renewed and remade in the inner man after

69. There is a resemblance between the thoughts expressed here and later views developed by Ambrosiaster and Augustine of the solidarity of the human race in Adam, and of Adam's guilt being imputed to his descendants who were in his loins. Origen may be attributed with passing down the exegetical material for the doctrine of original sin. However, scholars are generally agreed that inherited guilt is not stressed in Origen's thought. As J. N. D. Kelly, *Early Christian Doctrines*, revised edition (New York: Harper & Row, 1978), p. 182, observes, "Even in that [sc. Romans] commentary . . . his whole emphasis is on the personal sins of individuals who have followed Adam's example, rather than on their solidarity with his guilt; and, while admitting the possibility that we may be in this vale of fears [(sic), cf. 5.4.3] because we were in Adam's loins, he does not conceal his belief that each one of us was banished from Paradise for his personal transgressions." Cf. Teichtweier, *Sündenlehre*, p. 99, "It must be conclusively said that a doctrine of inherited guilt based on descent from Adam's lineage is unknown to Origen." See also Schelkle, *Paulus, Lehrer*, p. 163; N. P. Williams, *The Ideas of the Fall and of Original Sin* (London: Longmans, Green and Co., 1927), p. 217.

70. Cf. 5.4.3; *Cels* 7.28. 71. 1 Cor 15.22.
72. 1 Tm 2.14. 73. 1 Cor 15.47, 49.
74. Cf. 5.9.8; 9.1.9; *Hom in Gn* 9.2; *Comm in Jn* 19.20; 20.25; *Cels* 4.40.

the image of God, who created him.⁷⁵ This man, then, who is already being remade and restored in the image of God is neither earthly nor in this world, but his citizenship is said to be in heaven;⁷⁶ and therefore death cannot pass through to him according to him who said, "But you are not of this world."⁷⁷ Of the one who is still in this world, however, and who is earthly and who bears the image of the earthly,⁷⁸ it is said of him that sin entered into this world, and through sin death.⁷⁹

(16) But if sin and death entered into this world and inhabit this world, it is certain that those who are dead to this world through Christ, or rather with Christ, are strangers to death and sin. Having been raised with him,⁸⁰ they have even merited to sit with him in the heavenly places.⁸¹ Their citizenship is no longer in this world but in heaven,⁸² from which, by an equal consequence, it is made known first of all that every man "of the earth," as the same Apostle says elsewhere, "is earthly,"⁸³ since he walks in the image of the earthly and thinks according to the flesh and considers the things that are of the flesh⁸⁴ and very seldom is it that he is converted to the Lord and led by the Spirit of God⁸⁵ and made into a spiritual "last Adam, into a life giving Spirit."⁸⁶

(17) He says that sin entered this world through one man, and it is certain [M1011] that he designates this place in which men live as the earthly world. Because of this you will ask, of course, whether sin entered no other place⁸⁷ or whether it is not also found in those places where "the spiritual forces of evil in the heavenly places"⁸⁸ are named? A further question you should consider for yourself is: From where did sin enter this world?⁸⁹ Where was it prior to its entrance here? Did it even exist at all? Or was it prior to him to whom it is said, "Up to the time when iniquities were found in you"; and, "for this reason I

---

75. Cf. Col 3.10; 2 Cor 3.18; 4.16.
76. Cf. Phil 3.20.
77. Jn 15.19.
78. 1 Cor 15.47, 49.
79. Cf. 1.19.8.
80. Cf. Rom 6.8; Col 2.20.
81. Cf. Eph 2.6.
82. Cf. Phil 3.20.
83. 1 Cor 15.47, 49.
84. Rom 8.5.
85. Cf. Rom 8.14.
86. 1 Cor 15.45.
87. Cf. 3.6.6; *Comm in Mt* 13.20.
88. Eph 6.12.
89. Cf. *Comm in Jn* 2.15; *Princ* 1.5.2–5.

cast you to the earth"?[90] But it is not safe for us to discuss these things further, because we may observe that the Apostle has scarcely touched these matters in individual discourses.[91]

(18) "Therefore through one man sin entered into the world." But as we have said,[92] the "world" should be interpreted as either the place in which men dwell or the earthly and bodily life[93] in which death has a place. To this world, i.e., to the earthly life, saints claim to have been crucified and to have died.[94]

(19) "And through sin," he says, "death." Without a doubt this is the death concerning which the prophet says, "The soul which sins will die."[95] Of this death one could rightly say that bodily death is a shadow.[96] For wherever the one goes, the other necessarily follows, just as the shadow follows the body. But if someone may raise the objection that the Savior committed no sin[97] and death did not come to his soul through sin and yet he still endured bodily death, we shall respond to that one that just as the Savior, though he did not commit sin, is nevertheless said to have become sin[98] through his taking on flesh for our salvation, so also, although he owed death to no one and was not himself subject to it, nevertheless for our salvation the [death] of that condition taken up by him, of which we have spoken above, he took upon himself freely, not under compulsion like [it was] his shadow. As he himself said, "I have authority to lay down my life, and I have authority to take it up again."[99]

(20) Now let us see how "death passed through to all men." He says, "in that[100] all sinned." With an absolute pronounce-

---

90. Ezek 28.15, 17. Origen interprets this passage as referring to the devil. Cf. 5.10.13; *Princ* 1.5.4; *Hom in Ezek* 1.3.

91. Erasmus, CWE 56:143, reasonably conjectures that Rufinus has omitted material at this point.

92. Cf. 5.1.17. 93. Cf. *Comm in Mt* 13.21.

94. Cf. Gal 6.14. See also 5.1.16; *Hom in Nm* 7.3.

95. Ezek 18.4. Cf. 4.5.10; 5.10.9; 6.5.4; 6.6.4–5; *Dial* 25.13ff.; Clement, *Stromateis* 3.9.64.1.

96. Cf. 5.2.5; 5.4.2; 5.10.8–9; 6.5.4.

97. Is 53.9; 1 Pt 2.22. 98. Cf. 2 Cor 5.21.

99. Jn 10.18.

100. *In quo*. Or "in whom." See 5.1.1 n. 1. The causal meaning makes better sense in this paragraph. Heither in Origenes, *Commentarii*, 3:53, renders it *dadurch daß*. Cf. *Comm in Jn* 20.39, 42.

ment the Apostle has declared that the death of sin passed through to all men in this, that all sinned. As he says elsewhere, "For all have sinned and lack the grace of God."[101] Therefore even if you should call Abel righteous, he cannot be excused. For "all have sinned." For why was it only "after days" that he offered the sacrifice from his firstborn and not immediately? Why did he offer it after Cain and not before him?[102] Even if you cite Enosh who "hoped to call upon the name of the Lord,"[103] still, he *hoped*. And why does he not immediately [M1012] call? Instead he neglects and delays. Even if you bring up Enoch, it is not written that he had pleased God until after he became the father of Methuselah.[104] But Methuselah is interpreted to mean "emission of death," from which it is shown that death, which passed through to all men, came to him as well. But hardly at any time did [Enoch] feel death within himself; and having been converted to the Lord he emitted it from himself and cast it out through repentance.[105] And that is why it is said he became the father of Methuselah, because he had cast out from himself the death which had besieged him. It is therefore rightly said that God translated him so that he would not see death,[106] since he was no longer liable to death but had cast it out from himself and had escaped.[107] And even if you conduct a careful investigation of the case of Noah, you will find that it was not until his five hundredth year[108] that it is written of him that "Noah found grace in the sight of the Lord God,"[109] and that "he was a righteous man in his own generation," and that "he pleased God."[110] In my opinion, had he merited it prior to this, certainly the Holy Scripture would never have been silent about it. In addition if someone wants to charge that he drank wine and became drunk and naked,[111] he will find in all of these actions as well that it was not undeservedly said by the Apostle, "in that all sinned," even if Noah woke up from his

101. Rom 3.23.
102. Gn 4.3–4 LXX. Cf. 5.1.35.
103. Gn 4.26 LXX.
104. Gn 5.22.
105. Sir 44.16.
106. Cf. *Hom in Nm* 27.12
107. Cf. Gn 5.24; Heb 11.5; Sir 44.16.
108. Cf. Gn 5.32.
109. Gn 6.8.
110. Gn 6.8–9.
111. Cf. Gn 9.21.

wine.[112] What should I say about Abraham, to whom it is said, "Depart from your land and your kindred and your father's house"?[113] Assuredly this would not have been said if he had been able to please God in his father's house.

(21) But it is not necessary, with its great danger, to enumerate each of the saints in these matters. For the opinion which says that death passed through to all men suffices, both that of the Apostle and of him who said, "No one is pure from uncleanness, even if his life should be one day long."[114] But when that death of sin which passed through to all had come to Jesus and had attempted[115] to pierce him with its sting—"for the sting of death is sin"[116]—it was repulsed and broken. "For he was life,"[117] and death was inevitably destroyed by life. At that time it is said to [death], "Where, O death, is your sting? Where, O death, is your victory?"[118] Because death had conquered all, it is said to death here, "Where, O death, is your victory?"

(22) Moreover, he has not said that sin came to all men, but "into the world," and death, on the other hand, not "into the world," but "to all men," and it did not "come," but "passed through." I do not think that Paul has made use of this variety of expressions here in vain. I think, therefore, that "world" designates here certain earthly people, those who remain in an earthly way of life.[119] On the other hand he calls "men" those who are already beginning to know and understand that they have been made in the image of God.[120] He says that sin had come into those [M1013] who are called "the world," that is to say, those who are earthly, and at no time does he record its solution. But in those whom he wants to be understood as men already, he says sin passed through, that is to say, it was indeed there but through the repentance of conversion it was expelled

---

112. Cf. Gn 9.24.
113. Gn 12.1.
114. Jb 14.4–5 LXX. This passage is cited five times in the *Commentary* to prove the universality of sin: 5.1.21; 5.9.4; 5.9.11; and 7.18.3.
115. *Temtasset.* Erasmus, CWE 56:144, assumes he means when Christ was tempted by Satan (Mt 4.1–11; Lk 4.1–13). This may be right. Cf. also 5.2.5.
116. 1 Cor 15.56.   117. Jn 1.4.
118. 1 Cor 15.55; Cf. Hos 13.14.   119. Cf. 5.1.18; 3.1.13; *Princ* 2.3.6.
120. Cf. Gn 1.27. See also 2.13.34; 5.1.28; *Comm in Jn* 10.45.

and passed through[121] and did not remain any longer in them. Thus it is apparent that in Paul's writings not even one syllable should be understood as devoid of mysteries.[122]

(23) Now let us consider the sense of what was said, "For sin was in the world until the law, but sin is not imputed when there is no law." In this passage it appears to me that Paul, in accordance with the parable we told above,[123] has gone in through one entrance and exited by another. For who is able to follow him through that entrance through which, as it seems to many, he has entered, namely that he should be understood to speak of the law of Moses, that, "Sin was in the world until the law, but sin is not imputed when there is no law"? As if sin did not exist before the law! [As if], too, no one sinned, and sin was not reckoned to anyone before the law of Moses was given![124] Even though we read that sin was reckoned both to Cain and Lamech[125] and, lest we be delayed by all the individual instances, God was provoked by the sins of men to such a degree that he brought the flood upon the world and said, "I should destroy all flesh on the earth."[126] What is more, a rain of fire and burning sulfur devastated the residents of Sodom.[127] How then can it be said that in sins of this type there was no sin? Or how will it be denied that sin was reckoned when there were such acts of retribution? And therefore, because Paul has exited by a secret door, we need to keep searching for his meaning in what he says, "For sin was in the world until the law, but sin is not imputed when there is no law." Later in this very epistle we find him speaking in the following way, "For sin is dead apart from law; but I was once alive apart from law."[128] It seems to me that the meaning of each passage is identical. For what was here missing from his expression he has filled in there. "For sin was in this world until the law"; but "dead" is missing. He expressed

---

121. Cf. 5.1.32.
122. For the "nothing superfluous" theme cf. 1.8; 2.6.1; 4.11.2; 5.3.5; 5.8.8; 5.10.18; 6.5.6; 7.7.4f.; 9.41.8; 10.25.
123. Cf. 5.1.9.
124. For the theme of sin before the law of Moses, cf. 4.4.4 n.
125. Gn 4.8ff.; 23.   126. Gn 6.7, 17.
127. Cf. Gn 19.24.   128. Rom 7.8–9.

this more openly in the latter passage. So then, if we add that later expression to the present one and say, "Sin was dead in the world until the law, but sin is not imputed when there is no law," notice how complete the sense can now stand. [M1014]

(24) But we have already frequently said this,[129] that Paul indeed discusses many different kinds of law in this epistle but very frequently he is speaking about natural law, which can especially be detected here in this passage. For until natural law enters,[130] which takes place at a certain age when a person begins to be capable of reason and to be able to discriminate right from wrong and justice from injustice, at that time sin, which previously was considered as if dead amongst man, is said to revive.[131] This happens because there is now an internal law which prohibits; the faculty of reason points out what ought not be done.

(25) But in order that what we are saying may be understood more plainly, let us make use of a clear example.[132] It is written, "Whoever strikes father or mother shall surely be put to death";[133] and, "Whoever curses his father or mother shall surely be put to death."[134] Now suppose a small boy of say four or five years of age, becoming angry from a whipping, as is normal to occur, strikes his father or mother. As far as the precept of the commandment is concerned he deserves death. But because natural law does not yet exist in him, which would teach him that he ought not to inflict an injury upon his father or mother, he is not aware that he has committed an impious crime in this action. To be sure what he is doing has the appearance of sin, for he is striking or cursing his mother, but sin is dead in him, for through the absence of natural law which does not yet exist in him, sin cannot be reckoned to him. For the reasoning capacity in him is not yet great enough to teach him that what he is doing ought not be done. And therefore not only is the boy's action not reckoned as a fault by his parents, but it is taken graciously and with joy. In my opinion what the

129. Cf. Preface of Origen (8); 3.6.1; 3.7.5; 4.4.2–10; 4.5.7.
130. Cf. 3.2.8; 3.6.1.   131. Cf. Rom 7.8–9.
132. This example is picked up again in 6.8.7 on Rom 7.8ff.
133. Ex 21.15.   134. Ex 21.17.

Apostle says can be logically interpreted in this manner, "For until the law sin was"—here should be supplied "dead"[135]—"in the world; but sin is not reckoned when there is no law."

(26) It is also fitting to interpret in accordance with this explanation what the Apostle says, "I was once alive apart from the law."[136] For how can Paul be found ever to live apart from the law of Moses, seeing that he claims concerning himself that he is a Hebrew of Hebrews and that, having been circumcised immediately on the eighth day, he has lived, from birth on, in the observation of the Mosaic law?[137] It is accepted, however, that he once lived apart from natural law, namely in his childhood, before he was capable of reason. For at that age the power of distinguishing right and wrong was not yet dwelling within him, nor [M1015] was the ability to consider what is proper and what is improper accessible. That what follows is being said about natural law he plainly shows when he says, "But when the commandment came, sin revived, but I died."[138] By these words he is making clear that at that age, sins were certainly there, but they were considered dead, because they were not reckoned as a fault. But, he says, when I began to know what ought to be done and what must be avoided, and when I began to accept the commandment of the law growing powerful in me, then sin revived within me, which previously seemed dead due to the absence of law. Thus he says, "I died."[139] For now sin began to be reckoned against me.

(27) Now Basilides,[140] failing to observe that these things ought to be understood of natural law, drags the Apostle's discourse down into senseless and godless fables[141] and attempts to build out of this utterance of the Apostle the doctrine called μετενσωμάτωσις, i.e., that souls are transferred into one body

---

135. Rom 7.8.
136. Rom 7.9. Cf. 3.2.7–8; 6.8.7.
137. Cf. Phil 3.5–6.
138. Rom 7.9–10. Cf. 3.2.9; 6.8.3.
139. Rom 7.10.
140. Cf. 5.9.11; 6.8.8; *Comm in Mt* 13.1. According to Irenaeus, *Against Heresies* 1.24.3, Basilides (fl. 120–40) was a gnostic teacher of the second century in Alexandria. Accounts of his teaching are diverse.
141. Cf. 1 Tm 4.7.

BOOK 5, CHAPTER 1   319

after another. For he says that the Apostle says, "I was once alive apart from the law,"¹⁴² that is: Before I came into this body, I lived in a bodily form which was not under law, namely that of a cow or a bird. But he has failed to look at what follows, namely, "But when the commandment came, sin revived."¹⁴³ For Paul did not say that he came to the commandment, but the commandment came to him; and he did not say that sin did not exist in him, but that it was dead and revived. By these statements he is assuredly showing that he was saying both things about one and the same life of his. But let Basilides and those who share his perceptions be left to their own impiety. Let us, however, turn to the sense of the Apostle in accordance with pious reverence toward ecclesiastical doctrine.¹⁴⁴

(28) We need to examine the sense of the fact that he says, "Sin was in the world," and that he did not say, "in men." Although, of course, there are in this world cattle, other animals and trees, and whatever else this world consists of, yet no one believes that sin is in these things. It seems to me that the Apostle thinks of "men" as those who are already capable of reason and who comply with the laws of nature.¹⁴⁵ But that age which has not yet reached the capacity of reason he calls not so much "men" as "the world," in that they are indeed part of the world but they have not yet reached the point of exhibiting the image of God in them *qua* reasoning capacity, in which man is said to have been made.¹⁴⁶

(29) Moreover, unless it seems improperly curious, I would like to inquire,¹⁴⁷ in response to those who wish the law of Moses to be understood in these matters through what he says, "But sin is not reckoned when there is no law," whether the dev-

142. Rom 7.8–9.
143. Rom 7.9.
144. Cf. 2.7.3; *Comm in Jn* 6.11; *Comm in Mt* 11.17. See also *Hom in Lk* 16.6 (= FOTC 94:67–68), "Although they [the heretics] seek to expound it, they will be unable to succeed. But I hope to be a man of the Church. I hope to be addressed not by the name of some heresiarch, but by the name of Christ. I hope to have his name, which is blessed upon the earth. I desire, both in deed and in thought, both to be and to be called a Christian."
145. Cf. 5.1.22.   146. Cf. Gn 1.27.
147. Cf. 3.6.4.

il and his angels seem to be absolved if sin is not reckoned [M1016] when there is no law. But why then was the serpent condemned even before the law of Moses?[148] Or why did death enter the world through the devil's envy?[149] What is more, how is it possible to explain what the apostle Jude says in the general epistle? For he says the following: "Even the angels who did not keep their own position, but left their proper dwelling, he has kept bound in eternal chains in deepest darkness for the judgment of the great Day."[150] From all of which it is more definitely established that the Apostle is saying these things about the law which every being, both men and also angels, bears naturally within itself by a certain divine dispensation and gift. The strength and power of this law is so great that it convicts even angels. It excludes no one, no matter what their dignity. It accomplished that which the apostle Jude says above, "Angels who did not keep their own position, but left their proper dwelling, were kept bound in eternal chains for the judgment of the great Day."[151] This is the law which drags even the devil and his angels into the eternal fire which has been prepared for them.[152] And it is certain that those angels would not be kept bound in eternal chains for judgment nor would those others be thrown into the eternal fire prepared for them if it were not for the fact that they have not kept the law given to them by God, nor would they come to judgment unless they had done something contrary to law. In the same way it seems certain that if they would have kept the law given to them, they would not have fallen into the eternal fire nor would they have gone down in deepest darkness in eternal chains.

(30) It still remains for us to discuss, as well as we can, this, the sense of what was said, "But death exercised dominion from Adam until Moses in those who sinned in the likeness of Adam's transgression, who is a type of that which was to come." The Apostle now mentions death for the third time. First he said, "Through sin death came into this world." Then he says,

---

148. Cf. Gn 3.14. See also *Comm in Jn* 2.15.
149. Cf. Wis 2.24.
150. Jude 6.
151. Jude 6.
152. Cf. Mt 25.41.

"Death passed through to all men." And now he says, "Death exercised dominion from Adam until Moses." Knowing that there exist certain distinctions in each of these things, he has now made known the time when it entered and when it began to exercise dominion. It entered, he says, at that time when the first man transgressed. He has also told us how it entered. He says, "through sin." And now he is designating the time period of its rule as being from Adam until Moses. But as to when it will have passed through to all men he has not made known.

(31) Therefore it seems to me that in these matters the Apostle is describing death as if the hostile entrance of some tyrant who wanted to invade the dominions of a rightful king.[153] First he would seize the very passes and entrances into the kingdom by means of collusion with the guard. Then he would attempt to turn the hearts of everyone [M1017] in the kingdom to himself and, for the most part, he would succeed. In this way he would lay claim to a kingdom not his own. Therefore, while he is ruling through tyranny a commander chosen by the rightful king is sent—Moses, who must call back the people who have been taken over by the [tyrant] to the laws of civilized rule and must teach them to make use of the laws of the true king. But that tyrant, i.e., the death of sin, who had stolen his way in because of the collusion of the first guard, was ruling over all those who had fallen away by a transgression similar to that of the first man. But the commander of the lawful ruler does everything in order that he might lead at least some of the people out of the kingdom of sin and death. He succeeds at last in converting one nation and anyone else who wants to join himself to that nation. And by an order of the king, first of all he instituted sacrifices, by means of which, when they are offered according to certain formalities, he could say, "and their sin shall be forgiven them."[154] And so it was only then that a certain part of mankind began to be liberated from the kingdom of sin and death. For that tyrant, who is called death, was exercising do-

---

153. Cf. 3.7.14; 4.8.1; 5.1.10; 5.1.37; 5.10.11; *Comm in Jn* 20.39; Irenaeus, *Against Heresies* 3.19.6.
154. Cf. Lv 4.

minion from Adam, who was the first to give entrance to him by his own collusion, so that he could pass through to all men, up to Moses, the one we called a commander, who, sent by God, the king of all, began to weaken the tyrant's kingdom and to call the people back under the law of the just ruler.[155]

(32) "Therefore death exercised dominion from Adam until Moses" in the form we have set down above, not over all people, but "over those who sinned in the likeness of Adam's transgression." For death did indeed enter the world and it passed through to all, but it did not exercise dominion in everyone. For it is one thing to pass through and another to exercise dominion. To be sure sin passed through even the righteous and grazed them with a certain light infection.[156] But in transgressors, i.e., in those who surrender themselves to it with their entire mind and allegiance, it seizes dominion and rules over them with complete authority. "Death, therefore, exercised dominion from Adam," who first opened up the passage-way for sin into this world by his transgression, "until Moses," that is, until the law.[157] For through the law the cleansing of sins began to be ushered in, and from a certain part of his tyranny resistance began through victims, various acts of expiation, sacrifices, and commands.

(33) But because his power of domination was so great, greater even than the strength of the law, prophets are sent as reinforcements to the law. But even they, realizing that the tyrant's power exceeded their strength, pray for the coming and presence of the king, calling out to God, "Send your light and your truth!"[158] and again, "Bow the heavens and come down!"[159] and once more, "Arise, O Lord, bring help to us!"[160] Therefore Jesus Christ, the Son of God, came and "in that the law was weak [M1018] through the flesh, God, by sending his own Son in the likeness of sinful flesh on account of sin, condemned sin in the flesh."[161] Indeed he also reconciled the

---

155. Cf. 5.10.11. Origen's assessment of Moses' role in salvation history is strikingly positive. See also *Hom in Ex* 4.6; *Cels* 4.31; 5.42.
156. Cf. 5.1.22. 157. Cf. 5.1.34.
158. Ps 43.3. 159. Ps 144.5.
160. Ps 44.26. 161. Rom 8.3.

world to God[162] and disarmed the principalities and powers of the tyrant, triumphing over them in himself.[163] However in these matters we seem to have slipped into a bit of a digression.[164] But let us return to the main argument.

(34) Therefore the "death" of sin "exercised dominion from Adam until Moses," that is, until the coming of Christ.[165] For it is called the law of Moses and the law, as is written, held its place until John the Baptist, from which time Jesus began to proclaim the kingdom of God.[166] But the fact that [Paul] has made particular mention of certain ones in whom death exercised dominion when he says, "Death exercised dominion in those who sinned in the likeness of Adam's transgression," does not seem to me to be said without reference to a certain mystery.

(35) Perhaps there were some, up to that time when men were living under law as under a pedagogue,[167] who performed something similar to what Adam is said to have performed in Paradise, to touch the tree of knowledge of good and evil and to be ashamed of his own nakedness and to fall away from the dwelling in Paradise.[168] Or perhaps it seems this ought to be interpreted in a simpler way and the likeness of Adam's transgression is to be received without any further discussion. This would mean that everyone who is born from Adam, the transgressor, seems to be indicated and retain in themselves the likeness of his transgression, taken not only by descent from him but also by instruction. For all who are born in this world are not only raised by their parents but instructed as well;[169] and not only are they sins' children but also sins' pupils. But when a person matures and the freedom of doing what one likes comes

---

162. Cf. 2 Cor 5.19.   163. Cf. Col 2.15.
164. For other digressions see 2.13.8–33 (circumcision); 3.8.2–8 (atonement); 7.1.2–4 (Spirit); also 2.14.25; 3.1.15–19; 4.5.12; 5.3.6; 6.7.16; 7.5.4.
165. Cf. 5.1.8; 5.1.36; 5.2.10; 5.4.7; *Hom in Jos* 1.3; *Comm in Jn* 20.39.
166. Cf. Lk 16.16.   167. Cf. Gal 3.23–24.
168. Cf. Gn 3.6–7, 23. Of the several interpretations offered in this section, this first one appears to be a reference to Origen's belief in the pre-existence of souls, some of whom may have literally copied Adam's sin in a manner left unexplained.
169. Cf. 5.2.10.

around, a person either goes the way of his fathers, as is written of several kings,[170] or he advances along the road of his Lord God. After all, it seems to me that something like this is also indicated concerning Abel in that which is written, "But after days Abel offered a sacrifice to God from the first-born of his sheep and from their fat portions."[171] Thus, what he says, "after days," shows that in the early days of his life he was being held fast by the lessons he learned from his father's transgression. But after those days he came to his senses and looked to God, having been admonished by the law of nature, and then he offered a sacrifice to God.

(36) It is possible, then, either for this passage to be explained in this fashion simply, or to be considered a mystery, hidden in that which he says, "in the likeness of Adam's transgression," and almost ineffably concealed by a certain thin line of understanding. It is just as if anyone suggests that here death,[172] [M1019] which is said to have exercised dominion from Adam until Moses, i.e., until the end of the law[173] and the beginning of Christ,[174] is said of that death about which it is written in the prophet, as if under the *persona* of the Lord, saying, "I shall rescue them from the power of the underworld and I shall deliver them from death."[175] Or, to put it another way, that there would be certain persons noted and described by means of a quite hidden mystery, who are recorded as having sinned in the likeness of Adam's transgression, in whom alone death would exercise dominion.

(37) If, on the other hand, as it reads in some manuscripts, "even in those who did not sin in the likeness of Adam's transgression,"[176] *this* death, namely that which was keeping souls bound in the underworld, is said to exercise dominion, then we shall understand it to mean that even the saints had fallen prey

---

170. Cf. e.g. 1 Kgs 15.26, 34.
172. Cf. 5.10.9; 6.6.6ff.
174. Cf. 5.1.34.
171. Gn 4.4 LXX.
173. Cf. Rom 10.4.
175. Hos 13.14.
176. Origen knew of both readings and did not decide on which was correct. Bammel, *Römerbrieftext*, p. 205, says that this discussion of the textual variant was probably Origen's (not Rufinus's). On Origen's respect for the divergent manuscript readings preserved in the churches, see 3.1.6.

to that death certainly under the law of dying, even if not under the punishment of sin. But it was on this account that Christ descended into the underworld, not only because he would not be held by death,[177] but also in order that he might release those who were held there,[178] as we said, not so much through the crime of transgression as much as by the condition of dying. As it is written, "Many bodies of saints who were sleeping were resurrected with him and entered into the holy city."[179] In this as well the prophet's sayings were fulfilled, in which he said of Christ, "In ascending on high he led captivity captive."[180] Thus by his own resurrection he has already destroyed the dominions of death, which is also why it is written that he set captivity free. Listen now to when the Apostle says that the enemy and tyrant, whose dominions [Christ] destroyed, is going to be destroyed:[181] He says, "The last enemy is destroyed, death."[182] The kingdom of death has already been destroyed, then, and the captivity which was being held under its authority has been led away. But because that enemy and tyrant is still ultimately to be destroyed at the end of the age,[183] that is why we see him even now, I do not say reigning so much as robbing. Having been expelled from his kingdom, we see him going around through deserts and wastelands[184] seeking to gather to himself a band of unbelievers. That is why the Apostle cries out, "Therefore do not let sin exercise dominion in your mortal bodies any longer, to make you obey its desires."[185] Content, however, with having lightly touched upon a few of these things which the Apostle wanted concealed, let us continue our investigation of the things which follow.

(38) After these things he says additionally, "who is a type of that which was to come." This expression certainly seems ambiguous to me. Is Adam said to be a type of that which was com-

---

177. Cf. Acts 2.24.
178. Cf. 5.10.12; *Comm in Mt* 12.43; *Comm in Cant* 3.
179. Mt 27.52–53. Cf. 1.6.3. 180. Ps 68.18; Eph 4.8.
181. Cf. *Comm in Jn* 20.39. 182. 1 Cor 15.26.
183. Cf. 5.3.7.
184. Cf. Mt 12.43; Lk 11.24; 1 Pt 5.8.
185. Rom 6.12.

ing in the future from the time the Apostle was writing these things, or of an age to come? Or is it of a future from himself, that is, from the time of Adam, so as to be interpreted of Christ, a time which, for the Apostle as he wrote these things, was not the future but the past? Although in another passage as well the same Apostle, while speaking of Adam and Eve, would say, "This is a great mystery; but I am speaking of Christ and the Church."[186] In that passage he appears to have given us to understand that Adam is being called a type of that which was to come, in that [M1020] Christ came to unite the Church with himself.[187] Admittedly, I do not know how anyone can link Adam's transgression and sin and the fact that death passed through him to all men to a type of Christ except on the basis of contraries,[188] as the same Apostle explains later when he says, "For just as death came through one man, so also is the resurrection of the dead through one man."[189] And again, "For just as through the disobedience of the one man many were made sinners, so also through the obedience of the one many will be made righteous."[190] But if we understand that the Apostle was saying that Adam is a type of that which was to come, from the time when he was writing these things, then it should be understood all the more that, just as death exercised dominion in this age through one man, Adam, and the whole human race became mortal, so also in the future age life shall reign through Christ and the whole human race will be bestowed with immortality.[191]

(39) I have said that Paul's expression here is ambiguous when he says, "who is a type of that which was to come." Similarly, I find that what he wrote to the Colossians is also ambiguous, where he says, "Therefore do not let anyone condemn you in matters of food and drink or with regard to festivals, new moons, or Sabbaths, which are a shadow of things to come."[192] And in another place the same Apostle says likewise, "For the law contains the shadow of the good things to come."[193] In both

---

186. Eph 5.32.
187. Cf. *Comm in Mt* 14.17.
188. Cf. 5.1.8; 5.2.2.
189. 1 Cor 15.21.
190. Rom 5.19.
191. Cf. 5.1.5; 5.10.3.
192. Col 2.16–17. Cf. *Comm in Cant* 3.
193. Heb 10.1.

texts, at any rate, there is a similar lack of certainty as to whether food and drink and festivals and new moons and Sabbaths contain the shadow of the things to come in the sense that at the coming of Christ the reality of the shadow itself would be fulfilled, or whether it is to be fulfilled in the age to come. But as for the entire law, which the Apostle says contains the shadow of the good things to come, it is uncertain whether the reality to which the shadow belongs is to be fulfilled at the coming of Christ or in the age to come. For in another passage it is written concerning those who are under the law that they serve as types and shadows of the heavenly things.[194]

(40) So then anyone who wants to claim that these things have been fulfilled at the coming of Christ will assert that the matters of food and drink were fulfilled where Peter sees in a vision every sort of animal lowered in a sheet, and he hears a voice, "What God has made clean, you should not call common."[195] Doubtless this refers to the different customs of men. He will call the cup of the new covenant the drink.[196] He will approve of a festival if it be the one where "Christ our Passover lamb was sacrificed."[197] The festival we celebrate "not with the old yeast but with the unleavened bread of sincerity and truth."[198] In a similar way he will show that new moons, i.e., new months, are accomplished through Christ, "the sun of righteousness,"[199] and his [twelve] apostles. What is more he will teach that Sabbaths are to be observed by not carrying around the burden[200] of sin, but by standing in one's own place[201] steadfastly, not the kindling fire[202] of which it is said through the prophet, "Go in the light of your fire and in the flame which [M1021] you have kindled in yourselves."[203]

(41) On the other hand someone else who transfers these types and the shadow[204] of the law to the future age[205] considers them to be images of the heavenly ministries which are to be

---

194. Cf. Heb 8.5.
195. Acts 10.9ff.; 15.
196. Cf. 1 Cor 11.25; Lk 22.20.
197. 1 Cor 5.7.
198. 1 Cor 5.8. Cf. *Hom in Nm* 23.5–7.
199. Mal 3.20; cf. Wis 5.6.
200. Cf. Jer 17.21, 27.
201. Cf. Ex 16.29.
202. Cf. Ex 35.3.
203. Is 50.11. Cf. *Hom in Nm* 23.4.
204. Col 2.17; Heb 10.1.
205. Cf. *Comm in Jn* 10.14–15.

fulfilled in that heavenly Jerusalem.[206] He will try to assign a meaning to food and drink in accordance with what the Lord says, "Until I shall drink it with you anew in the kingdom of my Father."[207] Moreover he will speak of a festival in accordance with the saying of the prophet, "What will you do on the day of the appointed festival and on the feast day of the Lord?"[208] He will look for new moons, that is, new months, in those eternal years of which the prophet says, "I have called to mind the eternal years and have meditated";[209] and again in the song of Deuteronomy, "Remember the eternal days."[210] And of the Sabbath it is said, "So then a Sabbath rest remains for the people of God."[211] He will go on to say that just as each of these things contains a type of the age to come, so also can Adam, of whom it is said, "who is a type of that which was to come," be referred to the matter of the future age. And this is why, after it was first set out about those "who sinned in the likeness of Adam's transgression," it was added, "who is a type of that which was to come."

2. *But the gift is not like the trespass. For if the many died through the trespass of the one, much more surely will the grace of God and the gift in the grace of the one man, Jesus Christ, abound for very many. And the gift is not like the one man who sins. For the judgment from the one brought condemnation, but the grace following many trespasses brings justification.*[212]

(2) Above, the Apostle had said of Adam, "He is a type of that which was to come,"[213] seeing that it was possible that if Adam is a type of Christ, then, in that he sinned, he must preserve the type of Christ. And in that death reigned from Adam until Moses[214]—but it seemed absurd to think this about Christ—he immediately adds, "But the gift is not like the trespass." And he begins with this expression, just as if explaining in what sense he might call Adam a type of Christ. He says, "For

---

206. Cf. Heb 12.22.
207. Mt 26.29.
208. Hos 9.5.
209. Ps 77.5. Cf. 1.4.1.
210. Dt 32.7.
211. Heb 4.9.
212. Rom 5.15–16.
213. Rom 5.14.
214. Rom 5.14. Cf. 5.1.8.

if the many died through the trespass of the one," i.e., in Adam, obviously, "much more surely will the grace of God and the gift in the grace of the one man, Jesus Christ, abound for very many." That is to say: If death, finding room, by the one who sins was able to be spread to very many, how much more will the grace of God, which has abounded in greater supply and more broadly in Christ, in comparison with death in Adam be diffused to very many. Furthermore, the extent of the situations brought about respectively by the transgression and the gift is not the same. For when judgment comes from Adam's single act of transgressing[215] the result is that condemnation came to all men. In contrast, however, justification was given to all through Christ from many transgressions, in which the whole human race was being held [M1022] so that, just as death had exercised its dominion in transgressions through the one, so also through the obedience of the one, life would reign through righteousness.[216] It was therefore not without profound skill in speaking that the Apostle calls Adam a type of Christ.[217] The type is similar in genus but contrary in species.[218] For the type is similar in genus in that, just as something is diffused to very many men from the one Adam, so also something is diffused to very many men from the one Christ. But the species is contrary because the transgression which began with Adam "made the many sinners," whereas by Christ's obedience "many will be made righteous."[219]

(3) Since it has been explained the extent to which Adam was a type of Christ, whether in points of similarity or in points of contrast, in accordance with [Paul's] method of discourse, let us now consider as well what the interior meaning of the Apostle is making known or, rather, concealing in these matters. And though to uncover things which lie concealed in the Apostle's writings may be risky, nevertheless I do not think it will seem absurd to gather certain indications of the divine goodness from these things, to the extent that this is possible.

---

215. Rom 5.17.
216. Cf. Rom 5.21.
217. Rom 5.14. Cf. 4.1.2.
218. Erasmus, CWE 56:168, calls this, "elegantly written."
219. Rom 5.19.

(4) The Apostle has set out to make known what "the first Adam," who "became a living soul," brought to the human race, and also what "the second Adam," who is a "life-giving spirit," brought about.[220] He says that, through the transgression of the one, sin appeared, and through sin death entered and passed through to all men; to be more precise and so that we might preserve the restraint found in Paul's letters, which he has preserved in this passage, I should say, "to *many* men."[221] But through Christ's obedience justification abounded and through justification life abounded much more for very many.[222]

(5) He wants also to show that life is much stronger than death, and righteousness than sin, and by this means to teach that if sin and death were able to exercise dominion in this way in men, having received a beginning from the disobedience of the one man, how much more powerfully and deservedly will life reign through righteousness,[223] receiving its beginning through the obedience of the one, namely Christ; Christ, I say, who came to this task not from the compulsion of his nature but moved by compassion alone. For he was "in the form of God"; and when he sees that death is exercising dominion through the people by the transgression of the one man, he is not oblivious to his own creation, nor does he "regard equality with God as something to be held fast to," that is, he does not consider it a matter of any great importance to himself that he is indeed equal to God and is one with the Father, but rather that death is laying waste to his own work, having gained entrance through one man's transgression.[224] Therefore "he empties himself" from the equality and form of God and takes "the form of a slave"[225] and becomes man. He who was exercising his dominion over everyone even dared to tempt him, but he could not enter him.[226] Yet he accepts that common death,[227] since he would not receive the death of sin which [M1023] was ruling over everyone, in order that, just as "death came through a man, so also

---

220. 1 Cor 15.45; cf. 1 Cor 15.47.   221. Cf. Rom 5.12, 15.
222. Rom 5.15, 19.   223. Cf. Rom 5.21.
224. Rom 5.12, 17.   225. Phil 2.6–7.
226. Cf. 5.1.21.
227. Cf. 5.1.19; 5.4.2; 5.10.8–9; 6.5.4.

the resurrection of the dead might come through a man";[228] and just as "many died by the transgression of the one, much more surely might the grace of God and the gift in the grace of the one man Jesus Christ abound to very many."

(6) It is not without that profound wisdom which Paul claims to speak among the perfect[229] that he has moderated his words in this passage.[230] And what he had elsewhere called "all men,"[231] he has designated here as "many" or "very many," where he makes a comparison between the sin and death, which was diffused from Adam to all men, and the justification and life which derived from Christ. He did this lest he soften his audience, had he pronounced without qualification that, in an identical manner and in the same measure in which the death of sin was diffused from Adam unto all men, so also will the justification and life which come from Christ be diffused to all men, lest they become more lazy in obedience, being certain of a guarantee of life which was to be given to all men through Christ's grace.

(7) For this reason he restrains his words and does not put down "all men," as is usual in other places, but "many," who have been made sinners through the transgression of the one. Similarly he does not assert that the gift in the grace of God through the one man Jesus Christ abounds to "all" but to "very many," in order to keep the more negligent of his hearers in check with fear and to make them apprehensive, without closing the mysteries of the divine goodness for those who are more perfect.[232] It is well that he has set down that those to whom the gift of grace will reach are more than those who were made sinners by the transgression of the one.[233] Indeed I am convinced that there is also some hidden mystery in this, because elsewhere he says that death had exercised dominion from Adam until Moses, not in all but only in those who sinned according to the likeness of Adam's transgression.[234]

(8) Yet even by the simpler interpretation it can seem they

---

228. 1 Cor 15.21.
229. Cf. 1 Cor 2.6. Cf. 7.7.4.
230. Cf. 5.1.6–7.
231. Cf. 1 Cor 15.22.
232. Cf. 2.2.2; 2.3.2; 5.1.7. Here again appears the theme of God's hidden goodness which, in Origen's view, offers the possibility, but not the absolute certainty, of universal restoration. The argument here is resumed in 5.5.2.
233. Rom 5.15, 19.
234. Rom 5.14.

are called "more" since, even though those who became sinners from Adam are many, yet those who are being made alive through the grace of Christ are called "more" because [Adam] himself, from whom the death of sin was diffused to the others, is added to their number. For he himself will be saved with all those whom he had made subject to his transgression,[235] just as it is said about wisdom, "She protected the first-formed father of the world, when he alone had been created; and she delivered him from his own sin."[236] But what wisdom is this which delivered the first man from his own sin if not Christ, who is "the power of God and the wisdom of God"?[237] So then Christ leads back more to life than Adam led into death because Christ has called even Adam himself, who [M1024] was the cause of death for the others, back to life so that what the Apostle writes in what follows is true, "Through the grace of the one comes the justification of life for all men."[238] But Adam is also a man; therefore the justification of life shall reach him as well.[239]

(9) But you will perhaps say: If death passed through to all men because of one who sinned, and likewise by the righteousness of the one the justification of life reached unto all men,[240] then we have done nothing that we should die or that we should live, but indeed Adam is the cause of death, and Christ, the cause of life.

(10) Certainly we have already said above[241] that parents not only produce sons but they also educate them. And those who are born become not only sons of their parents but also their pupils; and they are not prodded into the death of sin so much by nature as by instruction. For example, if someone, falling away from God, worships idols, will he not immediately teach his sons as well, if he has begotten any, to venerate idols and to offer sacrifices to demons? He has done this according to Adam, and in these persons death reigns from Adam,[242] that is

---

235. According to Irenaeus, *Against Heresies* 3.36–37, a heretic named Tatian denied Adam's salvation. This opinion was rejected by the Catholic Church.

236. Wis 10.1.   237. 1 Cor 1.24.
238. Rom 5.18; cf. Rom 5.16.   239. Cf. *Cels* 4.40.
240. Rom 5.12, 18.   241. Cf. 5.1.35.
242. Rom 5.14.

from birth, until the time of the law,²⁴³ when, since he reaches the point of being able to discern between right and wrong, he is enabled to receive Christ's grace. At that point he leaves behind Adam, who had begotten or taught him unto death, and he follows Christ, who teaches him and gives birth to him unto life.

(11) Now do you wish to understand that it was not only by birth but also by instruction that death exercised its dominion from Adam?²⁴⁴ This can be learned from the contraries. For when the Lord Jesus Christ had come to amend what had been done wrongly, in view of the fact that the first birth, which came from Adam, was born to death, he introduces a second birth, which he called not so much being born as being reborn.²⁴⁵ Doubtless it was through this second birth that he wiped away the blemish of the first birth. And just as he substituted birth with re-birth, so also he replaced one doctrine with another. For when he sent his own disciples to do this task, he did not merely say, "Go, baptize all nations," but, "Go, teach all nations, baptizing them in the name of the Father and the Son and the Holy Spirit."²⁴⁶ Therefore, because he knew that both were at fault, he gave a remedy for both, so that even our mortal birth would be changed by the re-birth of baptism, and the teaching of godliness might shut out the teaching of godlessness.²⁴⁷

(12) Death exercised dominion in us,²⁴⁸ therefore, not without our own active engagement in sin; just as, on the other hand, life will reign in us not by our being idle and not by our doing nothing. But indeed the beginning [M1025] of life is given by Christ not to those who are unwilling, but to those who believe. It spreads to the perfection of life by means of the perfecting of the virtues, just as formerly a beginning of death had spread by means of the imitation of transgression and by the carrying out of the vices. And even though the Apostle Paul, as a wise steward of God's word,²⁴⁹ wanted these things in his letters to be kept secret, nevertheless he did include even what

---

243. Cf. 5.1.34.
245. Cf. Jn 3.3; Ti 3.5.
247. Cf. 1 Tm 6.3.
249. Cf. Lk 12.42.

244. Rom 5.14.
246. Mt 28.19.
248. Cf. Rom 5.14.

had been covered up and he was not silent about this when he said, "But death exercised dominion from Adam until Moses over those who sinned in the likeness of Adam's transgression."[250]

(13) Do you see how Paul excuses no one from sin? Moreover he designates the class of sin by assigning to each individual an imitation of Adam's transgression, granted that he did not consider it safe to speak out more openly about the question of where, when, or how this imitation of Adam's transgression may have been committed by each person.[251] But he who has been instructed from the law of the Lord[252] knows how to understand obscure speech and the sayings and riddles of the wise.[253] Finally, this is why he speaks even of the salvation in Christ in a somewhat hidden manner, and when he said, "For just as in Adam all die," he did not say, "so also in Christ all are being made alive," but, "will be made alive."[254] And again when he said, "For just as by the sin of the one death exercised dominion through the one, so also through the justification of the one," he has not said, "life reigns," but, "life will reign through the one Jesus Christ."[255] For he knows, as I have said, that it is written, "A faithful man conceals matters in his spirit";[256] and again elsewhere, "How great is the multitude of your kindness, O Lord, which you have hidden for those who fear you."[257]

(14) For if you should ask: When will life reign through Jesus Christ? and: When will his righteousness become effective in all men in the justification of life? and: When will that blessedness spread to all? learn [the answer] from the words of the Lord Jesus Christ himself, in which he says to his disciples, "'Have you heard all these things?' They answered him, 'Yes, Lord!'[258] And he said to them, 'You are blessed if you do these things.'"[259] Therefore we shall be blessed at that time when we

---

250. Rom 5.14.
251. Cf. 5.1.36; 5.3.3; 5.4.3; C. P. Bammel, "Adam in Origen," in *The Making of Orthodoxy: Essays in Honour of Henry Chadwick*, ed. R. Williams (Cambridge: Cambridge University Press, 1989), pp. 81–82.
252. Cf. Ps 94.12.
253. Cf. Prv 1.6.
254. 1 Cor 15.22.
255. Cf. Rom 5.17, 18, 21.
256. Prv 11.13.
257. Ps 31.19.
258. Mt 13.51.
259. Jn 13.17.

are able not only to hear and understand the Word of God, but also to do it. For although it is promised that a person may eventually come out of prison, nevertheless it is ordained that no one can come out from there unless each one pays back even the last penny.[260] But if not even the penalty of one penny, which is that of the smallest sin, is remitted until it is atoned for in prison by means of punishments,[261] how is it possible for someone to be set free by the hope of being exempted from punishment, or how will he regard the gift of grace as a license to sin?[262] [M1026]

(15) Therefore sin did indeed begin to exercise dominion in this world from the one Adam. And it reigned in those who pursued the imitation of Adam's transgression; and for that reason, "judgment came from the one leading to condemnation." But on the other hand through our one Lord Jesus Christ grace began to reign through righteousness. It will reign in all who obey him and keep his words, and by this means they come from many transgressions to the justification of life.[263]

3. For *if, by the trespass of the one, death exercised dominion through that one, much more surely will those who receive the abundance of grace and of the gift of righteousness reign in life through the one, Jesus Christ.*[264]

(2) If the gift were just like the transgression, the Apostle would assuredly have said that, just as by the transgression of the one, death exercised dominion through the one, so also through the righteousness of the one, life will reign through the one, Jesus Christ. But now he says, "Death indeed exercised dominion by the transgression of the one through the one." But as for "those who receive the abundance of grace and of the gift of righteousness," not only does death no longer exercise dominion over them, which would certainly even in itself be no small grace, but also two other goods are conferred on them. First, instead of death, life reigns in them, namely Christ

---

260. Cf. Mt 5.26. 261. Cf. *Hom in Lk* 35.
262. Origen's unique eschatological views are seen here: A future restoration is promised, but it is conditional and not necessarily abiding. Cf. 5.2.6.
263. Rom 5.14, 16, 18, 21. 264. Rom 5.17.

Jesus. Second, they themselves will likewise reign through the one, Jesus Christ. Then, since these necessary goods come to them, i.e., in order that they might flee the dominion of death, and, instead of death, life might reign in them, nay rather in order that they themselves might reign in life through the one, Jesus Christ,[265] it is clear in what sense "the gift is not like the trespass";[266] and also how it may be said, "much more surely will the grace of God and the gift in the grace of the one man Jesus Christ abound to very many";[267] and also these words, "But grace came from many transgressions leading to justification";[268] and also what he says in the present passage, "Much more surely will those who receive the abundance of grace and of the gift of righteousness reign in life through Jesus Christ" our Lord.

(3) Well then, what he says, "By the transgression of the one, death exercised dominion through the one," shows that dominion is granted to death through transgression; it cannot exercise dominion in anyone unless it receives the right to rule from transgression. What seems to be made known in this is that since a soul created by God is itself free, it leads itself into slavery by means of transgression and hands over to death, so to speak, the IOU[269] of its own immortality which it had received from its own Creator. "For the soul that sins will [M1027] die."[270] That soul, after all, cries out through the prophet, saying, "You have led me down to the dust of death."[271] This assuredly could not have come to pass to the person except as a result of transgression. Therefore it seems plain that the soul had composed its own IOU with death by means of transgression, so that, having lost the freedom of immortality, it took up the yoke of sin and the dominion of death.

(4) Because the Apostle wanted to show how much more a soul has received through Christ than it had lost through Adam, he repeats these expressions to say, "much more surely,"

---

265. Cf. 5.2.15.   266. Rom 5.15.
267. Rom 5.15.   268. Rom 5.16.
269. Cf. Col 2.14. See 5.9.8; 9.30.4; *Hom in Jer* 15.5; *Orat* 28.5; *Hom in Gn* 13.4.
270. Ezek 18.4. Cf. 5.1.19.   271. Ps 22.15. Cf. 5.9.10.

"the abundance of grace and of the gift of righteousness," and "they shall reign through the one, Jesus Christ," all of which most certainly declare how much more abundant the gifts are than the losses.

(5) But as for those whom he says are going to reign in life through Jesus Christ, I ask: Over whom are they going to reign? It seems to me that just as he shows that the dominion of death[272] was in those whom, by sinning, it made subject to it,[273] so also with regard to those who receive the abundance of grace and of the gift of righteousness and who are said to be going to reign through the one Jesus Christ, he is pointing to a future dominion over those who become subjected to them in instruction in the kingdom of God; over those who, as I might say, will have been found capable of receiving wisdom, righteousness, and life, which is in them and through which they reign.[274] This is also why it does not seem to me to be to no purpose that the Apostle, who in other passages had said, "death passed through to all men";[275] and again, "abounded to very many,"[276] and again, "from many transgressions leading to justification,"[277] in this passage has recorded neither "all" nor "many" nor "more." For he was aware that the apex of that blessedness reaches to few, namely to those "who, by receiving the abundance of grace and of the gift of righteousness shall reign in life through the one, Jesus Christ."[278]

(6) The dominion of that death is described here, which is said elsewhere to be Christ's ultimate or last enemy to be destroyed.[279] He is destroyed in that he would no longer exercise dominion. But if he no longer exercises dominion, it is certain that transgression, in which alone the dominion of death consists, will no longer exist in the future. Doubtless it will be at that time when it will be said to it, "Where, O Death, is your sting?" For indeed, as the Apostle himself says, "The sting of

---

272. Rom 5.14.
274. Cf. *Princ* 2.11.3.
276. Rom 5.15.
278. Cf. 5.2.6–7; 5.2.14. The passage seems to imply that not all will attain the highest blessedness.
279. Cf. 1 Cor 15.26.

273. Cf. 5.3.3.
275. Rom 5.12.
277. Rom 5.16.

death is sin, but the power of sin is the law."²⁸⁰ It follows, therefore, that at that time there will be no law, if indeed it is called the power of sin, so that when the power of sin has been put away, even the dominion of death could be deservedly abolished.²⁸¹ But these matters have been mentioned here only as a digression; they need to be examined more appropriately in their own passages.

(7) But I would like to ask particularly: Since we have indeed said that death had held dominion until the arrival of Christ,²⁸² who is life,²⁸³ [M1028] but the Apostle says that Christ had come not only to destroy death but also him who was holding the power of death, i.e., the devil,²⁸⁴ who is reigning? That is, before that which is written happens, "Then comes the end when he hands over the kingdom to God the Father."²⁸⁵ For if we should say what seems logical, that life reigns when death has been destroyed, it could be objected to us: Why then is sin still being committed? It is clear that death exercises its dominion through sin. But if we should say that Christ, i.e., life, reigns in certain souls, and death in certain others, what persons shall we find in whom the dominion of life exists in such a way that the dominion of death has no authority in them? In other words, who is entirely free from sin? These matters seem to me to pertain instead to the future kingdom, and there those things are to be fulfilled where it is said, "That God may be all in all."²⁸⁶ For this is why we are taught to say in the Lord's prayer, "Your kingdom come!"²⁸⁷ as if it has not yet come.²⁸⁸ And the Lord himself, when he began to preach, does not say: The kingdom of heaven has come, but: "The kingdom of heaven has come near."²⁸⁹ The present time, however, I would say seems not so much a time of reigning as of war.²⁹⁰ Through this war the future kingdom is being striven for. Yet Christ can be said to reign even in this time of war, since the dominion of

---

280. 1 Cor 15.55–56.
281. Cf. 5.7.8; *Princ* 3.6.5.
282. Cf. 5.1.34.
283. Cf. Jn 14.6.
284. Heb 2.14.
285. 1 Cor 15.24. Cf. *Princ* 1.6.2.
286. 1 Cor 15.28. Cf. *Princ* 3.6.3.
287. Mt 6.10; Lk 11.2.
288. Cf. *Orat* 25.2.
289. Mt 4.17.
290. Cf. 5.1.37; *Hom in Jos* 8.4.

death is now broken in part and being gradually destroyed, a dominion which had previously spread itself out to all men. This agrees with the words of Scripture, "For he must reign until he puts every enemy under his feet."[291] He likewise says in another passage, "But now we do not yet see everything subjected to him."[292] Whence it appears that what he says, "For he must reign,"[293] he used instead of, "He [must] prepare a kingdom." For it is certain that the strong man first must be fought and bound and in this way his property must be plundered.[294] For this reason as well the Savior himself says, "I have not come to bring peace but a sword."[295] Therefore the fight must be fought for a long time by those who want to reign in life through Jesus Christ, until "death, the last enemy, should be destroyed."[296]

(8) Moreover, concerning "the abundance of grace and of the gift of righteousness," it needs to be known that someone does not enter this kingdom, which we said is being prepared by means of war,[297] who has attained [only] a single grace, that is to say, who has pleased God in respect to only one work. On the contrary, an abundance of grace is required according to him who says, "But I labored more abundantly than all of them; but not I but the grace of God with me."[298] He prays similar things as well for those whom he instructed [M1029] when he says, "Grace to you and peace be multiplied!"[299] Therefore grace is multiplied and abounds if our speech is always seasoned in grace as with salt[300] and if our deeds are done with the grace of humility and sincerity, and if everything we do, we do for the glory of God.[301] The gift of righteousness should be interpreted in a similar way. For one who is justified by Christ should do nothing without righteousness, according to him who says, "Blessed are those who practice judgment and preserve righteousness at all times,"[302] and according to what wis-

---

291. 1 Cor 15.25.
292. Heb 2.8.
293. 1 Cor 15.25.
294. Cf. Mt 12.29; Mk 3.27; Lk 11.22.
295. Mt 10.34.   296. 1 Cor 15.26.
297. Cf. 5.4.7.   298. 1 Cor 15.10.
299. 1 Pt 1.2. Cf. 9.2.6 for the same mistaken citation.
300. Cf. Col 4.6.   301. Cf. 1 Cor 10.31.
302. Ps 106.3.

dom declares when she says, "Even if someone is perfect among the sons of men, if he does not have the righteousness from God it shall be reckoned to him as nothing."[303] In this way, those who will have had the abundance of grace and of the gift of righteousness will reign in life through the one, Jesus Christ.

4. *Accordingly just as through the trespass of the one came condemnation to all men, so also through the righteousness of the one comes the justification of life to all men.*[304]

(2) We have already said above[305] that by means of Adam's transgression a certain access, as it were, was given by which sin, or the death of sin, or condemnation, spread to all men. Thus, in contrast, Christ opened up an access to justification, through which life would enter to men. This is why he was saying about himself, "I am the door. If anyone enters through me he will be saved."[306] But enough has already been said about these things above. Nevertheless it should be noted that he has not said "the condemnation of death came unto all men" like he said "the justification of life comes unto all men." On the contrary, he said merely "condemnation" in order, obviously, to demonstrate how much more abundant the gift to all is than the transgression.[307] How, or rather which, condemnation would come to all men must of course be seen. Perhaps it can suffice us according to the simple interpretation to say that the condemnation of transgression is that common death[308] which comes to all and will come to all, even if they seem righteous.[309]

(3) But if perhaps anyone would object to this over the cases of Enoch and Elijah, who were translated so as to not see death,[310] this will be disposed of in the following manner: things that are said about all men shall not immediately be deemed false if any dispensation of God has been made in the case of one or two men. But someone could reasonably, as I

---

303. Wis 9.6.
305. See 5.1.8; 5.1.31; 5.2.2.
307. Rom 5.15.
308. See 5.1.19; 5.2.5; 5.10.8–9; 6.5.4.
309. Cf. 5.1.37.
310. Cf. Gn 5.24; Heb 11.5; 2 Kgs 2.11.

304. Rom 5.18.
306. Jn 10.9.

judge, suggest in this place, that when Adam had transgressed it is written that the Lord God expelled him from paradise and established him in that land opposite to the paradise of delights.[311] And this was the condemnation for his transgression which doubtless spread to all men. For everyone was fashioned in that place of humiliation and in the valley of tears;[312] whether because all who are born from him were in Adam's loins and were equally expelled with him or, in some other inexplicable fashion known only to God, each person seems to be driven out of paradise and to have received condemnation.[313]

5. *For just as by the one man's disobedience* [M1030] *many were made sinners, so by the obedience of the one many will be made righteous.*[314]

(2) It can indeed be that, according to the matters which we have noted above, Paul, wanting to cover up the more secret mysteries,[315] those whom he has called in some passages "all," he puts down elsewhere as "many," lest, perchance, had he said, "By the disobedience of the one all were made sinners," and then out of logical necessity had joined to this, "so also by the obedience of the one all will be made righteous," it would have seemed, in view of the security offered in a promise of this sort, to relax the minds of those whom it is more expedient to keep under fear.[316] And therefore even we who preserve the counsel of this faithful and wise steward of the word of God[317] must also endeavor all the more to explain how it is that by the disobedience of the one, not all but many have been made sinners. For there will be no difficulty in understanding how, by the obedi-

---

311. Cf. Gn 3.23–24.
312. Cf. Ps 43.20, 26 LXX; Ps 83.7 LXX. Cf. 5.1.14.
313. Cf. 5.9.10; *Princ* 2.8.5. N. P. Williams, *The Ideas of the Fall and of Original Sin*, p. 228, gives a helpful summary of this passage: "Here two alternative methods of conceiving a pre-natal and transcendental Fall are indicated: the first being the hypothesis of a collective pre-natal Fall of the whole race, contained in Adam, from the heavenly place; the second being the theory which has been already expounded in the *De Principiis*, that of a never-ending series of individual falls into this vale of tears, which is the world of matter."
314. Rom 5.19.
315. Cf. 5.2.7.
316. Cf. 5.1.7; 5.2.6–7.
317. Cf. Lk 12.42.

ence of the one, not all but many are made righteous according to what the Lord says in the Gospel, "For many will come from the east and west and will recline with Abraham and Isaac and Jacob in the kingdom of God."[318] And he did not say, "All will come." But we need to show how it can be that many, and not all, seem to be sinners, although the same Apostle says that "all have sinned."[319]

(3) It is one thing to have sinned, another to be a sinner. One is called a sinner who, by committing many transgressions, has already reached the point of making sinning into a habit[320] and, so to speak, a course of study. Just as, on the other hand, one is not called righteous who has once or twice done some righteous act, but who continually behaves justly and keeps righteousness in use and makes it habitual. For if someone is unjust in nearly all other matters but should carry out some just work one or two times, he will indeed be said to have acted justly in that work in which he practiced justice; nevertheless he will not on that basis be called a just man. Similarly it will indeed be said that a righteous man has sinned if he has at some time committed what is not lawful. But he will not on that account be labeled a sinner, since he does not hold fast to the practice and habit of sinning. Just as one is not called a physician who knows how to place a bandage lightly upon the skin of a head wound, or who can sooth the swelling of an injury with hot water, even though this seems to belong to the art of medicine. Rather one is called a physician who maintains the use and study and instruction of medical science.

(4) By all this I think it has been sufficiently shown that it is one thing to sin and another to be a sinner. For it can happen that all people commit sin, even if they are holy, since "no one is pure from uncleanness, not even if his life should be one day long."[321] For who is there who does not sin either in deed or in word or, if one is extremely cautious, at least in thought? Therefore, as I have said, everyone will deservedly be said to have sinned, but not all have become sinners, only many. And by a

318. Mt 8.11.
320. Cf. 6.9.8.
319. Rom 5.12.
321. Jb 14.4–5 LXX.

similar pattern many shall be deemed righteous but not all, even though all may do something righteous.

(5) However [M1031] the reckoning of time is also well preserved by the Apostle. For since he referred to the past as the time when many were made sinners, he transferred to the future the time when many are to be made righteous, knowing, doubtless, that by the progression of the proclamation of the gospel the multitude of the righteous would grow larger. But, that many were righteous even before the coming of the Savior, the Lord likewise testifies in the Gospels when he says, "Many prophets and righteous men longed to see what you see."[322] However the Savior says the righteous are "many" here in one way, while the Apostle puts it in a different way. For the Savior calls them many righteous men and prophets in comparison to the number of the apostles, the number of whom he had in mind. In the present passage, however, the Apostle should be understood to have called them many in comparison with all who have been born into this world and who will be born. Therefore "by the disobedience of the one many have been made sinners." Here the many sinners must be interpreted in accordance with that observation we set forth above[323] concerning the one who sins and the one who is a sinner.

(6) But suppose someone objects to us that the Apostle says even about himself, "Christ Jesus came into this world to save sinners—of whom I am the foremost,"[324] as if he seems to call himself a sinner. Then we shall say that it is one thing for someone to be designated as a sinner under the *persona* of the Scripture or a prophet or the Lord,[325] but it is another matter for a righteous man to become his own accuser[326] and to humble himself, so that he might be exalted by God.[327] Although Paul, in that he says that he had persecuted the church of God and had fought against it[328] and had even dragged off men and women and had them thrown in prison,[329] indeed would have

---

322. Mt 13.17.
324. 1 Tm 1.15.
326. Cf. Prv 18.17.
328. 1 Cor 15.9; Gal 1.13; Acts 8.3; 9.2.
329. Cf. Acts 9.2; Gal 1.13.
323. Cf. 5.5.3.
325. Cf. 6.9.12.
327. Cf. Mt 23.12; Lk 18.14.

done this out of ignorance and he would attain mercy;[330] nevertheless it must be admitted that while he was doing these things, he had to be called a sinner perhaps not undeservedly.

(7) But in order that the grounds for this distinction, which we have given between one who sins and one who is a sinner, might become even clearer, consider Cain who, although he was openly a sinner, still did something right, on account of which the Lord said to him, "If you bring an offering rightly."[331] And Pharaoh is doing something just when he says, "The Lord is righteous, but I and my people are ungodly";[332] but he will not be called a just man on that basis. You may find in the Holy Scriptures many things of this sort in which you will discover both that the righteous man has committed sin and the sinner has done some righteous things. Nevertheless you will not find either the righteous man called a sinner because he sinned in some matter, or the sinner designated as a righteous man because he did something just.

(8) Now not even this ought to escape the notice of the attentive hearer, that where he says, "disobedience of the one," he adds, "man, through whom [M1032] many have been made sinners." But when he records, "obedience of the one," he does not add, "man," through whom many will be made righteous.[333] For the one through whom they become righteous is doubtless righteousness itself,[334] as the same Apostle also says about Christ, "Who has become for us righteousness from God."[335]

(9) So then Adam offered sinners a model through his disobedience; but Christ, in contrast, gave the righteous a model by his obedience. As it is written in another passage, "But you have become obedient from the heart to the same model of teaching to which you were entrusted."[336] It is also on this account that he "became obedient unto death,"[337] in order that those who follow the example of his obedience might be made righteous by righteousness itself, just as those others were made sinners by following the model of [Adam's] disobedience.[338]

---

330. Cf. 1 Tm 1.13.
331. Gn 4.7.
332. Ex 9.27.
333. Rom 5.19. Cf. *Comm in Jn* 10.6.
334. Cf. *Cels* 5.39.
335. 1 Cor 1.30.
336. Rom 6.17.
337. Phil 2.8.
338. Rom 5.19.

6. *But law entered by stealth, so the trespass might abound; but where sin abounded, grace superabounded so that, just as sin exercised dominion in death, so grace might also reign through righteousness leading to eternal life through Jesus Christ our Lord.*[339]

(2) Indeed, if no one had sinned before the law was given through Moses, then Marcion and the other heretics,[340] who want to accuse the law based on these words of the Apostle, seem to seize this opportunity, as if the reason the law was given was in order that sin, which did not exist before the law, might abound. Yet I do not know what time period they could find prior to the giving of the law which was void of sins. When Cain was murdering Abel and defiling the earth with his brother's blood so that it was said to him, "The ground is cursed, which opened its mouth to receive your brother's blood,"[341] was not sin abounding?[342] Plainly it was abounding; and this was so in spite of the fact that there was not an abundance of men. Or take the time when Lamech was saying, "I killed a man for my wound and a young man for my bruise";[343] and indeed, "On Cain's behalf it has been avenged seven times, but Lamech seventy-seven times."[344] So much did transgression abound at the time of Noah that it says, "The Lord saw that the wickedness of men had multiplied on the earth, and that every man had set his heart intently upon evil all the days of his life. And the Lord reconsidered that he had made man on the earth, and it grieved him in his heart and he said, 'I must blot out man whom I have created from the face of the earth—from men to cattle and from creeping things to the birds of the sky, for it grieves me that I have made them.'"[345] And again [we see sin abounding] when it is said, "The earth was corrupt in the sight of the Lord, and the earth was filled with iniquities. And God saw that the earth was exceedingly corrupt; for all flesh had corrupted its way upon the earth."[346] Who then can be so stupid [M1033] as to deny that sin abounded in all these instances? Or certainly when God

---

339. Rom 5.20–21.
340. Cf. 3.6.9; 4.4.3.
341. Gn 4.11.
342. For the recurring theme of sin before the law of Moses, see 4.4.4 and 5.1.23.
343. Gn 4.23.
344. Gn 4.24.
345. Gn 6.5–7.
346. Gn 6.11–12.

said of the residents of Sodom, "I have come down to see if, according to the outcry of the Sodomites, their iniquities have been finished off";[347] or when they surrounded Lot's house, endeavoring to commit acts of lewdness even against angels.[348] Was sin possibly not abounding then, when Pharaoh was afflicting the sons of Israel with mud and brick and was giving orders to have their infants killed in the river?[349] Assuredly the law of Moses had not yet entered by stealth when such a blot of sins were being diffused throughout the earth.

(3) From all these testimonies it is deduced that the heretics whom we mentioned above,[350] and whoever there is who agrees with them in interpreting these words as spoken about the law of Moses, have been unable to touch even remotely upon the Apostle's meaning.[351] Instead, this passage ought to be understood, as we have already repeatedly said,[352] of the law of nature which is written "not on stone tablets but on the fleshly tablets of the heart, not with ink but with the Spirit of the living God."[353] This law has been inscribed by the one who created man in the beginning[354] on the governing part of man's heart[355] so that at the proper time, when the pages of that mind will have matured, or rather, as the Scripture has designated it, when the tablets of the fleshly heart should begin to be opened with the advancement of age, this law would begin to be diffused in the inner workings of the conscience and to fill the mind with reason. Then the will of the flesh arises and suggests other desires which are contrary to the commands naturally suggested by this sort of law.[356] And this is what this Apostle himself has designated as the law in the members, resisting the law of the mind.[357]

---

347. Gn 18.21.
348. Cf. Gn 19.4ff.
349. Cf. Ex 1.14, 22.
350. Cf. 5.6.2.
351. Cf. 1.18.3; 3.7.4.
352. Cf. 2.8.2; 2.9.1; 3.2.7–8; 3.6.1; 5.1.24.
353. 2 Cor 3.3.
354. Cf. Mt 19.4.
355. *In principali cordis*. The Greek term is *hegemonicon*. Lewis in Origen, *Philocalia* (Edinburgh: T & T Clark, 1911), p. 49 n. 4, notes, "The Stoics taught that the soul had eight parts, the *hegemonicon* or governing part, the five senses, the faculty of speech, and the generative force."
356. Cf. 3.2.9; 5.1.26.
357. Cf. Rom 7.23. See also 4.4.5–6.

(4) It seems that the Apostle here in this passage has described a law of the members which, he says, entered by stealth so sin might abound. Even the word he has used seems to me to be pointing very clearly to what we are saying. For it is one thing to enter but another to enter by stealth; just as it is one thing to lead away and another to lead away by stealth; or to drag off and to drag off by stealth.[358] After all, to enter by stealth means that when the one thing had entered the other came in under the cover of the first.[359] The meaning which we explained above is what is plainly pointed to, that under the cover of natural law, which the Apostle named the law of the mind which consents to the law of God,[360] the law of the members has arisen which, by suggesting the desires of the flesh and by leading man captive, inclined toward lust and pleasures, makes sin abound in him. In this way then "the law entered by stealth so the trespass might abound."

(5) "But where sin abounded," he says, "grace superabounded." As we have taught above,[361] when [Paul] makes the comparison with each of the things [M1034] which seem to have occurred as a result of Adam's transgression, he shows that what has been amassed through the grace of Christ as a means of bringing healing is in opposition and much greater. Also in the same way, in the present passage when he had said that sin had abounded, he used an extremely worthy discourse in which he supercedes "abundance" and uses "superabundance." For the grace of Christ superabounded in that not only would it absolve man from past sins, but it would also fortify him against future ones.

(6) If in fact he wants to show that there are two kingdoms in man—one by which sin exercised dominion in death, the other by which grace would reign through righteousness in life—then it is grace which ejected and expelled sin from its

---

358. He uses the following forms in this sentence: *intrare, subintrare; ducere, subducere; trahere, subtrahere.*

359. Rufinus has consistently used *subintrare,* "to enter by stealth," up to this point. Later in 5.8.2 he will switch to *subintroire,* "to enter."

360. Cf. Rom 7.22–23.

361. Cf. 5.2.2; 5.3.2; 5.3.4; 5.4.2.

own kingdom,[362] i.e., from our members, since death necessarily was equally expelled with it. Not until then would grace lay claim to a kingdom for itself in us through righteousness; and where death had been, eternal life took up residence. This is what the Apostle also says elsewhere, "Therefore, do not let sin reign any longer in your mortal bodies";[363] and again in another passage, "For just as you presented your members as instruments of wickedness to sin, so now present your members as instruments of righteousness to God."[364] Therefore there is a marvelous superabundance, because where sin and death were, now there is grace and righteousness and eternal life. And these are all things which surpass the others through our Lord Jesus Christ.

(7) It may be the case that, just as he said that all these good things come into being through our Lord Jesus Christ, so also he wanted it to be understood that those evils have arisen through the devil. But he has remained silent about the name of the originator of those things in order that he might attribute the superabundance in all things to grace. For just as Christ is indeed one in essence but may be designated in many ways according to his virtues and operations[365] (for example he is understood to be grace itself, as well as righteousness, peace, life, truth, the Word[366]) so perhaps also the devil can himself be understood by various designations. For he should be thought of as the sin which is said to exercise dominion. Also one has to believe that he is that death of which it is said, "For the last enemy, death, will be destroyed."[367] Moreover he is understood to be a desolation according to what has been spoken by the prophet, "You have become a desolation and you will not exist in eternal time."[368] Furthermore I think that what the Apostle

---

362. Cf. 5.7.3; 6.1.2. 363. Rom 6.12.
364. Rom 6.13; cf. 6.19.
365. Cf. *Cels* 2.64; *Princ* 1.2.1; 1.2.13; 4.4.1; *Comm in Jn* 1.10; 1.19; 1.20. Scripture gives to the Son of God a number of titles (ἐπίνοιαι). These, according to Bigg, *Christian Platonists*, p. 168, refer to "his economic functions, his relations to the world."
366. Cf. 1 Cor 1.30; Eph 2.14; Jn 14.6; Jn 1.1.
367. 1 Cor 15.26. Cf. 5.1.31; 5.10.9.
368. Jer 51.26 (LXX 28.26); Ezek 28.19.

says, "Therefore, do not let sin reign in your mortal bodies,"[369] could be said even more about the devil.[370] For he is the author of sin and death and desolation, and the author of an invention is logically named after the things he has invented.

(8) So then, it is impossible that a soul exists at any time without having a ruler. But we must make provision that Christ should be that ruler, whose yoke [M1035] is easy and whose burden is light,[371] and not the devil, whose dominion is burdensome. For it is wickedness which sits enthroned upon a leaden weight;[372] but wherever Christ reigns, there grace and righteousness superabound unto eternal life.

7. *What then shall we say? Shall we continue in sin in order that grace may abound? By no means! How shall we who died to sin go on living in it?*[373]

(2) Since he had said above, "Where sin abounded, grace superabounded."[374] Now he poses to himself a question which arises from this, namely, that if the abundance of sin brings forth a superabundance of grace, should we not then commit sin in order that grace might abound all the more? But he furnishes a quick answer to the question when he says, "By no means!" And he supplies the reason immediately by saying that those persons in whom grace abounded are dead to sin. Now it is certain that one who is dead is not able to sin; therefore one who has died to sin cannot continue in sin.

(3) To make these matters clearer, let us examine what it means to live to sin and to die to sin. Just as a person is said to live to God who lives in accordance with the will of God, so also one is said to live to sin who lives in accordance with the will of sin. This is what the same Apostle makes known when he says, "Therefore do not let sin reign in your mortal bodies to obey its desires."[375] By this he is showing that to live to sin means to obey sin's desires. Now if to live to sin means to do the desires of sin, then to die to sin must refer to not carrying out sin's de-

369. Rom 6.12.
371. Cf. Mt 11.30.
373. Rom 6.1–2.
375. Rom 6.12.

370. Cf. 5.7.5.
372. Cf. Zec 5.6–8.
374. Rom 5.20.

sires and not obeying its will.[376] The Apostle says, however, that sin has, so to speak, established a throne and a seat of its dominion in our body.[377] For that part of the [man's] substance is more familiar to it and [forms] a kind of friendly association with the pleasure of the flesh. From this bond of friendship, while employing the opportunities given to it by nature's inducement, by means of a small detour it turns the order of nature over the precipice of death.

(4) But in order to explain what we are saying with greater clarity, as an example let us suggest this: The flesh has natural appetites[378] for food and drink which need to be kept within certain limits of satisfaction. But if someone, by the enticement of sin, should exceed these limits, he is no longer yearning after food and drink, a flesh which suffices nature, but after excess and drunkenness.[379] In a similar way there even exists in the flesh a natural drive by which it demands to be united with a woman for the sake of procuring offspring. But if he should be turned aside from the law, sin enticing in this occasion, and his impulses of natural lust should be roused to illicit things, he lives to sin, since he is not obeying the law of God in these instances but the persuasions of sin.

(5) Therefore, suppose someone, admonished by the death of Christ, [M1036] who "died for the ungodly,"[380] repents of all these things and he expels the one exercising dominion in his flesh like an extremely wicked king, and makes himself a stranger to his desires and commands. Then he will truly be said to have died to sin through the death of Christ. Now in this passage I believe the author of sin is being called sin.[381] If anyone dies to sin, it is certain that he dies by means of repen-

---

376. Schelkle, *Paulus, Lehrer*, p. 197, notes the un-sacramental stress of Origen's interpretation of Rom 6.2. For him "dying to sin is understood as an act of faith. No mention is made of the sacrament [of baptism]." Whereas for Origen death to sin must take place before baptism, for the other Fathers (Ephrem, Cyril of Jerusalem, Theodoret, Pelagius, Ambrosiaster, Chrysostom), the death takes place at the same moment of baptism. See 5.8.2 below.

377. Cf. 6.1.2.

378. Cf. Clement, *Stromateis* 3.4.37.1; 3.5.41.5; 3.5.44.4.

379. Cf. Gal 5.19–21.   380. Rom 5.6.

381. Cf. 5.6.7.

tance. How then will someone continue in sin so that grace may abound, when grace abounds because one dies to sin? For if we should continue in sin, as is proposed, it is certain that we are not dying to sin but living to it. But in those who are living to sin, it is impossible for grace to abound.[382]

(6) It is of course asked whether grace superabounds[383] only in human beings in whom sin formerly abounded, and whether grace superabounds in no one except in the one in whom sin had abounded; or whether it is possible for grace to superabound even in certain others in whom sin had never abounded or existed. If anyone takes into consideration what the Apostle says, "Christ made peace through his own blood not only with things on the earth but also with things in heaven";[384] and this, "so that apart from God he might taste death for all";[385] that person will be convinced that there, likewise, there was an abundance of sin so that there should no less be a superabundance of grace.[386] But if you pay attention to what the text just above this recorded, where sin is said to have entered into this world through one man, and through sin death, and in this way death to have passed through to all,[387] you would say that the matters at hand depend upon this starting point. Consequently, the Apostle seems to deal only with those matters which he proposed at that beginning point, that is to say, only what deals with human beings.

(7) It must certainly be noted how forceful the expression employed by the Apostle is that he would say, "Shall we continue in sin?" For to continue means not to cease from what was begun. Assuredly if someone should act in this way, it is obvious that he has not accepted the starting point of conversion. Now indeed it does occasionally happen that a person ceases to continue in sin, but after desisting from it, returns again to his own

---

382. Wiles, *Divine Apostle*, p. 115, comments on this passage that for Origen "[t]he question of continuing in sin that grace may abound is not therefore a regrettable counsel to be opposed but a logical impossibility to be exposed."
383. Cf. Rom 5.20.   384. Col 1.20.
385. Heb 2.9. For this reading cf. 3.8.1; *Comm in Jn* 1.35.
386. Cf. 1.4.4; 5.10.14; *Comm in Jn* 1.35.
387. Rom 5.12.

vomit[388] and becomes infinitely wretched so that, after having expelled from himself the kingdom of sin and death and after having received the kingdom of life and righteousness, the person surrenders himself all over again to the tyranny of sin and death. The Apostle calls this the shipwreck of one's faith.[389]

(8) Nevertheless no matter how much a person may continue in sin, no matter how much he should hold out under the dominion and authority of death, I do not think that the kingdom of death is therefore of eternal duration in the same way as that of life and righteousness, especially when I hear from the Apostle that the last enemy, death, is going to be destroyed.[390] [M1037] And in fact, if the duration of the eternity of death is supposed to be the same as that of life, death will no longer be the contrary to life but its equal. For an eternal will not be contrary to an eternal, but identical. Now it is certain that death is contrary to life;[391] therefore it is certain that if life is eternal, death cannot be eternal;[392] whence also the resurrection of the dead necessarily takes place. For when the death of the soul, who[393] is the last enemy,[394] should be destroyed, likewise this common death, which, we have said[395] to be like the shadow of the other one, shall necessarily be abolished. Logically, at that time room will be made for the resurrection of the dead, when the dominion of death has been destroyed equally with death.

(9) But we must not wait until that time when the last enemy is destroyed, we who "have once been enlightened, and have tasted the heavenly gift, and have become sharers of the Holy Spirit, and have tasted the good word of God and the powers of the age to come."[396] But let us continue in grace; and we should

---

388. Cf. Prv 26.11; 2 Pt 2.22.   389. Cf. 1 Tm 1.19.
390. Cf. 1 Cor 15.26.
391. Cf. *Comm in Jn* 20.39; *Comm in Mt* 12.33; 13.9.
392. Heither in Origenes, *Commentarii*, 3:132 n. 77, notes that this is a Platonic form of argumentation. Cf. *Phaedo* 105c–6d. Cf. M. B. von Stritzky, "Die Bedeutung der Phaidrosinterpretation für die Apokatastasislehre des Origenes" *VC* 31.4 (1977): pp. 287–88.
393. *Qui* is a masculine pronoun referring unambiguously to the devil. The Migne text changes this to the feminine *quae*, i.e., *mors* (death).
394. 1 Cor 15.26.   395. Cf. 5.1.19.
396. Heb 6.4–5.

not expect that we who re-crucify to ourselves the Son of God and hold him up to contempt[397] shall be restored again to repentance after falling away.[398] But may the kingdom of righteousness become in us an eternal kingdom. May we not take refuge again in the kingdom of death, delivered from which we have come to the kingdom of eternal life in order that grace might reign in us through righteousness [leading] to eternal life through Jesus Christ our Lord.[399]

(10) Therefore what he says, "We died to sin,"[400] is that which he says elsewhere, that we have become conformed to the death of Christ,[401] the one who "died to sin once for all."[402] When he says, "once for all," he means "completely." For Christ, who "committed no sin nor was deceit found in his mouth,"[403] has died completely to sin.[404]

8. *Do you not know that all of us who have been baptized into Christ Jesus were baptized into his death? Therefore we have been buried with him through baptism into death, so that, just as Christ rose from the dead through the glory of the Father, so we too might walk in newness of life.*[405]

(2) Observe carefully the order of words and the line of thought. For he compares the death which is through Adam with the life which is through Christ;[406] and he says, "The gift is not like the trespass."[407] And likewise after this he says that the law entered so sin might abound, but while sin was abounding grace superabounded.[408] By these words he solves the apparent contradiction[409] and says, "For how shall we who have died to sin go on living in it?"[410] Now then, because he wants to show in these matters what it means to be dead to sin, he says, [M1038]

---

397. Cf. Heb 6.6.
398. In 5.7.8 he seems certain that even the devil will cease to be God's enemy in the future. But here he shows that these hopes are conditional, not guaranteed.
399. Cf. Rom 5.21.
400. Rom 6.2.
401. Cf. Rom 6.5; Phil 3.10.
402. Rom 6.10.
403. 1 Pt 2.22.
404. Cf. 4.12.5.
405. Rom 6.3–4.
406. Cf. 5.1.8; 5.4.2.
407. Rom 5.15.
408. Cf. Rom 5.20.
409. Cf. 5.7.2.
410. Rom 6.2.

"Do you not know that all of us who have been baptized into Christ Jesus were baptized into his death? For we have been buried with him through baptism into death," teaching through these things that if someone has first died to sin, he has necessarily been buried with Christ in baptism. But if the person does not die to sin beforehand, he cannot be buried with Christ. For no one who is still alive is ever buried. But if one is not buried with Christ, he is not validly baptized.[411]

(3) But concerning the meaning of baptism, we have spoken to the best of our ability whatever was able to come or, rather, whatever the Lord freely granted, when we were explaining the Gospel according to John[412] when it came to the passage where he says of Jesus, "He himself will baptize you in the Holy Spirit";[413] and again where the Savior himself says, "Unless someone should be born anew of water and Spirit, he cannot enter into the kingdom of God."[414] In that passage we tried to reveal the force of that expression more profoundly, in which it is said, "unless someone should be reborn anew."[415] For what we Latin speakers use as "anew," the Greeks say ἄνωθεν, which means both "anew" and "from above." In this passage, that whoever is baptized by Jesus is baptized in the Holy Spirit, it is suitable to be understood not so much as "anew," as "from above"; for we say "anew" when the same things which have already happened are repeated. Here, however, the same birth is not repeated or done a second time, but this earthly one is laid aside and a new birth from above is received. For that reason we would more accurately read the text in the Gospel as, "Unless someone has been reborn from above, he cannot enter into the kingdom of

---

411. The un-sacramental stress of Origen's theology comes through clearly here. Without denying the efficacy of the sacramental act, Origen emphasized that moral conversion had to take place before baptism for any benefit to be derived from the rite. See 5.7.3; *Hom in Lv* 6.2.; *Hom in Lk* 21; *Hom in Ezek* 6–10; and esp. *Comm in Jn* 6.17 (= FOTC 80:215): "He is teaching that the benefit of baptism depends on the choice of the one who is baptized. It is a benefit for the one who repents, but it will result in more grievous judgment for the one who does not approach baptism in this way." Cf. also G. W. H. Lampe, *The Seal of the Spirit* (London: Longmans, Green & Co., 1951), pp. 163–70.

412. The corresponding volumes of Origen's *Comm in Jn* are not preserved.
413. Jn 1.33; cf. Mt 3.11.
414. Jn 3.3, 5.
415. Jn 3.3.

God."[416] For this refers to being baptized in the Holy Spirit. For this reason, that baptism is confirmed to be "from above," not unfittingly are even the waters, which are above the heavens and which praise the name of the Lord,[417] linked to the Holy Spirit. And although all of us may be baptized in those visible waters and in a visible anointing,[418] in accordance with the form handed down to the churches, nevertheless, the one who has died to sin and is truly baptized into the death of Christ and is buried with him through baptism into death, he is the one who is truly baptized in the Holy Spirit and with the water from above.

(4) Consider the logic of the sequence of this mystery even more carefully: First you must die to sin so that you can be buried with Christ; for a burial is required for a dead person. For if you are still living to sin, you cannot be buried with Christ or be placed in his new tomb,[419] since your old man is still alive and cannot walk in newness of life. This is why it was important to the Holy [M1039] Spirit to hand down in the Scriptures even the fact that it was a new tomb in which Jesus was buried, and that he was wrapped in clean linen so that everyone who wants to be buried with Christ through baptism might know that nothing of the old should be laid in the new tomb and nothing unclean should be brought to a clean linen.[420] This, then, is that blessed death[421] of which the Apostle says, "We always carry around the death of Jesus Christ in our body";[422] and again, "I die daily."[423] Moreover he lists this death by which we die to sin and are buried with Christ when he says the following, "All things are yours, whether Paul or Apollos or Cephas or this world or life or death."[424]

(5) But one can ask why the Apostle, when speaking in these passages about our baptism, should also speak of Jesus, "We were buried with him through baptism"; and then elsewhere,

---

416. Jn 3.3, 5.
417. Ps 148.4–5. Cf. *Cels* 5.44; 6.19; 6.20.
418. Cf. *Hom in Lv* 6.5; *Cels* 6.79.   419. Cf. Mt 27.60.
420. Cf. Mt 27.59–60.   421. Cf. 6.5.4; 6.6.5.
422. 2 Cor 4.10.   423. 1 Cor 15.31.
424. 1 Cor 3.21–22.

"If we die together with him, we shall also live together"; and again, "If we suffer together, we shall also reign together";[425] but at no time did he say: We have been baptized together with Christ. But surely just as death is compared with death and life with life, it seems that baptism ought to be compared with baptism. Notice, however, what great caution there is in the Apostle's letters. For he says, "We who have been baptized in Christ Jesus." [Paul] says that our baptism, therefore, is in Christ Jesus.

(6) Christ himself, however, is related to have been baptized by John not with the baptism which is in Christ but with the one which is in the law. For this is what he himself says to John, "Let it be so; for in this way it is fitting for us to fulfill all righteousness."[426] In that passage he is making known that John's baptism was a fulfillment of the old, not a beginning of the new. After all, it is related in the Acts of the Apostles why certain disciples who had been baptized with John's baptism were rebaptized in the name of Jesus by a determination made by the apostles.[427] "Therefore we who have been baptized into Christ Jesus were baptized into his death."

(7) You may perhaps also be asking this: Since the Lord himself told the disciples to baptize all nations in the name of the Father and of the Son and of the Holy Spirit,[428] why does the Apostle employ here the name of Christ alone in baptism? For he says, "We have been baptized into Christ," although surely it should not be deemed a legitimate baptism unless it is in the name of the Trinity. But look at Paul's good sense since, indeed, in the present passage he was not interested in discussing the subject of baptism as much as the death of Christ, in whose likeness he argues that we should die to sin and be buried with Christ. Obviously it was not appropriate to name either the Father or the Holy Spirit in a passage in which he was speaking about death. [M1040] For "the Word became flesh";[429] and where there is flesh, it is fitting to treat the subject of death. But it was not fitting for him to say, "We who have been baptized in the name of the Father or in the name of the Holy Spirit, have

---

425. 2 Tm 2.11–12.
426. Mt. 3.15.
427. Cf. Act 19.3–5. See also *Comm in Jn* 6.33.
428. Cf. Mt 28.19.
429. Jn 1.14.

been baptized into his death." Consequently, in this passage one should keep in mind the Apostle's custom in other places, that when he cites the Scriptures, he does not always cite the complete wording of the text as it is found in the original passage, but he takes only as much as is called for by his current argument.[430] Thus in the expression we have mentioned here, because he desired to teach about the death of Christ, it is sufficient for him to say, "We who have been baptized into Christ were baptized into his death."

(8) But it seems to me that the Apostle did not pointlessly prefix in this section what he says, "Do you not know?" For he is showing by this question that back then, i.e., in the age of the apostles, not only was the form of the mysteries given to those who were baptized, as we see happening in the present time, but also their effective power and meaning were imparted, as if to those who knew and had been instructed that those who are baptized are baptized into the death of Christ and are buried with him through baptism into death; and that "just as Christ rose from the dead through the glory of the Father," so those who were baptized "ought to walk in newness of life." For the Apostle writes these things.

(9) Yet it may still perhaps be investigated in this current section: If we died to sin and were buried together with Christ and were resurrected with him, it will seem necessary to show the manner in which we also became buried with him for three days and three nights in the heart of the earth.[431] Consider whether we can spend three days buried together with Christ when we receive complete knowledge of the Trinity. For the Father is light[432] and in his light, which is the Son, we see the light of the Holy Spirit.[433] And we spend three nights when we destroy the father of darkness and ignorance together with the lie which is born from him—"For he is a liar as also his father," and, "when he tells a lie he speaks from what is his own"[434]—

---

430. For the theme of Paul's use of his own apostolic authority in citing Scripture, cf. 3.2.5; 7.18.7; 8.8.4; 10.8.4–5.
431. Cf. Mt 12.40.
432. Cf. 1 Jn 1.5.
433. Cf. Ps 36.9.
434. Jn 8.44. Cf. *Comm in Jn* 20.21; 20.29; *Comm in Mt* 11.6; 12.20.

and, in the third place, the spirit of error,[435] who inspires false prophets to say, "'Thus says the Lord,' though the Lord has not sent them."[436] For we destroy these things and trample upon them if we have been buried with Christ according, as well, to what he himself says, "Behold I have given you authority for trampling upon serpents and scorpions and upon every power of the enemy."[437] Each of these things is as contrary to the Trinity as the night is to the day, as darkness is to light, [M1041] as lying is to truth. For the moment, these thoughts for the present passage have occurred to us. If, however, someone discerns something better, let the reader not feel reluctant to receive those things, leaving behind the things [I have said].[438]

(10) Nevertheless the following is deduced from the Apostle's statements by way of a deeper interpretation: Just as no living man can be buried with a dead man, so no one who is still living to sin can be buried together in baptism with Christ,[439] who has died to sin.[440] Therefore those who are hastening to baptism ought to take care as a matter of first importance that they should first die to sin. And in this way they can be buried with Christ through baptism[441] so they might say, "Always carrying around the death of Jesus Christ in our body so that the life of Jesus Christ might be manifested in our mortal flesh."[442] Now the manner in which the life of Jesus Christ is manifested in the body, Paul himself makes known when he says, "But no longer do I live, but Christ lives in me."[443] This is the same thing the apostle John also writes in his epistle when he says, "Every spirit which confesses that Jesus Christ has come in the flesh is from God."[444] Surely in that passage it is not the one who shall have declared these syllables and pronounced them in this common confession that shall seem to be led by the Spirit of God,[445] but the one who has fashioned his life in such a way and has pro-

---

435. Cf. 1 Jn 4.6.
436. Ezek 13.6.
437. Lk 10.19.
438. The writer's humility is evident in these addresses to the reader. Cf. 2.13.33; *Princ* 2.6.7.
439. Rom 6.4.
440. Rom 6.10.
441. Rom 6.2, 4.
442. 2 Cor 4.10.
443. Gal 2.20.
444. 1 Jn 4.2.
445. Cf. Rom 8.14.

duced the fruit of works such that he has demonstrated by the very devotion of his own works and thoughts that Christ has come in the flesh and that he is dead to sin and alive to God.[446]

(11) Now that we have explained as well as we could what it means to be buried with Christ, let us consider what else he says, "So that just as Christ rose from the dead through the glory of the Father, so we too might walk in newness of life." If we were buried together with Christ according to what we said above, namely according to the fact that we died to sin, it is certainly consistent with this that since Christ rises again from the dead, we also shall rise together with him. And since he ascends to heaven, we shall ascend together with him. And since he is sitting at the right hand of the Father, we too shall be said to sit together with him in the heavens, according to what the same Apostle says elsewhere, "He raised us together with Christ and made us sit together in the heavenly places."[447]

(12) But Christ rose through the glory of the Father; and we, if we have died to sin and been buried together with Christ, because all who see our good works glorify our Father in heaven,[448] we shall deservedly be said to have been raised together with Christ through the glory of the Father that we might walk in newness of life. Now the newness of life is when we lay aside "the old man with his deeds" [M1042] and put on "the new, who has been created according to God"[449] and "who is being renewed in the knowledge of God according to the image of him who created him."[450]

(13) For you must not imagine that the renewing of the life, which is said to have been done once, suffices. On the contrary at all times and daily, this newness must, if it can be said, be renewed. For this is what the Apostle says, "Even if he who is our outer man is being corrupted, but he who is inner is being renewed from day to day."[451] For just as the old is constantly aging and from day to day becoming older, so also this new one is constantly being renewed and there is never a time when his re-

---

446. Cf. Rom 6.10. 447. Eph 2.6.
448. Cf. Mt 5.16.
449. Eph 4.22, 24; Col 3.9–10. Cf. 1.19.8.
450. Col 3.10. 451. 2 Cor 4.16.

newing is not increasing. Just consider those who are making progress in the faith and who daily shine forth in the virtues, how they are always adding better things to their good works and eagerly searching for more noble things to add to their noble deeds, how they grow rich in understanding, in knowledge, and in wisdom. The things which previously seemed to be less clearly understood, they later discern as things plain to see and distinctly evident. Consider whether you would not say that a man of this sort is in his affairs being daily renewed—just as, on the contrary, as we have said, the person who has begun to grow old shall continue to get worse and is found daily to grow older and to deteriorate further in himself. So then let us walk in newness of life, showing ourselves daily to him who raised us with Christ[452] as new persons and, so to speak, as increasingly more beautiful people,[453] uniting the beauty of our face with Christ, as in a mirror and, beholding the Lord's glory, let us be transformed into the same image[454] by which Christ, rising from the dead, has ascended from earthly lowliness to the glory of the Father's majesty.

(14) But up to what he says, "Let us walk in newness of life," consider whether perchance it may mystically point out that as long as someone is making progress, he is said to be walking. Yet it ought not be imagined that he walks without a goal but in order that they who are walking in progressive steps might come at some time to that place where one must stand still. After all, Christ, "standing at the right hand of the power,"[455] appeared to the first martyr, Stephen, who had already reached the stage of perfection. And the Lord says to Moses, who had himself also attained to perfection after much progress, "But you stand here with me!"[456] Moreover Paul, when he recognized the completion of perfection in himself, says, "I have completed the race."[457] But to those who imagined themselves to be perfect but were not, he says, "Let him who thinks he is standing firm take heed lest he fall."[458] [M1043] To the imper-

---

452. Eph 2.6.
453. Cf. 9.1.10.
454. Cf. 2 Cor 3.18.
455. Acts 7.55.
456. Dt 5.31. Cf. *Comm in Mt* 12.32; *Hom in Ezek* 2.4; *Cels* 6.64.
457. 2 Tm 4.7.
458. 1 Cor 10.12.

fect, in fact, and to those who are still at the beginning stages, it is said that they must walk behind the Lord their God.[459] And concerning others it is said, "I do not want to send them away hungry lest they should faint along the way."[460]

9. *For if we have been planted together into likeness of his death, we will also be of his resurrection. We know that our old man was crucified together with him so that the body of sin might be destroyed, and we might no longer be enslaved to sin.*[461]

(2) All these things have in view his original question, lest he seem to grant room for sinning, in the place where he says, "But where sin abounded, grace superabounded."[462] For it is on that account that he says that we are dead to sin, and he says that we who have been baptized into Christ have been baptized into his death.[463] And now he writes that we have been planted together into the likeness of his death, adding that if we bear the likeness of his death, by which he died to sin, we ought also to hope for the likeness of his resurrection. But he shows how this can come about when he says that our old man needs to be crucified together with Christ. Our old man[464] should be understood to refer to our previous life which we led in sins and whose end and destruction, so to speak, we fashioned when we received within ourselves the faith of the cross of Christ, through which the body of sin is destroyed in such a way that our members which were enslaved to sin should no longer serve it but God.

(3) But taking up the expression once again, let us now see what it means to be planted together into the likeness of Christ's death. In this he exhibits the death of Christ like the sprout of some tree in which he wants us to be planted together, so that our root as well, by receiving some of the sap from that root, might bring forth branches of righteousness and bear the fruits of life. Now if you want to find out from the Scriptures which sprout it is in which we are supposed to be planted

459. Dt 13.4.
461. Rom 6.5–6.
463. Cf. Rom 6.2, 3, 5.
460. Mt 15.32.
462. Rom 5.20.
464. Cf. 5.9.8.

together and what sort of tree it may be, listen to what is written about wisdom, "She is a tree of life for all who hope in her and for those who trust in her as in the Lord."[465] So then Christ, who is the power of God and the wisdom of God,[466] is the tree of life in which we must be planted together; and his death becomes for us a tree of life by a certain new and a wonderful gift from God.[467]

(4) The Apostle, knowing very well that he was not treating the subject of the common death in the present passage, but rather that of sin, did not say, "For if we are planted together into his death," but instead, "into the likeness of his death." For Christ has died to sin once and for all[468] in such a way that he committed absolutely no sin whatsoever nor was deceit found in his mouth.[469] It is not possible for this to be found at all in any other man. "For no one is pure from sin, not [M1044] even if his life should be one day long."[470] Therefore it is not possible for us to die that same death which Jesus died to sin, so that we would be completely unacquainted with sin. However it is possible for us to possess the likeness so that, by imitating him and following in his footsteps, we may keep ourselves from sin.[471] This is something, therefore, which human nature is capable of receiving: It may become in the likeness of his death, when by imitating him it does not sin. But to be absolutely and entirely unacquainted with sin belongs to Christ alone.[472]

(5) But certain heretics[473] who do not understand this have tried to assert from this passage of the Apostle that Christ did not truly die, but had the likeness of death and that he appeared to die rather than truly died. Since it is very easy to respond to such persons, I do not think it necessary to call in a mass of testimonies from other sayings of the Apostle or of the Gospels where simply "death" is written, and not "the likeness

---

465. Prv 3.18 LXX.
466. Cf. 1 Cor 1.24.
467. Cf. *Comm in Jn* 20.36.
468. Cf. Rom 6.10.
469. Cf. 1 Pt 2.22. See also 4.12.5; 5.7.10.
470. Jb 14.4–5 LXX.
471. 1 Pt 2.21.
472. Cf. *Comm in Cant* 3.
473. The heresies of Marcionism and Docetism. Cf. *Cels* 2.16; *Comm in Jn* 10.6; Ignatius of Antioch, *Trallians* 10; *Smyrnaeans* 2.

of death" since we can say to them: If his was the likeness of death and not true death, then his was also a likeness of a resurrection and not a true resurrection. Consequently we also will only seem to rise again and will not truly rise again, and we shall seem to die to sin and not truly die. So then everything which has been done and is being done has *seemed* to be done but has not *been* done. It follows then that, in that we have been saved, it seems that we have been saved, but we were not truly saved. Since these ideas are so preposterous that they do not even require proofs, let us return to our commentary on what is found in the next section.

(6) Therefore he wants us to be planted together into the likeness of his death by which he died once and for all to sin, so that we might be able also to be planted together into his resurrection.[474] For to each must be supplied the expression "planted together." Notice how out of necessity he has taken up the figure of planting. For every plant awaits the resurrection in the spring after the death of winter. If then we also have been planted together into the death of Christ in the winter of this age and of the present life, we shall also be found bringing forth from his root the fruits of righteousness in the coming spring. And if we have been planted together in him, it is necessary that the Father, as the vinedresser, should prune us as branches of the true vine so that we might bear more fruit; just as he himself says in the Gospels, "I am the true vine, you are the branches, my Father is the vinedresser. My Father will cut off every branch which does not abide in me. But whoever abides in me he will prune that he might bear more fruit."[475] In this way, then, we have been planted together into the likeness of his death so that we might also be planted together into the likeness of his resurrection.

(7) The apostle John shows what it means to be planted together into the likeness of his resurrection: [M1045] "Little children, we do not yet know what we shall be. But if he is revealed to us, we shall be like him."[476] And again the Savior him-

---

474. Rom 6.5, 10. 475. Jn 15.1–2.
476. 1 Jn 3.2.

self says, "Father, I want that where I am they might be with me as well";[477] and once more, "Just as I am in you and you are in me, that they also might be one in us."[478] Surely he is saying this about those who have been planted together into the likeness of his death in the present life. Now I think that this could deservingly be said also about that thief who was hanging alongside Jesus on the cross. It seems that he had been planted together into the likeness of his death by his own confession, in which he said, "Lord, remember me when you come into your kingdom";[479] and by the fact that he rebuked the other one who was blaspheming.[480] He was also planted together in his resurrection through what is said to him, "Today you will be with me in paradise."[481] For he was a sprout worthy of paradise, which was joined to the tree of life.

(8) Because of this, then, what the Apostle had called, "planted together in the likeness of Christ's death," he repeats again with another figure and has said, "Our old man was crucified together with him so that the body of sin might be destroyed." Frequently and in many other places[482] we have spoken already about what it means to be crucified together with Christ. And we have also frequently dealt with the subject of the old man.[483] Therefore in the present passage we speak only briefly about the old man who lived, like Adam, subjected to transgression and sin and over whom the death of sin exercised lordship and about whom he who was holding the power of death[484] possessed the IOU of sin.[485] But because Christ, erasing this IOU with his own blood, affixed it to his own cross,[486] we ought to be crucified according to the old man, who was subject to sin, so that "the body of sin may be destroyed and we might no longer be enslaved to sin." Now I think it needs to be noted that the Apostle records here "body of sin" where he is speaking of what needs to be destroyed; but where he is not

---

477. Jn 17.24.
478. Jn 17.21.
479. Lk 23.42.
480. Lk 23.40.
481. Lk 23.43.
482. Cf. 4.12.5; *Comm in Jn* 10.35; *Comm in Mt* 12.24–25; *Hom in Jos* 8.3.
483. Cf. Eph 4.22; Col 3.9. See also 1.19.8; 4.7.7.
484. Cf. Heb 2.14.
485. Cf. 5.3.3.
486. Cf. Col 2.14.

speaking of what needs to be destroyed, he does not say it is the "body of sin" but we ourselves who ought not to be enslaved to sin. In this way he is showing that if the body of sin is destroyed, we shall no longer be enslaved to sin, to which, of course, we have been enslaved, as long as it was not destroyed in us and our earthly members were not put to death.[487]

(9) Yet we need to go over again with greater attentiveness how he said, "the body of sin." A double understanding seems to be given here: Either because he said that our body is the body of sin, or because he says that sin itself has its own certain body which must be destroyed in those who ought no longer to be enslaved to sin. Because both meanings can be admitted in this passage, [M1046] from each we set forth what appears to us. Now if we assume that sin has its own body, it will appear that just as it was said of those who have been restored in the new man, "You are the body of Christ and members individually,"[488] so it can be said of those who have not yet crucified the old man that they are the body and members of sin. Of that body the head is the devil, just as Christ is the head of [his] body, the Church, "without spot or wrinkle."[489] The members from which that body of sin consists might seem to be those earthly members which the Apostle has enumerated above, namely, fornication, uncleanness, immodesty, greed, contention, wrath, deceits, quarrels, dissensions, heresies, envy, revels, and similar things.[490] It will be rightly said that the body of sin consists of all these members and this is called the body of the old man.[491] But if someone destroys [the old man] through the cross of Christ and is changed into the new man, who has been created according to God,[492] he will no longer be said to be enslaved to sin, to which doubtless he is enslaved as long as he is subject to any of these things which, as we have explained above, are the members of sin.

(10) But if instead the Apostle should be understood as having called our body the body of sin, it will assuredly be taken in

---

487. Col 3.5.
488. 1 Cor 12.27.
489. Eph 5.23, 27.
490. Cf. Col 3.5; Gal 5.19–21; Rom 1.29–31.
491. Eph 4.22; Col 3.9.
492. Cf. Eph 4.24.

agreement with the understanding which David speaks of in reference to himself, "For I was conceived in iniquities and in sins did my mother conceive me."[493] And the Apostle himself says elsewhere, "Who will rescue me from the body of this death?"[494] and again he calls our body "the body of lowliness."[495] Moreover, he says of the Savior in a certain passage that he came "in the likeness of the flesh of sin, so that with respect to sin he might condemn sin in the flesh."[496] He is showing by this that our flesh is indeed a flesh of sin, but Christ's flesh is similar to the flesh of sin.[497] For he was not conceived from the seed of a man, but the Holy Spirit came upon Mary and the power of the Most High overshadowed her so that what was born from her should be called the Son of the Most High.[498] In this way, then, Paul, through the inexpressible wisdom of God which was given to him,[499] and looking at something secret, who knows what, calls our body "the body of sin" and "the body of death" and "the body of lowliness."[500] Moreover David, practiced in the heavenly mysteries by the same Spirit, was speaking of the body, "And you have led me down to the dust of death";[501] and again, "Our soul has been brought down to the dust."[502] Jeremiah, also [M1047] aware of a similar mystery through the Spirit of God, says in his Lamentations that all men are captives to the earth, naturally because of the body. He says, "in order that he might lay low all the captives of the earth under his feet because they have turned aside a man's rights in the presence of the Most High and they have condemned a man by their judging."[503]

(11) Therefore our body is the body of sin, for it is not written that Adam knew his wife Eve and became the father of Cain until after the sin.[504] After all, even in the law it is commanded that sacrifices be offered for the child who was born: a pair of turtledoves or two young doves; one of which was offered for

---

493. Ps 51.5.
494. Rom 7.24.
495. Phil 3.21.
496. Rom 8.3.
497. Cf. 6.12.4.
498. Cf. Lk 1.35. See also 3.8.4; 6.12.4.
499. 2 Pt 3.15. Cf. *Comm in Jn* 20.25.
500. Rom 6.6; 7.24; Phil 3.21.
501. Ps 22.15.
502. Ps 44.25. Cf. 5.3.3.
503. Lam 3.34–36.
504. Cf. Gn 4.1.

sin and the other as a burnt offering.⁵⁰⁵ For which sin is this one dove offered? Was a newly born child able to sin? And yet it has a sin for which sacrifices are commanded to be offered, and from which it is denied that anyone is pure, even if his life should be one day long.⁵⁰⁶ It has to be believed, therefore, that concerning this David also said what we recorded above, "in sins my mother conceived me."⁵⁰⁷ For according to the historical narrative no sin of his mother is declared. It is on this account as well that the Church has received the tradition from the apostles to give baptism even to little children.⁵⁰⁸ For they to whom the secrets of the divine mysteries were committed⁵⁰⁹ were aware that in everyone was sin's innate defilement, which needed to be washed away through water and the Spirit.⁵¹⁰ Because of this defilement as well, the body itself is called the body of sin; it is not because of sins the soul committed when it was in another body, as they who introduce the doctrine of μετενσωμάτωσις imagine.⁵¹¹ But because the soul was fashioned into the body of sin, and the body of death and lowliness,⁵¹² and just as he said, "You have lowered our soul to the dust."⁵¹³ For the present these are the things which could come to us concerning "the body of sin." But which explanation of the two may agree with the apostolic meaning, or if it be neither, let the reader examine.

(12) Now in other passages the Apostle says that we have already been resurrected together and raised together with Christ and that we sit together with him in the heavens.⁵¹⁴ And here he says, "For if we have been planted together in the likeness of his death, we shall also be of the resurrection." That is,

505. Cf. Lv 12.8.
506. Cf. Jb 14.4–5 LXX. See also *Cels* 7.50.
507. Ps 51.5.
508. Cf. *Hom in Lv* 8.3; *Hom in Lk* 14.5. Origen's statement here is "our earliest witness to the belief that the Apostles themselves commanded the baptism of infants"; G. Beasley-Murray, *Baptism in the New Testament* (Grand Rapids, Mich.: Eerdmans, 1962), p. 306.
509. Cf. 1 Cor 4.1.   510. Cf. Jn 3.5.
511. Cf. 5.1.27.   512. Rom 7.24; Phil 3.21.
513. Ps 44.25.
514. Cf. Eph 2.6; Col 3.1; Col 2.12–13. See also *Comm in Jn* 10.35; *Hom in Jos* 8.4.

what elsewhere he had said has already been carried out, here he now says is yet to come and is to be hoped for. This is the reason why a twofold resurrection is understood: the first in which we rise with Christ from earthly things in mind, purpose, and faith as we ponder heavenly things and seek after what is future; the second which will be a general resurrection in the flesh of all. Consequently the resurrection which is according to our mind from faith would seem already to be fulfilled in those who "set their minds on the things above where Christ is at the right hand of God."[515] [M1048] But that general resurrection of the flesh which pertains to all is still yet to come. For the former is fulfilled at the Lord's first coming, the latter at the second coming.

10. *But if we have died with Christ, we believe that we will also live together with him. We know that Christ, in rising from the dead, will no longer die; death will no longer have dominion over him. For what he died, he died to sin once for all; but what he lives, he lives to God.*[516]

(2) In everything that the Apostle has said above, he wanted to show that if Christ had first died to sin, we also have died to sin with him.[517] And when he says, "We were baptized into his death,"[518] and, "we were planted together in the likeness of his death,"[519] he is showing through all these things that we have died to sin with Christ, because indeed Christ has died for our sins according to the Scriptures[520] and by his own death has freely bestowed his death of sin as if a certain reward of faith to every believer, namely to those who believe that they have died with him and have been crucified and buried together with him. And through these things sin is not able to operate in them who are, as it were, dead persons, and thus they are said to be dead to sin.[521]

(3) For this reason, then, in the present text the Apostle draws the conclusion to everything he had asserted above and says, "But if we have died with Christ"—namely through the

515. Col 3.1–2.
516. Rom 6.8–10.
517. Rom 6.2.
518. Rom 6.3.
519. Rom 6.5.
520. 1 Cor 15.3.
521. Cf. Rom 6.11.

BOOK 5, CHAPTER 10

things we have pointed out above—"we believe that we will also live with him." He did not say, "and we have lived together with him" as he said "we have died with him," but, "we will live together," in order to show that death is at work in the present but life in the future, namely, at that time "when Christ who is our life hidden in God will be revealed."[522] Therefore now, as Paul himself teaches, "death is at work in us."[523] What is more, death itself, which is at work in us, seems to me to have certain differences. For just as there was one moment of death in Christ when it says, "And crying out with a loud voice he breathed his last";[524] and there is another [moment of death] when he was lying in the tomb with the closed entrance;[525] yet there was another [moment of death] when he had been sought for in the tomb and was not found because he was already resurrected[526]—the beginning of his resurrection was not visible to any human being[527]—in this same way it should be held that the matter of death in us who believe in him is also threefold.

(4) Certainly in the first instance the death of Christ must be manifested in us by the confession of the voice, since "with the heart one believes and with the mouth confession is made leading to salvation."[528] But in the second instance, since "we always carry about the death of Christ in our body,"[529] [his death is manifested] by means of the mortification of our members which are on the earth,[530] and this is what he says: "Death [M1049] is at work in us."[531] Yet in the third instance [his death is manifested] when we are now resurrected from the dead and walk in newness of life.[532] And that we might explain this more concisely and clearly: The first day of death is to have renounced the world; the second is to have renounced the vices of the flesh as well; the third day of the resurrection, however, is the fullness of perfection in the light of wisdom. But what the

---

522. Col 3.3–4. Cf. 5.1.5; 5.1.38.
523. 2 Cor 4.12.
524. Mt 27.50; Lk 23.46.
525. Mt 27.60.
526. Mt 28.5–6; Mk 16.6; Lk 24.6.
527. Cf. Lk 24.1–5.
528. Rom 10.10.
529. 2 Cor 4.10.
530. Col 3.5.
531. 2 Cor 4.12. Cf. 5.8.4.
532. Cf. Rom 6.4.

differences are in the individual believer and the degrees of progress, the only one able to know and distinguish this is the one to whom alone the secrets of the heart are revealed.

(5) But consider Paul's wisdom in the way he writes. When writing to Timothy he said, "If we die together we shall also live together."[533] As if he was adding a logical necessity, namely, those who die together with Christ will live together with him, here he added, "we believe," so as to show that even though it may be logically necessary that one who dies together also lives together, nevertheless this is brought about by means of faith and trustfulness. We are certain, he says, and we know "that Christ in rising from the dead no longer dies." For if he were to die again, then just as we showed the logical necessity that those who die together shall also live together with him,[534] so the logical inference was undoubtedly seeming to be that if, after his resurrection and life, he were again to die, then even those who are going to live together with him would also have to die again together with the one who dies. This is why the Apostle makes the unqualified pronouncement that Christ no longer dies, so that those who will live together with him might be untroubled about the eternity of life.

(6) Now it is after these things that, if I may borrow the Apostle's own words where he says, "But Isaiah is so bold as to say,"[535] I say too, Paul is so bold as to say, "Death will no longer have dominion over him." Are you so bold, O Paul, as to say of Christ, "Death will no longer have dominion over him," as if at some time it *had* dominion over him? His voice is reported throughout the Gospels to be brighter than any flash of lightning that with it he says, "No one takes my life from me; I have authority to lay it down and I have authority to take it up again."[536] Are you saying that death had dominion over this man who received it not only voluntarily but also with authority; who alone was "free among the dead";[537] the only one whom death was not able to hold fast?[538] I believe that those who are held fast to Jesus by a tender affection and cannot bear to hear

---

533. 2 Tm 2.11.
535. Rom 10.20.
537. Ps 88.5.
534. 2 Tm 2.11.
536. Jn 10.18.
538. Cf. Acts 2.24.

anything base or unworthy said about him will bring these and similar observations against Paul.

(7) But when we consider Paul, we do not think that [M1050] another exists who could surpass him in love for Christ; therefore we must not think that [Paul] would declare anything about [Christ] other than what is worthy of him. By the grace of the Holy Spirit, then, let us investigate the word of wisdom,[539] in order that we might be able to turn to Paul's mind, or rather the mind of Christ who is in him, according to what he himself confesses, "But we have the mind of Christ."[540]

(8) Someone could say then very briefly that he is speaking here about the common death,[541] and the part in which, as the same Apostle says, he "died according to the Scriptures."[542] And it does not seem absurd if he who took the form of a slave[543] endured the dominion of death which, doubtless, exercises dominion over everyone who is placed in the flesh in slave form. Moreover, it will be added to this assertion that because of this, that form of the slave, that is, this flesh of ours, is sown in corruption that it might rise in incorruption; and it is sown in weakness that it might rise in power; and it is sown in dishonor that it might rise in glory; and it is sown a natural body that it might rise as a spiritual body.[544] Doubtless the result of this is that even death itself will no longer have dominion, though it did exercise dominion over it while it was in the state of weakness and dishonor and corruption. Of such flesh, which is still in the vices of the passions, Paul himself says, "Flesh and blood cannot inherit the kingdom of God, nor will corruption inherit incorruption."[545] Moreover, because elsewhere the same Apostle has called it "the body of death,"[546] he who asserts these things says that here he must be understood [to be speaking] of this neutral kind of death which dominates a body of this sort, for as long a time as it is natural and corruptible and has not yet been changed by the glory of the resurrection and made incorruptible from corruption and glorious from dishonor.

539. Cf. 1 Cor 12.8.
540. 1 Cor 2.16.
541. Cf. 5.1.19; 5.2.5; 5.4.2; 6.5.4; *Cels* 2.16.
542. 1 Cor 15.3.
543. Cf. Phil 2.7.
544. 1 Cor 15.42–44.
545. 1 Cor 15.50.
546. Rom 7.24.

(9) But that which strongly contradicts the above assertion, i.e., that we have died with Christ and have been buried with him,[547] because there is no possible way for this to be understood of the common death, I shall attempt to explain in the following manner. Just as above, when we were interpreting the varieties of "law," we showed that the Apostle in one and the same passage refers now to the natural law, now to the law of Moses, now even to the law of sin,[548] and we taught from other passages as well, called in to bear witness, that this is the custom of the Holy Scripture,[549] in the same way it may be firmly established in the present passage that the Apostle has referred now to the common death, now to the death of sin,[550] now even to the very author of death, who is also called the last [M1051] enemy to be destroyed.[551] Sometimes he even means that place in the underworld where the devil is said to have the power of death.[552] It shall therefore be firmly established that what he says, "Death will no longer have dominion over him," has been spoken with reference to the common death which Christ is believed to have died. The soundness of this assertion is for the reader to examine.

(10) But someone else, who looks at Paul's mind, more deep in these matters by the power of the Spirit, will say that, when it is said that here death will no longer have dominion over Christ, this must be understood of that last enemy himself,[553] who contained a figure of that sea monster that swallowed Jonah,[554] of whom it is written in Job, "But let him that curses that day curse it, even he who is going to slay the great sea monster."[555] Christ, like a Jonah in the belly of the sea monster, entered into this death, namely to that place which the Savior himself called the heart of the earth, where he says the Son of Man was going to spend three days and three nights, following the precedent of Jonah[556] in order to release those who were being held there by death. For it was on this account that he

547. Rom 6.4, 8.
549. Cf. 3.7.7.
551. Cf 1 Cor 15.26.
553. 1 Cor 15.26.
555. Jb 3.8 LXX.
548. Cf. 3.6.1; 3.7.5.
550. Cf. 6.6.4.
552. Heb 2.14. Cf. 6.6.5.
554. Cf. Jon 2.1.
556. Cf. Mt 12.40.

also took up the form of a slave,⁵⁵⁷ that he might be able to enter that place where death was holding dominion, in accordance with what the prophet also says under the *persona* of [Christ], "And I was reckoned with those who go down to the pit",⁵⁵⁸ and again, "What profit is there in my blood when I go down to corruption?"⁵⁵⁹

(11) In order that this might be perceived still more clearly, we shall again make use of this kind of parable.⁵⁶⁰ Let us imagine an upright and noble king who wants to wage a war against some unjust tyrant, but in such a way that he should not seem to conquer by means of a violent and bloody conflict; for even the soldiers serving under the tyrant were his own men whom he was not desiring to destroy but to liberate. Therefore under a better plan he assumes the dress of those who were under the tyrant, and in appearance he becomes like them in every way⁵⁶¹ until, while placed under the tyrant's sphere of rule, he persuades at least those who were serving him to leave off and turn back to the rightful kingdom. Then at the opportune time he binds the strong man⁵⁶² and despoils his powers and principalities⁵⁶³ and leads away the captives⁵⁶⁴ which had been seized and were being held by the tyrant.

(12) It was certainly in this way, then, that Christ also emptied himself voluntarily and took the form of a slave⁵⁶⁵ and endured the dominion of the tyrant, having become obedient unto death. Through that death he destroyed him who was holding [M1052] the power of death, i.e., the devil,⁵⁶⁶ so that he could liberate those who were being held fast by death. For when [Christ] had bound the strong man⁵⁶⁷ and triumphed over him by means of his cross,⁵⁶⁸ he even advanced into his house, the house of death in the underworld, and from there he plundered his possessions, that is, he led away the souls which [the devil] was keeping. This is what he was speaking

---

557. Phil 2.7.
558. Ps 28.1.
559. Ps 30.9.
560. See the related parable of 5.1.31.
561. Heb 2.17.
562. Cf. Mt 12.29.
563. Cf. Col 2.15.
564. Eph 4.8; Ps 68.18. Cf. 5.1.37.
565. Cf. Phil 2.7–8.
566. Heb 2.14–15.
567. Mt 12.29.
568. Cf. Col 2.15.

about in an enigmatic way in the Gospel when he said, "Who is able to enter the house of a strong man and plunder his possessions unless he first binds the strong man?"[569] So then, first he bound him at the cross and thus he entered his house, the underworld, and from there "ascending on high he led captivity captive,"[570] namely those who have been raised together with him and have entered the holy city, the heavenly Jerusalem.[571] Therefore it is right that the Apostle says in the present passage, "Death will no longer exercise dominion over him." For he will no longer give himself over to the tyrant's sphere of lordship nor will he empty himself again by taking the form of a slave and by becoming obedient unto death.[572] Never again will he endure the domination of the tyrant and of death in the form of a slave, even though he was put in this position voluntarily and not by compulsion.

(13) This is why I am amazed that certain people want to claim, in contradiction to this absolutely clear pronouncement of Paul, that in the future age it should be necessary for Christ to suffer the same things or similar things all over again, so that those whom his medicine was not able to heal in the life of the present dispensation might be freed. For they say:[573] Can there be any age in the future when neither good nor evil are committed, but instead things are brought to a standstill and pro-

---

569. Mt 12.29   570. Eph 4.8; Ps 68.18.
571. Cf. Mt 27.52–53; Heb 12.22. See also *Comm in Mt* 12.43.
572. Cf. Phil 2.7–8.
573. Cf. *Princ* 3.3.5. Unless Origen has repudiated his earlier speculation (which is by no means impossible; cf. Molland, *Alexandrian Theology*, pp. 161–64), it appears that Rufinus may have put Origen's own opinions into the mouths of others here. For according to Jerome, *Ep* 124.13, the Alexandrian himself expressed these speculations in *Princ* (in a passage omitted in Rufinus's translation). Jerome quotes Origen, "Now if we extend our inquiry to the passion of our Lord and Savior, it may indeed be overbold to suppose that He will suffer in heaven; yet if there is spiritual wickedness in heavenly places and if we confess without a blush that the Lord has once been crucified to destroy those things which He has destroyed by his passion; why need we fear to imagine a like occurrence in the upper world in the fullness of time, so that the nations of all realms shall be saved by a passion of Christ?" (NPNF2 6:243). Origen's earlier suggestion (which in the current passage is repudiated) seems to be an adaptation of the Stoic doctrine of endlessly repeating world-cycles; cf. H. Koch, *Pronoia und Paideusis: Studien über Origenes und sein Verhältnis zum Platonismus* (Berlin: Walter de Gruyter & Co., 1932), p. 92.

found silence remains? This, they claim, appears absurd. We shall therefore grant that something will happen. And where something is happening it is inevitable, they say, that some things would be done rightly, some things less rightly, and that in this very act some would make progress and become better, whereas others would become worse.[574] For freedom of will shall always remain in rational natures. It was possible even for him who was Lucifer, owing to the splendor of his glory,[575] and who rose in the morning because of the light of knowledge, to be changed from his own glory and become darkness because of the evil which he received.[576] And to him who was without stain from the day of his birth and dwelled with cherubim and lived in the midst of the fiery stones and was clothed with the entire adornment of the virtues[577] in the paradise of God, there was no tree of virtues which could compare.[578] But later, iniquities were found in him and he was cast from heaven to earth.[579] In the same way [M1053] it can come to pass that in whatever state a soul exists and in whatever degree of perfection of the virtues, it can still experience a fall, owing to the fact that virtue is changeable.[580] So just as the [soul] is moved from the vices to virtue, so also from the virtues to the vices.[581] If this is the case, the inference will seem to be that where there is sickness a physician will be needed, for according to the voice of the Savior himself, "There is need of a physician for those who are sick."[582]

(14) By proposing these and similar things, they surmise that these same arrangements will have to be repeated by Christ even in the future ages.[583] But we shall respond briefly to these things as well as we can. We certainly do not deny that free will always will remain in rational natures, but we affirm that the power of the cross of Christ[584] and of his death which

---

574. Cf. *Princ* 2.3.3.
575. Cf. Is 14.12.
576. Cf. *Princ* 1.5.5.
577. Ezek 28.13–15.
578. Ezek 31.8.
579. Cf. Ezek 28.15, 17. Cf. *Princ* 1.5.4.
580. Cf. *Comm in Jn* 32.19.
581. Cf. *Cels* 4.69; 8.72.
582. Mt 9.12.
583. There is a similar refutation of these views in *Princ* 2.3.4 but there again it appears that Rufinus may have put Origen's own tentative views into the mouths of others.
584. Cf. 6.1.4.

he undertook at the end of the ages[585] is so great that it suffices for the healing and restoration not only of the present and the future but also for the past ages. It suffices not only for our human order, but also for the heavenly powers and orders.[586] For according to the Apostle Paul's own pronouncement: Christ has made peace "through the blood of his cross" not only with "the things on earth" but also with "the things in heaven."[587]

(15) Now precisely what it is that would restrain the freedom of will in the future ages to keep it from falling again into sin, the Apostle teaches us with a brief statement, saying, "Love never falls away."[588] For this is why love is said to be greater than faith and hope,[589] because it will be the only thing through which it will no longer be possible to sin. For if the soul shall have ascended to this state of perfection, so that it loves God with all its heart and with all its mind and with all its strength, and loves its neighbor as itself,[590] what room will there be for sin? After all, it is on this account as well that in the law [love] is said to be the first commandment, and in the Gospels love is commanded above everything else.[591] And when the supreme authority for feeding the sheep was given to Peter and the Church was founded upon him as upon the rock,[592] the confession of no other virtue is demanded of him except of love.[593] And John, when he says many things concerning love, even says this: "He who abides in love abides in God."[594] Rightly then love, which alone is greater than all, will keep every creature from falling away[595] at that time when God will be all in all.[596] For the Apostle Paul had ascended to this degree of perfection,[597] and standing in it he was confidently saying, "For who will separate us from the love of God which is in Christ Jesus? Will affliction, or distress, or famine, or nakedness, or peril, or sword?" and again, "But I am certain [M1054] that neither life,

---

585. Cf. Heb 9.26.
586. Cf. *Princ* 2.3.5.
587. Col 1.20.
588. 1 Cor 13.8.
589. Cf. 1 Cor 13.13.
590. Cf. Mt 22.37–39.
591. Mt 22.38.
592. Mt 16.18.
593. Cf. Jn 21.15–17.
594. 1 Jn 4.16.
595. Cf. *Princ* 2.6.5–6, where Origen discusses how Christ's soul became immutable and incapable of sinning through its being on fire with love for God and righteousness.
596. Cf. 1 Cor 15.28.
597. Cf. Preface of Origen (3).

nor death, nor things present, nor things to come, nor angels, nor powers, nor height, nor depth, nor any other creature, will be able to separate us from the love of God in Christ Jesus our Lord."[598] From all of this it is plainly shown that if none of these things enumerated by the Apostle can separate us from the love of God, when someone shall have ascended to the peak of perfection, how much more impossible shall it be for the freedom of will to separate us from his love![599] For even though this is also a virtue and abides in nature, nevertheless the power of love is so great that it draws all things to itself[600] and joins all persons to itself and conquers the virtues, especially since God has first given to us the grounds of love, "He who did not spare his only Son but handed him over for us all and with him has freely given all things to us."[601]

(16) He who was Lucifer and who arose into heaven,[602] he who was without stain from the day of his birth and who was among the cherubim,[603] was able to fall with respect to the kindness of the Son of God before he could be bound by chains of love. But after the love of God shall have begun to be shed abroad in the hearts of everyone through the Holy Spirit,[604] what the Apostle has declared will become settled, "Love never falls away."[605] We have said these things to the best of our ability in response to questions generated by the passage, so that it might become more plainly clarified in what manner Christ has died to sin once and for all and how he dies no longer, and why it is the life he lives, he lives to God.

(17) To live to God should be understood by this being fulfilled, that he who was in the form of God emptied himself

598. Rom 8.35, 38, 39.
599. Cf. 7.12.3.
600. Cf. Jn 12.32.
601. Rom 8.32.
602. Cf. Is 14.12.
603. Cf. Ezek 28.14–17.
604. Cf. Rom 5.5.
605. 1 Cor 13.8. It is difficult to read this passage without recalling Koch's characterization of Origen as an "eternal optimist"; *Pronoia und Paedeusis*, p. 32. Some scholars take the present passage as Origen's final opinion on the subject of restoration and have concluded that the Alexandrian believed that there would be a final end of history, evil would never rise again and God's love will ultimately prevail in restoring all creatures; for example, Bigg, *Christian Platonists*, pp. 233; 300 n. 2; Molland, *Alexandrian Theology*, p. 164; Teichtweier, *Sündenlehre*, p. 81; Vogt, *Kirchenverständnis*, pp. 343–46.

and took the form of a slave and became obedient unto death,[606] as if he must again continue in the form of God, equal to the Father. Thus it is fitting that he records in what follows, "So you also must consider yourselves to be dead to sin and alive to God in Christ Jesus our Lord."[607] This means of course that we should die to sin in imitation of Christ, having become estranged from it; and we should live to God by being yoked together with him and by becoming one spirit with him.[608] But it was not without reason that he said, "Consider yourselves to be dead to sin,"[609] which is rendered better in Greek, "Think yourselves to be dead to sin." For the essence of this expression consists more in thinking and reason, because a death of this sort will be experienced not in fact but in thought. For whoever thinks and considers within himself that he is dead does not sin. For example, if lust after a woman entangles me [M1055] or greed for silver or gold or possessions agitates me, and if I should put it into my heart that I have died with Christ and I should think about death, immediately the desire is extinguished and sin flees. Or if I am provoked to kill my enemy while inflamed with hatred and anger, if I should consider myself to be dead with Christ and I put thoughts of death into my mind, doubtless the rage is extinguished, the anger ceases, the hatred dies down, and no room is given to sin. And whoever in this way is found to be dead to sin is alive to God.[610]

(18) Nor do his additional words, [M1056] "alive to God in Christ Jesus,"[611] seem to me to be superfluous. For in my opinion it is just as if he had said, "alive to God in wisdom, in peace, in righteousness, in sanctification, all of which are Christ."[612] To be alive to God in these things, therefore, is what it means to be alive to God in Christ Jesus. But if no one is alive to God without righteousness, without peace, without sanctification, and without the rest of the virtues, it is certain that no one may live to God except in Christ Jesus. Amen.

606. Cf. Phil 2.6–8.
607. Rom 6.11.
608. Cf. 1 Cor 6.17.
609. Rom 6.11.
610. Cf. Rom 6.11.
611. Rom 6.11.
612. Cf. 1 Cor 1.30; Eph 2.14.

INDICES

GENERAL INDEX

ep refers to Epilogue, int to Introduction, n to notes, pr Or to Preface of Origen, pr Ruf to Preface Rufinus. The Introduction is referenced by page number. The Prefaces and Epilogue are referenced by section number. All other entries are referenced by book, chapter, and paragraph numbers.

Aaron, 1.5.4; 2.13.12,13; 3.2.11
Abel, 5.1.20,35; 5.6.2
Abihu, 2.2.2
Abraham, int 43; pr Or 9; 1.8.1;
   1.9.3; 1.10.3; 2.13.8,11,13,16;
   2.14.9; 3.8.14; 3.9.5;
   4.1.1,2,2n,5–12; 4.2.1–11,11n;
   4.3.1–2; 4.4.1–2,10; 4.5.1–14;
   4.6.1–9; 4.7.1–4,9–10; 5.1.14,20;
   5.5.2
Abram, pr Or 9; 4.1.8; 4.2.11,11n
Achilles, 3.3.4n
Adam, int 16; 1.13.4; 3.3.1; 4.4.4;
   5.1.1,1n,3,5,7,8,12,14,14n,16,
   30–32,34–38,35n,41;
   5.2.2–4,6–8,8n,9–13,13n,15;
   5.3.4; 5.4.2–3,3n; 5.5.9; 5.6.5;
   5.8.2; 5.9.8,11
Adamantius, pr Ruf 1,1n
Admetus, 4.11.4n
Adoption, 1.1.1,4; 4.9.11
Adultery, 2.7.7; 2.9.1;
   2.11.1,5–6,9,11; 2.13.35;
   2.14.22; 3.9.7; 4.2.9
Affliction, pr Or 4,6; 1.13.4; 1.16.3;
   2.4.3; 2.5.1,2; 2.6.1,5,6; 2.7.4,5;
   3.5.1; 3.6.1; 4.9.1,2,4,7–10;
   5.6.2; 5.10.15
Agamemnon, 4.11.4n
Ahaziah, 1.5.5
Alcestis, 4.11.4n
Amaziah, 1.5.5
Ambrose, int 7,11; 2.13.8n; 2.13.9n
Ambrosiaster, int 45n; 5.1.1n;
   5.1.14n; 5.7.3n
Amorite(s), 2.3.2; 4.2.9

Anastasius I, Pope, int 6
Angels, pr Or 6; 1.4.3; 1.5.4; 1.9.4;
   1.16.3; 1.17.1n; 1.18.6,10; 2.4.6;
   2.13.7,18,21; 3.1.12; 3.6.4; 4.1.4;
   4.7.2,3; 4.8.9; 4.10.1; 5.1.29;
   5.6.2; 5.10.15
Anselm, 4.11.4n
Anthropomorphites, 1.19.8
Apocatastasis (restoration), int 6n;
   2.2.2; 2.4.4n; 5.1.7n; 5.2.7n,14n;
   5.10.14–16,16n
Apollos, 5.8.4
Apostle, derivation of term, 1.7.1n
Appeasement, 3.8.12,13
Arabs (Arabia), int 5; 2.13.28
Arbiter (Paul sits between Jews and
   Gentiles), 2.14.1–5; 3.1.2,3; 3.2.2
Aristotle, pr Or 3n; 3.1.7n; 4.1.2n
Arius (Arian heresy), int 11; 1.5.5n
Ark (of the covenant), 3.8.2,2n;
   3.8.7,8
Article(s), use of, 3.7.9,9n
Astrology, 2.4.5; 2.13.28
Astronomy, 2.13.28
Athanasius, int 10; 1.5.1n
Atonement, see Propitiation
Attributes, sharing of, 1.6.2,2n
Augustine, int
   2,16,17,20n,23,24,30,32,44n,47,
   47n; 5.1.1n; 5.1.14n
Aulis, 4.11.4n
Aurelian, pr Or 9n
Azariah, pr Or 10; 1.5.5

Baal, 2.14.7
Balaam, 1.11.2

GENERAL INDEX

Balak, 1.11.2
Balthasar, H. Urs, von, int 8,31; 1.5.5n; 1.18.5n; 4.1.14n
Bammel, C.P., *see* Hammond Bammel, C.P.
Baptism, int 41,44,47,48; pr Or 7; 2.1.2; 2.11.9; 2.12.4; 2.13.2,32; 3.1.11,12; 5.2.11; 5.7.3n; 5.8.1–10; 5.9.2,11,11n; 5.10.2; of children, 5.9.11; in the name of the Trinity, 5.8.7
Barbarian(s), 1.13.1,3,6; 1.14.2; 1.15.1
Barnabas, Epistle of, 2.9.1n; 2.13.21n; 2.13.28n
Basil of Caesarea, int 7,17
Basilides, int 28,28n; 2.4.7n; 5.1.27,27n
Bathsheba, 2.14.22
Beasley-Murray, G., 5.9.11n
Belief/believe, *see* Faith
Beza, T., int 30n,33,48
Bigg, C., int 5n; pr Or 1n; 1.5.1n; 5.6.7n; 5.10.16n
Blessing (bless),1.8.1; 1.12.1; 1.18.1,9; 2.6.4; 2.7.1,2; 2.13.14; 3.2.11; 3.4.2; 3.8.6,7; 4.4.1,9,17,19,20; 4.2.1,2,4; 4.3.1; 4.5.4,5,9; 4.6.4; 4.7.10; 4.8.8; 4.10.2; 5.1.27n; 5.2.14; 5.3.5,8; 5.8.4
Blood, 1.1.2; 1.4.4; 1.9.5; 1.16.3n; 2.4.3; 2.5.3; 2.13.9,9n,13,14,29,32; 3.2.1,6; 3.4.3; 3.7.14; 3.8.1,2,10,11,14; 4.8.1; 4.11.1,4–6; 4.12.3,3n,4; 5.6.2; 5.7.6; 5.9.8; 5.10.8,10,11,14
Boast(ing), int 41–42; 1.17.2; 1.19.1; 2.9.3; 2.11.1,5,8,9,12; 2.14.19; 3.9.1–8; 4.1.1–6; 4.2.8; 4.4.5; 4.5.14; 4.8.1,6,7,9; 4.9.1–6,10; 4.12.1,5
Body (bodies), pr Or 3,4,6; 1.1.2,4; 1.2.1; 1.3.3; 1.5.3; 1.6.1n,3; 1.10.2; 1.12.1; 1.16.3,3n; 1.17.2; 1.18.1,2,5,9,10; 1.19.2,4,7,8; 2.4.6; 2.5.5,7; 2.6.3; 2.7.6; 2.9.2; 2.13.20,24,27,29–31,35; 2.14.5,14; 3.1.10n,16,17; 3.2.13,14; 3.4.1,3; 3.5.3; 3.7.7; 3.8.4,11; 4.5.10; 4.6.1,6–9; 4.7.7; 4.9.3,9,10; 4.12.4; 5.1.18,19,27,37; 5.6.6,7; 5.7.3; 5.8.4,10; 5.9.1,2,8–11; 5.10.4,8
Bohlin, T., int 16n
Bullinger, int 33
Butterworth, int 8n

Cain, 1.13.4; 3.2.9; 3.6.1; 4.1.15; 4.4.4; 5.1.20,23; 5.5.7; 5.6.2; 5.9.11
Called, distinct from chosen, 1.2.1; 1.3.1
Calvin (Calvinism), J., int 23,30n,33,48
Canaan, 4.2.9
Captives (captivity), 1.4.3; 3.7.14; 3.8.1; 4.4.5,6; 5.1.37; 5.6.4; 5.9.10; 5.10.11,12
Caracalla, int 5,8; pr Or 9n
Cassian, John, *see* John Cassian
Cassiodorus, int 12
Catechumens, 2.13.2
Catena, int 17–18
Cenchreae, port of Corinth, pr Or 7
Cephas, 5.8.4
Chadwick, H., int 4,8n,9,9n,14; 1.18.7n; 2.7.6n; 3.1.17n; 4.5.10n; 5.1.19n
Chemnitz, M., int 33
Cherubim (cherub), 3.8.2,5,6,8; 3.10.3n; 5.10.13,16
Childhood (child, children), 3.2.8,9,9n; 3.6.3; 3.11.5; 5.1.25,26,28,35; 5.2.10; 5.6.3; 5.9.11
Choose, Chosen, *see* Election
Christian(s), 1.12.1; 2.7.2,3n,4–6; 2.11.11,11n; 3.7.12n; 3.9.7n; 4.5.11n; 5.1.27n
Chrysostom, John, int 2,7,45n; 4.1.18n; 5.7.3n
Church (ecclesiastical), int; pr Or 5,7; 1.2.1; 1.6.3; 1.8.1; 1.9.1; 1.18.1; 1.19.6,8; 2.2.1; 2.4.5; 2.6.4; 2.7.3; 2.11.2,3,9–12; 2.13.2,3,14,15,26; 3.1.6,18; 3.2.3,12; 5.1.27,27n,37n,38; 5.2.8; 5.5.6; 5.8.3; 5.9.9,11; 5.10.15
Cicero, 3.1.16n

GENERAL INDEX

Circumcision, int 25,40,41; pr Or 8; 2.8.3,7; 2.9.1; 2.11.3,4,9; 2.12.1,2,4; 2.13.1–6,8–33,35,36; 2.14.1–7; 3.2.2,7; 3.6.1; 3.9.1,2; 3.10.1,2,4,5; 3.11.1; 4.1.4; 4.2.1–11; 4.5.9; 4.7.10; 4.12.4; 5.1.26; excursus on, 2.13.8–33
Clement of Alexandria, int 4; 1.1.3n; 2.9.1n; 2.11.11n; 2.13.3n; 2.13.19n; 2.13.22n; 2.14.19n; 3.1.15n; 3.5.2n; 3.6.4n; 3.6.9n; 3.8.5n; 4.1.20n; 4.4.9n; 4.5.7n; 4.5.11n; 4.9.9n; 5.1.19n; 5.7.4n
2 Clement, 4.5.12n
Cocchini, F., int 22
Cochleus, int 33
Codrus, 4.11.4n
Compulsion, 1.18.7; 5.1.19; 5.2.5; 5.10.12
Concealment of God's goodness and mercy (conceal, cover, hide, hidden), 1.13.1,6; 1.16.6; 2.4.4–8; 2.7.3; 2.8.4; 2.11.7; 3.7.11; 3.8.5; 5.1.2,4,7,10,36,37; 5.2.3,7,7n,13; 5.5.2; 5.9.10; 5.10.3
Conscience (awareness, consciousness), int 28; pr Or 6; 1.16.1,3; 2.2.1; 2.6.6; 2.8.2; 2.9.1,3,3n,4; 2.10.1,2; 3.2.7–9; 4.1.20; 4.3.2; 4.4.9; 4.5.7; 5.1.25; 5.6.3
Contention, 2.5.1,2; 2.6.1,4,5; 2.7.5; 2.14.1; 5.9.9
Continence (self control), 1.1.2; 2.13.31,35; 2.7.5; 4.6.7
Corinth, pr Or 7
Cornelius, 2.7.7
Covenant, 1.7.1; 1.13.1; 2.13.8,11,27; 3.1.3; 3.8.2,2n,7,8; 4.12.4; 5.1.4,40
Cranfield, C., 2.2.1n; 3.9.3n
Creation ex nihilo, 4.5.13,13n
Crispus, pr Or 7,
Cross (of Christ), int 42,48; 1.4.4; 2.13.29; 3.9.3,6,7; 4.1.16; 4.8.1,2; 4.12.4; 5.9.2,7–9;5.10.12,14
Crouzel, H., int 4n,5n,6,6n,7,9n,21n,28n
Cyril of Jerusalem, 5.7.3n

Damascus, 4.6.2
Daniélou, J., int 4n,7
Dassmann, E., int 20n
David, 1.5.1–5; 1.6.1; 1.16.3; 2.8.4; 2.14.20–24; 3.8.11; 4.1.1,17,19; 4.5.10; 5.9.10,11
Day of Wrath, 1.16.3; 2.4.1,3–6; 2.9.1; 2.10.1; 2.14.17; 3.6.4; 5.1.7,29
Death, int 25,32,45,46; pr Or 3,4,6; 1.4.1; 1.5.2; 1.6.1; 1.10.2; 1.18.7; 2.4.5; 2.5.4; 2.8.6; 2.9.4; 2.13.7,18,35; 2.14.19; 3.1.9; 3.2.13; 3.8.1; 3.9.8; 3.11.3; 4.1.15; 4.5.10,12; 4.6.7; 4.7.6–8; 4.10.1,2; 4.11.4; 4.12.1–5; 5.1.1,2,3,3n,8,9n,12–22,25,29–38; 5.2.2–13; 5.3.1–7; 5.4.2,3; 5.5.9; 5.6.1,6,7; 5.7.3,3n,5–10; 5.8.1–10; 5.9.1–12; 5.10.1–17; not of eternal duration, 5.7.8
Decius, int 5
Deeds, see Works
Deity/divinity, 1.17.1,2; 1.18.1; 1.19.6; 2.7.1; 2.14.11; 3.8.4,6,7,9,11; 4.9.12
Delarue, Dom, int 22
Descent into hell, see Underworld
Destine (determine, determinism), int 22; 1.5.1,1n,2,3; 1.6.2; 2.1.2; 3.8.9
Determinism, see Destine, Predestination
Devil, int 29; 1.18.6,7; 2.6.6; 2.13.29; 3.1.9; 3.3.3; 3.4.1; 4.8.1,4; 5.1.12,17n,29; 5.3.7; 5.6.7,8; 5.7.8n,9n; 5.9.9; 5.10.9,12
Didache, 1.18.6n
Didymus the Blind, int 7,10
Disease, see Medicine
Docetism, 5.9.5n
Drewery, B., int 48

Ebion, 3.11.2
Ebionites, 1.5.4n
Eck, int 33
Egypt(ians), int 3,6,10,11; 2.13.26,28,28n; 3.5.2; 3.6.1
Eight(h), 2.9.1; 2.12.2;

GENERAL INDEX

Eight(h) *(continued)*
 2.13.8,9,11,12,21,29; 3.2.7;
 4.2.4; 5.1.26
Election (choosing, chosen), int
 27,29,30; pr Or 1n; 1.2.1;
 1.3.1–3; 2.14.7; 3.3.4; 3.9.7;
 4.5.14; 5.1.31
Eliezer, 4.6.2
Elijah, 1.10.3; 2.5.4; 5.4.3
Enoch, 1.13.4; 5.1.20; 5.4.3
Enosh, 1.13.4; 5.1.20
Ephraim the Syrian, 5.7.3n
Epictetus, 2.1.2n; 2.9.3n; 4.9.3n
Epicurus (Epicurean philosophy),
 3.1.15n
Erasmus of Rotterdam, 1.5.1n;
 4.2.11n; 5.1.9n; 5.1.17n;
 5.1.21n; 5.2.2n
Erastus, pr Or 7
Essence, *see* Substance
Esther, 4.5.5
Eternal duration of death denied,
 5.7.8
Eternal gospel, 1.4.1,3; 1.14.1
Eternal life, 1.18.7n; 2.5.1,2,5,6,8;
 2.6.1; 2.7.4–6; 3.1.15; 4.1.15;
 5.6.1,6,8; 5.7.9
Ethiopian(s), 2.13.28
Eusebius of Caesarea, int 3–5,7,8; pr
 Ruf 1n; 1.1.3n; 1.5.1n; 1.5.4n
Evagrius Ponticus, int 7
Eve, 2.5.7; 4.4.4; 5.1.12–14,38; 5.9.11
Expiation, 3.8.13; 5.1.32

Fairweather, W., 2.7.6n; 4.11.4n
Faith (belief, believe, believer, infidel), int 25–48; pr Or 9; 1.1.2;
 1.2.1; 1.7.1; 1.9.1,4,5; 1.12.1;
 1.13.1,3; 1.14.1,2; 1.15.1; 1.18.1;
 1.19.6,7; 2.4.2,7,7n; 2.5.2,7;
 2.6.1,5; 2.7.2–8; 2.9.1,4,4n;
 2.11.2,6–12; 2.12.4;
 2.13.1–4,11,14,16,23,26,29,30;
 2.14.1,3,8,9,13–15,17,19,24;
 3.1.3,11,12,14; 3.2.2,3,12;
 3.7.1,2,4,12,12n,13,14;
 3.8.1,2,9–14; 3.9.1–8; 3.10.1–5;
 3.11.1–5; 4.1.1–18; 4.2.1–11;
 4.3.1,2; 4.4.1–5,8,10,11;
 4.5.1–7,9,12,14; 4.6.1–9;
 4.7.1–10; 4.8.1,3,4,6,10; 4.9.1;
 4.10.1,2; 4.11.2,5,6; 4.12.5;
 5.1.2,37; 5.2.12; 5.7.3n; 5.7.7;
 5.8.13; 5.9.2,12; 5.10.1–5,9,15
Faith alone, int 33–48; 3.7.12,12n;
 3.9.2,2n,3,3n,4; 3.10.1; 4.1.18
Fate (chance), int 1.3.2,3
Father, God the, 1.1.1; 1.3.5;
 1.5.1,1n; 1.7.1; 1.8.1; 1.10.1,2;
 1.13.4; 1.16.5,6; 1.18.4,6,10;
 2.5.5,6; 2.7.4,8; 2.10.1; 2.11.2;
 2.13.32; 3.1.15,17; 3.2.11;
 3.8.8,12; 3.11.2; 4.4.11; 4.6.9;
 4.7.4,5,10; 4.8.5,9,10;
 4.9.7,11,12; 4.10.1,2; 4.11.4;
 4.12.4; 5.1.7,41; 5.2.5,11; 5.3.7;
 5.8.1,7–13; 5.9.6,7; 5.10.17
Fear (afraid), int 27; pr Ruf 2; 1.1.1;
 1.3.3; 1.16.2; 2.4.3,8; 2.5.7;
 2.8.4; 3.1.7; 3.2.1,6; 3.5.3;
 4.9.11; 5.1.7; 5.2.7,13; 5.5.2;
 5.8.10
Fifth Ecumenical Council, int 6
Fire, 1.13.4; 1.18.2,7; 2.2.2; 2.3.2;
 2.4.3,6; 2.6.2; 2.11.9; 2.14.14;
 3.2.9; 4.4.7; 4.10.2; 4.11.6;
 5.1.23,29,40
Flesh, int 41; pr Or 4,5,8; 1.1.4;
 1.4.3; 1.5.1–5; 1.6.1,1n,2; 1.10.2;
 1.13.5; 1.18.5–9; 2.4.1–3; 2.5.3;
 2.9.2; 2.11.2,4; 2.12.1,2,4;
 2.13.1,3,7–14,18–26,34–36;
 2.14.4,5,15; 3.5.3; 3.6.1,7;
 3.8.4,7; 3.10.5; 4.1.1,7;
 4.2.3,5–10; 4.5.6,14;
 4.8.1–4,9,10; 4.11.2; 4.12.4;
 5.1.16,19,23,33; 5.6.2–4;
 5.7.3–5; 5.8.7,10; 5.9.10,12;
 5.10.4,8
Foreknowledge of God, int
 16,27,29,30; 1.2.1; 1.3.1–4; 1.5.1
Forgiveness (absolve, remission), int
 36,40,41,45,48; 1.4.3; 2.1.2,3;
 3.6.1; 3.8.1,10,11,14; 3.9.4;
 4.1.1,15,17–20; 4.2.2; 4.11.4;
 5.1.31,32; 5.2.14; 5.6.5
Free will (freedom of will), int
 16,23,26,28–30,47; pr Or 1,1n;
 1.18.7; 4.10.1; 4.12.1;
 5.10.13–15; to be restrained by
 the love of God, 5.10.15–16
Freedom (free, license, liberty),

GENERAL INDEX

1.1.1–4; 1.2.1; 1.16.2; 2.9.3;
3.1.18; 3.7.14; 3.9.4,8; 4.1.14n;
4.9.9; 4.10.2; 4.11.1;
5.1.19,35,37; 5.2.6,12,14; 5.3.3;
5.10.2,6,15
Fremantle, W., int 10,12n; 5.10.13n

Gaius, pr Or 7
Gennadius, int 11
Gentile(s), int (6); pr Or 8,10; 1.3.5;
1.7.1; 1.13.3; 2.4.7; 2.5.2;
2.7.1–9; 2.8.2; 2.9.1;
2.11.1,8,10–12;
2.13.1–4,9,11,14–16;
2.14.1–9,13; 3.1.2,3; 3.2.2,3,7,9;
3.6.1; 3.7.2,12; 3.9.1,2; 3.10.1;
4.1.7; 4.2.7,8; 4.4.9; 4.5.9,12,14;
4.11.3; 4.12.4
Geometry, 2.13.28
Geta, int 5
Glory, pr Or 4; 1.3.5; 1.5.2; 1.6.1,3;
1.10.3; 1.16.1; 1.17.1,2; 1.18.1,8;
1.19.2–4,7,8; 2.1.2; 2.5.1–6;
2.6.1; 2.7.1–6; 2.11.5; 2.13.36;
2.14.2,3,12; 3.1.1,14,18,19;
3.2.3; 3.7.1,13; 3.9.2; 3.11.3–5;
4.1.4; 4.6.1,6–8; 4.7.2;
4.8.1,7–10; 4.9.1; 5.3.8;
5.8.1,8,11–13; 5.10.8,13
Golden Rule, 2.9.1n
Goodness (divine goodness), int 27;
1.3.1; 1.5.2; 2.3.1; 2.4.4,8,8n;
2.5.6; 2.7.3; 2.8.4; 3.2.1,6; 4.1.6;
4.10.1; 5.1.7,7n; 5.2.3,7,7n
Gorday, P., int 24,25n
Gordian III, int 8; pr Or 9n
Gospel (message), int 23,27;
1.3.1,3,5; 1.4.1,3,5; 1.7.1;
1.9.1; 1.10.1; 1.11.1; 1.13.1,7;
1.14.1; 1.15.1; 2.2.1; 2.9.1;
2.10.1; 2.13.29; 3.3.1; 4.1.7;
5.5.5
Gothicus, int 5,8; pr Or 9
Goths, int 5,8; pr Or 9
Grace, int
16,16n,23,27,30–34,37,41,46–
48; 1.2.1; 1.7.1; 1.8.1; 1.12.1,1n;
1.13.6; 2.1.2; 2.12.4; 2.13.2;
2.14.19; 3.1.12; 3.7.1,2; 3.8.7,13;
3.9.2,4,5; 3.11.4; 4.1.14n,15;
4.2.2,3; 4.5.1–7,10; 4.6.7;

4.8.1,5,6,9,10; 4.9.1;
5.1.6,7,7n,20;
5.2.1,2,5–8,10,14,15; 5.3.1–5,8;
5.6.1,5–8; 5.7.1,2,5,6,9; 5.8.2;
5.9.2; 5.10.7
Grant, M., int 9
Greek(s), int 32; pr Ruf 1; pr Or 10;
1.13.1,3,6; 1.14.1,2; 1.15.1;
2.5.1,2; 2.7.1,2,5,5n,6,6n,9;
2.14.1,2; 3.2.1,2,3,6,9; 3.3.2;
3.4.3; 3.5.4; 3.6.9; 3.7.13; 3.9.2;
4.11.4; 5.8.3
Greek textual tradition, int 14–15;
1.5.1n; 2.14.18; 3.1.2n,6,6n;
3.2.4; 3.6.5,5n; 3.7.9; 3.8.5n;
3.8.12; 4.1.20; 4.9.6n; 4.10.1n;
5.6.3n; 5.8.3; 5.10.17
Greek words cited,
ἀδιάφορα, 4.9.3n
ἀκολουθία, 1.1.2n
ἀνομία, 4.1.20
ἄνωθεν, 5.8.3
ἀόρατα, 1.17.2n
ἀποστέλλω, 1.7.1n
ἀπόστολος, 1.7.1n
ἄρθρον, 3.7.9
δικαιοσύνη, int 36
ἐπίνοια, int 36,38; 5.6.7n
εὐώνυμος, 3.8.5n
ἐφ' ᾧ, 5.1.1n
ἡγεμονικόν, 5.6.3n
ἦν ποτε ὅτε οὐκ ἦν, 1.5.1
ἥ τε ἀΐδιος αὐτοῦ δύναμις, 1.17.2n
θέσει νόμον, 3.2.9n
ἱλαστήριον, 3.8.2n
καταχρηστικῶς, 4.9.6n
κυρίως, 4.9.6n
μετενσωμάτωσις, 5.1.27; 5.9.11
νόμος, int 23
ὅρασις εἰρήνης, 3.5.2n
ὁρισθέντος, 1.5.1n
παιδαγωγός, 2.9.3n
προορισθέντος, 1.5.1n
στενοχωρία, 2.6.6n
σχολάσατε, 2.5.8n
ὑπέρβατον, 1.13.1
ὑπόδικος, 3.6.5n
χάρις, int 23
χάριτι θεοῦ, 3.8.1n
χωρὶς θεοῦ, 3.8.1n
Gregory of Nyssa, int 7

Gregory Thaumaturgus, int 7; 3.1.7n

Hammond Bammel, C.P., int *passim;* pr Or 11n; 3.1.6n; 3.1.10n; 3.6.9n; 4.1.2n; 4.12.3n; 5.1.3n; 5.1.6n; 5.1.37n; 5.2.13n
Hammond, C.P. *see* Hammond Bammel, C.P.
Hanson, R., int 22n; pr Or 1n, 2.9.1n
Harl, M., int 36n
Harnack, A., int 8n; 2.13.21n
Health, healing, *see* Medicine
Heart, definition of, 2.9.2,3; hard, soft, fat, 2.4.1; 2.8.7
Hebrew textual tradition, 2.13.8,8n; 2.13.25; 2.13.25n; 3.1.4n
Hebrews, customs of the, pr Or 10
Hebron, 4.1.9
Heine, R., int 13n; 3.1.16n; 5.8.2n
Heither, T., int *passim;* pr Or 3n; 1.4.5n; 1.5.4n; 1.10.3n; 1.18.5n; 2.5.8n; 2.6.1n; 2.7.2n; 2.11.11n; 2.14.20n; 3.1.2n; 3.1.6n; 3.1.9n; 3.6.5n; 3.8.2n; 4.9.6n; 5.1.9n; 5.1.20n; 5.7.8n
Hell, *see* Underworld
Heraclius, int 12,13; pr Ruf 1
Heretic(s), int *passim;* pr Or 1,1n; 1.3.1,3; 1.18.2; 1.19.6; 2.4.7; 2.11.11,11n; 2.13.27; 2.14.11; 3.4.1; 3.6.9; 3.10.1; 4.4.3; 4.7.4; 4.10.2; 5.1.27n; 5.2.8n; 5.6.2,3; 5.9.5
Hermas, int 29; 1.3.3n
Herodotus, 2.13.28n
Hieroglyphics, 2.13.28
Hippolytus, int 5
Historia Augusta, int 3n,5n,8n; pr Or 9n
Hittite(s), 2.14.22,23; 4.2.9
Holy Spirit, *see* Spirit
Homer, 3.3.4n
Honor, 1.16.1; 1.17.1; 1.18.8; 1.19.2,5; 2.5.1,2,5,6; 2.6.1,2; 2.7.1–6; 2.9.1; 2.11.1,10; 2.14.2; 3.5.1; 5.10.8
Hope, 1.16.6; 3.2.2; 4.1.3; 4.3.1; 4.4.1,11; 4.5.7; 4.6.1–7; 4.7.10; 4.8.1,7–10; 4.9.1,4,7,9,10; 4.11.4; 4.12.4,5; 5.1.2,20; 5.9.2,12; 5.10.15
Horoscopes, 2.13.28
Hort, F., int 8n
Humility (humble), pr Or 3; 1.1.1; 3.9.6; 4.1.12; 4.8.5; 4.11.3; 5.3.8; 5.5.6; 5.8.9n
Hyperbaton, 1.13.1

Idolatry (idols), 1.16.1; 1.19.6–8; 2.11.1,7,9–11; 2.13.14,26; 2.14.23; 4.5.10,11; 5.2.10
Ignatius of Antioch, 1.5.4n; 5.9.5n
Image(s), 1.3.4; 1.5.2; 1.16.1,5; 1.17.1,2; 1.18.8,10; 1.19.2–4,8; 2.4.1; 2.5.4,5; 2.13.34; 3.2.3; 4.5.10,11; 4.7.6; 4.8.9,10; 5.1.15,16,22,28,41; 5.8.12,13
Immortality, 5.1.38; 5.3.3
Incarnation, *see* Flesh
Incoherence/incompleteness of Paul's thought, pr Or 1; 1.9.6; 1.13.1,2; 3.1.2,3,6; 4.8.7; 4.9.1; 4.12.5; 5.1.2,3,5,6,23; 5.8.2
Incorruption, 2.5.1–7; 2.6.1; 5.10.8
Indifferent matters (neutral), 4.9.3–9; 5.10.8
Infernal regions, *see* Underworld
Iniquity, distinguished from sin, 4.1.20
Inner man, *see* Man, inner
Intention, *see* Purpose
Interpolation, int 13–14; pr Ruf 2,2n
Iphigenia, 4.11.4n
Irenaeus, 1.5.3n; 2.13.30n; 5.1.8n; 5.1.27n; 5.1.31n; 5.2.8n
Isaac, 1.8.1; 1.9.3; 2.14.9; 4.2.4; 4.5.12; 4.6.7,8,9; 4.7.3,9,10; 5.5.2
Ishbak, 4.6.7
Ishmael, 4.1.7; 4.5.6,9
Israel, Israelite, pr Or 8,9; 1.2.1; 1.5.4; 1.7.1; 1.8.1; 1.11.2; 2.5.4; 2.7.1; 2.8.4,5; 2.11.2; 2.13.9,12–15,18,22,23,26; 2.14.9,23; 3.1.3; 3.8.2,10; 3.11.3; 4.1.7,12; 4.2.7–9; 4.8.7; 4.12.4; 5.6.2

GENERAL INDEX   387

Jacob, pr Or 9; 1.8.1; 1.9.3; 2.13.36; 2.14.9; 4.5.12; 4.7.9; 5.5.2
Jansen, C., int 30n
Japheth, 1.8.1
Jedidiah, pr Or 10
Jehoiachin, pr Or 10
Jehoshaphat, 1.5.5
Jerome, int 4,4n,6,7,10–12,14n; pr Ruf 1n; 1.4.1n; 1.4.4n; 2.13.8n; 4.10.1n; 4.10.2n; 5.10.13n
Jerusalem, int 43; 1.10.1; 2.13.15,17; 2.14.7; 3.2.10,11; 3.5.2,2n; 4.11.4n; 5.1.41; 5.10.12
Jesse, 3.5.3
Jews (Jewish, Judaic), int 25,32,39,40,42,48; 1.10.2n; 1.13.1; 1.14.1,2; 1.15.1; 2.5.1,2; 2.7.1–5,9; 2.9.1; 2.11.1–12; 2.12.1; 2.13.1,3,7,11,17,34,36; 2.14.1–13,17; 3.1.2; 3.2.1–3,6–9; 3.3.2; 3.4.3; 3.5.4; 3.6.1,9; 3.7.2,12,13; 3.9.1–3,7,7n; 3.10.1; 4.1.4; 4.2.8; 4.5.14; 4.11.3,4n; 5.1.9n
Joab, 1.16.3
John Cassian, int 7,12
John of Jerusalem, Bishop, int 6,11
John the Baptist, 3.2.13; 4.5.9n; 5.1.34; 5.8.6
Jokshan, 4.6.7
Jonah, 4.2.5; 5.10.10
Joram, 1.5.5
Joseph (husband of Mary), 1.5.4,5
Joseph (patriarch), 3.6.1; 4.5.4; 4.7.9
Josephus, 1.14.2n; 2.13.30n; 4.11.4n
Joshua, 2.13.26; 3.8.6
Jotham, 1.5.5
Judah, 2.11.4; 2.13.36; 3.2.11; 4.2.9; 4.7.9
Judas (son of James), pr Or 10
Judas Iscariot, 1.2.1
Judea, 2.14.7
Judgment, int 28,30,31,34,38,42; 1.3.2; 1.16.5; 1.19.1; 2.1.1–3; 2.2.1–2; 2.4.1–8; 2.5.2; 2.6.5; 2.7.6,7; 2.8.4,6; 2.10.1; 2.11.3,10; 2.13.2,3,6; 2.14.17; 3.1.3,4; 3.3.2; 3.6.1–5; 3.7.5,7,12n; 3.8.14; 4.1.4; 4.8.9; 4.9.2,6; 5.1.7,29; 5.2.1,2,15; 5.3.8; 5.8.2n

Justification, int 26–48; 1.4.3; 2.4.7n; 2.7.6n; 2.8.1,3; 2.9.1; 2.13.4,23; 2.14.1,16,17,22,24; 3.1.3; 3.2.10–13; 3.3.1; 3.6.1,2,7,8; 3.7.1,2,13; 3.8.1,14; 3.9.1–8; 3.10.1–5; 3.11.1; 4.1.1–6,9,13,16–18; 4.2.2,3,8; 4.3.2; 4.4.1,10; 4.5.6,7; 4.7.1,7,8,10; 4.8.1–4; 4.9.1; 4.11.1,4,5; 5.1.2,6,8; 5.2.1–15; 5.3.2,5; 5.3.8; 5.4.1,2
Justin Martyr, 1.5.4n
Justinian, Emperor, int 6

Kelly, J., int 11n; 12n; 5.1.14n
Keturah, 4.1.7; 4.5.6,9; 4.6.7
Kingdom, 1.12.1; 1.13.2; 2.4.2; 2.7.3,6,6n; 2.13.21,31; 2.14.9,13,14; 3.2.13; 3.9.3; 4.1.16; 4.6.3; 4.11.4; 5.1.7,31,34,37,41; 5.3.5,7,8; 5.5.2; 5.6.6; 5.7.7–9; 5.8.3; 5.9.7; 5.10.8,11
Koch, H., 5.10.13n; 5.10.16n

Lamech, 5.1.23; 5.6.2
Lampe, G., 5.8.2n
Lange, N., de, 1.10.2n; 2.14.10n
Latin textual tradition, int 14–15; 1.5.1; 2.6.5; 2.14.18; 3.1.6; 3.2.4; 3.8.12; 5.8.3
Law, int 23,41–42; pr Or 8,10; 1.1.1; 1.5.4; 1.10.2,3,3n; 1.13.1,3; 1.14.2; 1.15.1; 1.18.4; 2.2.1; 2.4.8; 2.5.4; 2.6.4; 2.7.1,2,5,6; 2.8.1–7; 2.9.1–3; 2.11.1–12; 2.12.1,2,4; 2.13.1–19; 22,23,27,29–31,35; 2.14.1–4,6,9–13,15,19; 3.1.3,15; 3.2.2,3,7–9,12; 3.5.3; 3.6.1,1n,3–7,7n,9; 3.7.1–3,5–10,12,12n,13; 3.8.2,10; 3.9.1–8; 3.10.1,5; 3.11.1–5; 4.1.2,7,18,20; 4.2.8,11; 4.3.1,2; 4.4.1–10; 4.5.1,6–9,14; 4.6.6; 4.7.4,10; 4.8.1–3,10; 4.9.3; 4.10.1,2; 4.11.3; 4.12.4; 5.1.1,2,8,9n,23–41; 5.2.10,13; 5.3.6; 5.5.3; 5.6.1–4; 5.7.4; 5.8.2,6; 5.9.11; 5.10.9,15

Lawson, R., 3.5.2n
Laxness, see Negligence
Laziness, see Negligence
Lebbaeus, pr Or 10n
Left (opp. right), 1.14.1; 3.3.1; 3.7.5; 3.8.5,5n
Lemma (lemmata), definition of, int 14n
Leonides, int 3,4
Levi (Matthew), pr Or 10
Levi (OT priest), 5.1.14
Levites, 2.13.12
Lewis, G., 5.6.3n
Lienhard, J., 5.1.27n
Likeness of God, distinct from image, 4.5.11,11n
Logos, see Word of God
Lommatzsch, int 22
Lot, 4.1.9; 5.6.2
Love, pr Or 6; 1.8.1; 1.13.2,5; 2.7.5; 3.5.2; 4.6.3,5; 4.7.8; 4.8.2; 4.9.1,4,7,10–12; 4.10.1; 4.11.1,4,6; 4.12.1; 5.1.2; 5.10.7,15,16
Lubac, H. de, int 10
Lucifer, 5.10.13,16
Lucius Verus, pr Or 9n
Lucretius, 3.1.16n
Luther, M., int 23,30n,33,48; 3.9.3n
Lutheran theology, int 23,47
LXX, see Septuagint

Magic, 2.4.5
Mamre, 4.1.9
Man, inner, pr Or 8; 1.19.8; 2.13.34–36; 4.1.4; 4.4.5; 5.1.5; 5.8.13
Mani (Manichean Gnosticism), 3.6.9n
Marcella, int 6
Marcion (Marcionites), int 14,20,21,23,23n,24,27,28,28n, 38; pr Ruf 2n; 1.18.2n; 1.18.3; 2.4.7n; 2.4.8n; 2.10.2; 2.13.9n; 2.13.27; 2.14.11; 3.6.9n; 3.7.12n; 3.10.1n; 3.11.2; 4.4.3n; 4.7.4n; 4.10.2n; 4.12.1; 5.6.2; 5.9.5n
Marcus Aurelius, pr Or 9n
Marcus Curtius, 4.11.4n
Marqah, 2.14.10n

Marriage, 1.1.2–3; 1.2.1; 1.12.1; 2.13.21,31; of the Apostle Paul, 1.1.3,3n; 4.6.7
Martyr (martyrdom), 1.2.1; 2.1.2; 2.7.4; 2.13.30; 2.14.15; 4.10.2; 5.8.14
Mary (mother of Jesus), 1.5.4,4n; 3.8.4; 5.9.10
Masech, 4.6.2
McSorley, H., int 30–31
Medan, 4.6.7
Median, 4.6.7
Medicine, art of, 2.2.2; 2.6.3,3n,4; 3.1.7; 3.6.9; 3.7.5,7; 4.6.3,4; 4.9.3n; 5.2.11; 5.5.3; 5.6.5; 5.10.13,14
Melanchthon, P., int 30n,33,46–48; 3.7.6n
Melania, int 11
Melchizedek, 1.8.1; 4.1.9; 5.1.14
Mentally incompetent, 3.6.3
Mercy Seat, see Propitiatory
Merit (desert, deserve, earn), int 27,29–33,45–48; 1.3.2,3,3n,4; 1.11.1; 1.18.1,7; 1.19.1,4; 2.1.2; 2.5.6; 2.7.1,6; 3.1.1,4,9,19; 3.4.2; 3.6.2; 3.7.13; 3.8.6; 4.1.3,12,20; 4.2.3,7; 4.3.1,2; 4.4.1,2; 4.5.3,4,9,10,14; 4.7.7; 4.8.10; 4.11.6; 4.12.1–3; 5.1.5,16,20; 5.2.5; 5.3.6; 5.5.3,6; 5.8.11; 5.9.7
Methuselah, 5.1.20
Metzger, B., pr Or 10n
Migne edition, int 2,22,22n; textual readings of the, 1.5.5n; 1.19.1n; 2.13.9n; 2.13.27n; 3.1.15n; 4.1.20n; 4.2.8n; 4.5.9n; 5.1.7n; 5.7.8n
Mind, pr Or 8; 1.1.2; 1.3.3; 1.4.2; 1.18.4; 1.19.1,2,4,5,7; 2.1.1–3; 2.3,2; 2.4.1,6; 2.5.2; 2.13.18,20; 2.14.19; 3.2.3,14; 3.5.3; 3.6.1; 3.7.5; 4.1.17; 4.2.12; 4.4.5,9; 4.6.9; 4.7.5; 4.8.3,4,9,10; 4.9.1; 4.11.6; 5.1.12,16,32; 5.5.2; 5.6.3,4; 5.8.10; 5.9.11,12; 5.10.7,10,15,17
Miriam, 3.2.11
Molland, E., int 23,25n; E., 5.10.13n; 5.10.16n
Montague, R., int 33

Montanists (Montanus), 2.7.8n
Moses (Mosaic), int 43; pr Or 8;
  1.8.1; 1.10.3; 1.13.1; 1.15.1;
  2.5.4; 2.8.1,3; 2.9.1; 2.11.8;
  2.13.9,12,13,15,18,25,26;
  2.14.6,8,10,12; 3.2.7,8,9,11;
  3.6.1; 3.7.2,3,6,7,8,9,10;
  3.8.2,6,8,13; 3.9.8; 3.11.1,3,4,5;
  4.1.12; 4.3.1; 4.4.2,3,4,4n,5,
  7,8,10,11; 4.5.4; 4.7.1;
  4.8.7,8,9,10; 4.11.6; 4.12.2;
  5.1.1,8,23,23n,26,29,30,31,31n,
  32,34,36; 5.2.2,7,12; 5.6.2,2n,3;
  5.8.14; 5.10.9
Mother of God, *see* Theotokos
Murphy, F., int 11n,12n
Mystery (mysteries, mystical),
  1.13.2,6; 2.4.5,6,8; 2.7.2,2n;
  2.13.21,27–29,36; 2.14.4; 3.1.11;
  3.7.14; 3.8.1,6,13; 4.2.4,8,10;
  4.5.6; 4.7.3; 4.8.8;
  5.1.2,10,11,22,34,36,38; 5.2.7;
  5.5.2; 5.8.4,8,14; 5.9.10,11

Nadab, 2.2.2
Nathaniel, 4.8.10
Nature(s), heretical doctrine of, int
  22–30,33,34; pr Or 1,1n;
  1.3.1–3; 2.4.7; 2.10.2; 4.12.1;
  5.2.10
Negligence (lax, lazy), int 41,48;
  2.3.2; 2.14.14; 3.3.4; 3.9.4;
  5.1.4,7; 5.2.6,7
Nestorius (Nestorian heresy), int
  17n,
Neuschäfer, B., 1.13.1n; 2.6.3n;
  3.1.2n
New Testament, int 38; 1.18.3,4;
  3.7.12n
Nicaea (Nicene), Council of,
  1.5.1n
Noah, 1.8.1; 1.13.4; 3.1.11; 4.5.4;
  5.1.20; 5.6.2
Novatians (Novatus), 2.7.8n

Obedience (obey), 1.7.1; 2.6.5;
  2.9.4; 4.4.8; 5.1.6,37,38;
  5.2.2,4–6,15; 5.5.1,2,5,8,9;
  5.7.3,4; 5.10.12,17
Old Latin versions, int 14,14n,15
Old Testament, int 38; 1.18.3,4;

  2.13.27; 3.7.12n
Oracle(s), 2.5.2; 2.7.1; 2.13.11;
  2.14.1,6–11,14,15; 3.2.2; 3.9.2;
  4.11.4n
Original sin, doctrine of, 5.1.1n;
  5.1.14n

Pagan(s), int 44; 1.19.6,7; 2.7.6n;
  2.13.27,28,29; 2.14.23; 3.2.12;
  4.11.4n
Palace, 2.6.6; 5.1.9,10,10n,23
Palladius, int 11
Pamphilus the Martyr, int 7; 1.5.1n
Parables of Origen; of the king's
  palace and steward (Paul),
  5.1.9–11,23; of the soul as a
  house, 1.18.9–10; 2.1.3; of the
  tyrant and the rightful king,
  5.1.31–33,37; 5.2.5; 5.10.11,12
Paradise, int 39,46; 2.4.3; 2.5.6;
  3.3.1; 3.9.3; 5.1.12,14,14n,35;
  5.4.3; 5.9.7; 5.10.13
Parker, H., int 5n,9n
Parthians, pr Or 9
Parthicus, pr Or 9
Passover, 2.13.17; 5.1.40
Paul (consul in Cyprus), pr Or 9
Peace, int 36; 1.4.4; 1.8.1; 1.9.5;
  1.13.5; 2.5.1; 2.7.3,5,6;
  2.14.2,18; 3.2.1,6; 3.5.1,2; 3.9.4;
  4.8.1–5; 4.11.5; 4.12.4; 5.3.7,8;
  5.6.7; 5.7.6; 5.10.14,18
Pedagogue, 2.9.3; 3.11.4,5;
  5.1.35
Pelagius (Pelagian), int
  16,17,29–33,47,48; 1.3.3n;
  5.7.3n
Perfection, pr Or 3–7; 1.6.1; 1.10.3;
  1.13.3,5,6; 2.12.2; 2.14.14;
  3.3.2,4; 3.5.3; 3.6.5; 3.7.12;
  3.10.3,5; 3.11.2,4;
  4.1.10,12,16,20; 4.5.3,11n;
  4.6.3,4,9; 4.7.3; 4.8.1; 4.9.11;
  5.2.6,7,12; 5.3.8; 5.8.14;
  5.10.4,13,15; in Paul, pr Or 3n
Peripatetics, 3.1.16n
Perseverance, 2.5.1–5; 2.6.1,6;
  2.7.4,5; 4.8.4
Persona, 2.11.2,3,5; 5.1.36; 5.5.6;
  5.10.10
Peter, pr Or 9; 2.5.4; 2.7.3; 2.7.7;

GENERAL INDEX

Peter, pr Or *(continued)*
 2.13.3; 2.13.29; 3.1.11; 3.3.4;
 3.7.14; 4.9.12; 5.1.40; 5.10.15
Pharaoh, 5.5.7; 5.6.2
Philip I, Emperor, int 9
Philo, 2.13.19n; 2.13.28n; 3.2.9n;
 3.5.2n; 3.6.4n; 3.8.3n; 3.8.5n;
 3.8.8n; 3.10.3n
Philosophers (Philosophy),
 1.16.1,2,2n; 1.17.1; 1.19.6; 2.4.5;
 2.13.26; 2.7.6n; 2.14.19;
 3.1.9,14,15; 3.2.9; 3.6.4;
 4.5.11n,14
Phineas, int 43; 4.1.12n
Phoebe, pr Or 7
Phoenician(s), 2.13.28
Plato, 2.13.28n; 5.7.8n
Prayer, pr Ruf 3; pr Or 1n,2; 1.1.2;
 1.11.1; 1.13.3; 3.9.6; 4.1.15;
 5.1.33; 5.3.7,8
Predestination (predestine, predetermine), int
 16,22,23,26n,29,30; pr Or 1n;
 1.3.3n,4; 1.5.1,1n; 3.8.1,2,9,10
Prepositions, Paul's use of, 3.10.2–5
Priest(hood), 1.7.1; 1.9.2; 2.4.3;
 2.13.15,23,28; 3.8.10,11,13
Probus, pr Or 9n
Promise(s), 1.4.1,5; 2.14.1,2,4;
 3.2.2; 3.8.6; 4.1.20; 4.3.1;
 4.4.1,2; 4.5.1–9; 4.6.1–6; 4.7.3;
 4.12.4; 5.1.2; 5.2.14; 5.5.2
Promised land, 2.13.26; 3.5.2
Proper/improper sense of words
 (strict), 4.9.3,6,6n,8,9
Propitiation (propitiator, propitious,
 atonement), 2.13.13; 3.8.1–3;
 10–14; 3.9.2; 4.11.4n; 5.1.33n;
 5.2.14
Propitiatory (mercy seat), 3.8.2–10;
 3.8.2n
Psalms, titles of, 2.10.22–24
Punishment (penalty), 1.16.3,4;
 1.18.7; 1.19.4; 2.1.2; 2.2.2n;
 2.3.1,2n; 2.4.4n; 2.7.1,2; 2.8.6;
 2.14.1; 3.1.4,10n; 3.8.14; 4.1.15;
 4.3.1; 4.4.4,7,7n; 5.1.7n,37;
 5.2.14
Purification (purging), 2.2.2n;
 2.13.3,18,32; 2.14.14; 4.6.8;
 4.8.5; 4.11.4

Purpose (intention), int 26,29; pr
 Or 1,3; 2.3.2; 2.4.4,6; 5.9.12
Pyghius, int 33

Quasten, J., int 5
Queen, 2.13.2; 4.5.5; 5.1.9
Quintilian, 1.13.1n

Ramsbotham, A., int 17n
Ransom, *see* Redemption
Reconciliation (reconcile), int
 27,34,35; 4.8.1,2; 4.11.4;
 4.12.1–5; 5.1.2,33
Redemption (redeem, redeemer),
 int 23; 1.5.3; 2.13.29,32;
 3.7.1,2,10,14; 3.8.1,13; 3.9.2;
 4.7.7; 4.10.1; 4.11.1
Remission, *see* Forgiveness
Repentance, int 36; pr Or 5; 1.9.4;
 2.1.2; 2.3.1,2; 2.4.1; 3.8.14;
 3.11.2; 5.1.20,22; 5.7.5,9; 5.8.2n
Restoration, *see* Apocatastasis
Resurrection, pr Or 3; 1.6.1,1n;
 2.5.5,7; 3.1.12; 4.6.3,9;
 4.7.2,3,5,8; 4.12.5; 5.1.37,38;
 5.2.5; 5.7.8; 5.9.1,2,5–7,12;
 5.10.3–5,8
Revelation (reveal, manifest), 1.3.1;
 1.4.1,3; 1.13.1,3; 1.15.1;
 1.16.1–6; 1.17.2; 1.18.1,4;
 2.4.1,3,4,6; 2.6.2; 2.7.1,2n,4,6n;
 2.10.1,2; 2.14.24; 3.1.5; 3.7.5,11;
 3.8.5,8,13; 3.11.5; 4.8.9; 5.1.2,7;
 5.9.7; 5.10.3,4
Riches, *see* Wealth
Roukema, R., int 25n; 1.16.2n
Rufinus of Aquileia, int *passim;* pr Or
 8n,11n; 1.3.5n; 1.4.5n; 1.5.1n;
 2.6.5n; 3.1.6n,9n; 3.6.5n; 3.8.2n;
 5.1.17n,37n; 5.6.4n;
 5.10.13n,14n
Rule of faith, int 7; 2.7.3; 5.1.27

Sabbath(s), int 42; 1.10.2; 2.8.3;
 2.9.1; 2.13.9; 5.1.39–41
Sacrifice(s), 1.9.2; 2.4.3; 2.9.1;
 2.13.3,15,17,32; 3.8.1,10,11,13;
 4.7.3; 4.8.1; 4.11.4,4n;
 5.1.20,31,32,35,40; 5.2.10;
 5.9.11
Saint(s), 1.1.4; 1.4.1; 1.6.3; 1.7.1;

1.8.1n; 1.9.3,4; 1.10.1; 2.4.4,6;
  2.6.6; 2.13.31; 3.1.12; 3.8.6,8;
  3.10.1; 3.11.4; 4.5.4,12; 4.6.7;
  4.7.10; 4.8.9; 4.9.8,12;
  5.1.18,21,37
Samaria, 1.10.1; 2.14.10,10n
Samaritan(s), 1.10.2; 2.14.9,10,10n
Sanday & Headlam, int 1; 2.9.3n;
  2.10.1n; 3.6.7n; 3.7.9n
Sarah, pr Or 9; 4.6.1,6,7
Sarai, pr Or 9
Satan, int 6; pr Or 5; 1.1.2; 1.13.3;
  2.11.4; 4.11.4; 5.1.21n
Saul (king), 2.14.22
Saul (Paul's Hebrew name), pr Or
  9,10,
Schelkle, K., int
  1,17,18,29,30n,42,45; 1.3.3n;
  1.5.1n; 1.15.1n; 1.17.1n;
  1.17.2n; 2.7.4n; 3.6.7n; 3.6.9n;
  3.9.7n; 4.1.18n; 5.1.14n; 5.7.3n
Scherer, J., int 17,17n,18,39n
Scholasticism, pr Or 3n
Scourge, 2.2.2; 4.9.8,9,9n
Seal, 2.4.1; 3.2.11; 4.2.1,5–8; 4.5.9
Sects, 2.14.10n,23,24; 3.1.14;
  3.7.4
Self control, *see* Continence
Septuagint (LXX), int 14n,15
Serpent(s), 1.16.4; 2.4.3; 2.5.7;
  2.6.6; 3.3.1; 3.4.1; 5.1.12,14,29;
  5.8.9
Seth,1.13.4
Severus Alexander, pr Or 9n
Severus Septimius, int 3,3n,4; pr Or
  9n
Shem, 1.8.1
Shepherd of Hermas, see Hermas
Shuah, 4.6.7
Sign, 1.13.3; 2.10.1;
  2.13.8,11,27,28,30; 3.2.7; 3.9.5;
  4.2.1,3,5,6,8; 4.4.11; 4.10.1
Simon (Peter), *see* Peter
Simon (the Cananaean), pr Or 10
Sin and Sinner, distinction of,
  5.5.3–7
Sinlessness, possibility of, int 16;
  2.7.8
Socrates (church historian), int
  17,17n
Sodom (Sodomites), int 43,44;

2.3.2; 3.2.9,10,11; 4.4.4; 5.1.23;
  5.6.2
Solomon, pr Or 10; 2.6.6; 2.13.2;
  2.13.24; 2.14.6; 2.14.23; 3.7.14
Son of God, 1.1.1; 1.3.1,4,5; 1.5.1–3;
  1.6.1,2; 1.10.1,2; 1.16.5,6;
  1.18.10; 2.5.5,6; 2.7.4,5,7;
  2.10.1; 2.11.2; 3.1.15; 3.2.11;
  3.7.10,14; 3.8.5,6,8; 3.11.2;
  4.4.11; 4.9.12; 4.10.1,2; 4.11.1,4;
  4.12.1–3,5; 5.1.2,33; 5.2.11;
  5.6.7n; 5.7.9; 5.8.7,9; 5.9.10;
  5.10.15,16
Son of Man, 1.9.4; 2.8.4,5; 4.2.5;
  4.8.9; 5.10.10
Soul(s), int 28,34,37,44,46,48; pr Or
  10n; 1.5.2,3; 1.6.1n; 1.10.2;
  1.16.5; 1.18.5–10; 1.19.5; 2.1.3;
  2.4.2,7; 2.5.1,3; 2.6.4,6; 2.7.4,5;
  2.9.2–4,4n; 2.10.1,2; 2.11.5;
  2.12.2; 2.13.8,13,18,20,27;
  2.14.3; 3.1.10n,16; 3.2.14;
  3.4.1,3; 3.6.1; 3.7.14;
  3.8.3–7,9,13; 4.1.17,18,20;
  4.5.6,10; 4.8.6; 4.11.6;
  5.1.19,27,35n,37; 5.2.4;
  5.3.3–5,7; 5.6.3n,8; 5.7.8;
  5.9.10,11; 5.10.12,13,15,15n,17;
  pre-existence of the, int 6,7;
  3.1.10n; 5.1.35n; 5.4.3,3n
Spirit, (Holy Spirit, spirit), int
  24,25,31,47; pr Or 2,4–6;
  1.1.1,4; 1.2.1; 1.4.1,3; 1.5.1–4;
  1.8.1; 1.10.1–3; 1.13.3,5,6;
  1.14.1; 1.16.5; 1.18.4–6,8–10;
  2.1.1; 2.2.2; 2.4.8; 2.5.2,4,7;
  2.6.1; 2.7.3,6; 2.9.1,3,4; 2.11.2,4;
  2.12.1; 2.13.6,7,12,32,34,35;
  2.14.4,5,12,13,15; 3.1.3; 3.2.3,8;
  3.5.1,3; 3.6.5,7; 3.7.6,8;
  3.8.4–8,13; 3.9.8; 3.10.2;
  3.11.2,3; 4.1.4,7,15; 4.5.3,6,12;
  4.6.9; 4.8.1,3,9,10; 4.9.1–12;
  4.10.1; 4.12.4; 5.1.16,33n;
  5.2.4,11,13; 5.6.3; 5.7.9;
  5.8.3,4,7,9,10; 5.9.10,11;
  5.10.7,8,10,16,17
Stars, *see* Astrology
Stephen, 5.8.14
Stoics, pr Or 3n; 2.13.27n; 3.1.17n;
  5.6.3n; 5.10.13n

GENERAL INDEX

Substance (essence), 1.5.2; 1.16.6; 2.5.5; 2.13.20; 3.8.12; 3.11.2; 4.5.12; 4.8.8; 4.10.1; 4.12.1; 5.6.7
Superfluous (vain, purposeless) words/syllables not found in Scripture, int 21,21n; 1.5.2; 1.8.1; 1.9.3; 2.6.1; 2.13.15; 3.10.2; 4.2.11; 4.11.2; 5.1.22; 5.3.5; 5.8.8; 5.10.18
Synagogue(s), 2.11.4,5

Tartarus, 3.6.4
Tatian, 5.2.8n
Teichtweier, G., 5.1.14n; 5.10.16n
Tertullian, pr Or 1n; 1.5.4n; 1.15.1n
Thaddeus, pr Or 10,10n
Theodoret, 5.7.3n
Theotokos, int 17n
Thief on the cross, int 39,45,46; 3.9.3; 4.1.16; 5.9.7
Thomas (apostle), pr Or 10
Tollinton, R., 2.9.1n; 2.9.4n; 3.7.4n; 5.1.11n
Transgression (transgressor), 1.16.3; 2.3.2; 2.7.8; 2.8.6; 2.11.1,3,8; 2.12.1,4; 2.13.1–7,18; 2.14.3; 3.2.2,7; 3.8.10,13; 4.4.1–8; 4.5.10; 5.1.1,8,12,14,14n,30–38,41; 5.2.2–8,12,13,15; 5.3.2–6; 5.4.2,3; 5.5.3; 5.6.5; 5.9.8
Treasure, pr Or 7; 2.4.1,2,8; 2.6.1; 3.8.2,5; 4.5.4; 5.1.9
Tree, 2.5.6; 2.7.2; 3.6.9; 5.1.12,35; 5.9.3,7; 5.10.13
Trent, Council of, int 47–48
Trichotomous understanding of man, 1.18.5n
Trigg, J., int 21
Trinity, int 19; 3.8.4; 3.11.2; 5.8.7,9
Tübingen school, int 24
Tura Papyrus, 17
Turner, C., int 13
Two ways, 1.18.6,6n
Tyrant, 3.8.1; 4.8.1; 4.10.2; 5.1.31–33,37; 5.7.5; 5.10.11,12

Underworld, 1.5.2; 1.9.5; 2.13.28; 3.6.6; 4.2.5; 4.11.6; 5.1.36,37; 5.10.9,10,12

Unity of divine and human natures in Christ, 1.5.3; 1.6.2; 3.8.9
Uriah, 2.14.22,23
Uzziah, pr Or 10; 1.5.5

Valentinus, int 27,28,28n; 2.4.7n; 3.10.1n; 4.12.1
Variant textual readings respected, 3.1.6n; 5.1.37n
Verfaillie, C., int 26,31–34,37,39n,42n,44n,46–48
Virginity (virgin), 1.2.1; 1.12.1; 2.13.31; 3.3.1; 3.8.4; 4.5.5; 4.8.6
Virtues, pr Or 3,3n; 1.1.2–4; 1.3.4; 1.18.7,9; 2.1.3; 2.5.6,7; 3.2.9; 3.6.2; 3.8.4; 3.9.6; 4.1.12; 4.6.5,9; 4.9.3–10; 4.12.2,5; 5.2.12; 5.6.7; 5.8.13; 5.10.13,15,18
Vogt, H., 4.5.11n; 5.10.16n
Von Stritzky, 5.7.8n
Vulgate, Latin, int 14n; 2.13.24n

Wagner, M., int 12n
Wax, 2.4.1; 2.10.1; 4.5.6
Wealth (riches), 1.12.1; 1.13.3; 2.3.1; 2.4.2,4,8; 3.7.14; 4.9.2–6; 5.1.7,9,10
Westcott, B., int 12n,14,15
Wiles, M., int 2,32,36,37; pr Or 3n; 3.6.7n; 3.7.9n; 5.7.5n
Williams, N. 5.1.14n; 5.4.3n
Windisch, H., 2.7.8n
Wisdom, int 36,42,43; pr Or 2,3; 1.5.2,3; 1.12.1; 1.13.3,6; 1.14.1; 1.16.5; 1.17.2; 2.1.3; 2.5.6; 2.6.5,6; 2.7.6; 2.8.5; 2.9.2; 2.13.2; 2.14.14,19,23; 3.1.6,7,14,15,18; 3.6.7; 3.7.6,10,14; 3.8.5; 3.9.6,7; 3.10.2; 4.1.12; 4.2.5; 4.5.14; 4.7.5; 4.8.1,6; 4.9.2,4–6; 4.11.4; 5.2.6,8; 5.3.5,8; 5.8.13; 5.9.3,10; 5.10.4,5,7,18
Wolfram, H., 8n
Word of God (divine Logos), pr Or 3; 1.3.5; 1.4.3,5; 1.6.1n,2; 1.13.2; 2.5.3; 2.14.21; 3.1.14; 3.3.3; 3.8.5–9; 3.10.2; 4.5.10; 4.6.4; 4.7.5; 5.1.7,15; 5.2,12,14; 5.5.2; 5.6.7; 5.7.9; 5.8.7

Work(s)/deed(s), int 34–48; 1.3.3;
  1.10.2; 1.11.1; 1.12.1; 1.13.4,5;
  1.16.2; 1.18.7n; 1.19.5,8; 2.1.1,2;
  2.2.1; 2.4.1,2,7,7n,8; 2.5.1–3,5;
  2.6.1,3–5; 2.7.4,4n,5–7; 2.8.2;
  2.9.1,3; 2.11.8,9; 2.12.2;
  2.12.3,4; 2.13.7,23,35; 2.14.2,15;
  3.1.9; 3.2.10,12; 3.3.1–3; 3.6.1,7;
  3.7.2,12n,13,14; 3.8.1–3;
  3.9.1–8; 3.10.5; 3.11.1,2;
  4.1.1–6,9,13–18; 4.2.2,8,9;
  4.4.1,3,5–7,9,10;
  4.5.2,7,7n,10,11n; 4.6.3,8,9;
  4.7.6,8,10; 4.8.1,6,6n; 4.9.6,8;
  4.10.1; 4.11.5,6; 4.12.1,3;
  5.1.5,7,27n; 5.3.8; 5.5.3,4;
  5.8.10,12,13
Works of the Law, int 41–42
Wrath, 1.1.4; 1.16.1,3,3n,4;
  2.4.1–4,6; 2.5.1,2; 2.6.1,5,6;
  2.7.1,5; 2.14.1;
  3.1.1,4,6,8–10,12;
  4.4.1,3,6,7,7n,10; 4.11.1,4–6,6n;
  5.1.7; 5.9.9

Zebedee, pr Or 9
Zedekiah, pr Or 10
Zimran, 4.6.7
Zipporah, 2.13.18

INDEX OF HOLY SCRIPTURE

ep refers to Epilogue, int to Introduction, n to notes, pr Or to Preface of Origen, pr Ruf to Preface Rufinus. The Introduction is referenced by page number. The Prefaces and Epilogue are referenced by section number. All other entries are referenced by book, chapter, and paragraph numbers.

Old Testament

Genesis
  1.26–27: 4.5.11
  1.27: 1.19.8;
    2.13.34; 5.1.22;
    5.1.28
  2.7: 2.13.34
  2.8ff.: 2.5.6
  2.17: 5.1.12
  3.1: 5.1.12
  3.4–5: 5.1.12
  3.6–7: 5.1.35
  3.14: 5.1.29
  3.23: 5.1.35
  3.23–24: 5.4.3
  4.1: 5.9.11
  4.2: 4.1.15
  4.3–4: 5.1.20
  4.4: 5.1.35
  4.7: 5.5.7
  4.8ff.: 5.1.23
  4.11: 5.6.2
  4.13: 3.6.1
  4.23: 5.1.23; 5.6.2
  4.24: 5.6.2
  4.26: 5.1.20
  5.22: 5.1.20
  5.24: 5.1.20; 5.4.3
  5.32: 5.1.20
  6.3: 1.18.5
  6.5ff.: 2.3.2
  6.5–7: 5.6.2
  6.6–7: 3.1.11
  6.7: 5.1.23
  6.8: 4.5.4; 5.1.20

6.8–9: 5.1.20
6.11–12: 5.6.2
6.14: 3.1.11; 3.1.12
6.17: 5.1.23
9.21: 5.1.20
9.24: 5.1.20
9.26–27: 1.8.1
12.1: 4.4.2; 4.7.10;
  5.1.20
12.1ff.: 4.1.9
12.1–3: 4.3.1
12.2–3: 4.7.10
12.3: 4.2.4; 4.5.9
12.4: 4.7.10
13.14–15: 4.1.9
13.15: 4.6.8
13.18: 4.1.9
14.18–20: 1.8.1
14.19–20: 4.1.9
15.2–3: 4.6.2
15.3–6: 4.1.8
15.4–6: 4.6.2
15.5: 4.6.7
15.6: 3.8.14; 4.1.2;
  4.1.10; 4.1.12;
  4.2.11n 4.3.1;
  4.6.2; 4.7.1;
  4.7.9
15.16: 2.3.2
17.5: pr Or 9; 4.2.7;
  4.2.11; 4.5.9
17.9–12: 2.13.11
17.9–14: 2.13.8
17.12: 2.9.1; 2.12.2

17.12–13: 2.13.11
17.14: 2.13.8n
17.15: pr Or 9
17.17: 4.6.7
18.11: 4.6.7
18.20ff.: 2.3.2
18.21: 5.6.2
19.4ff.: 5.6.2
19.24: 5.1.23
21.2–4: 4.2.4
22.2: 4.7.3
23.1: 4.6.7
25.1–2: 4.6.7
25.1ff.: 4.1.7; 4.5.6
25.12ff.: 4.5.6
25.20: 4.6.7
25.23: 2.7.2
27: 2.7.2
27.28–29: 1.8.1
35.10: pr Or 9
39.4: 4.5.4
39.21: 4.5.4
42.21: 3.6.1
49.1–28: 1.8.1
49.8–9: 2.11.4;
  2.13.36

Exodus
  1.14: 5.6.2
  1.22: 5.6.2
  3.6: 1.9.3
  3.14: 4.5.12 4.10:
    2.13.25
  4.13: 2.13.25

INDEX OF HOLY SCRIPTURE 395

4.24–25: 2.13.18
6.12: 2.13.25
6.30: 2.13.25
8.12: 2.13.12
9.27: 5.5.7
12.15–20: 2.9.1
12.48: 2.13.17
12.48–49: 2.13.17
14.31: int 43;
    1.13.1; 1.15.1;
    4.1.12; 4.4.10;
    4.4.11
16.29: 1.10.2;
    5.1.40
20.12–16: 2.9.1
21.13: 2.8.6
21.15: 5.1.25
21.17: 5.1.25
23.1: 2.13.24
23.15: 2.9.1
25.9: 3.8.13
25.10ff.: 3.8.2
25.17–22: 3.8.2
25.18–19: 3.8.5
25.19: 3.8.5
25.21: 3.8.7
25.22: 3.8.8
25.40: 3.8.13
26.30: 3.8.13
28.18: 3.8.5
31.18: 2.12.1;
    2.14.12
32.19: 2.14.12
33.11: 4.12.2
33.13: 4.5.4
34.29: 2.5.4
35.3: 5.1.40
40.34: 2.5.5; 4.8.7

Leviticus
1.2: 2.13.13
4: 5.1.31
4.1–2: 2.13.13
4.3ff.: 3.8.13
4.13–14: 3.8.10
4.13ff.: 3.8.13
4.16: 3.8.10
4.20: 3.8.10; 3.8.13
4.22ff.: 3.8.13
4.27ff.: 3.8.13
6.1–2: 2.13.13

6.17–18: 2.13.13
9.1: 2.13.13
9.3: 2.13.13
9.23: 4.8.7
10.1–2: 2.2.2
10.3: 2.2.2
10.8–9: 2.13.13
11.1–2: 2.13.13
12.1–4: 2.13.9
12.2: 2.13.12
12.3: 2.13.12
12.3: 2.9.1; 2.12.2
12.4: 2.13.9n
12.8: 5.9.11
13.48ff.: 1.10.2
14.37ff.: 1.10.2
17.1–2: 10–12:
    2.13.13
17.8–9: 2.13.15
17.13–14: 2.13.14
18.22: 4.4.9
19.15: 2.5.6
20.2: 2.8.6; 4.4.7
20.14: 2.8.6; 4.4.7
20.27: 2.8.6; 4.4.7
21.9: 2.8.6; 4.4.7
26.12: 2.6.6; 3.8.6

Numbers
6.2: 2.13.12
6.23: 2.13.12
17.7: 4.8.7
18.7: 2.13.23
18.26: 2.13.12
22.7ff.: 1.11.2
23.8: 3.4.2
35.11ff.: 2.8.6
36.8–9: 1.5.4
36.13: 2.13.6

Deuteronomy
2.9: 2.11.5
5.31: 5.8.14
9.10: 2.12.1
13.4: 5.8.14
13.11: 4.4.7
16.5–6: 2.13.17
17.5: 4.4.7
22.11: 2.9.1
28.43: 2.13.18
28.43–44: 2.13.14;

    2.13.18
29.17: 3.4.2
29.28: 4.1.3
30.15: 1.18.7,7n
32.7: 5.1.41
32.22: 4.11.6
32.33: 1.16.4
33: 1.8.1

Joshua
1.5: 3.8.6
5.2ff.: 2.13.26
5.6: 2.13.26
5.9: 2.13.26
6.27: 3.8.6
20: 2.8.6

Judges
2.12: 4.11.3

1 Samuel
2.30: 2.6.2
16.7: 4.1.3

2 Samuel
11.2–4: 2.14.23
11.3: 2.14.23
11.26–27: 2.14.22
12.18,24: 2.14.23
12.25: pr Or 10
24.1: 1.16.3

1 Kings
4.29: 2.6.6
8.10–11: 2.5.5
8.11: 4.8.7
8.39: 1.3.3; 2.1.1;
    2.10.1; 4.1.5
11.1–8: 2.14.23
13.9,19,24: 1.2.1
15.26: 5.1.35
15.34: 5.1.35
19.18: 2.14.7

2 Kings
2.11: 5.4.3
8.25: 1.5.5
11.2: 1.5.5
14.1: 1.5.5
15.1: 1.5.5
15.1,7,32,34: 1.5.5

INDEX OF HOLY SCRIPTURE

2 Kings *(continued)*
  15.1–7: pr Or 10
  15.32–34: pr Or 10
  25.7: pr Or 10
  25.27: pr Or 10

1 Chronicles
  3.11–12: 1.5.5
  28.9: 1.3.3

2 Chronicles
  5.13–14: 2.5.5
  5.14: 4.8.7
  7.1–2: 2.5.5
  7.3: 4.8.7
  7.22: 4.11.3
  24.18: 4.11.3
  24.24: 4.11.3
  28.6: 4.11.3

Tobit
  1.17: 3.3.2
  4.15: 2.9.1; 3.7.6
  12.7: 2.4.5; 5.1.10
  12.11: 5.1.10
  12.15: 4.12.2

Esther
  2.15: 4.5.5
  2.17: 4.5.5

2 Maccabees
  7.1–42: 4.10.2

Job
  1.1: 2.12.3
  3.8: 5.10.10
  5.13: 2.14.24
  6.4: 1.16.3
  14.4–5: 5.1.21; 5.5.4; 5.9.4; 5.9.11
  23.8: 3.2.13
  25.5: 3.6.8
  29.12: 3.3.2
  31.33–34: 3.6.1
  32.8: 2.9.4

Psalms
  2.1: 3.7.6
  4.1: 2.6.6
  5.9: 3.2.6; 3.3.3
  10.7: 3.2.6
  12.7: 2.14.14
  14.2: 3.2.6
  14.3: 2.3.1; 3.2.4; 3.2.6
  14.5: 3.5.3
  15.3: 2.13.24
  16.10: 1.5.2
  18.1: 2.14.22
  18.7: 2.14.22
  18.10: 2.14.22
  18.11: 2.14.22
  19.4: 1.4.5; 1.7.1; 1.9.4
  19.9: 3.1.3
  22.15: 5.3.3; 5.9.10
  27.3: 3.5.3
  28.1: 5.10.10
  30.9: 5.10.10
  31.19: 2.4.4; 2.4.8; 2.7.3; 2.8.4; 5.2.13
  32.1: 4.1.19
  32.1–2: 2.1.2; 2.1.3; 4.2.2
  32.2: 4.2.2
  32.10: 4.9.8
  34.10: 3.5.3
  34.19: 4.9.8
  36.1: 3.2.6
  36.6: 3.7.5
  36.9: 5.8.9
  37.27: 2.12.2
  43.3: 5.1.33
  43.20: 5.4.3
  43.26: 5.4.3
  44.25: 5.9.10; 5.9.11
  44.26: 5.1.33
  45.2: 1.7.1
  45.13: 2.11.5
  46.10: 2.5.8
  49.12,20: 2.5.6; 3.5.1
  50.16: 3.7.13
  50.17: 4.11.2
  51.4: 2.14.22; 2.14.24; 3.6.1
  51.5: 5.9.10; 5.9.11
  51.17: 3.5.1
  53.2: 3.2.6
  53.5: 3.5.3
  56.3–4: 3.5.3
  58.3: 1.3.1
  59.11: 1.14.1
  68.11: 1.4.5
  68.18: 5.1.37; 5.10.11; 5.10.12
  72.14: 3.3.2
  73.2: 3.4.3
  73.8ff.: 1.19.6
  73.9: 2.3.1; 2.14.11
  76.2: 3.5.2
  77.5: 1.4.1; 5.1.41
  78.38: 4.11.6
  78.49: 1.16.3,38 2.6: 2.14.21; 3.1.10; 3.1.11
  82.7: 3.1.11
  83.7: 5.4.3
  88.5: 5.10.6
  94.10: pr Or 2; 2.14.19
  94.10–11: 2.14.19
  94.12: 3.5.3; 5.2.13
  103.2–3: 2.6.4
  106.3: 5.3.8
  106.31: int 43; 4.1.12n
  110.4: 3.8.11
  115.4–6: 4.5.10
  115.8: 4.5.10
  116.2: 2.14.19
  116.11: 2.14.19
  116.13: 2.14.19
  116.15: 2.14.19
  118.6: 3.5.3
  119.165: 3.5.2
  119.176: 2.8.4
  122.7: 2.14.18
  128.2: 1.13.5
  139.7: 2.2.2
  140.3: 3.2.6
  141.3: 2.13.25
  143.2: 3.2.10; 3.2.13
  144.4: 5.1.33
  147.15: 1.4.5
  148.4–5: 5.8.3

INDEX OF HOLY SCRIPTURE

Proverbs
 1.6: pr Or 2; 1.4.2;
  5.2.13
 1.16: 3.2.6
 3.12: 2.2.2
 3.13–14: 4.5.4
 3.18: 5.9.3
 11.13: 5.2.13
 13.8: 3.7.14
 16.23: 2.14.6
 18.17: 5.5.6
 19.14: 1.12.1
 20.9: int 42; 3.9.7
 26.11: 5.7.7
 31.10,22: 2.14.23

Ecclesiastes
 4.2–3: 3.2.13
 7.29: 3.3.1

Wisdom
 1.1: 3.7.6
 1.7: 3.2.9
 2.17: 3.2.13
 2.24: 5.1.29
 5.6: 5.1.40
 7.25–26: 1.5.2
 9.6: 5.3.8
 9.15: 3.2.14
 10.1: 5.2.8
 11.20: 2.3.2
 12.1: 2.9.4
 12.1–2: 2.9.3

Sirach
 4.25–27: 2.5.6
 11.28: 3.2.13
 12.16: 3.3.4n
 15.9: 3.7.13
 15.16–17: 1.18.7
 20.10: 1.12.1
 25.24: 5.1.12
 28.28 Vlg: 2.13.24
 44.16: 5.1.20

Isaiah
 1.18: 2.14.17
 3.1–3: 2.14.7
 3.14: 2.14.17
 5.21: 2.6.4; 4.9.5
 6.2: 3.8.6

 6.10: 2.4.1
 8.14: 1.18.4
 8.20: 2.8.4
 11.1: 3.5.3
 11.3: 3.5.3
 13.9: 2.4.3
 13.13: 2.4.3
 14.12: 5.10.13;
  5.10.16
 26.20: 2.4.4
 29.14: 2.8.5
 33.15: 2.13.24
 35.10: 4.8.8
 39.2: 5.1.9
 40.5: 2.13.36
 40.6: 2.13.36; 3.6.7
 43.12: 1.10.1
 43.26: 2.14.17
 44.22: 3.1.11
 50.11: 2.6.2; 5.1.40
 51.7: 1.14.1
 51.11: 4.8.8
 52.5: 2.11.12
 52.7: 1.4.553.4:
  4.11.4
 53.9: 3.3.4; 3.8.3;
  5.1.19
 58.7: 3.3.2
 59.7: 3.2.6
 59.7–8: 3.2.6
 61.1–2: 1.4.3
 64.6: int 42; 3.9.7

Jeremiah
 2.20: 3.5.1
 5.5: 3.5.1
 6.10: 2.13.24
 9.2: 2.3.1
 9.22–24: 4.9.2
 9.23: 4.9.5
 12.10: 2.11.5
 13.17: 2.11.5
 16.16: 1.4.5
 17.21: 5.1.40
 17.27: 5.1.40
 23.24: 3.2.9
 51.26: 5.6.7

Lamentations
 3.34–36: 5.9.10

Baruch
 3.36: 4.11.3
 3.38: 4.11.3
 4.4: 2.7.1

Ezekiel
 2.10: 1.4.1
 11.19: 2.4.1
 13.6: 5.8.9
 16.3: 4.2.9
 16.51–52: int 43;
  3.2.10; 3.2.11
 18.4: 4.5.10; 5.1.19;
  5.3.3
 18.20: 4.5.10
 18.24: 2.4.7
 28.13: 5.10.13
 28.14: 5.10.13
 28.14–17: 5.10.16
 28.15: 5.1.17;
  5.10.13
 28.17: 5.1.17;
  5.10.13
 28.19: 5.6.7
 31.8: 5.10.13
 34.3–4: 1.2.1
 34.4: 2.8.4
 34.16: 2.8.4
 36.26: 2.4.1
 44.9: 2.13.22;
  2.13.23; 2.13.24

Daniel
 2.21: 1.12.1
 3.20ff.: 4.10.2
 3.27: 3.1.3
 3.86: 1.10.2; 2.9.4
 7.9: 3.2.11
 7.10: 1.4.1; 4.12.2
 7.13: 3.2.11
 13.42: 1.3.2
 13.56: 4.2.9

Hosea
 2.20–21: 2.11.6
 9.5: 5.1.41
 13.14: 5.1.21;
  5.1.36

Joel
 1.14–15: 2.4.3

INDEX OF HOLY SCRIPTURE

Joel *(continued)*
  2.1–5: 2.4.3
  2.11: 2.4.3
  2.25: 1.14.1

Amos
  5.18–20: 2.4.3
  6.1: 2.14.10

Jonah
  2.1: 5.10.10

Micah
  4.2: 3.6.5
  6.8: 2.7.5

Habakkuk
  2.4: 1.13.1; 1.15.1; 4.1.4,4n
  3.2: 3.8.8

Zephaniah
  1.7: 2.4.3
  1.14–18: 2.4.3

Zechariah
  5.6–8: 5.6.8
  11.16: 1.2.1

Malachi
  3.20: 2.6.6; 5.1.40

New Testament

Matthew
  1.6–16: 1.5.4
  1.8: 1.5.5
  1.18: 1.5.4
  3.7: 4.11.6; 4.2.4; 4.5.9
  3.10: 1.13.4
  3.11: 5.8.3
  3.15: 5.8.6
  4.1–11: 5.1.21n
  4.17: 5.3.7
  5.8: 4.8.8
  5.16: 5.8.12
  5.17: 2.13.6; 3.11.4
  5.18: 2.6.1; 4.2.11
  5.26: 5.2.14
  5.28: int 42; 2.13.35; 3.9.7
  5.45: 2.3.1; 3.1.15
  6.1: 3.7.6
  6.2: 2.1.1
  6.3: 3.7.6
  6.4: 4.1.3
  6.6: 4.1.3
  6.10: 2.14.18; 5.3.7
  6.12: 4.1.15
  6.16: 1.2.1
  6.18: 4.1.3
  6.19: 2.4.2
  6.19–20: 2.4.2
  6.20: 2.4.2
  6.23: 2.11.5
  7.2: 4.1.15
  7.7–8: 5.1.4
  7.12: 2.9.1,1n; 3.7.6
  7.13: 3.8.4
  7.13–14: 1.18.6n; 2.3.1; 4.9.8
  7.18: 3.6.9
  7.23: 4.1.15
  7.24: int 35; 2.13.23
  8.4: 2.13.15
  8.10: 2.14.9
  8.11: 5.5.2
  8.11–12: 2.14.9
  8.13: 4.6.3
  8.17: 4.11.4
  9.9: pr Or 10
  9.12: 5.10.13
  9.22: 3.9.4; 4.6.3
  9.29: 4.6.3
  10.3–4: pr Or 10
  10.26: 2.4.4; 3.7.11
  10.29: 3.1.15
  10.32: 1.10.1; 4.10.1
  10.34: 5.3.7
  10.39: 2.13.29
  11.11: 3.2.13
  11.27: 1.16.6; 3.8.8
  11.28: 1.15.1
  11.29: 1.1.1; 4.8.5
  11.30: 5.6.8
  12.28: 2.12.1
  12.29: 5.3.7; 5.10.11; 5.10.12
  12.33: int 28; 3.6.9
  12.34: 3.3.3
  12.36: 2.13.25
  12.40: 5.8.9; 5.10.10
  12.39–40: 4.2.5
  12.42: 2.13.2
  12.43: 5.1.37
  12.45: 3.2.13
  12.50: 4.6.9
  13.15: 2.4.1
  13.17: 5.5.5
  13.44: 2.4.8; 4.5.4
  13.45–46: 1.13.5
  13.51: 5.2.14
  15.14: 2.11.5
  15.24: 2.8.4; 2.8.5; 4.7.3
  15.32: 5.8.14
  16.18: 5.10.15
  16.25: 2.13.29
  17.1–3: 2.5.4
  17.3: 1.10.3
  18.10: 1.18.6; 4.12.2
  19.4: 5.6.3
  19.6: 1.5.3
  19.12: 2.13.21; 2.13.31
  20.16: 2.7.2; 2.13.18
  20.22: 2.14.19
  21.19: 2.7.2
  21.43: 2.14.13
  22.14: 1.2.1
  22.20: 3.1.12; 4.8.9
  22.30: 2.13.21
  22.37–39: 5.10.15
  22.38: 5.10.15
  23.4: 1.18.3; 3.7.4
  23.5: 2.11.4
  23.12: 5.5.6

INDEX OF HOLY SCRIPTURE

23.27: 3.3.3
23.38: 2.7.2
24.2: 2.13.17
24.24: 3.1.14
24.40–41: 2.9.4
24.45: 3.3.1
25.1–12: 4.8.6
25.21: 3.3.1
25.31: 4.8.9
25.33: 1.14.1
25.35–36: 3.3.2
25.41: 1.14.1; 2.4.6;
   5.1.29
26.7,10: 2.5.3
26.29: 5.1.41
26.38: 1.5.2
26.67: 2.5.6
27.29–30: 2.5.6
27.50: 5.10.3
27.52–53: 1.6.3;
   5.1.37; 5.10.12
27.59–60: 5.8.4
27.60: 5.8.4; 5.10.3
28.5–6: 5.10.3
28.19: 5.2.11; 5.8.7

Mark
1.1–2: 1.3.5
3.16–17: pr Or 9
3.18: pr Or 10
3.27: 5.3.7
5.34: 3.9.4
10.18: 4.10.1
10.29: 1.4.5
10.52: 3.9.4; 4.6.3
15.17,19: 2.5.6
16.6: 5.10.3

Luke
1.5: 1.5.4
1.19: 4.12.2
1.35: 5.9.10
1.36: 1.5.4
2.21: 2.13.29
2.33: 1.5.5
2.34: 4.2.5
2.48: 1.5.5
3.6: 2.13.36
3.7: 4.11.6
3.8: pr Or 5; 4.2.4;
   4.5.9

3.23–31: 1.5.4
4.1–13: 5.1.21n
4.18: 1.4.3; 1.7.1
5.27: pr Or 10
6.15–16: pr Or 10
6.16: 1.2.1
6.31: 2.9.1; 3.7.6
6.38: 4.1.15
6.40: 2.11.10
6.43: 3.6.9
6.46: int 35; 2.13.23
7.37–39: int 40;
   3.9.4
7.41–42: 4.1.15
7.47: 4.1.15
7.48: 3.9.4
7.50: 3.9.4
8.10: 1.13.2
8.17: 3.7.11
8.45: 4.9.8
8.48: 3.9.4
9.26: 4.8.9
9.30–31: 1.10.3
10.6: 1.8.1
10.18: 4.11.4
10.19: 5.8.9
11.2: 5.3.7
11.20: 2.12.1
11.22: 5.3.7
11.24: 5.1.37
11.26: 3.2.13
11.46: 1.18.3; 3.7.4
12.2: 2.4.4
12.8: 4.10.1
12.16–18: 2.4.2
12.20: 2.4.2
12.21: 2.4.2
12.42: 5.1.7; 5.1.9;
   5.2.12; 5.5.2
12.46: int 41; 2.9.4;
   2.12.4
12.47: 2.7.1
12.48: 2.7.1
13.27: 4.1.15
13.29: 2.14.9
13.30: 2.7.2
15.8: 2.8.4; 4.7.3
15.10: 1.9.4
15.12–13: 2.8.4
15.17: 2.1.3
15.31–32: 2.8.4

16.16: 5.1.34
16.24: 1.18.3; 3.7.4
17.5: 4.1.11; 4.5.3;
   4.6.4
17.10: 3.3.1
17.12–14: 2.13.15
17.15–18: 2.13.15
17.19: 3.9.4; 4.6.3
18.1off.: int 42
18.10–12: 3.9.6
18.14: 3.9.6; 5.5.6
18.19: 4.10.1
18.42: 3.9.4; 4.6.3
19.10: 2.8.4; 2.8.5;
   4.7.3
20.35: 2.5.7
21.19: 2.5.3; 2.7.4
22.27: 1.1.1
22.20: 5.1.40
23.39: 4.1.16
23.40: 5.9.7
23.42: int 39; 3.9.3;
   4.1.16; 5.9.7
23.43: int 39; 3.9.3;
   5.9.7
23.46: 5.10.3
24.1–5: 5.10.3
24.6: 5.10.3

John
1.1: 1.3.5; 4.7.5;
   5.6.7
1.1–3: 3.10.2
1.3–4: 3.10.2
1.4: 5.1.21
1.9: pr Or 2
1.14: 1.4.3; 4.8.9;
   4.8.10; 5.8.7
1.29: 3.8.11; 4.11.4;
   5.1.8
1.33: 5.8.3
1.45: 1.5.5; 4.8.10
1.51: 1.9.4
2.19: 2.11.7
3.3: 2.7.3; 5.2.11;
   5.8.3
3.5: 2.7.3; 2.7.6;
   5.8.3; 5.9.11
3.16: 4.11.1; 4.11.4
3.18: 2.7.7
3.30: 3.11.5

3.31: 2.4.2
3.34: 4.1.15
4.7: 3.7.7
4.10: 3.7.7
4.13–14: 3.7.7
4.23: 1.10.2
4.35: 3.7.7
5.19: 3.2.11
5.22: 2.10.1
5.23: 2.5.6
5.39: 3.7.10
5.46: 2.11.8; 2.14.8;
   3.11.1; 4.4.10;
   4.4.11
6.42: 1.5.5
6.63: 3.6.7
7.22–23: 2.13.9
8.39: 4.2.8
8.39–40: 4.7.10
8.44: 5.1.12; 5.8.9
8.56:1.10.3; 4.7.3
9.1ff.: 3.7.7
9.39: 3.7.7
10.9: 4.8.5; 5.4.2
10.11: 3.3.2
10.15: 1.18.6
10.17–18: 1.5.2
10.18: 5.1.19;
   5.10.6
10.30: 1.3.5
10.35: 2.14.21;
   3.1.10
12.27: 1.5.2
12.32: 5.10.15
12.44: 4.4.11
13.17: 5.2.14
14.6: 1.1.3; 1.18.7;
   2.5.6; 2.6.5;
   2.7.5; 3.1.15;
   3.6.5; 4.7.5;
   4.8.5; 4.9.8;
   5.3.7; 5.6.7
14.9: 4.4.11
14.15,21,23:
   2.13.23
14.23: 1.18.10
15.1ff.: 1.13.4
15.1–2: 5.9.6
15.1–8: 1.13.4
15.6: 1.13.4

15.15: 4.3.1; 4.12.2
15.19: 5.1.15
15.22: 3.2.9
16.11: 4.11.4
16.20,33: 2.7.4
17.3: 2.5.8; 2.7.4;
   2.7.5; 3.1.15
17.10: 1.3.5
17.12: 2.8.5
17.21: 4.9.12; 5.9.7
17.24: 5.9.7
21.15–17: 5.10.15

Acts
1.8: 1.10.1
1.24: 4.1.5
2.24: 5.1.37; 5.10.6
2.27: 1.5.2
4.12: 2.7.3
7.2–3: 4.3.1
7.55: 5.8.14
7.58: pr Or 9
8.3: 5.5.6
9.1: pr Or 9
9.2: 5.5.6
9.15: 2.14.7
10.9ff.: 5.1.40
10.11ff.: 2.13.3
10.15:
   5.1.4010.34–35:
   2.7.7
13.6–12: pr Or 9
13.9: pr Or 10
15.20: 2.9.1;
   2.13.14
15.29: 2.9.1;
   2.13.14; 3.7.6
16.7: 1.13.2
17.25: 2.14.19
19.3–5: 5.8.6
21.26: 2.13.3

Romans
lemmata in bold
1.1: int 27; **1.1.1**;
   1.2.1; **1.3.1**;
   1.7.1
1.2: **1.4.1**
1.3: **1.5.1**
1.3–4: 1.6.1

1.4: 1.5.1; **1.6.1**
1.5: **1.7.1**
1.6: 1.7.1
1.7: 1.7.1; **1.8.1**
1.8: **1.9.1**; 2.11.2
1.9: **1.10.1**
1.9–10: **1.11.1**
1.10–11: 1.13.3
1.11–12: **1.12.1**
1.13: 1.9.6; 1.13.3
1.13–15: **1.13.1**
1.15: 1.13.7
1.16: 1.13.1; **1.14.1**;
   1.14.2
1.17: 1.13.1; **1.15.1**;
   4.1.4
1.18: 3.1.9
1.18–19: **1.16.1**
1.18–2.1: 2.1.1
1.19: 1.16.6
1.20: 1.16.6; 2.7.1
1.20–23: **1.17.1**
1.21: 1.16.1; 2.7.6
1.21–23: 1.16.5
1.21–24: 1.19.2
1.22–23: 1.16.1;
   3.2.3
1.22–28: 1.18.2n
1.24–25: **1.18.1**
1.25–26: 1.19.2
1.26–27: 1.19.2
1.26–2.1: **1.19.1**
1.28: 3.2.3
1.28–29: 1.19.2
1.29–31: 5.9.9
2.1: 2.11.2
2.2: **2.1.1**
2.3: **2.2.1**
2.4: **2.3.1**; 2.4.4;
   3.8.14
2.4–5: 5.1.7
2.5: 1.16.3; 2.10.1
2.5–6: **2.4.1**
2.6: int 33
2.7: 2.6.1; 2.7.4
2.7–11: **2.5.1**
2.8–9: **2.6.1**; 2.14.1
2.9: **2.7.1**
2.9–16: 2.7.4n
2.10: 2.7.5; 2.14.2

INDEX OF HOLY SCRIPTURE

2.11: 2.7.7
2.12: 2.8.7; 2.14.2
2.12–13: **2.8.1**
2.13: 2.8.3; 2.9.1
2.14: 2.7.6
2.14–15: 2.8.2;
   2.14.2; 3.2.9;
   3.6.7; 4.4.9
2.14–16: **2.9.1**
2.15: 2.8.2; 3.2.7;
   4.3.2
2.15–16: int 27;
   1.16.3; 2.4.4;
   2.10.1
2.16: 1.3.5
2.17: 3.2.3
2.17–24: **2.11.1**;
   2.11.11n; 2.14.2
2.21: 3.2.3
2.25: 2.13.4; 2.14.3
2.25–29: **2.12.1**
2.26: 2.14.3
2.26–27: **2.13.1**;
   2.13.5; 3.2.2
2.27: 2.11.3; 2.14.3
2.28: 2.11.4
2.28–29: 2.13.34;
   2.14.4; 3.2.8
2.29: 2.7.2; 2.11.4;
   4.1.4; 4.2.6
3.1–2: 3.2.2; 3.9.2
3.1–4: **2.14.1**
3.2: 2.5.2; 2.7.1
3.4: 3.1.3; 3.1.6;
   3.6.1; 3.6.2;
   3.6.5
3.5: 2.14.17; 3.1.6
3.5–8: **3.1.1**
3.9ff.: int 43
3.9–11: 3.6.9
3.9–18: **3.2.1**
3.12: **3.3.1**
3.13: **3.4.1**
3.14: 3.4.2
3.15: 3.4.3
3.16–17: **3.5.1**
3.17: 3.5.2
3.18: 3.5.3
3.19: 1.9.5; 2.2.1;
   3.7.2

3.19–20: **3.6.1**
3.20: 2.13.23;
   3.11.1
3.21: int 38; 3.7.5;
   3.7.6
3.21–24: **3.7.1**
3.22–26: 3.9.2
3.23: 5.1.20
3.24: 3.7.14; 3.8.1
3.25: 3.8.2n; 3.9.4
3.25–26: **3.8.1**
3.27: 4.1.2; 4.4.2;
   4.4.5; 4.4.10
3.27ff.: 5.1.2
3.27–28: **3.9.1**
3.28: int 39; 3.9.3n;
   3.11.1; 4.1.2;
   4.5.7
3.29: 2.5.2; 2.7.9
3.29–30: int 40;
   3.10.1
3.31: **3.11.1**
4.1: 4.6.7
4.1–8: int 31; **4.1.1**
4.3: 3.8.14; 3.9.5;
   4.1.10; 4.1.12;
   4.2.2; 4.2.11n;
   4.3.1; 4.4.1;
   4.4.10; 4.7.1;
   4.7.4; 4.7.9
4.4–5: 4.5.1
4.5: 4.1.10; 4.1.12
4.6–8: 4.2.2
4.8: 4.2.2
4.9: 4.1.10; 4.1.12;
   4.6.5
4.9–12: **4.2.1**
4.11: 3.9.5; 4.2.7;
   4.5.9
4.13: **4.3.1**; 4.4.1;
   4.5.9
4.13ff.: 5.1.2
4.14: 4.5.7
4.14–15: **4.4.1**
4.15: 3.2.7
4.16–17: **4.5.1**
4.17: 4.2.7; 4.5.9;
   4.5.10
4.18–22: **4.6.1**
4.22: 4.6.2; 4.6.5

4.23–25: **4.7.1**
5.1: 4.8.1; 4.11.5
5.1–2: **4.8.1**; 4.9.1
5.3: 2.6.6
5.3–5: **4.9.1**
5.5: 4.9.11; 4.10.1;
   5.10.16
5.6: 4.11.1; 5.7.5
5.6–7: **4.10.1**
5.8: 4.11.3
5.8–9: **4.11.1**
5.9: 4.11.1
5.10: 4.8.1; 5.1.2
5.10–11: int 27;
   4.12.1
5.12: 5.1.1n; 5.1.7;
   5.2.4; 5.2.5;
   5.2.9; 5.3.5;
   5.5.2; 5.7.6
5.12–14: **5.1.1**
5.13: 3.2.8; 3.2.9
5.14: 5.2.2; 5.2.7;
   5.2.10; 5.2.11;
   5.2.12; 5.2.15;
   5.3.5
5.15: 5.1.6; 5.1.7;
   5.2.4; 5.2.7;
   5.3.2; 5.3.5;
   5.4.2; 5.8.2
5.15–16: **5.2.1**
5.16: 5.2.15; 5.3.2;
   5.3.5
5.17: 5.1.8; 5.2.2;
   5.2.5; 5.2.13;
   5.3.1
5.18: 5.1.6; 5.1.7;
   5.1.8; 5.2.8;
   5.2.9; 5.2.13;
   5.2.15; **5.4.1**
5.19: 5.1.6; 5.1.38;
   5.2.2; 5.2.4;
   5.2.7; **5.5.1**;
   5.5.8; 5.5.9
5.20: 5.7.2; 5.7.6;
   5.8.2; 5.9.2
5.20–21: **5.6.1**
5.21: 5.2.2; 5.2.5;
   5.2.13; 5.2.15;
   5.7.9
6.1: 5.9.2n

Romans (continued)
6.1–2: **5.7.1**
6.2: 5.7.3n; 5.7.10; 5.8.2; 5.8.10; 5.9.2; 5.10.2
6.3: 5.9.2; 5.10.2
6.3–4: **5.8.1**
6.4: 4.7.5; 4.7.8; 5.8.10; 5.10.4; 5.10.9
6.5: pr Or 4; 5.7.10; 5.9.2; 5.9.6; 5.10.2
6.5–6: int 45; **5.9.1**
6.6: 5.9.10
6.8: 5.1.5; 5.1.16; 5.10.9
6.8–10: **5.10.1**
6.8–11: 4.7.5
6.9: 1.6.1
6.10: 4.12.5; 5.7.10; 5.8.10; 5.9.4; 5.9.6
6.11: pr Or 5; 4.12.5; 5.10.2; 5.10.17; 5.10.18
6.11: int 36
6.12: int 29; 5.1.37; 5.6.6; 5.6.7; 5.7.3
6.13: 5.6.6
6.17: 5.5.9
6.19: 5.6.6
6.23: int 32; 4.1.15
7.8: 5.1.25
7.8–9: 5.1.23; 5.1.24; 5.1.27
7.9: 3.2.7; 3.2.8; 3.2.9; 3.6.1; 5.1.26; 5.1.27
7.9–10: 5.1.26
7.10: 5.1.26
7.13: 3.9.8
7.14: 1.10.2; 2.8.3; 2.11.2; 2.13.19; 3.7.8
7.22: 1.19.8; 2.13.34
7.22–23: 4.4.5; 5.6.4

7.23: 4.4.6; 4.4.10; 4.8.3; 5.6.3
7.24: 5.9.10; 5.9.11; 5.10.8
8.1: int 36
8.2: 3.9.8
8.3: 1.10.2; 2.13.7; 5.1.33; 5.9.10
8.5: 5.1.16
8.7: 3.6.7; 4.8.1
8.8: 2.13.7; 3.6.7
8.9: 1.5.3; 1.18.5; 2.13.35; 3.8.13
8.13: 1.10.2; 2.13.7; 2.13.35
8.14: 5.1.16; 5.8.10
8.15: 1.1.1; 4.9.11
8.16: 2.9.4
8.17: 1.3.5
8.24: 4.8.9
8.24–25: 4.6.3
8.29: 1.3.4; 1.5.1
8.29–30: int 26n; pr Or 1n
8.32: 4.10.1; 4.11.1; 4.11.4; 5.10.15
8.35: 5.10.15
8.35–9.1: pr Or 6
8.35ff.: 5.1.2
8.37: pr Or 6
8.38: 5.10.15
8.38–39: pr Or 6
8.39: 5.10.15
9.3: 1.5.4
9.7: 4.2.8
9.8: 4.2.8
9.20–23: int 28
9.27: 3.1.3
9.33: 1.18.4
10.4: 3.6.5; 5.1.36
10.9: int 35
10.10: 5.10.4
10.15: 1.4.5
10.18: 1.7.1; 1.9.4
10.20: 5.10.6
11.4: 2.14.7
11.6: int 41
11.11: 3.1.3
11.25–26: 4.2.7; 4.2.8

11.33: 3.7.5
11.36: 3.10.2; 3.10.3
12.2: 2.11.9
12.3: 4.5.3
12.6: 4.5.3
12.14: 3.4.2
13.3: 3.5.3
13.7: 2.5.6
13.14: 4.7.7
14.1–2: 4.6.4
14.2: 2.14.14; 4.6.4
14.10: 2.7.6
16.1: pr Or 7
16.17: 2.4.5
16.23: pr Or 7
16.25: 1.3.5; 5.1.2

1 Corinthians
1.3: 1.8.1
1.4: 1.9.1
1.10: 4.8.3
1.14: pr Or 7
1.19: 2.8.5
1.20: 4.5.14
1.21: int 42; 3.9.7
1.24: 1.5.2; 1.14.1; 3.1.15; 4.7.5; 5.2.8; 5.9.3
1.26–27: 4.5.14
1.27: 3.9.7
1.28–29: 4.5.14
1.30: int 25,36,48; 1.1.3; 1.5.3; 2.5.6; 2.6.5; 3.6.5; 3.7.10; 3.7.14; 4.7.5; 4.7.8; 4.8.5; 5.5.8; 5.6.7; 5.10.18
1.31: 3.9.7; 4.9.4
2.2: 1.13.3; 2.14.14
2.4: 1.14.1
2.6: 1.13.3; 2.14.14; 5.2.6
2.6–7: 1.13.6
2.7–8: 4.11.4
2.8: 1.6.2
2.10: 3.8.5; 3.8.8
2.11: 2.9.4

INDEX OF HOLY SCRIPTURE

2.13: 1.14.1
2.14: 2.14.15
2.14–15: 2.4.2
2.15: 2.4.1; 2.14.24; 4.6.4
2.16: 5.10.7
3.1: 2.4.2; 2.11.9
3.2: 2.14.14
3.16: 1.19.7
3.17: 2.5.7
3.18–19: 4.5.14
3.19: 2.14.24
3.21–22: 5.8.4
4.1: 5.9.11
4.3: 2.14.24
4.4: 2.14.24
4.5: 2.4.4
4.9: 1.9.4
4.15: 4.1.7
5.5: pr Or 5
5.7: 5.1.40
5.8: 5.1.40
5.12: 2.2.1
6.3: 2.13.7; 3.6.4
6.15: 1.18.10
6.16: 1.5.3
6.16–17: 1.18.5
6.17: 1.5.3; 3.6.5; 5.10.17
6.19: 1.18.10
7.4: 1.1.2
7.5: 1.1.2; 1.1.3
7.7: 1.12.1
7.9: 4.6.7
7.15: 1.1.2
7.21: 1.1.2
7.21–23: 1.1.2
7.23: 2.13.29
7.25: 3.3.1
7.27: 1.2.1
7.29: 4.6.7
7.32–33: 3.2.14
7.34: 1.2.1
7.40: 1.8.1
8.1: 2.14.19
8.6: 1.6.2
9.14–15: 3.3.1
9.16: int 27; 1.3.3; 1.13.7
9.17: 1.13.7

9.19: 1.1.1
9.20–21: 1.1.1
9.20–22: 2.13.3
9.21: 2.8.1
9.27: int 27; pr Or 3,6; 1.3.3; 4.9.9
10.12: 5.8.14
10.31: 5.3.8
11.8: 3.10.4; 3.10.5; 5.1.13
11.12: 3.10.2; 3.10.4; 5.1.13
11.25: 5.1.40
12.8: pr Or 2; 5.10.7
12.8ff.: 4.5.3
12.8–9: 3.10.2
12.8–10: 1.1.4
12.9: 4.5.3
12.27: 5.9.9
12.28: 1.2.1
13.2: 4.1.11; 4.6.4; 4.6.5
13.4: 4.6.5
13.5: 4.6.5
13.7: 4.6.5
13.8: 5.10.15; 5.10.16
13.8–12: 1.1.4
13.9: 3.2.14; 5.1.11
13.9–10: 3.11.4; 4.1.10
13.11: 3.11.5
13.12: 1.1.4; 1.4.2; 3.2.14; 4.8.8; 4.8.10; 5.1.11
13.13: 4.6.3; 4.9.1; 4.9.7; 5.10.15
14.18: 1.13.6
15.3: 5.10.2; 5.10.8
15.9: 5.5.6
15.10: int 27; 1.3.3; 1.7.1; 3.9.5; 4.8.6; 5.3.8
15.21: 5.1.38; 5.2.5
15.22: 5.1.3; 5.1.5; 5.1.7; 5.1.8; 5.1.14; 5.2.6; 5.2.13
15.23: 3.8.13

15.24: 5.1.7; 5.3.7
15.25: 5.3.7
15.26: 1.18.7; 4.12.2; 5.1.37; 5.3.6; 5.3.7; 5.6.7; 5.7.8; 5.10.9; 5.10.10
15.28: 3.1.11; 5.3.7; 5.10.15
15.31: 5.8.4
15.33–34: 5.1.7
15.41: 2.5.5; 4.6.9
15.42–43: 2.5.5
15.42–44: 5.10.8
15.45: 1.13.4; 5.1.8; 5.1.16; 5.2.4
15.47: 2.4.2; 5.1.15; 5.1.16; 5.2.4
15.49: 5.1.15; 5.1.16
15.50: 5.10.8
15.54: 1.4.1
15.55: 5.1.21
15.55–56: 5.3.6
15.56: 5.1.21

2 Corinthians
1.2: 1.8.1
1.12: 2.9.3
1.18: 4.8.3
2.8: pr Or 5
2.15: 4.5.10
3.2–3: 4.5.6
3.3: 1.4.1; 2.9.1; 2.12.1; 5.6.3
3.5–6: 5.1.4
3.6: 1.10.2; 2.12.1; 2.14.8; 2.14.10; 2.14.11; 3.1.3; 3.9.8
3.7: 4.8.8; 4.8.10
3.7–8: 3.11.3
3.7–9: 2.5.4
3.10: 2.5.4; 3.11.4; 3.11.5
3.11: 2.5.4; 3.11.3; 3.11.4
3.16: 2.5.4
3.18: 2.5.4; 4.8.9;

2 Corinthians *(continued)*
  4.8.10; 5.1.15;
    5.8.13
  4.3: 1.3.5
  4.8: 2.6.6; 4.9.10
  4.8–9: 4.9.10
  4.8–10: pr Or 4
  4.10: 5.8.4; 5.8.10;
    5.10.4
  4.12: 5.10.3; 5.10.4
  4.16: 1.19.8;
    2.13.34; 5.1.15;
    5.8.13
  4.18: 2.13.21; 4.8.7
  5.10: 2.7.6
  5.15: 4.12.5
  5.16: 1.6.1
  5.19: 5.1.33
  5.20: 4.8.1
  5.21: 4.11.3; 5.1.19
  6.12–13: 2.6.6
  6.14: 4.7.6
  6.14–15: 4.1.6
  6.16: 2.6.6
  8.19: 4.5.6
  10.3: 2.13.21
  11.3: 2.5.7
  11.6: 2.6.1; 4.11.2
  11.26: 4.8.6
  11.26,27: int 27;
    1.3.3
  12.9: 4.8.6
  13.3: 2.6.1; 5.1.4

Galatians
  1.3: 1.8.1
  1.6: 1.9.1
  1.13: 5.5.6
  1.15–16: 1.3.1
  2.2: 1.3.5
  2.15: 4.11.3
  2.16: 2.13.23
  2.19–20: 4.12.4
  2.20: 4.12.5; 5.8.10
  2.21: 3.9.4
  3.6: 3.8.14
  3.9: 3.8.14
  3.16: 4.6.8; 4.7.3
  3.23–24: 5.1.35

  3.24: 3.11.4
  3.24–25: 3.11.5
  4.1: 3.11.4
  4.2: 2.9.3
  4.4: 3.10.5; 3.11.4
  4.6–7: 1.1.1
  4.19: 4.6.9
  4.24: 2.13.19
  5.2: 2.13.3
  5.3: 2.8.7
  5.17: pr Or 4;
    1.18.5; 1.18.6;
    4.8.3
  5.19: 1.13.5
  5.19–21: 5.7.4;
    5.9.9
  5.22: 1.13.5; 4.6.9
  6.1: 1.19.6
  6.14: int 42; 3.9.6

Ephesians
  1.2: 1.8.1
  1.7: 4.11.1
  1.18: 4.8.10
  1.20: 4.7.5
  2.1: 4.5.10
  2.3: 3.1.10
  2.5: 4.5.10
  2.6: 1.6.3; 4.7.5;
    5.1.16; 5.8.11;
    5.8.13; 5.9.12
  2.8: 4.6.3
  2.11–18: 4.12.4
  2.12: 1.7.1
  2.14: int 36; 3.5.2;
    4.12.4; 5.6.7;
    5.10.18
  2.14–15: 4.8.2
  2.16: 4.12.4
  2.17: 1.4.4
  2.22: 1.19.8
  2.24: 1.19.8
  3.7: 4.5.6
  3.16: 2.13.34
  4.8: 5.1.37; 5.10.11;
    5.10.12
  4.11: 1.2.1
  4.14: 1.12.1
  4.22: 5.8.12; 5.9.8;
    5.9.9

  4.24: 5.8.12; 5.9.9
  4.27: 2.6.6
  4.31: 2.13.25
  5.4: 2.13.25
  5.14: 3.7.11
  5.23: 5.9.9
  5.27: 5.9.9
  5.32: 5.1.38
  6.12: 1.16.4; 1.18.6;
    2.5.3; 3.5.3;
    5.1.17
  6.16: 1.16.4

Philippians
  1.2: 1.8.1
  1.29: 4.5.3
  2.2: 4.8.3
  2.6–7: 4.11.4; 5.2.5
  2.6–8: 5.10.17
  2.7: 1.1.1; 4.11.3;
    5.10.8; 5.10.10
  2.7–8: 5.10.12
  2.8: 5.5.9
  2.10: 1.9.5; 3.6.6
  3.2–3: 2.11.4;
    2.12.1
  3.5: 3.2.7
  3.5–6: 5.1.26
  3.7–8: 4.6.7
  3.10: 5.7.10
  3.10–11: pr Or 3
  3.12–13: pr Or 3
  3.13–14: pr Or 3
  3.15: pr Or 3
  3.19: 1.9.3; 2.4.2
  3.20: 2.13.21;
    5.1.15; 5.1.16
  3.21: 5.9.10; 5.9.11
  4.3: 1.1.3; 1.4.1
  4.7: 4.8.1
  4.12: 4.9.10

Colossians
  1.2: 1.8.1
  1.3: 1.9.1
  1.13: 4.9.12
  1.16: 1.17.2
  1.18: 1.6.3
  1.19: 2.7.5; 3.8.7;
    3.8.11

INDEX OF HOLY SCRIPTURE

1.20: 1.4.4; 1.9.5;
    4.8.1; 5.7.6;
    5.10.14
1.23: 3.9.5
1.26: 5.1.2
2.3: 3.8.5
2.9: 3.8.7; 3.8.11
2.12: 4.7.5
2.12–13: 5.9.12
2.14: 5.3.3; 5.9.8
2.15: 5.1.33;
    5.10.11; 5.10.12
2.16: 2.9.1
2.16–17: 5.1.39
2.17: 5.1.41
2.18: int 42
2.20: 5.1.16
2.21–22: 2.11.8;
    2.11.9
3.1: 4.7.8; 5.9.12
3.1–2: 4.7.5; 5.9.12
3.3: 5.10.3
3.4: 5.10.3
3.5: 4.6.7; 4.6.9;
    4.12.4; 5.9.8;
    5.9.9; 5.10.4
3.8: 2.13.25
3.9: 2.13.26; 4.7.6;
    4.7.8; 5.9.8
3.9–10: 1.19.8;
    2.13.34; 4.7.6;
    4.7.7; 5.8.12
3.10: 5.1.15; 5.8.12
3.20: 2.4.2
4.6: 5.3.8

1 Thessalonians
  1.1: 1.8.1
  1.10: 4.11.5; 4.11.6
  2.18: 1.13.3
  5.17: 1.11.1
  5.21: 2.7.9
  5.23: 1.10.2; 1.18.5

2 Thessalonians
  1.2: 1.8.1

1 Timothy
  1.2: 1.8.1
  1.7: 2.14.6

1.9: 3.6.5
1.9–10: 4.4.8
1.13: 5.5.6
1.15: 4.11.3; 5.5.6
1.19: 5.7.7
2.5: 1.7.1; 3.8.4
2.6: 3.7.14; 3.8.1
2.14: 4.4.4; 5.1.12;
    5.1.14
2.15: 4.6.9
3.16: 1.4.3
4.7: 5.1.27
4.8: 4.12.5
5.24: 2.4.5
6.3: 5.2.11
6.11: 4.11.6

2 Timothy
  1.2: 1.8.1
  1.7: 4.9.12
  2.8: 1.3.5
  2.11: 5.1.5; 5.10.5
  2.11–12: 5.8.5
  2.19: 3.9.5
  2.20–21: int 28
  3.7: 2.14.6
  3.8: 3.1.18
  4.7: 5.8.14
  4.20: pr Or 7

Titus
  1.4: 1.8.1
  1.9: 3.1.18
  1.13: 4.6.4
  3.5: 3.2.2; 3.7.2;
    5.2.11

Hebrews
  1.3: 2.5.5; 4.7.5;
    4.8.8
  1.14: 1.18.6; 2.4.6
  2.8: 5.3.7
  2.9: 3.8.1; 5.7.6
  2.10: 1.6.1
  2.14: 4.12.5; 5.3.7;
    5.9.8; 5.10.9
  2.14–15: 5.10.12
  2.17: 3.8.11;
    5.10.11
  3.1: 1.7.1; 1.9.2

4.9: 5.1.41
4.12: 3.3.3
4.14: 1.7.1
5.12: 2.14.14
6.4–5: 5.7.9
6.5: 4.5.10
6.6: 2.5.6; 5.7.9
6.8: 1.19.5
7.1: 5.1.14
7.9–10: 5.1.14
8.3: 1.9.2
8.5: 2.8.6; 3.8.13;
    5.1.39
9.12: 2.13.32
9.14: 2.13.32
9.22: 3.8.11
9.26: 3.8.1; 5.10.14
10.1: 5.1.39; 5.1.41
10.36: 2.5.3
10.38: 4.1.4
11.1: 4.6.3
11.5: 5.1.20; 5.4.3
11.9: 2.13.26
11.17: 4.7.3
11.19: 4.7.3
12.4: 4.12.4
12.6: 2.2.2
12.15: 3.4.2
12.22: 3.5.2; 5.1.41;
    5.10.12
12.23: 1.6.3
13.6: 3.5.3

James
  1.21: 2.14.14
  1.22–25: 2.8.3
  2.17: int 35; 2.13.23
  2.21: 4.11.5
  2.21–22: 4.1.6
  2.23: 3.8.14; 4.3.2;
    4.4.2
  2.26: int 35,41;
    2.12.4; 2.13.23
  4.4: 4.8.2
  4.7–8: 4.8.4

1 Peter
  1.2: 1.3.1; 5.3.8
  1.18–19: 2.13.29;
    3.7.14

INDEX OF HOLY SCRIPTURE

1 Peter *(continued)*
  1.19: 2.13.32
  1.24: 2.13.36
  2.1: 2.14.14
  2.21: 5.9.4
  2.22: 3.3.4; 3.8.3;
    4.12.5; 5.1.19;
    5.7.10; 5.9.4
  3.20–21: 3.1.11
  4.17: 2.2.2
  5.8: 5.1.37

2 Peter
  1.1: 1.9.5
  1.4: 4.9.12
  2.22: 5.7.7
  3.15: 5.9.10

1 John
  1.1: 4.5.10
  1.5: 5.8.9
  1.8: 2.7.8
  1.8–9: 2.7.8
  2.1–2: 2.7.8; 3.8.12
  2.2: 3.8.13; 4.11.4
  2.15–16: 4.8.2
  3.2: 5.9.7
  3.9: 4.1.6
  3.21: 2.9.3
  4.1: 2.7.9
  4.2: 5.8.10
  4.3: 1.5.3
  4.6: 5.8.9
  4.8: 4.9.12
  4.16: 5.10.15
  4.18: 4.9.11
  4.19: 4.9.12
  5.1: 4.1.6
  5.18: 4.1.6
  5.19: 3.1.13

Jude
  6: 3.6.4; 5.1.29

Revelation
  1.5: 1.6.3
  2.9: 2.11.4; 2.11.5;
    2.11.8
  3.5: 1.4.1
  3.7: 3.2.11
  3.9: 2.11.4; 2.11.5;
    2.11.8
  5: 3.2.11
  5.1: 4.2.8
  14.6: 1.4.1; 1.4.3;
    1.14.1
  17.8: 1.4.1
  21.4: 4.8.8
  21.27: 1.4.1

INDEX OF ORIGEN'S WORKS

ep refers to Epilogue, int to Introduction, n to notes, pr Or to Preface of Origen, pr Ruf to Preface Rufinus. The Introduction is referenced by page number. The Prefaces and Epilogue are referenced by section number. All other entries are referenced by book, chapter, and paragraph numbers.

Against Celsus
1.4–5: 2.9.1n
1.21: 3.1.15n,17n
1.31: 4.11.4n
1.45: 2.9.1n
1.55: 2.9.1n
1.70: 3.10.5n
2.1: 2.13.3n;
　3.11.2n
2.5: 2.14.13n
2.9: 1.6.1n
2.16: 5.9.5n;
　5.10.8n
2.30: 3.8.1n
2.31: 2.9.1n
2.64: 5.6.7n
3.3: 2.6.3n
3.15: int 9
3.22–25: 2.6.3n
3.34: 3.8.4n
3.37: 1.16.1n;
　2.5.8n; 3.1.15n
3.41: 1.6.1n
3.42: 2.6.3n
3.47: 1.16.1n;
　1.17.1n
3.61: 2.6.3n
3.62: 3.2.9n
3.71: 2.1.1n
3.75: 3.1.15n,16n,
　17n
3.81: 2.7.4n
4.5: 3.2.9n
4.11: 1.16.1n
4.14: 3.1.17n
4.17: 2.8.4n

4.21: 1.14.2n
4.30: 1.16.1n;
　4.5.11n
4.31: 5.1.31n
4.37: 2.9.4n
4.40: 5.1.15; 5.2.8n
4.42: 2.14.13n
4.45: 4.9.3n,6n
4.64: 3.2.9n
4.69: 5.10.13n
4.72: 1.16.1n,3n;
　2.4.1n
5.12: 3.2.9n
5.37: 3.2.9n
5.39: 5.5.8n
5.41: 2.13.28n
5.42–44: 1.14.2n
5.42: 5.1.31n
5.44: 2.13.17n;
　5.8.3n
5.47: int 9; 2.13.8n
5.48: 2.13.18n,28n,
　32n
5.61: 3.10.1n;
　3.11.2n
5.64: 4.9.3n
5.65: 3.11.2n
6.3: 1.16.1n
6.4: 1.16.1n;
　1.17.1n
6.19: 5.8.3n
6.20: 5.8.3n
6.27: 2.11.11n
6.36: 5.1.8n
6.40: 2.11.11n

6.43: 3.6.1n;
　5.1.12n
6.47: 3.8.9n
6.54: 4.9.3n
6.63: 1.19.8n
6.64: 5.8.14n
6.65: 3.10.3n
6.68: 2.7.4n
6.69: 2.9.2n
6.71: 3.1.15n
6.79: 5.8.3n
7.4: 1.16.1n
7.13: 2.5.6n
7.21: 3.7.14n
7.27: 1.19.8n
7.28: 5.1.14n
7.29: 3.5.2n
7.34: 4.5.10n
7.46–47: 1.16.1n
7.46: 1.9.2n;
　1.17.1n
7.47: 1.18.1n
7.50: 5.9.11n
7.51: 2.9.4n
7.63: 3.1.15n;
　4.4.9n
7.68: 3.6.4n
8.9: 2.5.6n
8.10: 2.5.6n
8.29–30: 2.13.13n
8.34: 1.18.6n
8.65: int 9
8.70: 3.1.15n
8.72: 5.10.13n

INDEX OF ORIGEN'S WORKS

Commentary on John:
5.8.3n
    1.3: 3.8.13n
    1.4: 2.10.1n
    1.7: 1.4.1n; 2.13.3n
    1.10: 5.6.7n
    1.16: 1.16.6n
    1.17: 4.5.13n
    1.18: 3.10.3n
    1.19: 5.6.7n
    1.20: 2.5.6n; 2.6.3n; 5.6.7n
    1.22: 3.8.12n
    1.23: 2.11.4n
    1.33: 3.8.3n
    1.34: 3.7.14n
    1.35: 2.11.4n; 3.8.1n,11n; 5.7.6n
    1.37: 3.2.9n
    1.40: 3.6.8n
    1.46: 2.11.2n
    2.2: 3.7.9n
    2.7: 4.12.1n
    2.10: 3.10.3n
    2.13: 4.5.12n
    2.15: 3.2.9n; 3.6.2n; 5.1.17n,29n
    2.17: 3.2.11n
    2.20: 3.1.7n
    2.35: 2.9.2n
    5.6: 4.2.8n
    5.7: 1.4.1n
    6.7: 3.7.9n
    6.11: 5.1.27n
    6.17: 5.8.2n
    6.33: 5.8.6n
    6.39: 3.2.9n
    6.53ff.: 4.11.4n
    8.33: 3.1.10n
    10.6: 5.5.8n; 5.9.5n
    10.14–15: 5.1.41n
    10.35: 5.9.8n,12n
    10.45: 5.1.22n
    13.17: 3.10.1n; 3.11.5n
    13.20: 2.8.4n
    13.21: 3.1.17n
    13.37: 3.3.1n
    13.46: 2.4.5n
    13.58: 2.4.6n; 4.5.9n
    19.20: 5.1.15n
    19.21: 4.1.6n
    19.23: 4.1.6n
    20.3ff.: 1.13.4n
    20.7: 1.16.6n
    20.10: 4.7.10n
    20.13: 4.1.17n
    20.19: 1.7.1n
    20.21: 5.8.9n
    20.25: 5.1.15n; 5.9.10n
    20.26: 5.1.12n
    20.27: 2.14.21n
    20.29: 5.8.9n
    20.32: 4.5.3n
    20.36: 5.9.3n
    20.39: 5.1.1n,8n,20n, 31n,34n,37n; 5.7.8n
    20.42: 5.1.20n
    20.43: 4.5.10n
    28.13: 2.1.1
    32.15: 4.1.11n
    32.18: 1.18.5n; 3.1.10n
    28.19: 4.11.4n; 5.10.13n
    32.26–27: 2.5.4n
    32.26ff.: 4.8.7n
    32.28: 2.5.5n

Commentary on Matthew:
1.5.5n
    5.9: 3.7.4n
    10.5–6: 2.4.8n
    10.9: 1.13.5n
    10.14: 2.4.2n
    10.19: 4.9.5n
    11.5: 3.7.9n
    11.6: 5.8.9n
    11.11: 3.2.5n
    11.17: 5.1.27n
    12.3: 4.2.8n
    12.20: 5.8.9n
    12.24–25: 5.9.8n
    12.32: 5.8.14n
    12.33: 1.18.7n; 5.7.8n
    12.38: 1.10.3n; 2.5.4n
    12.43: 5.1.37n; 5.10.12n
    13.1: 5.1.27n
    13.2: 2.9.4n
    13.6: 2.6.3n
    13.8: 4.11.4n
    13.9: 5.7.8n
    13.16: 3.2.9n
    13.20: 5.1.17n
    13.21: 5.1.18n
    13.26: 2.9.3n
    14.2: 4.6.7n
    14.9: 1.4.1n; 3.7.11n
    14.16: 1.12.1n
    14.17: 5.1.38n
    15.3: 2.13.27n
    15.10: 4.9.6n; 4.10.1n
    15.11: 2.3.2n
    15.26: 2.13.18n
    15.31: 1.4.1n
    16.4: 1.14.1n
    16.8: 2.13.29n; 4.11.4n
    16.9: 3.9.5n
    16.14: 3.2.5n
    16.26: 2.7.2n
    17.7: 2.14.13n
    17.29–30: 2.13.36n
    17.32: int 9
    17.33: 2.13.36n; 3.2.9n
    17.36: 4.5.12n

Commentary on Song of Songs
    prol 2: 4.9.6n
    1: 3.8.11n
    2: 1.13.5n
    2.1: 3.5.2n
    2.2: 2.5.3n; 3.8.3n,5n
    2.3: 5.1.12n
    2.8: 1.18.10n; 2.6.6n
    3: 1.4.1n,5n; 2.4.6n;

INDEX OF ORIGEN'S WORKS

2.6.3n; 3.3.3n;
5.1.37n,39n;
5.9.4n

Dialogue with Heraclides
6.20–31: 2.9.4n
7.9–12: 2.9.4n
11.20–12.14: 1.19.8n
15.28–16.11: 1.19.8n
25.13ff.: 5.1.18n
25.13–15: 4.5.10n
25.13–18: 3.4.3n
27.9–15: 1.18.7n

Epistle to Africanus
1.18.6n

Exhortation to Martyrdom
18: 1.9.4n; 4.1.4n
22–27: 4.10.2n
28–29: 2.14.19n
42: 4.9.8n
47: 3.2.14n

Fragments on Hebrews
1.8: 1.5.1n

Homilies on Exodus
1.5: 1.19.8n
2.1: 4.7.9n
4.6: 5.1.31n
4.8: 3.2.9n
6.5: 3.1.10n
6.9: 2.13.29n
10.1: 2.13.6n
11.5: 2.14.24n

Homilies on Ezekiel
1.2: 2.2.2n
1.3: pr Or 1n; 2.4.7n; 5.1.17n
1.7: 3.1.10n
1.15: 3.8.5n
1.16: 2.9.3n
2.3: 1.4.1n
2.4: 5.8.14n

3.4: 2.11.11n
3.7: 2.6.2n
4.1: 3.6.4n
6–10: 5.8.2n
8.2: 1.13.5n
9.3: 3.2.11n
13:2: 2.4.1n; 3.9.5n

Homilies on Genesis
1.10: 3.1.7n
1.13: 1.19.8n; 2.6.6n
2.5: 3.8.4n
2.6: 1.10.2n
3: 4.2.10n
3.3: 4.1.8n
3.4–5: 2.13.22n
3.4–6: 2.13.8n,22n
3.5: 2.13.9n,25n
3.6: 2.13.26n
6.2: 4.6.8n
6.3: 4.6.9n
7.1: 4.6.9n
8.2: 4.7.3n
8.10: 4.6.9n
9.1: pr Ruf 2n; 2.14.13n
9.2: 1.19.8n; 4.6.8n; 5.1.15n
10.5: 1.15.1n
11.1: 4.6.7n
12.3: 2.7.2n
13.3: 2.13.17n
13.4: 1.4.1n; 5.3.3n
14.3: 3.1.16n

Homilies on Isaiah
6.5: 2.4.1n

Homilies on Jeremiah
2.12: 4.12.1n
5: 4.2.10n
5.2: 1.9.3n
5.14: 2.13.28n
5.15: 2.9.2n; 2.13.22n
7.3: 1.9.3n
8.2: 3.1.7n
8.6: 1.13.5n
8.7: 3.2.11n

9.1: 2.11.4n
9.2: 3.5.2n
10.5: 4.12.1n
11.4: 4.9.2n
12.8: 4.9.3n
14.1: 2.6.3n
14.12: 2.4.2n; 2.14.13n
15.5: 5.3.3n
16.1: 1.4.5n
16.3: 2.9.3n
16.10: 2.10.1n; 3.7.11n
17.5: 4.9.2n
18: 2.4.1n
18.9: 2.8.5n
19.8: 4.9.9n
18.10: 2.4.1n

Homilies on Joshua
1.3: 5.1.34n
1.7: 2.13.26n
4.3: 3.9.5n
5.5: 2.13.26n
5.6: 2.12.4n; 3.9.4n
8.3: 5.9.8n
8.4: 5.3.7n; 5.9.12n
16.5: 2.4.6n
21.2: 3.5.2n
22.4: 4.6.9n

Homilies on Judges
2.3: 1.9.3n

Homilies on Leviticus
1.2: 3.8.13n
1.3: 1.4.4n
2.2: 2.9.3n
3.5: 2.13.32n
4.7: 2.9.1n
5: 2.9.1n
5.1: 2.13.9n
5.2: 1.17.2n; 2.13.12n; 3.2.9n
6.2: 1.10.3n; 5.8.2n
6.5: 5.8.3n
7.1: 2.6.3n
8.3: 2.13.9n; 5.1.13n; 5.9.11n

Homilies on Leviticus (continued)
8.4: 2.13.21n; 4.2.4n
8.10: 2.6.3n
9.5: 3.8.1n
9.7: 3.7.14n
9.8: 2.6.3n
9.10: 3.8.1n
9.11: 3.1.11n
11.2: 1.18.2n; 3.8.14n
12.4: 1.5.5n
12.5: 2.5.7n
13.2: 4.8.6n
14.4: 3.8.14n
16.1: 1.8.1n
16.4: 2.13.17n

Homilies on Luke
2: 2.1.1n
2.3–4: 3.2.11n
8.1: 2.6.3n
11: 1.4.1n
14: 2.13.9n
14.5: 5.9.11n
16.6: 5.1.27n
17.1: 1.5.5n
17.4: 3.11.2n
21: 5.8.2n
21.6–7: 2.6.6n
22: 1.16.1n; 2.4.1n; 4.5.10n
22.7: 4.11.6n
25: int 6n
28: 1.5.5n
35: 5.2.14n
35.7: 3.7.9n
39: 2.4.1n

Homilies on Numbers
3.3: int 9n
5.3: 3.8.5n
7.1: 2.13.21n
7.2: 2.13.17n
7.3: 5.1.18n
7.4: 2.13.15n, 21n
9.2: 4.8.4n
9.7: 1.18.7n

10.1: 2.7.8n
10.2: 2.13.15n
10.3: 2.9.1n; 3.8.5n,7n
11.1: 2.13.6n
11.4: 2.10.2n
11.9: 1.9.2n
12.4: 3.9.5n
13.8: 1.11.2n
16.9: 2.13.14n
17.1: 2.6.3n; 2.13.32n
20.3: 2.14.23n
20.4: 2.9.3n; 2.10.2n
21.2: 3.8.4n
23.2: 2.14.19n
23.4: 5.1.40n
23.5–7: 5.1.40n
23.11: 3.2.14n
24.3: 2.10.2n
25.1: 2.14.10n
26.4: 2.5.6n
26.6: 2.4.6n
27.12: 5.1.20n
28.1–2: 2.8.6n

Homilies on Song of Songs
1.3: 2.14.18n
2.2: 4.8.6n

On First Principles
Entire text
3.1.10n; 5.4.3n; 5.10.13n
1.1.2: 1.5.1n
1.1.9: 2.9.2n; 4.5.10n
1.2.1: 5.6.7n
1.2.2: 2.14.20n
1.2.9: 1.5.1n; 1.17.2n
1.2.13: 4.9.6n; 5.6.7n
1.3.3: 4.5.13n
1.3.4: 3.8.6n
1.3.6: 3.2.9n; 4.5.12n

1.5.2–5: 5.1.17n
1.5.4: 5.1.17n; 5.10.13n
1.5.5: 5.10.13n
1.6.1: int 6n
1.6.2: 1.13.5n; 5.3.7n
1.7.1: 1.17.1n
1.7.2: 3.6.8n
1.8: 3.1.12n
1.8.3: 1.18.5n
2.1.1–2: 1.13.5n
2.1.2–3: 1.17.2n
2.1.5: 4.5.13n
2.3.3: 5.10.13n
2.3.4: 5.10.14n
2.3.5: 5.10.14n
2.3.6: 5.1.22n
2.4: 4.7.4n
2.4–5: 2.14.11n
2.4.4: 1.16.1n; 1.18.3n
2.5.1: 2.1.2n; 4.10.2n
2.5.1ff.: 1.18.2n
2.5: 2.4.8n
2.5.3: 2.2.2n
2.5.4: 3.6.9n
2.6.3: 1.5.3n; 1.6.2n; 3.8.4n,9n
2.6.5: 1.18.5n
2.6.5–6: 5.10.15n
2.6.7: 5.8.9n
2.8.4: 1.5.3n; 1.18.5n
2.8.5: 5.4.3n
2.9.2: 3.3.1n
2.9.5: 2.4.7n; 2.10.2n
2.10.4: 1.16.3n; 2.6.2n,3n; 2.10.1n
2.10.6: 2.2.2n
2.10.7: 2.9.4n
2.11.1ff.: 3.1.15n
2.11.3: 5.3.5n
2.11.5: 3.1.15n
2.11.7: 3.1.15n
3.1.1: 1.18.7n

INDEX OF ORIGEN'S WORKS

3.1.6: 1.18.7n; 2.4.7n
3.1.7ff.: int 26n; pr Or 1n
3.1.8: 4.12.1n
3.1.11: 1.18.7n
3.1.17: 2.3.2n
3.2.7: 3.1.15n
3.3.5: 5.10.13n
3.3.6: 1.18.6n
3.4.2: 1.18.5n
3.6.1: 3.1.15n; 4.5.11n
3.6.3: 5.3.7n
3.6.5: 5.3.6n
3.6.8: 1.4.1n
4.2.1: 2.6.4n
4.2.3: 2.6.1n
4.2.4: 1.10.2n
4.3.2: 1.10.2n; 2.9.1n
4.3.7: 1.13.4n
4.3.12: 2.13.32n
4.3.13: 1.4.1n
4.3.14: 3.8.6n
4.4.1: 1.5.1n; 5.6.7n

On Prayer

5.4: 1.3.1n
5.5: int 26n; pr Or 1n
10.2: 1.9.2n
11.1–2: 2.4.6n
24.2: pr Or 1on
24.5: 2.14.18n
25.2: 5.3.7n
28.5: 2.7.6n; 5.3.3n
29.2: 2.9.2n
29.12–13: 1.18.2n
29.15: 1.18.1n,7n
29.18: 5.1.12n
30.1: 2.6.6n; 4.9.1on

Philocalia

2.3: 5.1.1on

www.ingramcontent.com/pod-product-compliance
Lightning Source LLC
Chambersburg PA
CBHW032023290426
44110CB00012B/643